THE LANGUAGE OF THE NEW TESTAMENT

EUGENE VAN NESS GOETCHIUS

Episcopal Theological School
Cambridge, Massachusetts

The Language of

the New Testament

CHARLES SCRIBNER'S SONS, NEW YORK

PRINTED IN THE UNITED STATES OF AMERICA
ISBN 0-02-344530-0
Library of Congress Catalog Card Number 65-25867

To ANN

PREFACE

This book attempts to make use of modern linguistic analysis to introduce seminary students (and other interested persons) to the language of the Greek New Testament. It has passed through several provisional forms which have been used by myself and a few friends for four years in various schools. It is intended to be used in a one-semester course (three hours a week, preferably with an additional optional hour for less able students).[1] Students who have successfully completed this course have been able to proceed to introductory courses in New Testament exegesis in which the Greek text is used as the basis for study and, concurrently or alternatively, to courses in which the New Testament is read extensively, with exercises in translation.

Study preliminary to the preparation of this book was undertaken at the Linguistic Institute in 1959; this was made possible by a grant from the American Council of Learned Societies, which is hereby gratefully acknowledged.

This book would not have been brought to its present form without the help and encouragement of many people. I am particularly indebted to Robert T. Fortna, formerly of Union Seminary in New York and now of Vassar College, and to Edmund Deane, of the Perkins Institute of Theology at Southern Methodist University, both of whom used earlier manifestations of this book in their classes. They have made many invaluable suggestions, as has my colleague, Hubert L. Flesher, and far from least,

---

[1] This arrangement has proved to be satisfactory with small classes (less than twenty); modifications are, of course, possible.

Preface

my own students, including especially a small group of "volunteers" from the Massachusetts Institute of Technology, whose unexpected interest gave me great encouragement.

Professor J. Louis Martyn of Union Theological Seminary in New York, Professor Waldo E. Sweet of the University of Michigan, and Dean A. W. Argyle of Regent's Park College, Oxford, read the manuscripts of earlier rescensions, and I tremble to think of the pitfalls I would have tumbled into and the glaring errors I would have allowed to stand if I had not had the benefit of their searching and extensive comments. Needless to say, whatever shortcomings remain do so through my own grievous fault.

My special thanks are due to Miss Marcia Holden, faculty secretary of the Episcopal Theological School, who ran off thousands of stencils and stapled hundreds of lessons in the course of the past four years; without her assistance it is very doubtful whether any of this material would have made it much beyond my own typewriters.

Finally, I give affectionate thanks to my wife, who shared in the dreary business of shuffling and stapling, patiently endured the burning of much midnight oil, and managed somehow to make a happy home for my children while I wrestled with the demon Grammar.

EUGENE VAN NESS GOETCHIUS

Cambridge, Massachusetts

CONTENTS

Contents

[x]

INTRODUCTION

" Greek, Sir, is like lace; every man gets as much of it as he can." This remark seems originally to have been regarded as among the more penetrating of Samuel Johnson's *obiter dicta*, though at present it is hard to believe that it ever made much sense. Nowadays Greek is like lace in that few men care whether they " get" any or not. However, a little rummaging in the débris of history reveals that not so very long ago a knowledge of Greek, like the possession of an assortment of lace cuffs and jabots, was an indispensable mark of a gentleman. Things went from bad to worse, as they inevitably seem to do, so that by the middle of the last century only the clergy were making any effort to uphold Dr. Johnson's standards, and most of them had given up lace.

When the United States became an independent nation, most of the religious bodies existing within its borders found it necessary, even at that early date, to provide for the possibility of dispensing candidates for the ministry from the requirement of a knowledge of the Biblical languages, and such provisions for clemency have been retained, in almost all denominations, down to the present day. However, the theological seminaries which were established in later years made some effort to reaffirm the older standard. The earliest catalogues of these institutions make it clear that a knowledge of Greek was expected of all *entering* students; many seminaries offered no instruction at all in the Greek language, although some " lectures on the peculiarities of New Testament Greek" were occasionally included in the introductory New Testament course; knowledge of the " normalities" of the language of Homer and Plato was presumably taken for granted. Not only this, students were in many seminaries expected to add to their competence in Greek a competence in Hebrew as well.

By the end of the First World War most theological schools found themselves forced to adopt a more realistic attitude in the matter of entrance requirements, and many began offering introductory courses in Greek; these were at first noncredit courses, but in most places they have become regular parts of the curriculum. More and more chinks appeared in the Greek armor in succeeding years. Courses on the New Testament came to be offered in which an English translation, rather than the Greek text, was used as the basis of exegesis and interpretation; these courses were taught side by side with other courses of the older pattern and, in many schools, carried the same academic credit. Students might elect (or be required to take) one or the other, depending sometimes on personal preference and aptitude but frequently on outside ecclesiastical prescription or dispensation. Wherever this situation arose, with students divided, as it were, into half Greek and half barbarian, it gave rise to numerous administrative problems, was wasteful of faculty time, had a bad effect on student morale, and, most important, adversely affected the study of the New Testament itself.

It is obvious, of course, that all the problems resulting from having some students who do and some students who do not take Greek might most easily be avoided by the simple expedient of doing away with one or the other kind of student. However, it has been quite properly objected, on the one hand, that some students have little aptitude for languages and some may even have acquired a " psychological block" against them, so that to require such students to study Greek as it has been traditionally presented would be unreasonable. On the other hand, the total abolition of the Greek requirement does not seem to be the answer either, inasmuch as the study of the New Testament, if it is to be more than superficial, might reasonably be expected to entail some knowledge of Greek. Fortunately, it is possible to steer a middle course between these extremes.

After all, it is true of Greek—as it is true of other languages, other academic subjects, and other technical skills—that one may study it in various ways for various purposes, and may achieve different degrees—and even different kinds—of competence in it. Moreover, the degree and kind of competence in Greek which might be necessary in some circumstances might be quite superfluous—or totally inadequate—or merely beside the point—in other circumstances. It is thus not enough to inquire whether all students, or no students, or only some students, should have a knowledge of Greek. There are really a number of questions to be answered: What kind of competence in Greek is desirable for a Christian minister, especially for a parish minister? How much facility, in this special competence, is it desirable for him to have? Can such a competence, and such a degree of competence, be acquired in a reasonable length of time and at a reasonable expenditure of effort?

This textbook on the language of the New Testament has been designed with these questions in mind and with a view to providing them with reasonable answers. The author's basic assumption is that it is well for a minister of the Gospel to have some acquaintance with the language in which that Gospel was first put in writing and in which it was preached in the first age of the Church's expansion; this does not mean, of course, that a knowledge of Greek will make a man a better Christian or a better minister, or that such knowledge is absolutely indispensable for *all* Christian ministers. It is the purpose of this book to provide students with the kind of knowledge of Greek which it will be well for them, as Christian ministers—and, more particularly, as *parish* ministers—to have. It is taken for granted that few parish ministers will be moved to imitate Bishop Launcelot Andrewes by composing their private devotions in Greek; no effort is made in this book, therefore, to provide this kind and degree of competence, admirable though it may be from some points of view. Further, little emphasis is placed on translation from English into Greek, since it appears that occasions for practicing this skill arise but infrequently in the parish ministry. Somewhat surprisingly, perhaps, only slightly greater emphasis is placed on translation from Greek into English. It is true that occasions do arise in the parish ministry—generally in connection with the interpretation of some Biblical passage—when a clergyman finds it helpful to consult the Greek text on particular points; however, it is possible to be able to do this—and to do it quite *intelligently*, for that matter—without being able to translate the text " from scratch " or " at sight." When a clergyman does find occasion to consult his Greek Testament he is, we may normally assume, in his study or in some other situation in which he has access to a Greek dictionary in which he may look up the meaning of a word or words without having to feel furtive about it; indeed, when a clergyman has reason to believe that an examination of his Greek Testament will be valuable in some way, there is no reason whatever why he should not also consult one or several of the numerous English translations which exist. To use some already existing translation with *understanding* is hardly reprehensible. Even an interlinear translation may be used to advantage, though there are many who profess to despise such a " crutch." Perhaps it *is* a crutch, as are all translations, all dictionaries, all concordances, all commentaries, and all grammars. But, to press the figure a bit, it is sometimes easier to learn to use a crutch than to learn to use one's own legs and feet in unfamiliar ways, especially if there is only a short time available for learning and only short distances to be traversed at infrequent intervals; indeed, to use a crutch in such circumstances may very well be the most efficient and expedient thing to do.

What this book *does* aim to teach students is how to use the many crutches—including itself—which are available, when they may be used to advantage, and how to use them with understanding. One does not have to know a great deal of Greek to do this, but one does have to know *some*.

How much, exactly, is " some "? This question may be answered with some precision. First of all, except in rare instances, the Greek with which a Christian clergyman will have to deal is the Greek of the New Testament. There is, then, a *natural* limitation, so to speak, on the " quantity " of Greek he may find it desirable to know, for the New Testament is a relatively small linguistic corpus. The vocabulary of the New Testament comes to less than 5,450 words altogether, and the style is considerably less complicated than that of Homer or Plato.

In view of what has already been said about the propriety of a clergyman consulting a Greek dictionary whenever he feels inclined to do so, the absence of any emphasis on memorization of vocabulary should occasion little surprise. Students will be expected to acquire a reasonably exact knowledge of a small number of *grammatically* significant words (such as the prepositions, conjunctions, and pronouns), but even in the case of these the dictionary is seldom required to be shut. The principal thing that students are expected to learn about the vocabulary of the New Testament is not, however, any particular assortment of the separate words in it, but the fact that, generally speaking, *no* Greek word has an exact "literal" equivalent in English which may be used to render it in every context.

The main emphasis of this book, however, is upon *grammar*—the system of formal structural devices or "rules" which a language uses to indicate the relationships between words and arrangements of words. Now the grammar of a language, including New Testament Greek, consists of a definite and—happily—fairly small body of material. It is the mastery of this material which is essential for the understanding of Greek, for the differences which exist between the grammatical structure of Greek and the grammatical structure of English are precisely those differences which are least likely to be recognized and taken into account. It is the grammar of a language that enables us to understand what words mean in particular contexts and, hence, to understand at least to some extent what a word means *before* we look it up in a dictionary, and, finally, therefore, enables us to choose correctly from among the assorted meanings which a dictionary offers for a single word when we *do* look it up. Without some knowledge of the grammar of New Testament Greek it is not possible to make intelligent use of Greek dictionaries and commentaries on the Greek text of the New Testament. Here again, *some* knowledge does not mean exhaustive knowledge; the finer—and even the grosser—points of Greek grammar may be looked up too, but only by one who is sufficiently familiar with the structural system of the language to recognize a difficulty when he sees it and, further, who has some understanding of the structure, limitations, and scope of textbooks (like the present one) and reference grammars. More briefly, one should be able to tell when something needs looking up, and then should know how and where to do the looking.

In this book Greek grammar is presented, for the most part, "inductively"; that is, by means of analyzing the structure of a number of Greek sentences and smaller constructions. In keeping with the "natural" limitation of the book to the Greek of the New Testament, as many as possible of these sentences and constructions are taken directly from the

Introduction

New Testament itself. In this way the student is presented with *real* Greek at the very beginning, rather than with artificial models on the order of *la plume de ma tante*.

To sum up, then, it is the purpose of this book to provide *all* students with some knowledge of New Testament Greek, tailoring that knowledge at all points to the students' special needs. This knowledge should enable students to follow lectures and discussions in which reference to the Greek text is made, to understand commentaries on the Greek text and to make intelligent use of them, and to decide intelligently between the opinions of commentators who disagree on particular points. Mastery of the material in this book will not, generally speaking, enable a student to translate passages of the New Testament into English without the use of various crutches, but it should enable him to use the available crutches with reasonable efficiency. Moreover, it should make it possible for a student to understand the relationship of existing translations to the text they purport to render, to understand the criticisms which scholars make of one or another translation at particular points, and, to a more modest degree perhaps, to form an intelligent opinion of the relative merits of various translations in various circumstances.

So far as advanced study of Greek is concerned, it is anticipated that the material presented in this book will provide sufficient grounding not only to enable students to pursue with profit courses in the exegesis of the Greek text, but also for more intensive courses in Greek grammar and syntax.

This book is not intended to serve as a textbook in linguistic analysis, as any scientific linguist will readily see. The author has attempted to use linguistic analysis as a means of helping beginning students to acquire a knowledge of New Testament Greek and, specifically, the sort of knowledge described in this introduction. To this end a number of corners have been cut with what will doubtless appear to linguistic specialists as quite unwarranted abandon; to these scholars the author offers his humble apologies. To others, of course, the simplifications in the linguistic analysis may not seem to have been carried far enough, nor will the description of grammatical forms in terms of "morphemes" be found helpful to everyone. To all these the author suggests that the more technical linguistic sections of the book may be passed over rapidly and referred to later on, as and if necessary; more urgently, the attention of nonspecialists who use this book to teach from is drawn to the titles in §6 of the Selected Bibliography.

This textbook is divided into fifty lessons, the division being made on the basis of subject matter. The accompanying (and obviously indispensable) *Workbook* contains exercises correspondingly divided into sets. Clearly, in a one-semester course, the instructor will sometimes have to cover more than one lesson a day. This is not difficult to do, since some lessons are, in the nature of the case, shorter than others and have shorter sets of exercises. In the main, however, the lessons are all roughly the same length; longer lessons and exercises have been designed so that they may be easily divided if necessary or desirable. One word of caution may be added: the teacher should not make the mistake of starting too slowly. The first few lessons on linguistic structure are easily lingered over, but students usually grasp their content quickly and can be led on to the main subject matter.

1 | THE GREEK ALPHABET

1. The Greek alphabet consists of twenty-four letters. The pronunciation of these letters, briefly indicated in the right-hand column below, will be treated in detail in Lesson 2.

FORM				
CAPITALS	SMALL	NAME		PRONUNCIATION
A	α	ἄλφα	alpha	a in *father*
B	β	βῆτα	bēta	b in *baboon*
Γ	γ	γάμμα	gamma	g in *gag*
Δ	δ	δέλτα	delta	d in *dawdle*
E	ε	ἒ ψιλόν	epsilon	e in *egg*
Z	ζ	ζῆτα	zēta	z in *zoo*
H	η	ἦτα	ēta	a in *gate*
Θ	θ	θῆτα	thēta	th in *thug*
I	ι	ἰῶτα	iōta	i in *picnic*
K	κ	κάππα	kappa	k in *kumquat*
Λ	λ	λάμβδα	lambda	l in *lump*
M	μ	μῦ	mu	m in *mud*
N	ν	νῦ	nu	n in *nonsense*
Ξ	ξ	ξῖ	xi	x in *vex*
O	ο	ὂ μικρόν	omicron	ough in *ought*
Π	π	πῖ	pi	p in *pepper*
P	ρ	ῥῶ	rhō	r in *rarity*
Σ	σ, ς	σίγμα	sigma	s in *success*
T	τ	ταῦ	tau	t in *tight*
Υ	υ	ὒ ψιλόν	upsilon	German *ü*, French *u*
Φ	φ	φῖ	phi	ph in *phosphorus*
X	χ	χῖ	chi	German *ch* in *ach, ich*
Ψ	ψ	ψῖ	psi	ps in *tipsy*
Ω	ω	ὦ μέγα	ōmega	o in *oaf*

2. The student should practice writing the letters until he can do so with ease and speed. There should be no difficulty in imitating the printed forms of the capitals; the small letters may be written as indicated below. A small "s" indicates the point where each letter should be begun ("s₁," "s₂," etc., are used if it is necessary to lift the pen or pencil), and an arrowhead (——→——) indicates the direction in which the pen or pencil should move. For convenience, the letters may be divided into four groups:

(1) Eleven of the Greek small letters do not extend below the line of writing, and are approximately as wide as they are high (cf. English *a, c, e,* etc.). (The corresponding capitals are given first, then the printed forms of the small letters, then the "diagrams" for imitation.)

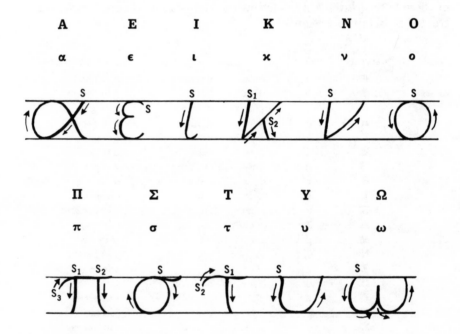

Note that ν has a point at the bottom, whereas υ is round. There are a large number of pairs of forms which are orthographically identical except for this small but important difference: e.g., **κόσμον — κόσμου, νόμον — νόμου, τύπον — τύπου.**

(2) Three of the Greek small letters rest on the line of writing but are twice as high as the letters in group (1):

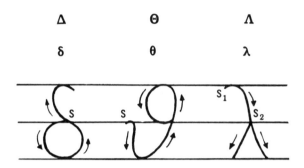

(3) Seven of the Greek small letters rest on the line of writing and extend below it, but do not extend above the letters of group (1):

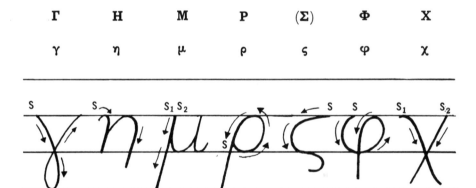

Notice (a) that η and ς are not usually made to extend as far below the line as the others and (b) that the form ς occurs *only* at the end of words (for the form used in other positions, see group (1)): σός, νόσος, συντάσσεις.

(4) Four of the Greek small letters extend both above and below the line of writing:

B	**Z**	**Ξ**	**Ψ**
β	ζ	ξ	ψ

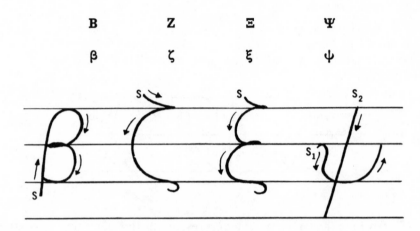

Notice that the first three do not extend quite as far below the line as does the last.

Every student will, of course, develop his own writing style, and slight variations from the method of forming the letters which has just been described will not, in general, cause confusion.

3. Transliteration. It is sometimes convenient to represent Greek words in Roman (English) letters: for example, when no Greek typewriter or type font is available. This method of representing Greek words, called *transliteration*, is ordinarily employed for single words or short phrases, but only rarely for longer passages. There are a number of systems of transliteration in use; that presented here is perhaps the most common.

α = a	η = ē	ν = n	τ = t
β = b	θ = th[2]	ξ = x	υ = u, y[3]
γ = g[1]	ι = i	ο = o	φ = ph[2]
δ = d	κ = k	π = p	χ = ch[2]
ε = e	λ = l	ρ = r	ψ = ps[2]
ζ = z	μ = m	σ, ς = s	ω = ō

The superscript numbers in the table above refer to the following notes.

[4]

NOTE 1: Greek γ is rendered by *n* when it immediately precedes κ, ξ, χ, or another γ; thus:

$$\text{γγ} = \text{ng} \qquad \text{γκ} = \text{nk} \qquad \text{γξ} = \text{nx} \qquad \text{γχ} = \text{nch}$$

NOTE 2: Greek θ, φ, χ, ψ are each represented by *two* English letters. This should be borne in mind when transliterating English into Greek.

NOTE 3: Greek υ is rendered by *u* in the combinations αυ, ευ, ου, υι, and ηυ; otherwise by *y*.

Further details of transliteration are given in the next lesson.

GREEK	TRANSLITERATION	MEANING
δόγμα	dogma	decree
γαστήρ	gastēr	stomach (cf. gastric)
ψυχή	psychē	soul (cf. psychology)
κρίσις	krisis	judgment (cf. crisis)
φθόγγος	phthongos	sound (cf. diphthong)

2 | GREEK PRONUNCIATION

4. Greek may be, has been, and is pronounced in a number of ways. Paul did not pronounce Greek as Plato did, any more than we now pronounce English as Chaucer did. However, although the written form—what we ordinarily refer to as the "spelling"—of English has been considerably modified since Chaucer's day, the written form of Greek remained very much the same from Plato to Paul and, indeed, has not been greatly altered down to the present time. This circumstance misleads some people into thinking that both Paul and Plato must have pronounced Greek in much the same way as modern Greeks do now, but this is not the case. It is possible to discover, by various methods and with considerable precision,[1] what the pronunciation of Greek was like in Plato's time and also in Paul's; however, for our purposes it would not be very useful to do so. In order that teachers and students may refer to Greek forms intelligibly without being reduced to pointing or passing notes, some system of pronunciation must be adopted, but this system need not have any relation to the actual pronunciation of Greek—by its native speakers—at any period. Some advantages would be gained if the pronunciation adopted reproduced all the significant contrasts represented in the written form of the language, i.e., if each symbol represented a single sound, and vice versa. The system described in this lesson falls somewhat short of this ideal, but it is more or less traditional in the English-speaking world.

5. The Vowels. The Greek vowels are represented by the symbols:

$$\text{A } \alpha, \text{ E } \epsilon, \text{ H } \eta, \text{ I } \iota, \text{ O } o, \text{ Y } \upsilon, \text{ } \Omega \text{ } \omega$$

A α is pronounced like *a* in *father*.

πάντα   μακράν   κατά

---

[1] For details, see, for example, E. H. Sturtevant, *The Pronunciation of Greek and Latin* (Baltimore: The Waverly Press, 1940).

E ε is pronounced like *e* in *get*.

  μένετε βλέπετε λέγετε

H η is pronounced like *a* in *gate*.

  λήθη πηγή θήκη

I ι is pronounced like *i* in *hit*. (When it bears the circumflex accent ~ it may be pronounced like *i* in *machine*.)

  τίνι κρίσις θλῖψις χρῖσμα

O ο is pronounced like *ough* in *ought*, *aw* in *awful*, *awl*.

  λόγος νόμος κόσμος

Y υ is pronounced like French *u* in *du*, *lu*, or German *ü* in *Mühe*. This un-English sound is made by holding the lips rounded (as when pronouncing English *oo* in *goose*) and *at the same time* saying—or attempting to say—the sound of English *ee* in *geese*. Greek **υ** is *not* pronounced like English *u* in *rule*, *mule*, etc. (The instructor's pronunciation, in this case as always, should be imitated.)

  σύν κύριος φυλακή

Ω ω is pronounced like *o* in *gold*.

  πρώτως πῶς ζώντων

Care should be taken to distinguish between:

    α and ο
  καλάς — καλός

    ε and η
  λέγετε — λέγητε

    ι and υ
  λίτρα — λύτρα

    ο and ω
  κόσμον — κόσμων

6. The Diphthongs. Diphthongs are compound sounds consisting of two vowels pronounced in rapid succession so that the first "glides" into the second without interruption. The Greek diphthongs are as follows:

[7]

αι ει οι υι αυ ευ ου[1] ηυ ωυ

αι is pronounced like *ai* in *aisle*.

καιρός καινός καί

ει is pronounced like *ei* in *weight*. (NOTE: This pronunciation for ει does not differ from that given for η. A rather large number of forms differ from each other only in that some have ει while the others have η; in general, the context will make clear which form is meant.)

γράφειν πειρασμός τηρεῖν

οι is pronounced like *oi* in *boil*.

πολλοί λοιποί ποιεῖν

υι is pronounced like *uee* in *queen* or *ui* in *quick*.

λελυκυῖα συνειδυίης

αυ is pronounced like *ow* in *owl*.

ταῦτα θαῦμα παύει

ευ is pronounced like the *e* in *get* followed immediately by the *w* in *wet* (i.e., like *ou* in *house*, as it is pronounced in parts of Virginia, or like *o* in certain hyper-British pronunciations of *Oh, no!*, or like *edw* in *Edward*, with the *d* left out).

λευκός βασιλεύς

ου is pronounced like *ou* in *soup*.

τούτου νοῦς

ηυ is pronounced like *ayw* in *wayward*.

ηὔξησα ηὐξήθην

ωυ is *o* in *gold* followed immediately by *ü* in German *üben*.

Μωυσῆς

(This is the only New Testament word containing this diphthong.)

---

[1] The sound represented by ου is not, properly speaking, a diphthong, but for simplicity it is described here.

Care should be taken to distinguish between:

υ and ου

νῦν — νοῦν

υ and ευ

πρεσβύτης — πρεσβεύτης

7. Improper Diphthongs. When a small ι (called **iota subscript**) is written beneath α, η, or ω (thus: ᾳ, ῃ, ῳ), the symbols so modified are called **improper diphthongs**. In the traditional "academic" pronunciation we are describing, ᾳ, ῃ, and ῳ are pronounced exactly like α, η, and ω, respectively. The ι-subscript is thus a useful sign for distinguishing between forms of the *written* language, but not of the spoken language. (An analogous situation exists in English, of course: we distinguish *sea* from *see*, *tea* from *tee*, *meat* from *meet*, *weigh* from *way*, etc., in the written language, but not in pronunciation.) Note that when the vowels are written in *capital* letters the ι is written on the line following them (and called **iota adscript**). In transliteration ᾳ, ῃ, and ῳ are written *āi*, *ēi*, and *ōi* (the long mark distinguishes them from the ordinary diphthongs *ai*, *ei*, *oi*).

σῴζω   μικρᾷ   τιμῇ   τούτῳ

8. The Consonants. The following Greek consonants are pronounced like the English letters below them:

β   δ   κ   λ   μ   ν   π   τ   φ   ψ

b   d   k   l   m   n   p   t   ph   ps

The other Greek consonants require special consideration.

Γ γ is pronounced like *g* in *gun*, never as in *gin*. (See also below, under combinations of consonants.)

γένεσις   γίνομαι

Z ζ is pronounced like *z* in *gaze*. (Students who have studied classical Greek may prefer to pronounce it like *dz* in *adze*; this is quite acceptable.)

βαπτίζω   ζητοῦμεν

Θ θ is pronounced like *th* in *thin*, *thigh*, never as in *then*, *thy*.

θεός   καθώς

[9]

Ξ ξ is pronounced like *x* in *vex*, never as in *exact*, nor as in *xylophone*.

τάξις   ξένος

P ρ was probably trilled (as it is in Modern Greek), but it will be sufficient for the purposes of this book to pronounce it as in English *roar*.

παρά   πατήρ

Σ σ is pronounced like *s* in *success*, never as in *rose*. When it is the last letter of a word, it always has the form ς.

σῶμα   μέσος

X χ is pronounced like *ch* in German *ich* (when it follows or precedes one of the vowels ε, η, ι, or υ) or in German *ach* (when it follows or precedes one of the vowels α, ο, ω, or the diphthong ου). Phonetically this sound is akin to English *k* (which also varies in pronunciation, e.g., in *keel* or in *cool*); to make it, raise the back of the tongue toward the roof of the mouth as for *k*, but do not entirely shut off the breath stream. The sound produced should not be harsh, but have only slightly more friction than is present in English *h*. Imitate the instructor's pronunciation.

χαρά   χρόνος   καύχησις

9. Combinations of Consonants. When γ is followed by another γ or by κ, ξ, or χ, it is pronounced like *ng* in *sing* and is transliterated by *n*. The combinations, then, are pronounced as follows:

γγ is pronounced like *ng* in *finger*.
γκ is pronounced like *nk* in *thinker*.
γξ is pronounced like *nx* in *lynx*.
γχ is pronounced like *ng* in *sing* followed by *ch* in German *ich*, *ach*, as described above.

φέγγος (phengos)   συγκοινωνός (synkoinōnos)

In all other combinations of consonants, in whatever position they occur, each consonant has its full value (i.e., there are no "silent" consonants).

βδέλυγμα   πνεῦμα   πτῶσις   κτίσις   φθάνω   πτύω

10. The Breathings. When a vowel or diphthong begins a word, it is always marked by a symbol called a **breathing**. There are two such symbols, the **smooth breathing** (') and the **rough breathing** ('). The breathing symbol is written *over* a vowel (before it, if it is a capital) or over the *second* vowel of a dipthong ("improper diphthongs" are treated as simple vowels). The smooth breathing is not pronounced at all and is ignored in transliteration; the rough breathing is pronounced like *h* in *help* and is transliterated as *h* (preceding the vowel or diphthong over which it stands). The rough breathing is, traditionally, always written over an initial ρ, thus: ῥ; this is always transliterated *rh*, not *hr*.

ἀδελφός (adelphos)	ἁμαρτία (hamartia)	ῥῆμα (rhēma)
ἐγώ (egō)	ὁδός (hodos)	Ἰησοῦς (Iēsous)
οὐρανός (ouranos)	ὑπό (hypo)	Ἑλλήν (Hellēn)
αἰώνιος (aiōnios)	εὐθύς (euthys)	

11. The Accents. The three accent marks (acute ['], grave ['], and circumflex [˜, ˆ, or ᷄]) were invented by the Hellenistic grammarians to indicate the type of musical pitch accent which characterized the classical language. It is usually difficult for a native speaker of English to imitate this pitch accent which had, moreover, probably developed into an ordinary stress accent (like that of English) by New Testament times. The student is advised, therefore, simply to stress (emphasize) the syllable of a word which contains an accented vowel or diphthong. In *writing* Greek the accents may be ignored, at least for the most part. In a few cases the accents serve to distinguish some words from others differently accented; these will be pointed out as they occur and should be learned. The general rules for the position of accents are taken up in Appendix I.

Note especially that the *breathings* are *not* accents; the breathings should always be written, whether the accents are ignored or not.

When a vowel is marked by a breathing *and* an accent, the breathing precedes, except for the circumflex accent, which is written *over* the breathing: ῎, ῞, ῍, ῝, ῏, ῟.

Accents may be ignored in transliteration, unless there is some special reason for writing them.

ἄνθρωπος (anthrōpos *or* ánthrōpos)	ἕν (hen *or* hèn)
ἅγιος (hagios *or* hágios)	οὖν (oun *or* oûn)
ἄν (an *or* àn)	αἷμα (haima *or* haîma)

12. Punctuation. Greek punctuation marks are like those of English, except that (;) is used for the question mark and (·) is used for both the colon and semicolon. The punctuation of our modern editions of the Greek New Testament is, in most instances, due to the modern editors. The oldest New Testament manuscripts have few marks of punctuation of any kind, and our earliest authorities are patristic comments and early versions (i.e., translations such as the Old Latin and the Old Syriac).

3 | LINGUISTIC STRUCTURE

13. A language may be defined as a system of habits of a very specialized sort. If we are native speakers of English, we are familiar with one such system, namely, that of the English language. Indeed, we are so familiar with the English system that it is second nature for us to use it. We use the English language with the same unconscious ease that we use our hands and feet; we use the latter without having to understand their anatomical structure, and we use the former without having to understand its grammatical structure. However, though it is second nature for us to speak English, it is not *really* natural for us to do so. For though anatomical structure varies only slightly from one human being to another, linguistic structure may vary enormously from language to language. It is therefore essential to study linguistic structure in detail for *each* language. We are safe in assuming that the structure of an Eskimo's foot will be quite similar to that of a Hottentot's, but we cannot even guess, from a study of the structure of the Eskimo language, what the Hottentot language is like. We must, therefore, in studying Greek, always be on guard against assuming that its structure is like that of English, merely because the latter is so familiar to us that it seems the "only natural way." The system of linguistic habits which make up the Greek language is similar in some respects to the system of habits which make up English, but in other respects it is quite different. It is the differences, obviously, to which we must pay special attention.

The system of habits of which a language consists may be analyzed into a number of subsystems, as follows:

(1) The phonological system, or system of *sounds.*

(2) The grammatical system, which may itself be divided into (a) the morphological system, or system of *forms*, and (b) the syntactic system, or system of *arrangements* of these forms.

(3) The semantic system, which relates the forms and arrangements of forms with *meanings.*

[13]

14. The Phonological System. In all language the *sounds* are primary; that is, real language is *spoken* language. The written form of a language is merely a representation of the spoken language and is usually an imperfect representation, at that. However, the written representation is all that we can deal with in the case of New Testament Greek, so that we may, for simplicity, proceed as if the Greek letters represented the sounds of spoken Greek exactly. As we have seen, the phonological system of Greek is not the same as that of English, though it resembles it in many respects. It would be possible for us to compare and contrast the phonological systems of the two languages in more detail, but for the purposes of this book this is not necessary.

15. The Grammatical System. The sounds of a language are combined in various ways to make grammatical *forms* (or, to put it more precisely for *written* Greek, the letters are combined in various ways to make written forms). Grammatical forms are of various kinds and of various degrees of complexity. The simplest grammatical form, the smallest element of language which has **meaning**, is called a **morpheme**.[1] Morphemes may be words or parts of words. In this book, for convenience, morphemes are usually represented in traditional orthography—English or Greek, as the case may require. Some English morphemes are *-ly* (occurring as an adverbial ending, e.g., in *badly, gravely, readily*), *-s* (occurring as a plural ending in *boys, hats, houses*), and *-ed* (occurring as the ending of the past tense, e.g., in *loved, wanted, hoped*). It should be noticed that two or more morphemes may have the same sound (or the same spelling, which is not at all the same thing): *-ly* in *lovely, bodily, manly* has the same pronunciation and the same spelling as *-ly* in *gravely, badly, readily*, but it is a different morpheme because it has a different meaning associated with it. Further, the *-ly* in *lily, fly*, is not a morpheme at all. It should also be noticed that a single morpheme may occur in two or more forms which differ from each other in spelling or pronunciation or both. Thus *-s*, which marks the plural or most English nouns, sometimes has the pronunciation of *s* in *success* (e.g., in *hats, peanuts, handicaps*) and sometimes has the pronunciation of *z* in *gaze* (e.g., in *boys, windows*). The English plural morpheme also has other forms, e.g., those which occur in *houses, churches, oxen, children,*

---

[1] For a more detailed discussion, see the appropriate chapters in Gleason or Hockett and E. A. Nida, *Morphology* (see Selected Bibliography, §6(b)).

men, women, etc. Variant forms of the same morpheme are sometimes called **allomorphs**.

16. The larger grammatical forms of a language consist of combinations of morphemes arranged according to the grammatical system of the language involved. These larger forms are **words, constructions**, and **sentences**.

A **word** consists of one or more morphemes:

> *kodak* (one morpheme)
> *princeling* (= *prince* + *ling*: two morphemes)
> *helpers* (= *help* + *er* + *s*: three morphemes)

In Greek, as in English and many other languages, the order of morphemes within a word is more rigidly determined than is the order of morphemes within constructions and sentences.[1]

17. A **construction** is a group of words which are interrelated by special grammatical devices, functioning as a single unit.

EXAMPLES: *The gloomy dean* is a construction in English, the interrelationship of the words being indicated by the order in which they occur (i.e., *the dean gloomy, gloomy the dean,* and *dean gloomy the* are not constructions); the construction *the gloomy dean* functions as a unit; i.e., it has the same function as a single word in:

> *The gloomy dean* came.   *He* came.
> We saw *the gloomy dean.*   We saw *him.*

18. A **sentence** is a construction which is marked as complete by special grammatical devices proper to the language in which it occurs. We use this, in place of the familiar definition of a sentence as "a group of words expressing a complete thought," because the latter cannot be applied in practice. For how can we tell when a *thought* is complete? Consider the examples below:

> (a)   The doctor came.
> (b)   The doctor came quickly.
> (c)   The doctor came quickly to bandage the wound.

---

[1] See the discussions in Hockett and Gleason (see Selected Bibliography, §6(b)).

[15]

Now (a), (b), and (c) are all sentences, but (a) and (b), understood as parts of (c), might reasonably be regarded as expressing less "complete" thoughts. What actually causes us to understand (a), (b), and (c) as sentences is the special intonation pattern (represented, in writing, by the period at the end) which accompanies them in English. The intonation pattern which accompanies each of the three sentences is a grammatical device which occurs in English and with which the meaning of "complete (declarative) sentence" is conventionally associated. ("Conventionally" here should not be taken to mean that speakers of English could change the convention by mutual agreement, but only that there is no *necessary* connection between this intonation pattern and the meaning described above. Many languages use other intonation patterns, or other grammatical devices altogether, to express the same meaning.)

A further example may make the matter clearer:

(d)   The mome raths outgrabe.

This is a sentence (and, indeed, an English sentence) because it is marked by English sentence intonation (or, rather, one type of English sentence intonation; there are several). Since it is nonsense, it can hardly be said to express a "complete thought," or any other kind of thought, for that matter.

19. The Semantic System. The relationship between the forms of a language and the meanings which they express is complex. It may most simply be described as (a) conventional, (b) seldom one-to-one, and (c) rarely the same in any two languages. Each part of this description will now be illustrated in detail.

(a) *The relationship between the forms of a language and the meanings which they express is conventional.*

Cratylus, in Plato's dialogue which bears his name, defended the position that all words in all languages are *naturally appropriate* to the meanings in which they are used. This view, which has been held by many persons of varying degrees of sophistication before and after Plato's time, is mistaken. Thus pigs are not, as the little girl is alleged to have believed, called pigs "because they are so dirty," but only because speakers of English habitually (and conventionally) use this particular term to refer to these particular animals.

It follows that it is nonsense to speak of the "real" meaning of a word or other linguistic form. A word or other linguistic form has whatever meaning its users understand it to have. This meaning is seldom sharply defined and may vary from time to time and from place to place.

EXAMPLES: (i) In the Authorized ("King James") Version of 1 Samuel 20:40, we read, *Jonathan gave his artillery to his lad.* From the context it is plain that *artillery*, here, means *a bow and arrow*; this is consistent with the general meaning of *artillery* in the sixteenth and seventeenth centuries, when it was used to refer to almost any instrument for hurling missiles.[1]

(ii) In America a *bonnet* is something to be worn on the head, but in England it may also be found on the front of a motorcar (or automobile); in England a *hood* is something to be worn on the head, but in America it may also be found on the front of an automobile (or motorcar).

(b) *The relationship between the forms of a language and the meanings which they express is seldom one-to-one.*

EXAMPLES: The English word *bank* has various meanings in the following sentences:

(i)	He works at the First National Bank.
(ii)	He likes to stretch out on the river bank.
(iii)	He banks at the Metropolitan Trust Company.
(iv)	That fast car banks sharply on curves.

With words of this kind ambiguities can easily arise:

(v)	I met him by the bank. (Savings bank, or river bank?).
(vi)	He skidded around the corner and banked at the Harvard Trust Company.

Sometimes the shades of meaning expressed by a word are not so clearly separate. The English preposition *in*, for example, expresses a relationship which has a very broad meaning. Within this area of meaning, however, it is possible to contrast certain shades by juxtaposing them. Thus we may say,

(vii)	She arrived in a flood of tears.
(viii)	She arrived in a sedan chair.

We cannot, however, say,

(ix)	She arrived in a flood of tears and a sedan chair.

---

[1] This example is from E. A. Nida, *Learning a Foreign Language*, p. 189. (see Selected Bibliography, §6(c).)

This use of a single word in two meanings simultaneously (technically called *zeugma*) may, if not carried to extremes, have a mildly humorous effect.

Some words have very wide ranges of meaning. Thus, in English, one may *take* a pill, a walk, measurements, cold, sick, first prize, after one's parents, a seat, notes, a picture, a nap, lunch, to one's heels, a wife, a magazine (i.e., subscribe to it), a bus, time, the floor, pride, in (i.e., understand), in (i.e., cheat), root, etc.[1]

(c) *The relationship between the forms of a language and the meanings which they express is rarely the same in any two languages.*

This fact may be regarded as a consequence of (a) and (b), but it deserves separate consideration because of its importance in language study. From this third fact it is, or should be, obvious that it is futile to search for *the* English equivalent for a Greek word, or vice versa.

EXAMPLES: The English word *left*, which occurs in each of the following verses quoted from the King James Version of the New Testament, translates a different Greek word in every case:

Mt 6:3 Let not thy *left* hand know what thy right hand doeth.	ἀριστερά
Mk 8:8 They took up of the broken meat that was *left* seven baskets.	περισσεύματα
Rom 11:3 I am *left* alone, and they seek my life.	ὑπελείφθην
Mt 4:20 They straightway *left* their nets.	ἀφέντες
Acts 23:32 They *left* the horsemen.	ἐάσαντες
Rom 9:29 Except the Lord of Sabaoth had *left* us a seed . . .	ἐγκατέλιπεν
Mk 14:52 And he *left* the linen cloth.	καταλιπών
Lk 5:4 When he had *left* speaking . . .	ἐπαύσατο
2 Tim 4:13 The cloke I *left* at Troas . . .	ἀπέλιπον

On the other hand, the Greek word **λόγος** is represented in the King James Version of the New Testament by the following English words:

word	218 times
saying	50 times
account	8 times
speech	8 times

---

[1] This example is from Waldo E. Sweet, *Latin: A Structural Approach* (Ann Arbor, Mich.: The University of Michigan Press, 1957), p. 14.

Word (i.e., Christ)	7 times
thing	7 times
matter	4 times
utterance	4 times
communication	3 times
reason	2 times

cause	tidings	
talk	intent	
question	work	
fame	preaching	} once each
rumor	doctrine	
treatise	show	

4 | GRAMMATICAL ANALYSIS

20. We shall study the grammatical and semantic subsystems of Greek by analyzing larger grammatical forms (words, constructions, and sentences) into their constituent parts and by examining the ways in which these parts are combined. We shall concentrate particularly on the way in which the *meanings* of the constituent parts, and the *meanings* of the grammatical devices which relate these parts to each other, contribute to the *meaning* of the larger forms.

21. Grammatical analysis is sometimes described as if it were a procedure which began with the total meaning of a grammatical form and which consisted almost entirely of assigning technical names to "portions" of this meaning. Since this kind of procedure has become traditional in many quarters, it is illustrated below in order that it may be sedulously avoided in the future.[1]

    (a)   God loves a cheerful giver.

In the "traditional" approach to grammatical analysis the example (a) above would be called a "sentence" because "it is a group of words expressing a complete thought"; it would be called a "declarative sentence" because "it makes a statement"; *God* would be called the "subject" because "it indicates the performer of the action"; *loves* would be called the "predicate" (or, perhaps, the "simple predicate") because "it asserts something about the subject" or "defines the action"; *giver* would be called the "direct object" because "it indicates that which receives the action of the verb." The analysis might proceed further by calling *cheerful* an "adjective" because "it qualifies or describes *giver*,"

---

[1] The discussion here is adapted from Charles C. Fries, *The Structure of English*, chap. IV (see Selected Bibliography, §6(b)).

and by calling *God* and *giver* "nouns" because each "is the name of a person, place, thing, quality, action, or idea."

As presented above, the "traditional" approach to grammatical analysis appears to be less a method for solving difficulties than one for naming difficulties after they have been solved by means which all too often remain obscure, even mysterious, to the student. The inadequacy of this method may be seen at once if we try to apply it to such a sentence as

    (b)   A cheerful giver is loved by God.

In (b) *God* still "indicates the performer of the action," but it is not the "subject," and *giver* still "indicates that which receives the action," but it is not the "object."

22. A more satisfactory approach to grammatical analysis is that of modern scientific linguistics. This is not so much a "new" method as it is an explicit formulation of procedures which underlie not only the "traditional" method we have rejected but also the everyday business of understanding what we read and hear and of making ourselves understood—in speech or in writing—by other people. In this "scientific" (or "common-sense") approach a distinction is drawn, first of all, between two *kinds* of meanings which contribute to the total meaning of an utterance such as the example we have discussed above,

    (a)   God loves a cheerful giver.

First, there are the meanings of the separate words as these are given in a dictionary. These are called **lexical** meanings. A dictionary includes definitions and explanations of the "persons, places, things, qualities, actions," and so forth, such as those referred to by *God, giver, cheerful*, and *love*, and gives details about the effect of placing *a* before such a word as *giver*.

23. These lexical meanings, however, are not the only ones communicated by the sentence. When we hear or read the sentence as it is printed above, we also learn that *God* performed the action, not the *giver*, that the action involved takes place in present time (or, in this case, habitually), that it is the *giver* who is *cheerful*, not *God*; we also understand the sentence as a statement, not as a question, and we understand it to be a complete utterance rather than one to which more has yet to be added. Meanings such as these are called **structural** meanings, since they are indicated by formal features of the structure of a grammatical form such as the sentence we are considering. Among these formal structural features or grammatical devices are **word order** or **position**, modifications in the **form** of individual words, and the **intonation** of the sentence. In the illustrative example it is the *order* of words which indicates that *God* is the "subject." If the order is changed, we get either a different meaning, as in

    (c)   A cheerful giver loves God.[1]

or else we get no structural meanings at all, as in

    (d)   Giver God cheerful loves a.

The *form* of the word *loves* (i.e., the ending *-s*) indicates that the action takes place at the present, or in general. The *intonation* indicates that the group of words (1) is a sentence and (2) makes a statement. With a different intonation the same words, in the same order, would form either some other kind of sentence, such as

    (e)   God loves a cheerful giver?

(with "rising inflection"), or only part of a sentence, as in

    (f)   God loves a cheerful giver and a repentant sinner.

(where the fact that the voice does not drop after *giver* makes it clear that the sentence is not finished). In written English, intonation is indicated, somewhat imperfectly, by the punctuation.[2]

24. The **total linguistic meaning** of an utterance consists of the lexical meanings of the separate words it contains plus the structural meanings of the grammatical devices connecting them. No utterance is fully intelligible without both kinds of meanings: thus the words strung together in

---

[1] In citing illustrative sentences set off as this one is, the period belonging to it is printed (to show the intonation), but is not to be understood as part of the punctuation of the citing material which introduces and comments on the illustrative sentence (unless, of course, a following capital letter indicates the beginning of a new sentence).

[2] For a discussion of English intonation, see, for example, Hockett, chap. 4 (see Selected Bibliography, §6(b)).

(d)   Giver God cheerful loves a.

have lexical meanings, but the group as a whole has no structural meanings; on the other hand, a sentence made up of nonsense words, such as Lewis Carroll's

(g)   The mome raths outgrabe.

has structural meanings, but no lexical meanings.

25. Lexical meanings, as we have already said, are to be found in dictionaries; structural meanings, however, are dealt with in grammar books like this one: the grammar of a language consists of the various devices the language employs to indicate structural meanings.

26. In the "scientific" approach to grammatical analysis we begin by examining the formal grammatical devices which are present in an utterance and then proceed to the structural meanings which are indicated by these devices. This approach may be illustrated by a brief consideration of the New Testament Greek equivalent of the English example we have been discussing:

ἱλαρὸν δότην ἀγαπᾷ ὁ θεός. (2 Cor 9:7)
God loves a cheerful giver.

If we compare the Greek example above with the English translation beneath it, we see that there are exactly the same number of words in the English as there are in the Greek. It would, however, be a mistake for us to imagine that each English word corresponds in meaning, or in any other way, to the Greek word immediately above it. If we looked up the Greek words in a lexicon, we would find that **ἱλαρόν** corresponds to *cheerful*, **δότην** to *giver*, **ἀγαπᾷ** to *loves*, and **θεός** to *God*. The little word **ὁ**, *the*, which appears in the Greek is not represented at all in the English, and the English word *a* is not represented in the Greek. Taking the Greek words as they come, we might expect them to mean "Cheerful giver loves the God." Why do we translate it by "God loves a cheerful giver"? The answer, of course, is that Greek and English, being different languages, have different *structures*. The *lexical* meanings of the Greek words are, in this particular case, very much the same as the lexical meanings of the English words with which a dictionary would equate them; however, the formal devices which relate the Greek words to each other in the Greek

[23]

sentence are entirely different from those which relate the English words to each other in the English sentence. Thus the lexical meanings are the same and the structural meanings are the same, but the formal devices which express these latter meanings are *not* the same.

27. When we examined the structure of the English sentence, we found that the **order of words** played a very important part. *God loves a cheerful giver* can only mean, in English, that *God* does the loving and that the loving is done to *a cheerful giver*. If we reverse the order and write *A cheerful giver loves God*, we have a sentence with a different meaning: the roles of "performer of the action" and "receiver of the action" are reversed when the positions of the words denoting them are interchanged. Further, if we alter the order of the words in the English sentence in a still more radical fashion, say to *Giver God cheerful loves a*, we no longer have a sentence at all.[1] Word order is so important in English that very little flexibility is *grammatically* permissible where it is concerned. Thus, broadly speaking, in "declarative" sentences, the subject must precede the verb, and the object must follow it.

28. In Greek, however, the order of words is not so significant. The meaning expressed in English by *God loves a cheerful giver* could be expressed in Greek not only by

(1) ἱλαρὸν δότην ἀγαπᾷ ὁ θεός.

but also by any one of the following:

(2) δότην ἱλαρὸν ἀγαπᾷ ὁ θεός.
(3) ἀγαπᾷ δότην ἱλαρὸν ὁ θεός.
(4) ἀγαπᾷ ἱλαρὸν δότην ὁ θεός.
(5) ὁ θεὸς δότην ἱλαρὸν ἀγαπᾷ.
(6) ὁ θεὸς ἀγαπᾷ δότην ἱλαρόν.
(7) ὁ θεὸς ἀγαπᾷ ἱλαρὸν δότην.
(8) δότην ὁ θεὸς ἱλαρὸν ἀγαπᾷ.
(9) ἀγαπᾷ ὁ θεὸς δότην ἱλαρόν.
(10) ἀγαπᾷ ὁ θεὸς ἱλαρὸν δότην.
(11) δότην ἱλαρὸν ὁ θεὸς ἀγαπᾷ.
(12) ἀγαπᾷ δότην ὁ θεὸς ἱλαρόν.
(13) ἱλαρὸν ἀγαπᾷ δότην ὁ θεός.

(14) δότην ἀγαπᾷ ἱλαρὸν ὁ θεός
(15) ὁ θεὸς ἱλαρὸν δότην ἀγαπᾷ.
(16) ὁ θεὸς ἀγαπᾷ ἱλαρὸν δότην.
(17) ὁ θεὸς δότην ἀγαπᾷ ἱλαρόν.
(18) ἱλαρὸν ὁ θεὸς δότην ἀγαπᾷ.
(19) ἱλαρὸν ὁ θεὸς ἀγαπᾷ δότην.
(20) δότην ὁ θεὸς ἀγαπᾷ ἱλαρόν.
(21) ἱλαρὸν δότην ὁ θεὸς ἀγαπᾷ.
(22) ἱλαρὸν ἀγαπᾷ ὁ θεὸς δότην.
(23) δότην ἀγαπᾷ ὁ θεὸς ἱλαρόν.
(24) ἀγαπᾷ ἱλαρὸν ὁ θεὸς δότην.

---

[1] See §23(d).

Some of these twenty-four possibilities are, of course, less likely to be encountered than others; moreover, they are not all *precisely* equivalent in meaning: the differences in meaning which are reflected by the different word orders above, however, are of the sort which in English would have to be expressed by intonation and emphasis, and by various paraphrases.

It should be noticed, further, that the order of words in Greek is not *completely* free: in every one of the twenty-four arrangements above, the two words ὁ θεός have keen kept together and in the same order; if they were to be separated, or if their order were to be changed, the resulting structure would be grammatically abnormal (although the meaning might still be intelligible to a native speaker).

29. A grammatical device found in both English and Greek is that involving **function words**. These are words which have little precise lexical meaning, but which have great importance as structural markers. The most important function words are prepositions (*to, for, with, by*, etc.), conjunctions (*and, or, but, because*, etc.), and the articles (*a, an, the*).

30. Important devices which are found more frequently in Greek than in English are those called **government** and **concord**. In government various **inflectional forms** are used to indicate the function of a word in the grammatical structure in which it occurs. Inflections are of several kinds. They may be easily distinguishable morphemes (or combinations of morphemes) added to the end of a word (suffixes), added to the beginning of a word (prefixes), or inserted into the middle of a word (infixes); they may involve the modification of the shape of a word in a more or less radical way, or even the substitution of an entirely different form (this last form of inflection is called **suppletion**).

EXAMPLES: (a) Suffixes: English *-s* in *hats*, indicating the plural; Greek -ς in θεός, indicating the subject of the verb.

(b) Prefixes: German *ge-* in *gesehen, gemacht*, indicating the past participle; Greek ἐ-, indicating a past tense of the indicative.

(c) Infixes: These are common in the Semitic languages; the tenses of the verb are indicated by various vowel infixes inserted into a consonantal "root": cf. Egyptian Arabic *katab*, "he wrote," *yektub*, "he is writing."

(d) Modification: English *sing — sang — sung*, where the alteration of the vowel serves to indicate the past tense (*sang*) and the past participle (*sung*); Greek λείπω — ἔλιπον — λέλοιπα, where the alteration indicates various tense forms of the verb.

(e) Suppletion: English *go — went — gone*; *went* is not related formally to *go* in any way, but simply replaces a lost form. A similar phenomenon is seen in Greek, where εἶπον, *I said*, is used to express the past tense (more precisely, the aorist) of λέγω, *I say*.

31. In the grammatical device called **concord** (or **agreement**) certain words are required to have forms (indicated by inflections) which correspond in specified ways with the forms of other words to which they are grammatically related.

EXAMPLES: In English, in the present tense, there is a concord of number between a verb and its subject (in the third person). Thus, in

> The boy runs.

the subject (*the boy*) is singular, and so the verb must have the inflectional ending -*s*, but in

> The boys run.

the subject (*the boys*) is plural, and so the verb must *not* have the ending -*s*. Other examples of concord in English may be seen in the alternation between singular and plural in

> this boy   these boys
> that girl   those girls

where the demonstratives *this* and *that* have special forms which must be used before plural nouns.

In Greek the devices called government and concord play a much larger role than they do in English. Some of their functions may be illustrated by the analysis of the example we have been discussing:[1]

> (α) ἱλαρὸν δότην ἀγαπᾷ ὁ θεός.

Starting at the beginning (as the Greeks did; they didn't hunt around for the subject), we learn at once from the morpheme -ν attached to ἱλαρόν and δότην that both these words belong to the "direct object" (this is the

---

[1] The statements which follow hold true in general, though they will have to be modified somewhat in details later on.

device called government) and also that they belong together (concord). Similarly, the ending of ἀγαπᾷ marks it as present tense, third person singular, and the -ς of θεός labels it as the subject in spite of its final position in the word order. (The word ὁ before θεός confirms, or duplicates, this last piece of information.)[1]

---

[1] For a more general discussion of grammatical devices, see Gleason, chap. 11 (see Selected Bibliography, §6(b)).

5 | THE PARTS OF SPEECH

32. Grammatical structures may be most conveniently described in terms of their constituent parts, much as a building may be described in terms of the bricks and mortar out of which it is built. Morphemes, the smallest grammatical "bricks," have already been discussed briefly, so that we may now proceed to examine the next larger grammatical unit, the **word**.

33. The basic classes of words, from the point of view of grammatical analysis, are the categories usually described as the **parts of speech**. These are frequently defined in terms of lexical meaning: e.g., a noun is usually defined as "a word which serves as the name of a person, place, thing, idea, action, or quality." The inadequacy of such definitions has been discussed in the previous lesson (in §21), but it can hardly be over-emphasized. Thus, if we wish to determine whether *toves* or *wabe* in Lewis Carroll's line,

> The slithy toves did gyre and gimble in the wabe.

are nouns, the definition cited above will not help us. Yet it is clear from the grammatical devices which are present (*-s* on *toves*, the article *the* before *wabe*, etc.) that these words are in fact nouns, even though we have to wait for Humpty Dumpty's explanation to discover their lexical meanings. In what follows we shall avoid definitions formulated in terms of meaning, and formulate them instead in terms of formal characteristics.

The formal characteristics which may serve as the bases for definition of the parts of speech are of two kinds: (1) **inflectional** or **paradigmatic** and (2) **distributional** or **syntactic**.

(1) **Inflectional or paradigmatic classification.** By way of illustration we may apply this method first to English. If we examine a few pages

of English (to speak in terms of the written language), we find some words which are similar, but not identical, to each other in **form**. It is possible, generally speaking, to arrange these words in larger or smaller sets (called **paradigms**) and to describe the members of any one set as consisting of an invariable part (called the **root**,[1] **base**,[2] or **stem**[3]) common to all members of the set and a variable part (called the **inflection**; see §30). Words which occur in such sets or paradigms are called inflected words; they can be grouped into classes on the basis of the patterns of the sets in which they occur. Examples of some English paradigms are given below:

(a)	man	cushion	shade	basket	
	man's	cushion's	shade's	basket's	
	men	cushions	shades	baskets	
	men's	cushions'	shades'	baskets'	
(b)	sing	help	want	propose	write
	sang	helped	wanted	proposed	wrote
	sung	helped	wanted	proposed	written
	singing	helping	wanting	proposing	writing
(c)	poor	rich	puny	strong	kind
	poorer	richer	punier	stronger	kinder
	poorest	richest	puniest	strongest	kindest

For English, words which occur in paradigms of type (a) are called *nouns*, those which occur in paradigms of type (b) are called *verbs*, and those which occur in paradigms of type (c) are called *adjectives*. Note that all possible contrasting forms need not occur; *man — man's — men — men's* illustrates all possible contrasts, but the contrasts marked by the apostrophe in various positions (in *cushion — cushion's*, etc.) do not appear in spoken English (in which *cushion's*, *cushions'*, and *cushions* are indistinguishable).

(2) **Distributional or syntactic classification.**[4]

(a) In this method of classifying parts of speech a **noun** is defined as a word which is appropriate (i.e., which is understood as appropriate by a

---

[1] See §166, fn. 1.

[2] See §§142, 164f.

[3] See §145, *Note* 2, and §168.

[4] Adapted from Fries, chap. V (see Selected Bibliography, §6(b)).

native speaker) in the blank space or "slot" in one of the following "frames":

Frame A.   The —— is (was) good.
           (The) ——s are (were) good.
Frame B.   The —— remembered the ——.
Frame C.   The —— went there.

For example, we may have the slots in the two variations of Frame A filled by *horse, cake, table, chair, lamp*, etc., those of Frame B by *judge, person, people, elephant*, etc., and so on.

(b) Similarly, a **verb** may be defined as a word which can fill the slot in one of the following frames:

Frame A.   (The) [noun] —— good.
Frame B.   (The) [noun] —— (the) [noun].
Frame C.   (The) [noun] —— there.

Only a somewhat limited number of verbs can fill the slot in Frame A; in addition to *is (are, was, were)*, we have *become(s), became, seem(s), seemed, taste(s), smell(s), feel(s)*, etc. Frame B can be filled by a great many verbs: *remember, see, want, write, manage*, and many others (in, of course, their proper inflectional forms). Frame C defines a somewhat special class, including *go (went), come, work, stand, live*, etc.

(c) Again, an **adjective** may be defined as a word which can fill the slots (both of them) in the following frame:

(The) —— [noun] is / was ——.
. . . are / were . . .

In general, the first method of classification is easier to apply, but the second must be used in the case of words which have no inflections (or which lack some inflections), or words which even with their inflections may be confused with other parts of speech. Thus *sheep* is classed as a noun although it lacks a distinct form for the plural, because the single form *sheep* will fill the slots in both forms of Frame A for nouns:

The *sheep* is good.
The *sheep* are good.

Similarly, *beautiful* is classed as an adjective, even though no such forms as *beautifuller, beautifullest*, are found, since we may have

The *beautiful* house is *beautiful*.

Finally, a word like *garden*, which occurs in two types of paradigms (*garden, garden's, gardens, gardens'* and *garden, gardened, gardening*) must be classified as a noun when it occurs in noun frames and as a verb when it occurs in verb frames.

34. We can now proceed to define the parts of speech for Greek. We begin with nouns, presenting for the present only as much of the complete paradigm as is necessary for the present purpose. Apart from the "possessive" forms indicated by *-'s* (or *-s'*), English nouns are inflected only for number (i.e., they have no ending in the singular and add *-s* or some other inflection to form the plural). Greek nouns are also inflected for number, and, in addition, their inflections serve as grammatical devices with much the same functions as those of word order in English. Thus, as we saw in our discussion of

ἱλαρὸν δότην ἀγαπᾷ ὁ θεός.

the endings **-ς** and **-ν** label the words which bear them as "subject" and "object," respectively. This function of the endings is called **case**; each ending of a Greek noun usually indicates both case and number, as the following paradigm illustrates:

	GREEK	ENGLISH
SINGULAR NOMINATIVE	θεός	God (in *God loves us.*)
ACCUSATIVE	θεόν	God (in *We love God.*)
PLURAL NOMINATIVE	θεοί	gods (in *The gods are angry.*)
ACCUSATIVE	θεούς	gods (in *Pagans worship gods.*)

The names of the cases are traditional; their uses will be described in more detail later on. Similar paradigms for other nouns are given below:

SG.N.	τιμή, *honor*	ὥρα, *hour*	δότης, *giver*
A.	τιμήν	ὥραν	δότην
PL.N.	τιμαί	ὥραι	δόται
A.	τιμάς	ὥρας	δότας

Nouns which have endings like those of **θεός** are said to belong to the **second declension**; nouns which have endings like those of **τιμή**, **ὥρα**, or **δότης** are said to belong to the **first declension**.[1] A **declension** is

---

[1] The division of the endings **-ος**, **-η**, **-ης**, etc., into morphemes will be dealt with in Lesson 19.

only a group of similar paradigms; regardless of which declension a noun belongs to, it can fill any slot in a grammatical construction that any other noun can fill.

35. The Dictionary Form. If we wish to look up the meaning of a word in a dictionary, we must know its **dictionary form,** since most dictionaries list only one form of each word rather than all the forms of every paradigm. Thus, in English, if we wish to find the meaning of *men*, we must look under *man*; if we wish to know the meaning of *sang*, we must look under *sing*, etc. In Greek, the dictionary form of a **noun** is its **nominative singular**. If we know only some other form of a noun we wish to look up, we must know how to discover its nominative singular. From the paradigms given in the preceding section it is obvious that the nominative singular is not always uniquely determined if we know only one other form; thus, if we find a word ending in -ας, we cannot tell whether it is the accusative plural of a word whose nominative singular ends in -η, in -α, or in -ης. Unless we have other clues to guide us, we must look up all the possibilities.

6 | NOUNS
GENDER
THE DEFINITE ARTICLE

36. Greek nouns, as we observed at the end of the last lesson, may be defined as words which are inflected for case and number (i.e., words which have inflections indicating case and number). We have also mentioned the division of nouns into declensions or groups of similar paradigms. We shall now consider a further category of nouns which cuts across the classification into declensions. This is the classification into **genders**. This classification has an important function which appears in connection with the grammatical device called **concord** or **agreement** (see §31).

37. Nouns are not inflected for gender as they are for number and case. Every Greek noun has, or belongs to, a gender, which it retains in all syntactic circumstances. There are three genders in Greek, the traditional names for which are **masculine**, **feminine**, and **neuter**. These names for the genders have given rise to much unnecessary confusion, the blame for which belongs to Protagoras of Abdera, who taught in Athens in the fifth century B.C. However, since it is much too late to change the names now, we shall have to be content with emphasizing that gender is a **grammatical** category, not a physiological one; gender is *not* the same thing as sex. Men and women do *not* have gender, they have sex; the *words* for "man" and "woman" in Greek (and in many other languages) have gender, but not sex. The grammatical terms masculine gender, feminine gender, and neuter gender are not synonymous with the terms male sex, female sex, and sexless. To say that one has a friend of the feminine gender is like saying that one has a friend in the accusative case, or in the past tense.

Gender is a partly systematic, but also partly arbitrary, classification of nouns which has, as we have said, some syntactic functions. In so far as the gender classification is systematic, it is *not* in relationship to the sex,

[33]

or sexlessness, of the persons or things to which nouns refer (using "things" in a very general sense). Thus κοράσιον is neuter, although it means *little girl*; παιδάριον, which means *little boy*, is also neuter. Χείρ, *hand*, κεφαλή, *head*, and γαστήρ, *stomach*, are all feminine, whether or not they refer to parts of a woman's body; similarly πούς, *foot*, and δάκτυλος, *finger*, are always masculine, and ὄμμα, *eye*, and στῆθος, *breast*, are always neuter.[1]

38. The best way to learn the gender of a Greek noun is to learn the form of the definite article which is grammatically associated with its nominative singular form: thus ὁ indicates that a noun is masculine (ὁ θεός), ἡ that it is feminine (ἡ τιμή), and τό that it is neuter (τὸ τέκνον). The definite article was considered by the ancient Greek grammarians to be a separate part of speech, all by itself; there is every reason to do so, since the definite article has syntactic functions unlike those of any other word. The article (we may omit the word "definite," since there is no "indefinite article" in New Testament Greek) is inflected for number, case, *and* gender. The form of the article is determined by the case, number, and gender of the noun with which it is associated (in traditional terms, the article **agrees** with the noun it **modifies** in case, number, and gender); this is an example of the grammatical device called concord. The important thing to remember here is that the number and case of a noun may vary in accordance with its grammatical function in particular instances, but that the gender of a noun is fixed.

EXAMPLES (only a few of the possible arrangements are given for the Greek examples):

τὸν μαθητὴν ἀγαπᾷ ὁ θεός.	God loves the disciple.
ὁ μαθητὴς ἀγαπᾷ τὸν θεόν.	The disciple loves God.
ἡ χήρα ἀγαπᾷ τὴν ἀδελφήν.	The widow loves the sister.
τὴν χήραν ἀγαπᾷ ἡ ἀδελφή.	The sister loves the widow.
αἱ χῆραι ἀγαπῶσιν τοὺς μαθητάς.	The widows love the disciples.
ἀγαπῶσιν οἱ μαθηταὶ τὰς ἀδελφάς.	The disciples love the sisters.

39. The paradigm of the article may be inferred from the sentences just given:

---

[1] Not all the examples cited here belong to the first or second declension.

	MASCULINE	FEMININE
SG.N.	ὁ	ἡ
A.	τόν	τήν
PL.N.	οἱ	αἱ
A.	τούς	τάς

Nouns of the neuter gender, however, behave differently from those of the masculine and feminine genders:

τὸ τέκνον ἀγαπᾷ ὁ θεός.	God loves the child.
τὸ τέκνον ἀγαπᾷ τὸν θεόν.	The child loves God.
τὰ τέκνα ἀγαπᾷ ὁ θεός.	God loves the children.
τὰ τέκνα ἀγαπῶσιν τὸν θεόν.	The children love God.

From these sentences it appears that for *neuter* nouns there is a difference between singular and plural, but no difference between nominative and accusative. This difference (and lack of difference) is reflected, by concord, in the article.

Contrast the neuter article with the article in the other genders:

	MASCULINE	FEMININE	NEUTER
SG.N.	ὁ	ἡ	τό
A.	τόν	τήν	τό
PL.N.	οἱ	αἱ	τά
A.	τούς	τάς	τά

40. Generally speaking, when rendering Greek into English, the Greek article should be translated by *the*, and when rendering English into Greek, *the* should be translated by some form of the Greek article. Exceptions to this rule will be considered in connection with the constructions in which they occur.

41. A noun which has no article is called an **anarthrous** noun; a noun which has an article is called an **articular** noun. The use of these terms will facilitate the statement of a number of definitions which must be introduced in future lessons.

42. The concord of the article with the noun may be illustrated by the following paradigms:

	MASCULINE	FEMININE	NEUTER
SG.N.	ὁ θεός	ἡ τιμή	τὸ τέκνον
A.	τὸν θεόν	τὴν τιμήν	τὸ τέκνον
PL.N.	οἱ θεοί	αἱ τιμαί	τὰ τέκνα
A.	τοὺς θεούς	τὰς τιμάς	τὰ τέκνα

The endings of the articles very frequently "rhyme" (or nearly rhyme) with the endings of the noun, as they do above. However, this is not necessarily the case. Many feminine nouns of the first declension have -α and -αν instead of -η and -ην, and there are also a number of masculine nouns in the first declension and some feminine nouns in the second declension.

43. Feminine nouns of the first declension which have -α and -αν in the nominative and accusative singular are of three types, examples of which are given below:

SG.N.	ἡ χήρα	ἡ καρδία	ἡ γλῶσσα
A.	τὴν χήραν	τὴν καρδίαν	τὴν γλῶσσαν
PL.N.	αἱ χῆραι	αἱ καρδίαι	αἱ γλῶσσαι
A.	τὰς χήρας	τὰς καρδίας	τὰς γλώσσας

The endings -α and -αν occur in feminine nouns of the first declension instead of -η and -ην (1) if ρ precedes (as in χήρα), (2) if a vowel precedes (as in καρδία), and (3) in a few other nouns (e.g., γλῶσσα).

44. Most masculine nouns of the first declension are declined like μαθητής, below, and feminine nouns of the second declension are declined exactly like masculine nouns of the second declension:

SG.N.	ὁ μαθητής	ἡ ὁδός
A.	τὸν μαθητήν	τὴν ὁδόν
PL.N.	οἱ μαθηταί	αἱ ὁδοί
A.	τοὺς μαθητάς	τὰς ὁδούς

NOTE: Neuter nouns like τὸ τέκνον are assigned to the second declension; there are no neuter nouns in the first declension.

7 | SUBJECT AND OBJECT

45. In Lesson 4 we noticed some of the difficulties which arise when we try to base definitions for grammatical terms like "subject" and "object" on the meanings they express, and we saw that it is more practical to base definitions for these and other grammatical terms on formal characteristics such as, in the case of English, word order. Grammarians of all schools would agree that the boldface words in the sentences below are the "subjects" of their respective sentences, but the meanings of these "subjects" are not all the same; what does remain constant in these sentences is a clear pattern in the word order:

(1) The **treasurer** misappropriated the funds.
(2) The **judge** coughed apologetically.
(3) The **child** gave the dog a bone.
(4) The **general** called the captain a fool.

In each of these four sentences the subject indicates "the performer of the action."

(5) His **wife** is a vegetarian.

In this sentence the subject indicates "that which is identified."

(6) This **room** is stuffy.

In this sentence the subject indicates "that which is described."

(7) The **funds** were misappropriated by the treasurer.
(8) A **bone** was given the dog by the child.
(9) The **captain** was called a fool by the general.

In each of these three sentences the subject indicates "that which receives or undergoes the action."

(10) The **dog** was given a bone by the child.

In this sentence the subject indicates "that to or for which the action is performed."

(11) The **professor** bathed hastily.

In this sentence the subject indicates both "the performer of the action" and "that which receives or undergoes the action."

[37]

46. In each of these eleven sentences the **position** of the boldface word marks it as the "subject"; in other types of sentences other positions serve to mark the subject. Thus, the interrogative sentences corresponding to those on the preceding page have a different, but still constant, characteristic pattern:

(1′)	Did the **treasurer** misappropriate the funds?
(2′)	Did the **judge** cough apologetically?
(3′)	Did the **child** give the dog a bone?
(4′)	Did the **general** call the captain a fool?
(5′)	Is his **wife** a vegetarian?
(6′)	Is this **room** stuffy?
(7′)	Were the **funds** misappropriated by the treasurer?
(8′)	Was a **bone** given the dog by the child?
(9′)	Was the **captain** called a fool by the general?
(10′)	Was the **dog** given a bone by the child?
(11′)	Did the **professor** bathe hastily?

47. The boldface words in all the sentences are in **subject positions**; their status as subjects is thus, in English, structurally defined. However, the structural **meanings** which are expressed by these subjects are not all the same; in order to be able to distinguish among these, we must be able to recognize still other characteristics of the different sentence structures. When taken together, these formal structural characteristics rarely leave us in doubt as to which of the possible meanings is actually intended in a given instance. As native speakers of English we recognize and "react" to these various structural signals quite unconsciously; it would not be easy for us to describe them in detail.

48. The subject of a Greek sentence also has distinctive formal features; these are not features of word order and are in general much easier to describe. In Greek the subject must be in the **nominative case** if it is expressed at all; if it is not expressed by a noun or pronoun in the nominative case, it must be inferred from the form of the verb or from the context. It may be stated as a general rule that:

The subject of a sentence in Greek is normally indicated by a noun or pronoun in the nominative case; conversely, the principal function of the nominative case is to indicate the subject of a sentence.

49. What we have said about subjects also holds for objects. The grammatical term "object" cannot be satisfactorily defined on the basis of meaning, but only on the basis of formal characteristics. In English the object is usually identifiable from its position in the word order. Thus, in the sentence

>   The dog bit the man.

dog is subject and *man* is object; in

>   The man bit the dog.

man is subject and *dog* is object. The reversal of the relative spatial positions of the words *dog* and *man* indicates the reversal of their grammatical functions.

Man in the first sentence and *dog* in the second are both "objects," and they are both the special sort of objects called **direct** objects. In Greek the direct object is not indicated by its position in the word order, but by its case, which is, in most instances, the **accusative case**; it should be noticed, however, that not all sentences contain direct objects (either in Greek or in English) and that the accusative case has other functions than that of indicating the direct object. Leaving aside these complications for the present, we may lay it down that:

The direct object in a sentence in Greek is normally indicated by a noun or pronoun in the accusative case; conversely, one of the principal functions of the accusative case is to indicate the direct object in a sentence.

50. A comparison of a few Greek sentences with their English equivalents reveals quite clearly the differences in the grammatical devices used in the two languages to indicate subjects and objects:[1]

	S V O	S V O
(1)	ἡ γῆ ἐβλάστησεν τὸν καρπόν. (cf. Jas 5:18)	The earth brought forth fruit.

	S O V	S V O
(2)	τὸ δένδρον καρποὺς ποιεῖ. (cf. Mt 7:17)	The tree bears fruits.

---

[1] The Greek New Testament sentences have been altered slightly for simplification; in no case, however, has the order of words been changed.

(3)	V S O ἠγάπησεν ὁ θεὸς τὸν κόσμον. (cf. Jn 3:16)	S V O God loved the world.
(4)	V O S φωνεῖ τὸν νυμφίον ὁ ἀρχιτρίκλινος (cf. Jn 2:9)	S V O The steward calls the bridegroom.
(5)	O V S ἐξουσίαν ἔχει ὁ υἱός. (cf. Mt 9:6)	S V O The son has power.
(6)	O S V ἄμπελον ἄνθρωπος ἐφύτευσεν. (cf. Mk 12:1)	S V O A man planted a vine.

Most native speakers of English will recognize that the six sentences at the right above all have the same structure. Each has three main constituents, and each of these occupies a characteristic position.[1] These characteristic positions, taken together, are parts of a characteristic structure or pattern which we may represent by the formula

(a) $N_1 - V - N_2$

in which N_1 and N_2 are **nouns** and V is a **verb** (defined in terms of paradigmatic or syntactic characteristics). If V is a **transitive**[2] verb, then N_1 is the **subject** and has the structural meaning "performer of the action," and N_2 is the **object** and has the structural meaning "receiver of the action." In this case we may use a less general formula

(b) $S - V - O$

---

[1] The English sentences also have the same intonation pattern; we cannot compare this with anything, however, as we do not know the intonation patterns of the Greek sentences.

[2] A transitive verb is one which has both active and passive forms. For example, the verb *rent* is transitive, since we can have

> The tenant *rented* the house. (Active)

and   The house *was rented* by the tenant. (Passive)

On the other hand, the verb *come* is *not* transitive, since we can have

> The collie *came* home.

but not   Home *was come* by the collie.

where S stands for **subject**, V for (**transitive**) **verb**, and O for **object**. Formula (b) represents the grammatical structure of each of the six English sentences above.

51. When we turn to the Greek sentences, however, we discover that the formal features which they share with each other are not features of word order. Each Greek sentence contains a noun in the nominative case (N_n), a noun in the accusative case (N_a), and a verb (V), but these three constituents do not appear in the same order in any two sentences. If we look up the lexical meanings of the Greek words, we find that English N_1 corresponds to Greek N_n, English N_2 to Greek N_a, and English V to Greek V.[1] It thus appears that in Greek, when V is a transitive verb, N_n indicates the subject (S) with the meaning "performer of the action," and N_a indicates the object (O) with the meaning "receiver of the action."

52. The structure S — V — O (with fixed order in English, variable order in Greek) is characteristic of a great many sentences in both English and Greek, but there are many other sentences which have different structures. The structural meanings we have found to be associated with subjects and objects which occur in sentences with the structure S — V — O will sometimes be associated with them in other kinds of sentences, sometimes not.[2] We must, therefore, first recognize which words are "subjects," "objects," etc., on the basis of formal characteristics such as word order in English or case in Greek, and then we must determine what structural meanings these "subjects," "objects," etc., bear, by examining the whole structure of the sentence of which they are constituent parts.

---

[1] At this stage we shall use only sentences in which the correspondence (Eng) N_1 = (Gk) N_n, (Eng) N_2 = (Gk) N_a, etc., holds true; the exceptions which may occur will be considered later.

[2] In English, for example, the subject indicates "the performer of the action" not only in sentences which are structurally parallel to sentence (1) of §45 (such as the six of §50), but also in sentences which are structurally parallel to sentence (2) of §45. These will be considered in Lesson 8.

8 | OTHER SENTENCE TYPES

53. Many English sentences occur which do not have the structure

$$S - V - O$$

which we examined in the preceding lesson. In some of these, namely, those which are structurally parallel to sentence (2) of §45,

(2)   The judge coughed apologetically.

the subject has the same structural meaning as that we have already learned: "the performer of the action." The structure of this sentence may be represented by the formula

$$S - V - [Adv]$$

in which S represents the subject and V the verb as before, and in which (Adv) stands for an adverbial adjunct.[1] Alternatively, with reference to the parts of speech rather than to the syntax, we may use the formula

$$N_1 - V - [Adv]$$

We continue to use the notation N_1, as the subscript provides a convenient indication that the subject comes first in the word order, but there is now

---

[1] We enclose the symbol Adv in square brackets to indicate that it is not "obligatory," i.e., it is not an essential part of the structure. We may also have, as a "complete sentence" in English,

The judge coughed.

Nonobligatory (or "optional") constituents may also occur in sentences of the S — V — O type; e.g.,

The treasurer maliciously misappropriated the funds.

[42]

no N_2. The verb in this sentence is **intransitive**, i.e., one which takes no object and which has no passive voice.[1]

54. Many Greek sentences have a structure which is comparable to this. In Greek, of course, the order of the constituents is not fixed, but once again the subject, which is indicated by a noun in first position in English, is indicated by a noun in the nominative case in Greek; the correspondence (Eng) N_1 = (Gk) N_n still holds. A few examples will suffice to illustrate this correspondence:

(1)	Lk 21:8	ὁ καιρὸς ἤγγικεν.	The *time* is at hand.
(2)	Lk 16:22	ἀπέθανεν ὁ πλούσιος.	The *rich man* died.
(3)	Mk 5:29	τὸ παιδίον οὐκ ἀπέθανεν.	The *child* is not dead.

From the third example above it will be seen that when the noun in a Greek sentence is neuter, we may not be able to tell whether it is the subject or the object (since we cannot tell whether it is nominative or accusative). However, it is clear from example (2) that the verb ἀπέθανεν is intransitive (it has no object), so that τὸ παιδίον must be the subject in sentence (3).

55. When we examine sentence (5) of §45, we find that the structural meaning indicated by the subject is not the same as it is in the first four sentences:[2]

(5) His wife is a vegetarian.

At first glance the structure of this sentence seems parallel to that of the sentences considered in Lesson 7; here again the basic pattern is certainly

$$N_1 - V - N_2$$

but in the case of sentence (5) this cannot be rewritten as

$$S - V - O$$

---

[1] See fn. 2, p. 40. Many verbs which are ordinarily intransitive may be used transitively with a restricted number of objects. Thus we may have

The judge coughed a great hacking cough.

Such exceptional examples may be included with sentences of the $S - V - O$ type. (The same kind of exceptional example is found in Greek.)

[2] Sentences (3) and (4) of §45 will be considered in Lesson 11.

as was done in §50. The first noun in sentence (5) ($N_1 = $ *wife*) may, indeed, be called the "subject" (as it traditionally is) because of its position in the sentence, but it does not have the meaning "performer of the action." Further, the second noun ($N_2 = $ *vegetarian*) does not indicate the "receiver of the action." In this sentence, as we said in §45, the "subject" indicates "that which is identified"; the second noun—which is called not an "object," but a "predicate nominative"—indicates "characteristics of identification" which are to be associated with the first noun.

56. Since this sentence (5) has the same *general* structure as sentence (1) of §45, viz., $N_1 - V - N_2$, how shall we account for the fact that it and its constituents express different structural meanings? It is to be explained as due to the presence, in sentences of this type, of a different *kind* of verb. Verbs of this kind are called **equative** verbs; equative verbs have structural meaning as well as lexical meaning and are, therefore, function words.[1] Equative verbs are like transitive verbs in that they may occur in structures of the general type $N_1 - V - N_2$, but like intransitive verbs in that they take no objects and have no passive voice. The distinguishing feature of equative verbs, however, is the structural meaning which they impart to a sentence, thereby determining the total structure. The way in which the presence of equative verbs affects sentence structure will be at once apparent if we rewrite sentence (5) with transitive verbs:

(5)	His wife *is* a vegetarian. (Equative verb)
(5a)	His wife *became* a vegetarian. (Equative verb)
(5b)	His wife *saw* a vegetarian. (Transitive verb)
(5c)	His wife *shot* a vegetarian. (Transitive verb)

The most important equative verbs in English are the verbs *to be* and *to become*; their equivalents are by far the most important equative verbs in Greek. In English we have to *know* whether a verb is equative or not; generally speaking, if we encounter a verb previously unknown to us, we will not be inclined to regard it as possibly equative, for the class of equative verbs is far too restricted. If we should come across a sentence like

(5d)	His wife *milvered* a vegetarian.

---

[1] See §29.

for example, we would be more likely to understand *milver* to indicate some action performed by the *wife* and received by the *vegetarian*, rather than that the *wife* is characterized, in some unfamiliar way, as a *vegetarian*.

57. In Greek sentences belonging to the corresponding structural type, there is an extra structural signal which helps us to recognize that a verb is equative, even if we have never seen the verb before. As we might expect, this extra signal is one of **case**. In Greek, when two nouns are joined by an equative verb, *both* nouns are in the **nominative** case. This extra clue is not generally very useful, however, as we are likely to know the whole stock of equative verbs in Greek fairly early in the game; on the other hand, the absence of a fixed word order in Greek makes it difficult for us to distinguish which of two nouns in the nominative case is the subject of an equative verb and which the predicate nominative.

A way out of this difficulty will be apparent if we will notice that in a sentence in which two nouns are joined by an equative verb, the two nouns are rarely simply equated in such a way as to be completely interchangeable. Thus,

> God is love.

does not mean the same thing as

> Love is God.

In sentences of this type, the "subject" is comparatively definite and special; the "predicate nominative" less definite and less special. The subject is, as it were, *identified* by being associated with a more general notion or class. Thus, in

> Thieves are cowards.

thieves is the subject, and the sentence indicates that they are to be included within the larger class, *cowards*. If, on the other hand, we have

> Cowards are thieves.

we make *thieves* the more general term, and we would infer from the statement that there are some thieves who are *not* cowards.

58. In Greek, since the word order is not fixed, some other way of identifying the subject of an equative verb must be sought. The notions of

" definiteness " and " indefiniteness " provide us with just such a way.[1] We may lay it down as a general principle that, if two nouns in the nominative case are connected by an equative verb in Greek, the more definite of the two is the subject. Thus:

(a) If one of the two nouns is a *proper name*, it is the subject.

                        S   PN   S   PN

Jn 18:40 ἦν ὁ **Βαραββᾶς ληστής.**   **Barabbas** was a **robber.**

(b) If only one of the nouns has the article, it is the subject:

                     S   PN   S   PN

1 Jn 4:8 ὁ **θεὸς ἀγάπη** ἐστίν   **God** is **love.**

(c) If both nouns are equally definite (or indefinite), the one which has the narrower reference is the subject:

                   S   PN   S   PN

1 Jn 3:4 ἡ **ἁμαρτία** ἐστὶν ἡ **ἀνομία.** **Sin** is **lawlessness.**

(i.e., there are other kinds of lawlessness besides sin).

(d) If one of the two nouns has been referred to in the immediately preceding context, it is the subject:

                   S   PN   S   PN

1 Cor 10:4 ἡ **πέτρα** ἦν ὁ **Χριστός.** The **rock** was **Christ.**

(In this particular example, since **Christ** may be regarded as a proper

                                   S   PN

name, the translation may be reversed: **Christ** was the **rock.**)

(e) If an equative verb joins a noun to a pronoun, the pronoun is the subject:

                   S   PN   S

Gal 4:24 **αὗταί** εἰσιν δύο **διαθῆκαι.** **These** [women] are two

                                               PN

                                              covenants.

---

[1] Cf. Otto Jespersen, *The Philosophy of Grammar* (London: Allen & Unwin, 1951), pp. 150–154.

59. It should be particularly noticed that when the predicate nominative precedes the verb in Greek, it generally does *not* have the article. Since this is true, it is frequently necessary to supply a definite article in English, even though there is none in Greek:

	S	PN		S	PN
Mk 15:39 οὗτος ὁ **ἄνθρωπος υἱὸς**			This **man** was **the son** of God.		
θεοῦ ἦν.			(*or* This **man** was **a son** of God.)		

9 | ADJECTIVES

60. Adjectives are important parts of speech in both English and Greek. A brief description of English adjectives is given first, so that we may then proceed to compare and contrast their characteristics with those of Greek adjectives.

English adjectives may be most satisfactorily defined in terms of their syntactic characteristics,[1] as follows: An **adjective** (in English) is a word which may occur in positions similar to those occupied by *hot* and *hostile* in the examples below:

(1) Immediately preceding a noun:

    (a) Without an article:

> *Hot* water dissolves sugar quickly.
> *Hostile* savages captured the missionaries.

    (b) With an article (*a, an,* or *the*):

> A *hot* cup of tea cheered him considerably.
> A *hostile* environment warped his personality.
> The *hot* poker bent near the end.
> The *hostile* gestures caused him to withdraw.

(2) Following an equative verb which has a noun as subject:

> The weather is *hot*.
> His attitude was *hostile*.

A number of English words occur in some, but not all, of the syntactic positions just described. These words may be classified in various ways; some of the most important are mentioned here:

---

[1] Some English adjectives are inflected for "degree of comparison" (e.g., *big — bigger — biggest*), but so are some adverbs (*well — better — best*). We shall postpone a consideration of this type of inflection until a later lesson.

[48]

(i) The articles (*a, an; the*) occur in position (1a), but not in (1b) or (2).

(ii) The demonstratives (*this, that; these, those*) do not occur in position (1b).

(iii) *Enough* occurs in (1a) or (2), but not in (1b):

> *Enough* time has elapsed.
> Ten people are *enough*.

(iv) *Only* occurs in (1a) and (1b), but not in (2):

> *Only* lawyers can understand it.
> The *only* person there is my uncle.

(v) *All* occurs only in (1a), but may also precede *the*.

Positions (1a) and (1b) are traditionally called **attributive** positions, and position (2) is traditionally called the **predicate** position. It should be noticed, however, that English adjectives occasionally occur in other positions (although we do not use these other positions to *define* the adjective):

(3) Some adjectives may follow a noun:

> I never seem to have money *enough*.
> He preached about life *everlasting*.
> The mailman collected three cents postage *due*.
> He is a devil *incarnate*.
> God *almighty* will protect you.

(4) Some adjectives may *precede* an equative verb, of which the subject then follows:

> *Blessed* are the peacemakers.

61. Whatever position an adjective has, it has the *meaning* of "modifying," i.e., qualifying, limiting, identifying, or describing, the meaning of the noun with which it is connected. It should be clear, however, that this meaning cannot serve as a basis for *defining* adjectives, since many words may have this meaning in particular instances, but do not qualify syntactically as adjectives. For example, in

> The *appointments* committee met yesterday.
> You are the *very* man I'm looking for.

appointments and *very* each has the meaning of "modifying" the following noun and each has a syntactic position which is appropriate for adjectives. However, neither *appointments* nor *very* can have the second or predicate position (with adjectival meaning), and they are on other grounds classified as noun and adverb, respectively. In such cases it is convenient (as well as traditional) to say that *appointments* and *very* are "used as adjectives" or "function adjectivally."

62. Conversely, and more important for us here, English adjectives (as defined in §60) may be "used as nouns" (or "have substantive functions"); i.e., they may sometimes occur in syntactic positions which are generally appropriate to nouns. For example, we may say,

> He hath put down the *mighty* from their seat,
> and hath exalted the *humble* and *meek*.

It is, of course, possible to say that nouns are "understood" here (though it would be difficult to give rules for deciding on just the right noun to "understand," in many situations), but the fact remains that, *as it stands*, the sentence quoted is structurally parallel to

> He hath put down the *kings* from their seat,
> and hath exalted the *beggars* and *slaves*.

We can still tell that *mighty, humble,* and *meek* are not nouns, because they do not have the plural morpheme *-s*, which would be appropriate if they were.

63. We are now ready to turn to a discussion of *Greek* adjectives. Unlike English adjectives, all Greek adjectives have characteristic inflections, so that it is convenient to define them in terms of these and then go on to describe their syntactic behavior. Greek adjectives are inflected for **case** and **number**, like nouns, and also for **gender**; that is, they have forms which indicate gender as well as forms which indicate case and number.[1]

64. The Greek adjectives we shall take up in this lesson are said to be of the first *and* second declensions: they have feminine forms like those of feminine nouns of the first declension, and they have masculine and neuter

---

[1] Greek adjectives are also inflected for degree of comparison. We shall consider this in a later lesson.

forms like the forms of masculine and neuter nouns of the second declension. The illustrative paradigms should be compared with the noun paradigms in Lesson 6.

Most adjectives are declined like **καλός**, *good*:

	MASCULINE	FEMININE	NEUTER
SG.N.	καλ-ός	καλ-ή	καλ-όν
A.	καλ-όν	καλ-ήν	καλ-όν
PL.N.	καλ-οί	καλ-αί	καλ-ά
A.	καλ-ούς	καλ-άς	καλ-ά

65. The **dictionary form** of an adjective is its nominative singular masculine (e.g., **καλός**); adjectives are frequently cited with the endings of the other genders indicated (e.g., **καλός, ή, όν**).

66. Adjectives which have **ρ** or a *vowel* (most frequently **ι**) immediately preceding the ending **-ος** of the dictionary form have **-α** in the feminine singular (all cases) instead of **-η**; thus (cf. §43):

	MASCULINE	FEMININE	NEUTER
SG.N.	μικρ-ός	μικρ-ά	μικρ-όν
A.	μικρ-όν	μικρ-άν	μικρ-όν
PL.N.	μικρ-οί	μικρ-αί	μικρ-ά
A.	μικρ-ούς	μικρ-άς	μικρ-ά

A (full) dictionary citation for this adjective would be **μικρός, ά, όν**, *small*. The most frequently encountered adjectives of this type are:

ἅγιος, *holy*	**νεκρός**, *dead*
ἴδιος, *one's own*	**ἕτερος**, *other*
δίκαιος, *just, righteous*	**πονηρός**, *evil, wicked*
δεξιός, *right (hand)*	**πρεσβύτερος**, *older, elder*
μακάριος, *blessed*	**μικρός**, *small, little*

67. Some adjectives have no separate form for the feminine gender:

	MASCULINE OR FEMININE	NEUTER
SG.N.	αἰώνι-ος	αἰώνι-ον
A.	αἰώνι-ον	αἰώνι-ον
PL.N.	αἰώνι-οι	αἰώνι-α
A.	αἰωνί-ους	αἰώνι-α

A (full) dictionary citation for this adjective is **αἰώνιος, ον,** *eternal*; that fact that the adjective has no separate feminine form is indicated only by the fact that no separate feminine ending is indicated. Adjectives of this type are not very common in the New Testament; **αἰώνιος, ον,** *eternal*, is the only one which occurs more than fifty times.

68. Syntactic Characteristics of Greek Adjectives. The most important details are given below:

(1) **Concord or agreement.** An adjective agrees with the noun it modifies, in case, number, and gender; that is, the form of the adjective is determined by the case, number, and gender of the noun it modifies.

EXAMPLES	πιστὸς διάκονος	a faithful servant
	καινὴ ἐντολή	a new commandment
	ἀγαθὸν ἔργον	a good work

Notice that the ending of the adjective is not necessarily the same as that of the noun it modifies:

	ἱλαρὸς δότης	a cheerful giver
	μικρὰ φωνή	a small voice
	ζωὴ αἰώνιος	eternal life
	ἡ καλὴ ὁδός	the good way

(2) **Position of adjectives.** (a) When an adjective modifies a noun which has no article, it may either precede or follow:

	Eph 6:21 πιστὸς διάκονος	a **faithful** minister
	1 Cor 5:6 μικρὰ ζύμη	a **little** leaven
	Rom 6:23 ζωὴ αἰώνιος	**eternal** life
	Phil 1:6 ἔργον ἀγαθόν	a **good** work

In all these examples the adjective is said to be **attributive**, and has the meaning of "modifying" the noun exactly as in the corresponding English constructions.

(b) When an adjective modifies a noun which has the definite article, it may have any one of four positions.

(i) It may come between the article and the noun, as in English:

	ὁ πιστὸς διάκονος	the **faithful** minister
	ἡ καινὴ ἐντολή	the **new** commandment
	τὸ ἀγαθὸν ἔργον	the **good** work

(ii) It may follow the noun, but in this case it must have the article repeated before it:

ὁ διάκονος **ὁ πιστός**	the **faithful** minister
ἡ ἐντολὴ **ἡ καινή**	the **new** commandment
τὸ ἔργον **τὸ ἀγαθόν**	the **good** work

Positions (i) and (ii) are called the first and second **attributive** positions, respectively.[1] When an adjective has one of these positions, it has the meaning of "modifying" the noun as in the equivalent English constructions indicated. The first attributive position is more common than the second.

The other positions an adjective may have with articular[2] nouns are called **predicate** positions.

(iii) In the first predicate position, the adjective precedes both the noun and its article, but has no article of its own:

1 Cor 1:9 **πιστὸς** ὁ θεός.	God **is faithful.**

(iv) In the second predicate position, the adjective again has no article, but follows the articular noun:

Rom 7:12 ὁ νόμος **ἅγιος.**	The law **is holy.**

69. It should be noticed that the English translations of the Greek examples in (iii) and (iv) above are sentences with structure parallel to that of sentence (6) of §45:

(6)   This room is stuffy.

Here we encounter an important difference between the structures of Greek and English. The English sentence (6) and those in (iii) and (iv) above all have a structure which may be represented by the formula

$$S - V - Adj$$

or, more generally, by

$$N_1 - V - Adj$$

---

[1] When an adjective which has an article follows a noun which does not, it is said to be in the third attributive position and has the same meaning as it does in the first and second. This position is rare in the New Testament. (Cf. John 14:27, 2 Timothy 1:13.)

[2] See §41.

where N_1 (the subject, S) is a noun in first position in the sentence, V is an equative verb, and Adj is an adjective. The structures of the Greek examples in (iii) and (iv), however, are entirely different; we may represent them as

(iii) $\text{Adj} - t - N_n$

and

(iv) $t - N_n - \text{Adj}$

where t represents the article, N_n a noun in the nominative case, and Adj an adjective (agreeing with the noun, of course). There is nothing in either Greek example to correspond to the equative verb in the English equivalents; yet the Greek examples are complete sentences just as much as their English equivalents are. It is not correct to say that a verb is "understood" in the Greek; it is true that we have to supply a verb (usually *is* or *are*) when we translate such Greek structures, but the Greeks were perfectly satisfied with them without any verb at all. The word order here, in the Greek this time, rather than in English, indicates the structural meaning.

70. Greek sentences with structure

$$N_n - V - \text{Adj} \ (\textit{or } S - V - \text{Adj})$$

(with variable order), where V is an equative verb, also occur:

	S	V	Adj	
Mt 17:2	τὰ ἱμάτια	ἐγένετο	λευκά.	The garments became white.

	V	Adj	S	
Mt 14:24	ἦν	ἐναντίος	ὁ ἄνεμος.	The wind was contrary.

	Adj	V	S	
Mt 17:26	ἐλεύθεροί	εἰσιν	οἱ υἱοί.	The sons are free.

71. Greek adjectives also occur in syntactic positions ordinarily occupied by nouns and may in such situations be said to be "used as nouns" or to have the functions of nouns. This use is quite similar to that of English (cf. §62), though occasionally a clearer translation results if a noun is supplied or if "one" or "ones" is added.

EXAMPLES   Mt 20:16 ἔσονται οἱ **ἔσχατοι** πρῶ-   The **last** shall be first.
τοι.

Mt 11:5 τυφλοὶ ἀναβλέπουσιν
καὶ χωλοὶ περιπατοῦσιν, λεπροὶ
καθαρίζονται καὶ κωφοὶ ἀκούουσιν
καὶ νεκροὶ ἐγείρονται καὶ πτωχοὶ
εὐαγγελίζονται.

Blind [men] receive their sight
and **lame** [men] walk, **leprous**
[men] (*i.e.*, lepers) are cleansed
and **deaf** [men] hear, and
dead [men] are raised up and
poor [men] have the Gospel
preached to them.

Notice that in Matthew 11:5 the Greek adjectives do not have the article; this is somewhat unusual, as the article is ordinarily used to indicate the substantive function of a word. In this passage, however, there is no obscurity, as there are no other possible subjects. The English translation, however, needs the article (*The blind receive their sight, the lame walk*, etc.) or some supporting word, like *men* or *people*.

72. Nouns are frequently used very much like adjectives, to "modify" other nouns, and when so used are called **appositives** or are said to be **in apposition**. An appositive usually has the article and usually follows the noun (or pronoun) to which it stands in apposition, and always agrees with it in case:

Ἰησοῦς ὁ **Χριστός**	Jesus, **the Christ**
Ἰωάννης ὁ **βαπτιστής**	John **the Baptist**
Φίλιππος ὁ **εὐαγγελιστής**	Philip **the Evangelist**
Ἀγρίππας ὁ **βασιλεύς**	Agrippa, **the king**
BUT: ὁ **βασιλεὺς** Ἡρῴδης	**King** Herod

10 | THE GENITIVE CASE

73. The third of the Greek cases to be considered is the **genitive**. Below are given a number of Greek expressions which contain nouns of the first two declensions in the genitive case (each is dependent on a noun in the nominative case, but this might have been accusative, genitive, or dative). The student should compare these with their indicated English equivalents. Reference may be made to the following vocabulary:

FIRST DECLENSION NOUNS	SECOND DECLENSION NOUNS
ἡ διαθήκη, *the covenant*	ὁ ἄνθρωπος, *the man*
ἡ ἐκκλησία, *the church*	ὁ δοῦλος, *the slave*
ἡ δόξα, *the glory; the angelic being* [in pl.]	ἡ ὁδός, *the way*
	τὸ τέκνον, *the child*
ὁ μαθητής, *the disciple*	

(1) ὁ δοῦλος τοῦ ἀνθρώπου
{ the man's slave
{ the slave of the man

(2) οἱ δοῦλοι τοῦ ἀνθρώπου
{ the man's slaves
{ the slaves of the man

(3) ὁ δοῦλος τῶν ἀνθρώπων
{ the men's slave
{ the slave of the men

(4) οἱ δοῦλοι τῶν ἀνθρώπων
{ the men's slaves
{ the slaves of the men

(5) ὁ δοῦλος τοῦ μαθητοῦ
{ the disciple's slave
{ the slave of the disciple

(6) ὁ δοῦλος τῶν μαθητῶν
{ the disciples' slave
{ the slave of the disciples

(7) ὁ δοῦλος τῆς διαθήκης
{ the covenant's slave
{ the slave of the covenant

(8) ὁ δοῦλος τῶν διαθηκῶν
{ the covenants' slave
{ the slave of the covenants

(9)	ὁ δοῦλος τῆς ἐκκλησίας	{ the church's slave / the slave of the church
(10)	ὁ δοῦλος τῶν ἐκκλησιῶν	{ the churches' slave / the slave of the churches
(11)	ὁ δοῦλος τῆς δόξης	{ [the] glory's slave / the slave of [the] glory
(12)	ὁ δοῦλος τῶν δοξῶν	{ the angelic beings' slave / the slave of the angelic beings
(13)	ὁ δοῦλος τῆς ὁδοῦ	{ the way's slave / the slave of the way
(14)	ὁ δοῦλος τῶν ὁδῶν	{ the ways' slave / the slave of the ways
(15)	ὁ δοῦλος τοῦ τέκνου	{ the child's slave / the slave of the child
(16)	ὁ δοῦλος τῶν τέκνων	{ the children's slave / the slave of the children

In the remaining illustrative expressions two Greek adjectives have been used:

καλός, ή, όν, *good*   **μικρός, ά, όν**, *small*

(17)	ὁ δοῦλος τῆς καλῆς ἐκκλησίας	} the slave of the good church
(18)	ὁ δοῦλος τῆς ἐκκλησίας τῆς καλῆς	
(19)	ὁ δοῦλος τῆς μικρᾶς ἐκκλησίας	} the slave of the small church
(20)	ὁ δοῦλος τῆς ἐκκλησίας τῆς μικρᾶς	
(21)	ὁ δοῦλος τῶν ἐκκλησιῶν τῶν μικρῶν	the slave of the small churches
(22)	ὁ δοῦλος τοῦ καλοῦ τέκνου	the slave of the good child

Before continuing with this lesson the student should complete Exercises 10-A, 10-B, and 10-C.

74. The Forms of the Genitive. The forms of the genitive have been presented in the preceding illustrative expressions and in the exercises (10-A, 10-B, and 10-C) based upon them; the following details should be noted:

(1) Feminine forms of the first declension which have the nominative singular in **-α** have the genitive singular in **-ας** if the **-α** is immediately preceded by **ρ** or a vowel; otherwise they have **-ης** (cf. §43):

EXAMPLES   ἡμέρα, ἡμέρας, *day*   BUT: δόξα, δόξης, *glory*
χαρά, χαρᾶς, *joy*   γλῶσσα, γλώσσης, *tongue*
ἐκκλησία, ἐκκλησίας, *church*   θάλασσα, θαλάσσης, *sea*
γενεά, γενεᾶς, *generation*   τράπεζα, τραπέζης, *table*

(2) A few masculines of the first declension which have their nominative singular in **-ας** have their genitive singular in **-α** (rather than **-ου**). These are for the most part proper names (e.g., Στεφανᾶς, genitive Στεφανᾶ), so that for practical purposes it is true to say that all masculine nouns of the first and second declension have **-ου** in the genitive singular.

75. The Syntax of the Genitive Case. In Greek, a noun in the genitive case may occur in the syntactic positions proper to adjectives and has in such positions a meaning which may be reasonably subsumed under that of " modification " which is expressed by adjectives in attributive positions. These semantic and syntactic characteristics of Greek nouns in the genitive are shared by the corresponding English constructions (viz., nouns in the " possessive case " (written **'s** or **(s)'**) and nouns preceded by the function word *of*).

76. In general it is true that, when a noun (in any case) is modified by a noun in the genitive case, the noun in the genitive is anarthrous if the noun it modifies is anarthrous, and articular if the noun it modifies is articular. Thus we have

               Mk 15:39 υἱὸς θεοῦ   **a** son of God[1]
    BUT: Mk 3:11 **ὁ** υἱὸς **τοῦ** θεοῦ   **the** son of God

77. With an anarthrous noun a noun in the genitive may either precede or follow:

           Rom 13:4 **θεοῦ** διάκονος   **God's** minister (= a minister **of God**)
           (cf. Eph 6:21 **πιστὸς** διάκονος   a **faithful** minister)
           Eph 6:6 δοῦλοι **Χριστοῦ**   **Christ's** slaves (= slaves **of Christ**)
           (cf. Lk 17:10 δοῦλοι **ἀχρεῖοι**   **worthless** slaves)

---

[1] Although, as this expression is a predicate nominative in this verse, it may very well mean " the son of God." Note the omission of English *the* with *God*, which is treated like an English proper name.

78. When an articular noun in the genitive modifies another articular noun, it may occupy any of the four positions which may be occupied by adjectives (as described in §68(2)). The similarities and differences between (a) constructions with genitive modifiers and (b) constructions with adjective modifiers are illustrated by the following examples:

(1) First attributive position:
   (a) With genitive:

   ὁ τοῦ κυρίου μαθητής   the disciple **of the Lord** (= **the Lord's** disciple[1])

   (b) With adjective:

   ὁ πιστὸς μαθητής   the **faithful** disciple

(2) Second attributive position:
   (a) With genitive:

   ὁ μαθητὴς ὁ τοῦ κυρίου   the disciple **of the Lord** (= **the Lord's** disciple)

   (b) With adjective:

   ὁ μαθητὴς ὁ πιστός   the **faithful** disciple

(3) First predicate position:
   (a) With genitive:

   τοῦ κυρίου ὁ μαθητής   the disciple **of the Lord** (= **the Lord's** disciple)

   (b) With adjective:

   πιστὸς ὁ μαθητής.   The disciple **is faithful**.

(4) Second predicate position:
   (a) With genitive:

   ὁ μαθητὴς τοῦ κυρίου   the disciple **of the Lord** (= **the Lord's** disciple)

---

[1] Notice that in English the definite article has the effect of making *both* nouns definite: *the Lord's disciple* does not mean either *a disciple of the Lord* or *the disciple of a Lord*, but only *the disciple of the Lord.*

(b) With adjective:

ὁ μαθητὴς **πιστός**.   The disciple **is faithful**.

79. It should be noticed that the meanings of constructions like those of
(1a) and (2a) of §78 are similar to the meanings of constructions like those
of (1b) and (2b), i.e., the noun in the genitive "modifies" the other noun
just as the adjective "modifies" its noun. On the other hand, the meanings
of constructions like those of (3a) and (4a) are not similar to the meanings
of constructions like those of (3b) and (4b); neither **τοῦ κυρίου ὁ μαθμτής**
nor **ὁ μαθητὴς τοῦ κυρίου** means "The disciple is the Lord's," as we
might expect, on the analogy of **πιστὸς ὁ μαθητής** and **ὁ μαθητὴς πιστός**.
To express such a meaning as "The disciple is the Lord's," an equative
verb is normally present.[1] For nouns in the genitive, positions (1), (2),
(3), and (4) are semantically equivalent, except for variations in emphasis.[2]
When a noun in the genitive modifies another noun, it most frequently
has position (4).

EXAMPLES

(1)	1 Pe 3:20 ἡ **τοῦ θεοῦ** μακροθυμία	**God's** patience
(2)	1 Cor 1:18 ὁ λόγος ὁ **τοῦ σταυροῦ**	the word **of the cross**
(3)	Mt 1:18 **τοῦ Ἰησοῦ Χριστοῦ** ἡ γένεσις[3]	the birth **of Jesus Christ**
(4)	2 Cor 13:13 ἡ ἀγάπη **τοῦ θεοῦ**	the love **of God**

80. As we have indicated, the Greek genitive case in the constructions we
have been discussing has meanings which are generally comparable to
those expressed by the English possessive or by English phrases with *of*.
Broadly speaking, we may define the meaning of the genitive in a construction of "modification" to be one of dependence or belonging; i.e.,
whatever is denoted by the noun which is modified is in some way de-

---

[1] Exceptionally, where the context is sufficient to make the meaning clear, no verb is
necessary; e.g.,

1 Cor 10:26 **τοῦ κυρίου** ἡ γῆ.   The earth is **the Lord's**.

[2] Positions (3) and (4) are always called "predicate positions," however, just as (1)
and (2) are called "attributive positions."

[3] This position is quite uncommon, and very emphatic. (ἡ γένεσις is a noun of the third
declension.)

pendent on, or belongs to, whatever is denoted by the noun in the genitive. In traditional grammars various subdivisions of this general meaning are listed, but we shall be content to give a few illustrative examples; the student may note the nuances of meaning for himself:

Rom 1:1 δοῦλος Ἰησοῦ Χριστοῦ	a servant **of Jesus Christ**
Rom 1:1 τὸ εὐαγγέλιον **τοῦ θεοῦ**	the gospel **of God**
Mt 4:23 τὸ εὐαγγέλιον **τῆς βασιλείας**	the gospel **of the kingdom**
1 Cor 15:9 ὁ ἐλάχιστος **τῶν ἀποστόλων**	the least **of the apostles**
Heb 12:15 ῥίζα **πικρίας**	a root **of bitterness**

Sometimes the Greek genitive is best translated by an English adjective:

Lk 18:6 ὁ κριτὴς **τῆς ἀδικίας**	the **unrighteous** judge (*literally,* the judge **of unrighteousness**)
Jas 1:25 ἀκροατὴς **ἐπιλησμονῆς**	a **forgetful** hearer (*literally,* a hearer **of forgetfulness**)

11 | THE DATIVE CASE

81. Each of the sentences below contains a noun (together with its article) in a case form we have not met before. These are forms of the **dative** case.[1] The student should compare these sentences with their English equivalents, making use of the vocabulary[2] provided.

ἀδελφή, ῆς, ἡ, *sister*
βασίλισσα, ης, ἡ, *queen*
δοῦλος, ου, ὁ, *slave*
χήρα, ας, ἡ, *widow*
προφήτης, ου, ὁ, *prophet*

τέκνον, ου, τό, *child*
τροφός, οῦ, ἡ, *nurse*
ἔδωκεν, *gave* (third person singular)

(1)   ἔδωκεν ἡ βασίλισσα τὸν δοῦλον τῇ χήρᾳ.
        The queen gave the widow the slave.
OR: The queen gave the slave to the widow.

(2)   ἔδωκεν ἡ βασίλισσα τῷ δούλῳ τὴν χήραν.
        The queen gave the slave the widow.
OR: The queen gave the widow to the slave.

(3)   ἔδωκεν τῇ βασιλίσσῃ τὸν δοῦλον ἡ χήρα.
        The widow gave the queen the slave.
OR: The widow gave the slave to the queen.

(4)   τῇ ἀδελφῇ ἡ βασίλισσα τὸν δοῦλον ἔδωκεν.
        The queen gave the sister the slave.
OR: The queen gave the slave to the sister.

(5)   τὸν δοῦλον ἔδωκεν ἡ χήρα τῷ προφήτῃ.
        The widow gave the prophet the slave.
OR: The widow gave the slave to the prophet.

---

[1] Consideration of the remaining case, the vocative, is postponed to Lesson 49.

[2] The nouns in this vocabulary are cited in the "full" dictionary form: (1) the nominative singular, (2) the ending of the genitive singular, and (3) the article of the nominative singular. (This is the citation form used by Bauer and other lexicons.)

(6)   τῷ τέκνῳ ὁ προφήτης τὸν δοῦλον ἔδωκεν.
       The prophet gave the child the slave.
OR: The prophet gave the slave to the child.

(7)   ἡ βασίλισσα ἔδωκεν ταῖς χήραις τοὺς δούλους.
       The queen gave the widows the slaves.
OR: The queen gave the slaves to the widows.

(8)   ἡ βασίλισσα ἔδωκεν τὰς χήρας τοῖς δούλοις.
       The queen gave the slaves the widows.
OR: The queen gave the widows to the slaves.

(9)   ταῖς βασιλίσσαις ἔδωκεν τοὺς δούλους ἡ χήρα.
       The widow gave the queens the slaves.
OR: The widow gave the slaves to the queens.

(10)   ἔδωκεν ταῖς ἀδελφαῖς ἡ βασίλισσα τοὺς δούλους.
       The queen gave the sisters the slaves.
OR: The queen gave the slaves to the sisters.

(11)   ἔδωκεν ἡ χήρα τοὺς δούλους τοῖς προφήταις.
       The widow gave the prophets the slaves.
OR: The widow gave the slaves to the prophets.

(12)   ἔδωκεν ὁ προφήτης τοῖς τέκνοις τοὺς δούλους.
       The prophet gave the children the slaves.
OR: The prophet gave the slaves to the children.

(13)   ἡ χήρα τῇ τροφῷ ἔδωκεν τὰ τέκνα.
       The widow gave the nurse the children.
OR: The widow gave the children to the nurse.

(14)   ταῖς τροφοῖς ἔδωκεν ἡ βασίλισσα τὰ τέκνα.
       The queen gave the nurses the children.
OR: The queen gave the children to the nurses.

In the remaining illustrative sentences the adjectives **καλός, ή, όν**, and **μικρός, ά, όν** have been used:

(15)   ἔδωκεν ἡ βασίλισσα τὸν δοῦλον τῇ καλῇ χήρᾳ.
       The queen gave the slave to the good widow.

(16)   τῇ μικρᾷ ἀδελφῇ ἡ βασίλισσα τὸν δοῦλον ἔδωκεν.
       The queen gave the slave to the little sister.

(17)   τῷ μικρῷ τέκνῳ ὁ προφήτης τὸν δοῦλον ἔδωκεν.
       The prophet gave the slave to the little child.

(18)   ἔδωκεν ἡ βασίλισσα τῷ καλῷ δούλῳ τὴν χήραν.
       The queen gave the widow to the good slave.

(19)   τὸν δοῦλον ἔδωκεν ἡ χήρα τῷ προφήτῃ τῷ καλῷ.
The widow gave the slave to the good prophet.

(20)   ταῖς καλαῖς τροφοῖς ἔδωκεν ἡ βασίλισσα τὰ τέκνα.
The queen gave the children to the good nurses.

(21)   ἔδωκεν ἡ χήρα τοὺς δούλους τοῖς προφήταις τοῖς καλοῖς.
The widow gave the slaves to the good prophets.

(22)   ἔδωκεν ὁ προφήτης τοῖς τέκνοις τοῖς μικροῖς τοὺς δούλους.
The prophet gave the slaves to the little children.

Before continuing with this lesson the student should complete Exercises 11-A, 11-B, and 11-C.

82. The Forms of the Dative. The only remarks that need be added here in regard to the forms of the dative case are (1) that the dative singular of first declension forms (masculine or feminine) has -ᾳ if the nominative singular ends in -α immediately preceded by a **vowel** or ρ and (2) that a few first declension masculine nouns, mainly proper names, have the dative singular in -ᾳ if their genitive is in -α.[1]

EXAMPLES SG.N.	ἡ τιμή, honor	ἡ χαρά, joy	ἡ δόξα, glory
G.	τῆς τιμῆς	τῆς χαρᾶς	τῆς δόξης
D.	τῇ τιμῇ	τῇ χαρᾷ	τῇ δόξῃ
A.	τὴν τιμήν	τὴν χαράν	τὴν δόξαν
	etc.	etc.	etc.

SG.N.	ὁ προφήτης, prophet	ὁ νεανίας, youth	ὁ Ἰούδας, Judas
G.	τοῦ προφήτου	τοῦ νεανίου	τοῦ Ἰούδα
D.	τῷ προφήτῃ	τῷ νεανίᾳ	τῷ Ἰούδᾳ
A.	τὸν προφήτην	τὸν νεανίαν	τὸν Ἰούδαν
	etc.	etc.	

The declension of Ἰησοῦς, *Jesus*, is irregular; the forms are given here for convenience:

SG.N.	ὁ Ἰησοῦς
G.	τοῦ Ἰησοῦ
D.	τῷ Ἰησοῦ
A.	τὸν Ἰησοῦν

---

[1] Cf. §§43, 74.

83. Syntax of the Dative. The Greek sentences in §81 all have a common structure, which corresponds to the structure of the English sentence (3) of §45:

(3)   The child gave the dog a bone.

In this English sentence the parts of speech occur in the order

$$N_1 - V - N_2 - N_3$$

and this order is an essential feature of the English structure. If we interchange N_2 and N_3, the structure will no longer express the same meaning. This is immediately evident when we compare two such sentences as

(3a)   The maharajah gave his mother-in-law a white elephant.

(3b)   The maharajah gave a white elephant his mother-in-law.

Examination of sentences (3), (3a), and (3b) reveals that the *second* of the two nouns following the verb (i.e., N_3) has the meaning "receiver of the action," which we have learned to associate with the structure called the (direct) object, and that the *first* noun following the verb (N_2) has a meaning which we may express as "that to or for which the action is performed." The syntactic functions of the nouns in this sentence are represented when we rewrite the formula as

$$S - V - IO - O$$

where IO ($= N_2$) stands for "indirect object."

84. As we have seen from our examination of the sentences in §81, the total structural meaning which is expressed by English sentences with structure

$$S - V - IO - O$$

may be expressed in Greek by sentences whose structure may be represented by the formula

$$N_n - V - N_d - N_a$$

where N_d is a noun in the dative case and where the order of the four constituents is not structurally significant. The meaning expressed by the "indirect object" in the English structure is the same as that expressed by the dative case in this Greek structure, namely, the meaning "that to or for which the action is performed."

Again it must be emphasized that this meaning cannot by itself serve as a basis for defining the grammatical term "indirect object" or the grammatical form "dative case." The indirect object is, in English, a noun or pronoun in a particular position in a particular structure; the meaning which is expressed by the structure can be expressed in other ways. For example, the sentences

(3)   The child gave the dog a bone.
(3c)   The child gave a bone to the dog.
(3d)   The dog was given a bone by the child.

all express the same total meaning, but with different structures.[1] The noun *dog* is the indirect object in (3), but not in (3c) or (3d). In (3c) the meaning expressed by the indirect object in (3) is expressed by a phrase introduced by the function word *to*; in (3d) it is expressed by the subject of the sentence, which itself has an entirely different structure from sentence (3).

85. The Greek dative in sentences with structure

$$N_n - V - N_d - N_a$$

can frequently be rendered as the indirect object in an English sentence with structure

$$S - V - IO - O$$

It can also be rendered by phrases with *to* or *for* (whether or not it can be rendered by the indirect object), and sometimes in other ways. The most common of these are illustrated below:

ὁ θεὸς **τῷ υἱῷ** ἐξουσίαν ἔδωκεν	God gave **the Son** authority *or* God gave authority **to the Son.**
ὁ θεὸς **τοῖς Ἰουδαίοις** νόμους ἔθηκεν.	God made **the Jews** laws *or* God made laws **for the Jews**).
ὁ κριτὴς κατέκρινεν **θανάτῳ** τον δοῦλον.	The judge condemned the slave **to death.**

---

[1] And, of course, differences of emphasis.

παρέδωκεν **τοῖς στρατιώταις** ὁ πονηρὸς μαθητὴς τὸν κύριον	The wicked disciple betrayed the Lord **to the soldiers.**
ὁ στρατιώτης **λόγχῃ** τὴν πλευρὰν ἔνυξεν.	The soldier pierced the side **with a spear.**
ὁ Ἰησοῦς **παρρησίᾳ** τὸν λόγον ἐλάλει.	Jesus was speaking the word **with boldness.**
μακάριοι οἱ καθαροὶ **τῇ καρδίᾳ.**	Blessed are the pure **in heart.**
Ζακχαῖος μικρὸς **τῇ ἡλικίᾳ** ἦν.	Zacchaeus was small **in stature.**
ὁ ἀπόστολος πιστὸς **τῷ κυρίῳ** ἦν.	The apostle was faithful **to the Lord.**
εἰρήνη ἐστὶν **τοῖς μαθηταῖς.**	**The disciples** have peace (*literally*, Peace is **to the disciples**).

It should also be noted that the dative case is not the only means by which the various meanings indicated above are expressed in Greek.

PRESENT AND FUTURE
INDICATIVE ACTIVE

86. The majority of sentences in English and in Greek contain **verbs** as essential constituents. Verbs in both languages may be defined paradigmatically as inflected words whose inflectional forms indicate certain grammatical categories. In English these categories are those of **person**, **number**, and **tense**. For example, the English verb *walk* has the form *walks* in which the morpheme -*s* indicates third person, singular number;[1] i.e., we have:

FIRST PERSON SINGULAR	I	
SECOND PERSON SINGULAR OR PLURAL	you	
FIRST PERSON PLURAL	we	walk
THIRD PERSON PLURAL	they	
	the soldiers	
	he	
THIRD PERSON SINGULAR	she	walks
	it	
	the soldier	

Similarly, the verb *walk* has the form *walked*, in which the morpheme represented by -*ed* indicates past time.

87. The inflectional system of Greek verbs is much more elaborate; inflectional forms serve to indicate not only person, number, and tense, but also mood, voice, and aspect, which are indicated in English by syntactic devices.[2]

---

[1] The morpheme written -*s* may also be said to indicate tense, since it occurs only in the present.

[2] E.g., structures such as *if I were you, we may not go, they have seen, he was seen, you were walking.* (The grammatical terms used in this paragraph will be explained as we proceed.)

A comparison of the Greek forms below with their English equivalents will reveal some of the similarities and differences between the verb systems of the two languages:

	λύω	I loose, I am loosing
	λύεις	you (sg.) loose, you (sg.) are loosing[1]
	λύει	he, she, it looses, he, she, it is loosing
ὁ προφήτης		the prophet
ἡ χήρα	λύει	the widow ⎬ looses, is loosing
τὸ τέκνον		the child
τὰ τέκνα	λύει	the children **are** loosing
	λύομεν	we loose, we are loosing
	λύετε	you (pl.) loose, you (pl.) are loosing
	λύουσιν	they loose, they are loosing
οἱ προφῆται		the prophets
αἱ χῆραι	λύουσιν	the widows ⎬ loose, are loosing
τὰ τέκνα		the children

The main points which stand out are the following:

(1) Each Greek expression corresponds to two[2] English ones; i.e., English has separate sets of forms to express "indefinite" action and "progressive" action in the present, while Greek has only one set of forms for both kinds or *aspects* of action in this tense.[3]

(2) In English the pronouns *I, you, he, she, it, we, they* must be expressed, but in Greek they need not be; the endings of the Greek forms indicate the person sufficiently (except that the third person singular is not definite as to whether *he, she,* or *it* is meant).

(3) In both English and Greek, the verb agrees with its subject in *person* and *number*. (That is, *the prophet* can only be the subject of a verb which is third person singular in form, and *the prophets* can only be the

---

[1] The archaic forms *thou loosest, thou art loosing* also belong here.

[2] Also to the emphatic forms *I do loose, you do loose,* etc., and, in the use called the "historical present," sometimes to *I loosed, you loosed,* etc. (The "historical present" is used for vividness by several New Testament writers. The context shows that it is to be translated by an English past tense.)

[3] Forms like *I loose* may be called "present indefinite," since they may refer to action in progress, action customarily engaged in, or action understood as taking place at the present instant; forms like *I am loosing* refer to action in progress in present time and are called "present progressive."

subject of a verb which is third person plural in form.) EXCEPTION: In Greek, a **neuter plural** subject *may* have a **singular** verb.

88. The six forms of the Greek verb given above make up the paradigm of the present tense, indicative mood, active voice. These terms refer to the sort of meanings which are usually associated with forms like these (i.e., forms with these endings but without further modifications). The present tense forms usually refer to action which takes place in present time; it may be understood as "action now going on" (= English present progressive, *I am loosing*) or " customary or indefinite action in the present " (= English "simple' present, *I loose*). Indicative forms occur in simple statements of fact (but also in other types of statement), and active forms occur in sentences of the type

$$N_n - V - N_a$$

where N_n is the subject and N_a the object as described in Lesson 7.

89. The dictionary form of an English verb is the infinitive (without the function word *to*); this is usually the same as the form of the first person singular, present indicative active; e.g.:

	(to) love	(I) love
	(to) sing	(I) sing
BUT:	(to) be	(I) am

The dictionary form of a Greek verb is[1] the first person singular, present indicative active, e.g., **λύω**. This form is also called the **first principal part** of the verb. The principal parts of a verb are those forms which one must know in order to be able to construct all the other forms. English verbs have three principal parts: (1) the first person singular present, (2) the first person singular past, and (3) the past participle. In the case of most English verbs the second and third principal parts are identical in form and may be constructed by adding -*d* or -*ed* to the first principal part:

love	loved	loved
kill	killed	killed

---

[1] At least in Greek–English dictionaries; German works usually cite the present active infinitive.

The remaining forms (*loves, loving; kills, killing*) are constructed from the first principal part by the application of simple rules. For some verbs, however, the second and third principal parts cannot be constructed from the first by any obvious method:

sing	sang	sung
bring	brought	brought
go	went	gone

For the verb *be* one must know not only the principal parts (*am, was, been*) but also the forms *be, is, are,* and *were.*

Verbs like *love* and *kill*, for which the first principal part is a sufficient basis for the construction of all the remaining principal parts and other forms, are sometimes called **regular** verbs; other verbs are called **irregular** and may be divided into subclasses according to the manner in which their second and third principal parts are formed from the first.

90. Greek verbs may be classified as regular or irregular in exactly the same way. The first principal part of the verb used in the illustrative paradigm is, as we said, **λύω**. If the ending **-ω** is dropped, we obtain the **present base λυ-**. If the endings of the present tense are added to this base, we have the paradigm of the verb in the present tense as this was presented in §87. The endings which are added to the present base to obtain this paradigm are as follows:

SG.1	-ω	PL.1	-ομεν
2	-εις	2	-ετε
3	-ει	3	-ουσι(ν)[1]

These are called the *primary (active) endings.* They are the endings not only of the present indicative active, but also of the *future* indicative active.

91. The paradigms of the present and future tenses are presented below for comparison (English equivalents are given here only for the future forms; for English equivalents of the present, see §87):

---

[1] A final **ν** may be added to any word ending in **-σι** and to third singular verb forms ending in **-ε** (which appear in certain other tenses; see §168, *Remark* 1). This **ν**, called "ν-movable," may be added if the following word begins with a consonant and is usually added if the following word begins with a vowel.

	PRESENT	FUTURE	
SG.1	λύω	λύσω	I shall loose, I will loose,[1] I shall be loosing, I will be loosing
2	λύεις	λύσεις	you (sg.) shall, will loose, etc.
3	λύει	λύσει	he, she, it shall, will loose, etc.
PL.1	λύομεν	λύσομεν	we shall, will loose, etc.
2	λύετε	λύσετε	you (pl.) shall, will loose, etc.
3	λύουσι(ν)	λύσουσι(ν)	they shall, will loose, etc.

92. When we compare the two paradigms above, we find that the **future base** (obtained by dropping -ω from the first person singular future λύσω) consists of the present base plus **σ**.

For a great many Greek verbs it is possible to form the future base in this way, by adding **-σ-** to the present base; for others, however, this is not the case, so that the first person singular of the future tense is a **second principal part** of a Greek verb.

93. Even when it is possible to form the future base from the present base by adding **-σ-**, it is sometimes necessary to make minor modifications of other kinds. Consider the following examples:

PRESENT	(PRESENT BASE)	FUTURE	(FUTURE BASE)
λύω	(λυ-)	λύσω	(λυσ-)
πιστεύω	(πιστευ-)	πιστεύσω	(πιστευσ-)
ἀκούω	(ἀκου-)	ἀκούσω	(ἀκουσ-)
παύω	(παυ-)	παύσω	(παυσ-)

From these examples it appears that when the present base ends in a **vowel**, the future base may be formed from it by adding -σ- as we stated in the preceding section. When the present base ends in a **consonant**, however, things are not quite so simple. Thus, for example, we find forms like:

---

[1] In ordinary English usage, "shall" and "will" are equivalent, although textbooks give various rules for distributing them among the persons. Notice that Greek employs a single form to express the future, while English employs a phrase (*shall loose*, etc.). The "future indefinite" (= *shall loose*) and the "future progressive" (= *shall be loosing*) are not differentiated in Greek.

PRESENT	(PRESENT BASE)	FUTURE	(FUTURE BASE)
πέμπω	(πεμπ-)	πέμψω	(πεμψ-)
διώκω	(διωκ-)	διώξω	(διωξ-)

The future forms of these verbs will not surprise us if we recall that the Greek letter ψ is pronounced *ps* (hence = π + σ) and the Greek letter ξ is pronounced *ks* (and hence = κ + σ). Present bases which end in consonants phonetically similar to π (i.e., β and φ) also have ψ in the future:

	PRESENT	(PRESENT BASE)	FUTURE	(FUTURE BASE)
BASE IN β:	τρίβω	(τριβ-)	τρίψω	(τριψ-)
BASE IN φ:	γράφω	(γραφ-)	γράψω	(γραψ-)

Bases ending in πτ are treated similarly:

καλύπτω	(καλυπτ-)	καλύψω	(καλυψ-)

Further, present bases which end in consonants phonetically similar to κ (i.e., γ and χ) also have ξ in the future:

	PRESENT	(PRESENT BASE)	FUTURE	(FUTURE BASE)
BASE IN γ:	ἄγω	(ἀγ-)	ἄξω	(ἀξ-)
BASE IN χ:	ἐλέγχω	(ἐλεγχ-)	ἐλέγξω	(ἐλεγξ-)

Bases ending in σσ are treated similarly (i.e., they have σσ of the present base replaced by ξ in the future):

PRESENT	(PRESENT BASE)	FUTURE	(FUTURE BASE)
κηρύσσω	(κηρυσσ-)	κηρύξω	(κηρυξ-)

If the present base of a verb ends in ζ, δ, or θ, this consonant is simply dropped before adding σ of the future base:

	PRESENT	(PRESENT BASE)	FUTURE	(FUTURE BASE)
BASE IN ζ:	βαπτίζω	(βαπτιζ-)	βαπτίσω	(βαπτισ-)
BASE IN δ:	ᾄδω	(ᾀδ-)	ᾄσω	(ᾀσ-)
BASE IN θ:	πείθω	(πειθ-)	πείσω	(πεισ-)

The manner of forming the future tense for other types of verbs will be taken up later.

94. The orthographic and phonological modifications described above may be summarized briefly as follows:

(a)   π, β, φ, or ππ + σ > ψ
(b)   κ, γ, χ, or σσ + σ > ξ
(c)   δ, θ, or ζ + σ > σ

13 | THE PAST TENSES OF
THE INDICATIVE ACTIVE

95. In the previous lesson we found that, in the present and future tenses, English verbs have separate sets of forms to express the two aspects of action we have called "indefinite" and "progressive," but that Greek verbs have only one set of forms in each of these tenses to express both of these aspects; i.e.,

λύω corresponds to both *I loose* ("indefinite aspect")
and *I am loosing* ("progressive aspect")

and

λύσω corresponds to both *I shall loose* ("indefinite aspect")
and *I shall be loosing* ("progressive aspect")

For indicating action in past time, however, Greek verbs have two sets of forms. Forms of one kind usually express the aspect we have called "progressive"; these forms make up the tense[1] called the **imperfect**. Forms of the second kind usually express the "indefinite" aspect; these forms make up the tense called the **aorist** (< Gk ἀόριστος, *indefinite*). More will be said a little later about the meanings of these two sets of forms; we proceed first to the forms themselves. For the model verb λύω they are:

	IMPERFECT		AORIST	
SG.1	ἔλυον	*I was loosing*, etc.	ἔλυσα	*I loosed*, etc.
2	ἔλυες		ἔλυσας	
3	ἔλυεν		ἔλυσεν	
PL.1	ἐλύομεν		ἐλύσαμεν	
2	ἐλύετε		ἐλύσατε	
3	ἔλυον		ἔλυσαν	

---

[1] In traditional grammatical terminology the imperfect and aorist are called *tenses*; they are actually sets of forms each of which (in the indicative mood) expresses (1) past time and (2) the particular aspect proper to the set.

Careful attention should be given to the following points:

(1) All the forms in both paradigms have a prefixed morpheme **ἐ-**. This is called the **augment**. The augment is present only in the past tenses[1] of the indicative mood. If a verb begins with a consonant, it has in the past tenses an augment in the form of a prefixed **ἐ-**, as here; if a verb begins with a vowel or diphthong, the augment consists of a modification of this vowel or diphthong, as follows:

INITIAL VOWEL OR DIPHTHONG		AUGMENTED VOWEL OR DIPHTHONG	EXAMPLES PRESENT	IMPERFECT
α	>	η	ἀκούω	ἤκουον
ε	>	η	ἐλπίζω	ἤλπιζον
ο	>	ω	ὀφείλω	ὤφειλον
ι	>	ῑ	ἰσχύω	ἴσχυον
υ	>	ῡ	ὑγιαίνω	ὑγίαινον

(The lengthening of ι and υ to ῑ and ῡ is not represented in ordinary texts, though it sometimes is in grammatical works.)

αι	>	η	αἴρω	ἦρον
αυ	>	ηυ	αὐξάνω	ηὔξανον
οι	>	ῳ	οἰκτείρω	ᾤκτειρον
ευ	>	ηυ	εὑρίσκω	ηὕρισκον

(ευ may sometimes be left unchanged: εὕρισκον)

ει is always left unchanged: εἰρηνεύω εἰρήνευον

(2) The forms of the imperfect are obtained by (a) augmenting the present base as described above and (b) adding the endings:

SG.1	–ον	PL.1	–ομεν
2	–ες	2	–ετε
3	–ε(ν)[2]	3	–ον

Note that the first person singular and third person plural are identical in form.

(3) The forms of the aorist are obtained by (a) augmenting the present base, (b) adding **-σ**, and then (c) adding the endings:

---

[1] I.e., the imperfect and aorist, and sometimes the pluperfect (in all voices, but only in the indicative mood).

[2] Cf. §90, fn. 1.

sg.1	-α	pl.1	-αμεν
2	-ας	2	-ατε
3	-ε(ν)[1]	3	-αν

Note that the endings of the imperfect are similar to (but not the same as) those of the aorist, but that neither set of endings is the same as that of the primary endings found in the present and future tenses.

(4) The rule given for the formation of the imperfect admits of few exceptions (e.g., εἶχον, rather than ἦχον, is the imperfect of ἔχω); the imperfect is, accordingly, not one of the principal parts of a verb. The rule for forming the aorist, on the other hand, admits of a number of exceptions of various kinds; the first person singular of the aorist (indicative active) is, hence, the **third principal part** of a verb.

(5) When σ is added to the augmented present base to form the aorist base, the same kind of modifications are made in the final consonants of the base as are made when σ is added to form the future base (cf. §§93f):

	PRESENT	FUTURE	AORIST
BASE IN π:	πέμπω, *send*	πέμψω	ἔπεμψα
BASE IN β:	τρίβω, *rub*	τρίψω	ἔτριψα
BASE IN φ:	γράφω, *write*	γράψω	ἔγραψα
BASE IN πτ:	καλύπτω, *hide*	καλύψω	ἐκάλυψα
BASE IN κ:	διώκω, *pursue*	διώξω	ἐδίωξα
BASE IN γ:	ἀνοίγω, *open*	ἀνοίξω	ἤνοιξα
BASE IN χ:	ἐλέγχω, *expose*	ἐλέγξω	ἤλεγξα
BASE IN σσ:	κηρύσσω, *preach*	κηρύξω	ἐκήρυξα
BASE IN δ:	σπεύδω, *hasten*	σπεύσω	ἔσπευσα
BASE IN θ:	πείθω, *persuade*	πείσω	ἔπεισα
BASE IN ζ:	βαπτίζω, *baptize*	βαπτίσω	ἐβάπτισα

(6) Verbs which have aorist forms with the endings given in (3), above, are said to have **first aorists**, and the forms are called first aorist forms. Most verbs have first aorists and the majority of these verbs form their first aorists regularly as set forth in (3), above. Some verbs, however, form their first aorists irregularly, or by suppletion (cf. §30(e)). It is advisable to commit the most important of these to memory; among the most common are the following:

---

[1] Cf. §90, fn. 1.

PRESENT	FIRST AORIST
δίδωμι¹, *give*	ἔδωκα
τίθημι¹, *put, place*	ἔθηκα
φέρω, *bring*	ἤνεγκα
κρίνω, *judge*	ἔκρινα
μένω, *remain*	ἔμεινα

The first aorist paradigms of verbs in the above list are formed by dropping
-α of the third principal part (given in the second column) and adding the
endings given in (3) above.

(7) A number of important verbs have **second aorists**; i.e., their aorists
are formed irregularly or by suppletion, and they have, instead of the
endings given in (3), above, the endings of the *imperfect* (given in (2),
above). Verbs of this type must be memorized. Some of the most important
are listed below:

PRESENT	FUTURE	AORIST
λείπω, *leave*	λείψω	ἔλιπον
ἄγω, *lead*	ἄξω	ἤγαγον
εὑρίσκω, *find*	εὑρήσω	εὗρον
ἔχω, *have*	ἔξω²	ἔσχον (Imperfect εἶχον)
ἁμαρτάνω, *sin*	ἁμαρτήσω	ἥμαρτον

Note that the imperfect always (except for a very few verbs) has the
augmented present base; the second aorist never has the present base,
but always some variation of it. The imperfect and aorist of **λείπω**, *leave*,
are given below for comparison:

	IMPERFECT	AORIST
SG.1	ἔλειπον	ἔλιπον
2	ἔλειπες	ἔλιπες
3	ἔλειπεν	ἔλιπεν
PL.1	ἐλείπομεν	ἐλίπομεν
2	ἐλείπετε	ἐλίπετε
3	ἔλειπον	ἔλιπον

96. Meaning of the Aorist and the Imperfect. The first aorist and the
second aorist are not two different tenses, but two different ways of forming

---

¹ For the conjugation of the present tense of these verbs, see Lesson 27.

² Note the *rough* breathing on this form.

the same tense. Thus **ἔλυσα** and **ἔλιπον** are both aorist forms, just as *walked* and *sang* are both forms of the English past tense. Very few verbs have both first and second aorists, just as few English verbs have two sets of past tense forms. When two sets of forms do occur, the difference in meaning is usually negligible.[1]

We have already said that the Greek imperfect usually expresses progressive action in past time and that the aorist refers to a less definite sort of action. When we come to render the Greek forms into English, we find that there is no one-to-one correspondence that will lighten our task. The table below illustrates something of the range of meaning of the Greek forms and some of the possible English equivalents:

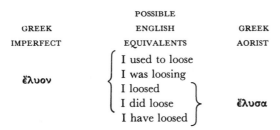

GREEK IMPERFECT	POSSIBLE ENGLISH EQUIVALENTS	GREEK AORIST
ἔλυον	I used to loose / I was loosing / I loosed / I did loose / I have loosed	**ἔλυσα**

In translating the Greek imperfect, the student should not limit himself to translations of the "I was loosing" type. The Greek imperfect does, of course, refer to action in progress, but various English expressions may be used to represent this. Sometimes the simple "I loosed" form is quite acceptable as a rendering of a Greek imperfect, as the context may make it quite clear that progressive action is meant, or that the activity was customary, or enduring, or something of the sort. When the context is sufficiently explicit, the "I was loosing" kind of translation frequently sounds awkward and overdone. Similarly, the Greek aorist very frequently refers to action which has been completed in the past, so that it often corresponds to the English perfect (*I have loosed*).

---

[1] Thus the past tense of *dive* may be *dived* or *dove*, and the aorist of **ἁμαρτάνω** may be **ἡμάρτησα** (first aorist) or **ἥμαρτον** (second aorist).

14

αὐτός
οὗτος and ἐκεῖνος

97. In Lesson 9 we defined adjectives as words which are inflected for case, number, and gender, and then described their various syntactic characteristics and functions.[1] A number of words are paradigmatically similar to adjectives as thus defined, but differ from them syntactically in one or more important respects.[2] Among the more important of these "semiadjectives" is the word **αὐτός**, which is declined as follows:

	MASCULINE	FEMININE	NEUTER
SG.N.	αὐτός	αὐτή	αὐτό
G.	αὐτοῦ	αὐτῆς	αὐτοῦ
D.	αὐτῷ	αὐτῇ	αὐτῷ
A.	αὐτόν	αὐτήν	αὐτό
PL.N.	αὐτοί	αὐταί	αὐτά
G.	αὐτῶν	αὐτῶν	αὐτῶν
D.	αὐτοῖς	αὐταῖς	αὐτοῖς
A.	αὐτούς	αὐτάς	αὐτά

It should be noticed that the endings of **αὐτός** are the same as those of an ordinary adjective like **καλός**, with the exception of those for the nominative and accusative singular neuter, where the ending is **-ο** instead of **-ον**.

98. Αὐτός occurs with articular nouns in each of the four positions previously described as appropriate for adjectives (§68(2)); the meanings

---

[1] Cf. §§63–68.

[2] Compare the similar situation that exists in English, as described above, §60.

[80]

of the resultant constructions should be compared and contrasted with the meanings of similar constructions with **καλός**:

(1) Compare **αὐτός** and **καλός** in:

(a) First attributive position:

ὁ **αὐτὸς** κύριος	the **same** Lord
ὁ **καλὸς** κύριος	the **good** Lord

(b) Second attributive position:

ὁ κύριος ὁ **αὐτός**	the **same** Lord
ὁ κύριος ὁ **καλός**	the **good** Lord

(2) Contrast **αὐτός** and **καλός** in:

(a) First predicate position:

αὐτὸς ὁ κύριος	the Lord **himself**
καλὸς ὁ κύριος.	The Lord **is good**.

(b) Second predicate position:

ὁ κύριος **αὐτός**	the Lord **himself**
ὁ κύριος **καλός**.	The Lord **is good**.

99. From these illustrative examples it appears that **αὐτός**, when it is in either *attributive* position, corresponds to the English adjective *same*. When **αὐτός** is in either *predicate* position, however, it does *not* function as a predicate adjective (i.e., **αὐτὸς ὁ κύριος** does not mean "the Lord is same," even if this made sense in English). Instead, when it is in either *predicate* position, **αὐτός** corresponds to English *himself, herself, itself, themselves,* depending on the noun with which it is associated. If the context permits, **αὐτός** may also (when in predicate position) be rendered by English *(the) very, (that) very,* in such constructions as *the very man, that very day*.[1] Thus we find

	Rev 21:3 **αὐτὸς** ὁ θεός	God **himself**
BUT:	1 Cor 12:6 ὁ **αὐτὸς** θεός	the **same** God
	Acts 16:18 **αὐτὴ** ἡ ὥρα	**that very** hour
	Jn 5:36 **αὐτὰ** τὰ ἔργα	the works **themselves**
OR:	Jn 14:11 τὰ ἔργα **αὐτά**	the works **themselves**

---

[1] Not, however, as in *the very good man*.

100. Αὐτός, like an ordinary adjective, may be "used as a noun."[1] In such cases it is preceded by the definite article:

Lk 6:33 οἱ ἁμαρτωλοὶ τὸ αὐτὸ ποιοῦσιν.	The sinners do **the same**.

101. Αὐτός sometimes occurs with proper names without an article; in such cases it usually precedes and has the meaning *himself*, *herself*, etc.

Mk 12:37 αὐτὸς Δαυίδ	David **himself**

102. The Greek demonstratives, οὗτος, *this* (pl. *these*), and ἐκεῖνος, *that* (pl. *those*), are declined as follows:

(1)

	MASC.	FEM.	NEUT.		MASC.	FEM.	NEUT.
SG.N.	οὗτος	αὕτη	τοῦτο	PL.N.	οὗτοι	αὗται	ταῦτα
G.	τούτου	ταύτης	τούτου	G.	τούτων	τούτων	τούτων
D.	τούτῳ	ταύτῃ	τούτῳ	D.	τούτοις	ταύταις	τούτοις
A.	τοῦτον	ταύτην	τοῦτο	A.	τούτους	ταύτας	ταῦτα

(2)

	MASC.	FEM.	NEUT.		MASC.	FEM.	NEUT.
SG.N.	ἐκεῖνος	ἐκείνη	ἐκεῖνο	PL.N.	ἐκεῖνοι	ἐκεῖναι	ἐκεῖνα
G.	ἐκείνου	ἐκείνης	ἐκείνου	G.	ἐκείνων	ἐκείνων	ἐκείνων
D.	ἐκείνῳ	ἐκείνῃ	ἐκείνῳ	D.	ἐκείνοις	ἐκείναις	ἐκείνοις
A.	ἐκεῖνον	ἐκείνην	ἐκεῖνο	A.	ἐκείνους	ἐκείνας	ἐκεῖνα

The paradigms of the demonstratives should be compared with those of αὐτός and the definite article, and the similarities and differences noted. The forms αὐτή and αὕτη, and αὐταί and αὗται, in particular, should be distinguished.

103. Syntax of the Demonstratives. (1) The Greek demonstratives may modify nouns and, when they do so, they agree with the nouns in case, number, and gender (compare αὐτός and ordinary adjectives like καλός).

(a) Οὗτος and ἐκεῖνος never modify anarthrous nouns.

(b) Οὗτος and ἐκεῖνος never occur in either of the **attributive** positions.

---

[1] Cf. §71.

(c) **Οὗτος** and **ἐκεῖνος** may occur in either of the **predicate** positions with meanings as indicated below:

(i) First predicate position:

Mt 7:6 **οὗτος ὁ λαός** (cf. Mt 15:8, below)	**this people**
Rev 22:6 **οὗτοι οἱ λόγοι** (cf. Lk 24:17, below)	**these words**
Lk 13:6 ἔλεγεν **ταύτην τὴν παραβολήν.**	He told **this parable.**
Mt 24:14 **τοῦτο τὸ εὐαγγέλιον** τῆς βασιλείας	**this gospel** of the kingdom
1 Cor 11:25 **τοῦτο τὸ ποτήριον** ἡ καινὴ διαθήκη ἐστίν.	**This cup** is the new covenant.

(ii) Second predicate position:

Mt 15:8 **ὁ λαὸς οὗτος**	**this people**
Lk 24:17 **οἱ λόγοι οὗτοι**	**these words**
Mt 13:53 ἐτέλεσεν ὁ Ἰησοῦς **τὰς παραβολὰς ταύτας.**	Jesus finished **these parables.**
Mt 13:44 ἀγοράζει **τὸν ἀγρὸν ἐκεῖνον**	He buys **that field.**
Lk 12:46 ἥξει ὁ κύριος **τοῦ δούλου ἐκείνου.**	The Lord **of that servant** will come.

(2) The Greek demonstratives also function as pronouns (i.e., without associated nouns).

(a) As a pronoun, **οὗτος** is equivalent to English *this* (not followed by a noun), *this one, this person, this man*; **αὕτη** is equivalent to *this one, this woman*; **τοῦτο** to *this, this one, this thing*; **οὗτοι** to *these, these men*, etc.; and **ἐκεῖνος** is equivalent to English *that, that one, that person, that man*, etc. Thus we have

Mt 3:17 **οὗτός** ἐστιν ὁ υἱός.	**This** is the son.
Mt 9:3 **οὗτος** βλασφημεῖ.	**This man** is blaspheming.
Acts 9:36 **αὕτη** ἦν πλήρης ἔργων ἀγαθῶν.	**This woman** was full of good works.

(b) The demonstrative pronouns are sometimes used to refer to persons mentioned in the immediately preceding context, and in such cases they are frequently best translated simply *he, she,* or *they*:

Jn 1:8 οὐκ ἦν ἐκεῖνος τὸ φῶς.	**He** was not the light. [ἐκεῖνος refers to John the Baptist.]

(c) When **οὗτος** and **ἐκεῖνος** do occur with anarthrous nouns, they are not modifiers of these nouns (see above, (1a)), but pronouns:

Jn 10:1 ἐκεῖνος κλέπτης ἐστὶν καὶ λῃστής.	**That man** is a thief and a robber (*not* That thief is also a robber).
Col 4:11 οὗτοι μόνοι συνεργοί.	**These** are **the** only workers. [*The* is supplied before *workers*, which is a predicate nominative; see §59.]
Rom 8:14 οὗτοι υἱοὶ θεοῦ εἰσιν.	**These** are sons of God (*or* the sons of God).
Lk 2:2 αὕτη ἀπογραφὴ πρώτη ἐγένετο.	**This** was the first enrollment.

(d) When **οὗτος** or **ἐκεῖνος** is connected to a predicate nominative by an equative verb (as in the last two examples above), the demonstrative usually has the gender, number, and case of the predicate noun; however, in the phrase **τοῦτ' ἔστιν** (= **τοῦτό ἐστιν**), *that is, i.e.,* the demonstrative is always neuter singular:

Heb 7:5 ἀποδεκατοῦν τὸν λαόν, **τοῦτ' ἔστιν**, τοὺς ἀδελφούς	to take tithes of the people, **that is,** the brethren

(3) **Οὗτος** may be used with **αὐτός** as in:

2 Cor 2:3 ἔγραψα **τοῦτο αὐτό**.	I wrote **this very thing**.

(4) **Οὗτος** and **ἐκεῖνος** may also modify nouns which are modified by other adjectives or which have other (ordinary) adjectives in one of the predicate positions:

Mt 24:18 ὁ κακὸς δοῦλος ἐκεῖνος	**that wicked** servant
Mk 12:43 ἡ χήρα αὕτη ἡ πτωχή	**this poor** widow
Mt 24:26 μακάριος ὁ δοῦλος ἐκεῖνος.	**Blessed** is **that** servant.

15 | PERSONAL PRONOUNS AND RELATED ADJECTIVES

104. It was pointed out in the preceding lesson that the demonstratives οὗτος and ἐκεῖνος are occasionally equivalent to English *he, she*, etc.[1] However, the English pronouns of the third person (i.e., *he, she, it, his, her, hers, its, him, they, their, theirs, them*) ordinarily correspond to forms of αὐτός.[2] When αὐτός functions as a personal pronoun, its syntactic behavior is like that of a noun, except that it has no article.

105. The *case* of the pronoun αὐτός is always the same as that which would be required of a noun with the same syntactic function:

(1) A nominative case form of αὐτός may function as the subject of a sentence.

Lk 19:2 αὐτὸς ἦν ἀρχιτελώνης.	**He** was a chief tax collector.
Lk 7:12 αὐτὴ ἦν χήρα.	**She** was a widow.
Lk 11:14 αὐτὸ ἦν κωφόν.	**It** was dumb.
Lk 8:13 αὐτοὶ ῥίζαν οὐκ ἔχουσιν.	**They** have no root.

NOTE: αὐτός, αὐτή, αὐτό, and αὐτοί could be omitted from these examples without obscuring the meaning, since the *person* of the verb is indicated by the form of the verb itself. Accordingly, the personal pronouns do not have to be expressed separately when they are subjects, except for emphasis or clarity.

(2) An accusative case form of αὐτός may function as direct object.

Jn 4:45 ἐδέξαντο αὐτὸν οἱ Γαλιλαῖοι.	The Galileans received **him**.

---

[1] Cf. §103(b).

[2] For the paradigm, see §97.

Mt 8:15 ἄφηκεν **αὐτὴν** ὁ πυρετός.	The fever left **her.**
Gal 1:12 παρέλαβον **αὐτό.**	I received **it.**
Mt 12:15 ἐθεράπευσεν **αὐτούς.**	He healed **them.**

(3) A dative case form of **αὐτός** may function as indirect object.

Rev 2:26 δώσω **αὐτῷ** ἐξουσίαν.	I shall give **him** power.
Jn 11:25 εἶπεν **αὐτῇ** ὁ Ἰησοῦς, ἐγώ εἰμι ἡ ὁδός . . .	Jesus said **to her,** "I am the way . . ."
Mt 10:1 ἔδωκεν **αὐτοῖς** ἐξουσίαν.	He gave **them** power.

(4) A genitive case form of **αὐτός** may be attributive to a noun; when it is so attributive, it may occupy the *first* attributive position (but not the second, in the New Testament) or either of the two predicate positions.

(a) In first attributive position:

1 Th 2:19 ἡ **αὐτοῦ** παρουσία	**his** appearing

(b) In first predicate position:

Jn 12:40 τετύφλωκεν **αὐτῶν** τοὺς ὀφθαλμοὺς καὶ ἐπώρωσεν **αὐτῶν** τὰς καρδίας.	He has blinded **their** eyes and has hardened **their** hearts.
Jn 9:21 [ὁ Ἰησοῦς] ἤνοιξεν **αὐτοῦ** τοὺς ὀφθαλμούς.	[Jesus] opened **his** eyes (i.e., the eyes of the blind man).

(c) In second predicate position:

Mt 1:2 Ἰακὼβ ἐγέννησεν τὸν Ἰούδαν καὶ τοὺς ἀδελφοὺς **αὐτοῦ.**	Jacob begat Judah and **his** brothers.
Lk 2:7 [Μαριάμ] ἔτεκεν τὸν υἱὸν **αὐτῆς.**	[Mary] bore **her** son.

NOTE: The equivalent of an English possessive (*his, her, its, their*) with an *anarthrous* noun is usually a Greek genitive (**αὐτοῦ, αὐτῆς, αὐτῶν**) with an *articular* noun. Thus we have

ὁ **αὐτοῦ** λόγος		
αὐτοῦ ὁ λόγος	BUT:	**his** (or **its**) word
ὁ λόγος **αὐτοῦ**		
ὁ **αὐτῆς** λόγος		
αὐτῆς ὁ λόγος	BUT:	**her** (or **its**) word
ὁ λόγος **αὐτῆς**		

ὁ αὐτῶν λόγος
αὐτῶν ὁ λόγος   } BUT: **their** word
ὁ λόγος αὐτῶν

When a Greek genitive form (αὐτοῦ, αὐτῆς, αὐτῶν) does occur with an anarthrous noun, the combination is frequently equivalent to an English anarthrous noun (or a noun with the *indefinite* article) followed by *of his, of hers, of theirs, of it(s)*. For example,

λόγος αὐτοῦ = a word **of his**
λόγος αὐτῆς = a word **of hers**
λόγοι αὐτοῦ = words **of his**
λόγοι αὐτῶν = words **of theirs**

106. The **gender** of the Greek pronoun of the third person depends on the gender of the Greek noun to which it refers, and not on the sex or sexlessness of the person or thing which the noun itself represents.[1] Thus αὐτός and αὐτή may correspond to English *it*, and αὐτό may correspond to *he* or *she*. The plural forms of the Greek pronoun also distinguish gender, whereas the English ones do not. The following examples will make this clearer:

Jn 12:24 ἐὰν μὴ ὁ κόκκος τοῦ σίτου ἀποθάνῃ, **αὐτὸς** μόνος μένει.	Unless the grain of wheat dies, **it** remains alone. [ὁ κόκκος, *grain*, is masculine.]
Jas 5:18 ἡ γῆ ἐβλάστησεν τὸν καρπὸν **αὐτῆς**.	The earth brought forth **its** fruit. [ἡ γῆ, *earth*. is feminine.]
Rev 6:13 συκῆ βάλλει τοὺς ὀλύνθους **αὐτῆς**.	A fig tree casts off **its** unripe fruit. [ἡ συκῆ, *fig tree*, is feminine.]
Lk 1:59 ἐκάλουν **αὐτὸ** Ζαχαρίας.	They called **him** Zacharias. [τὸ παιδίον, *child*, is neuter.]
Mk 16:8 εἶχεν **αὐτὰς** τρόμος.	Trembling seized **them**. [*Them* refers to the women at the tomb.]
Jn 10:12 ὁ λύκος ἁρπάζει **αὐτά**.	The wolf snatches **them**. [*Them* refers to *the sheep* = τὰ πρόβατα neuter plural.]

[1] Cf. §37.

107. The paradigms of the Greek pronouns of the first and second persons, singular and plural, are given below:

(1)	FIRST PERSON SINGULAR		(2)	SECOND PERSON SINGULAR	
N.	ἐγώ	I	N.	σύ	you (sg.), thou
G.	ἐμοῦ, μου	my, mine, of me, of mine	G.	σοῦ, σου	your, yours, of you, of yours, etc.
D.	ἐμοί, μοι	me, to me, for me	D.	σοί, σοι	you, to you, for you; thee, etc.
A.	ἐμέ, με	me	A.	σέ, σε	you, thee

(3)	FIRST PERSON PLURAL		(4)	SECOND PERSON PLURAL	
N.	ἡμεῖς	we	N.	ὑμεῖς	you (pl.), ye
G.	ἡμῶν	our, ours, of us, of ours	G.	ὑμῶν	your, yours, of you, of yours
D.	ἡμῖν	us, to us, for us	D.	ὑμῖν	you, to you, for you
A.	ἡμᾶς	us	A.	ὑμᾶς	you

108. The forms without accents in the paradigms above (i.e., the first and second persons singular, genitive, dative, and accusative) are called **enclitics**; they have no accent of their own, but affect the accent pattern of the preceding word. The details of this are discussed in Appendix I; for the present it is sufficient to point out that the accented forms are usually emphatic. Minor differences in the functions of the accented and unaccented forms are noted in the appropriate sections of this lesson.

109. Like αὐτός, the pronouns of the first two persons have syntactic functions similar to those of nouns, except that they do not have the article.

(1) The nominative case forms may function as subjects.

Jn 6:35 ἐγώ εἰμι ὁ ἄρτος τῆς ζωῆς.	**I** am the bread of life.
Lk 4:41 σὺ εἶ ὁ υἱὸς τοῦ θεοῦ.	**You** (sg.) are the Son of God.
Jn 19:7 ἡμεῖς νόμον ἔχομεν.	**We** have a law.
Jn 15:3 ὑμεῖς καθαροί ἐστε.	**You** (pl.) are pure.

NOTE: ἐγώ, σύ, ἡμεῖς, and ὑμεῖς could be omitted from these examples without obscuring the sense, since the person of the verb is indicated by the form of the verb itself (cf. §105(1), *Note*).

(2) The accusative case forms may serve as direct objects; notice that the accented and unaccented case forms are interchangeable in this use.

Mt 26:11 ἐμὲ οὐ πάντοτε ἔχετε.	You do not always have **me**.
Rom 7:11 ἡ ἁμαρτία ἐξηπάτησέν **με**.	Sin deceived **me**.
Jn 17:4 ἐγώ **σε** ἐδόξασα.	I glorified **you** (sg., = thee).
Mt 8:31 ἐκβάλλεις **ἡμᾶς**.	You are casting **us** out.
Jn 8:32 ἡ ἀλήθεια ἐλευθερώσει **ὑμᾶς**.	The truth will make **you** (pl.) free.

(3) The dative case forms may serve as indirect objects; again, notice that the accented and unaccented forms are interchangeable.

Lk 15:29 **ἐμοὶ** οὐδέποτε ἔδωκας ἔριφον.	You never gave **me** a kid.
Jn 4:29 εἶπέν **μοι** πάντα.	He told **me** everything.
Mt 16:19 δώσω **σοι** τὰς κλεῖδας τῆς βασιλείας τῶν οὐρανῶν.	I shall give **you** (sg.) the keys of the kingdom of the heavens.
Lk 24:32 διήνοιγεν **ἡμῖν** τὰς γραφάς.	He opened the scriptures **to us**.
1 Cor 15:51 μυστήριον **ὑμῖν** λέγω.	I tell **you** (pl.) a mystery.

(4) The genitive case forms may modify nouns; when they do so, they may occupy the *first* attributive position (but not the second) or either of the two predicate positions (cf. §105(4)).

(a) First attributive position:

2 Cor 12:19 ἡ **ὑμῶν** οἰκοδομή	**your** (pl.) edification

(b) First predicate position:

Lk 22:53 αὕτη ἐστὶν **ὑμῶν** ἡ ὥρα.	This is **your** (pl.) hour.

(c) Second predicate position:

Lk 1:46 μεγαλύνει ἡ ψυχή **μου** τὸν κύριον.	**My** soul magnifies the Lord.

(d) The genitive forms may occur with anarthrous nouns (cf. §105(4), *Note*):

Jn 8:31 μαθηταί **μού** ἐστε.	You are disciples **of mine**.

(e) If the noun modified has an adjective in first attributive position, the genitive case form of the pronoun comes between the adjective and the noun:

<table>
<tr><td>Rom 6:6 ὁ παλαιὸς ἡμῶν
ἄνθρωπος συνεσταυρώθη.</td><td>**Our old** man has been crucified.</td></tr>
</table>

(f) If the noun modified has an adjective in second attributive position, the genitive case form of the pronoun comes after the noun, preceding the article of the adjective:

<table>
<tr><td>Lk 3:22 σὺ εἶ ὁ υἱός **μου** ὁ
ἀγαπητός.</td><td>You (sg.) are **my beloved** Son.</td></tr>
</table>

(g) The emphatic form **ἐμοῦ** is not used to modify nouns except when it is joined to another pronoun (usually by **καί**, *and*):

<table>
<tr><td>Rom 16:13 ἀσπάσασθε ʽΡοῦφον
. . . καὶ τὴν μητέρα αὐτοῦ
καὶ **ἐμοῦ.**</td><td>Greet Rufus, . . . and his mother
and **mine.**</td></tr>
</table>

NOTE: Unlike the pronouns of the third person, the pronouns of the first two persons are not inflected for gender.

110. Possessive Adjectives. The English forms *my, mine, thy, thine, our, ours, your, yours* are usually represented in Greek by the genitive forms of the appropriate personal pronouns, as we have said; they may, however, also be represented by the possessive adjectives **ἐμός, ἡ, όν; σός, ἡ, όν; ἡμέτερος, α, ον;** and **ὑμέτερος, α, ον.** These possessive adjectives are inflectionally and syntactically similar to other adjectives; they occur much less frequently than the genitive forms of the personal pronouns.

(a) Possessive adjectives with anarthrous nouns:

<table>
<tr><td>Jn 13:35 γνώσονται πάντες ὅτι
ἐμοὶ μαθηταί ἐστε.</td><td>All shall know that you are **my**
disciples (= disciples **of mine**).</td></tr>
<tr><td>cf. Jn 8:31 μαθηταί **μού** ἐστε.</td><td>You are **my** disciples (= disciples
of mine).[1]</td></tr>
</table>

---

[1] Cf. §109(4d).

(b) Possessive adjectives with articular nouns:
  (i) In attributive position (either first or second):

Jn 7:6 ὁ καιρὸς ὁ ἐμός
Jn 7:8 ὁ ἐμὸς καιρός   } **my** time
cf. Mt 26:18 ὁ καιρός **μου**

  (ii) When possessive adjectives are used predicatively, a form of the verb **εἰμί**[1] is usually expressed (but see John 17:10, under (c), below):

Jn 7:16 ἡ ἐμὴ διδαχὴ οὐκ ἔστιν ἐμή.	My teaching is not **mine**.
Jn 17:6 **σοὶ** ἦσαν κἀμοὶ αὐτοὺς ἔδωκας.	They were **thine** and thou gavest them to me.
cf. Mt 6:13[2] **σοῦ** ἐστιν ἡ βασιλεία.	**Thine** is the kingdom.

(c) Possessive adjectives are also used substantively, like other adjectives (cf. §71):

Jn 17:10 τὰ ἐμὰ πάντα σά ἐστιν καὶ τὰ σὰ ἐμά.	All **that is mine** is thine, and **thine** is mine (= All **my things** are thine and **thy things** are mine).

---

[1] See Cf. §109. (4d).

[2] In the so-called Koinē text (i.e., of manuscripts EFGHSUVΩ, etc.).

16 | PRESENT AND IMPERFECT INDICATIVE PASSIVE

111. If we once more reexamine the sentences of §45, we find that sentences (1) and (7) are similar in meaning, but different in structure:

(1)   The treasurer misappropriated the funds.
(7)   The funds were misappropriated by the treasurer.

In sentence (1), as we have seen, the subject (*treasurer*) indicates "the performer of the action," and the object (*funds*) indicates "the receiver of the action." In (7), however, *treasurer* is no longer the subject and *funds* is no longer the object, even though the word *treasurer* still refers to the "performer" and the word *funds* still refers to the "receiver," and even though the total information content of the whole sentence is the same as that of sentence (1), with, perhaps, slight differences in emphasis.

112. The subject of (7) is *funds*; this grammatical fact is indicated in English by the position it occupies in the sentence structure (i.e., before the verb). It appears, then, that in sentences whose structures are similar to that of sentence (7), the subject indicates not the "performer," but the "receiver of the action." Moreover, in sentences with this structure, the *performer* of the action is indicated by a grammatical device we have not encountered before, namely, by the object[1] of the preposition *by*.

113. The relationship which holds between sentences (1) and (7) also holds between all sentences whose structures are similar to that of sentence (1) and the corresponding sentences whose structures are similar to that

---

[1] The "object" of a preposition is structurally very different from the object of a verb (in Greek as well as in English), but the same grammatical term has traditionally been used for both.

of sentence (7). Thus we can construct an indefinite number of sentences which are structurally similar to sentence (1), and for each one of these we can construct a sentence with the same information content, but with a structure similar to that of sentence (7):

SIMILAR TO (1)	SIMILAR TO (7)
Cats catch mice.	Mice are caught by cats.
The dog is chasing a cat.	A cat is being chased by the dog.
The merchant was selling coffee.	Coffee was being sold by the merchant.
The secretary will write a letter.	A letter will be written by the secretary.

114. Comparing the sentences on the left with those on the right, we find:

(a) The objects of the former are the subjects of the latter.

(b) The subjects of the former appear in the latter preceded by the preposition *by* (or, in grammatical terminology, the subjects of the former are objects of the preposition *by* in the latter).

(c) The verb forms of the former are replaced in the latter by verb phrases consisting of forms of the verb *be* (e.g., as in the examples above, *are, is being, was being, will be*) plus the past participle of the original verb (e.g., *caught, chased, sold, written*).

115. Verb forms such as those in sentence (1) and sentences of similar structure are said to be in the **active voice**; verb forms such as those in sentence (7) and sentences of similar structure are said to be in the **passive voice**. Verbs which have both active and passive forms are called **transitive** verbs.

116. In general, if we let X represent *treasurer, cats, dog, merchant, secretary*, or the subject of any other sentence whose structure is similar to that of sentence (1), and if we let Y represent *funds, mice, cat, coffee, letter*, or the object of any other sentence whose structure is similar to that of sentence (1), we can then represent sentence (1) itself and all sentences of similar structure (such as those at the left in §113) by the formula

$$(A) \qquad X_s - V_{act} - Y_o$$

where the subscripts s and o indicate that X and Y are the subject and object, respectively, in this sentence structure, and where V_{act} is a verb in the **active** voice. Sentence (7), on the other hand, as well as any other sentence of similar structure, can be represented by the formula

(B) $\qquad\qquad Y_s - V_{pass} - by + X_o$

where X and Y refer to the same nouns as before and where V_{pass} is a verb in the **passive** voice. Here, moreover, the subscript $_s$ indicates that Y, which was the object in formula (A), is now the subject, and the subscript $_o$ shows that X, which was subject in (A), is now the object of *by*.

117. Formula (A) can, obviously, be changed or transformed into formula (B) by:

(a) Moving X from subject position to a position after *by* (note that *by* is the only *new* constituent).

(b) Moving Y from object position to subject position.

(c) Changing the verb from active to passive (note that the verb is the only element which is changed in form).

This transformation may be represented symbolically as follows:

ACTIVE   PASSIVE

$$X_s - V_{act} - Y_o \quad > \quad Y_s - V_{pass} - by + X_o$$

The applicability of this transformation may be readily tested:

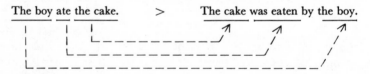

The boy ate the cake.   >   The cake was eaten by the boy.

If the transformation is applied to sentences containing pronoun subjects or objects, the case forms of these must be adjusted:

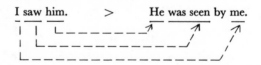

I saw him.   >   He was seen by me.

We heard her.   >   She was heard by us.

118. As we have seen, many Greek sentences share a structure which has a structural meaning similar to the English structure of sentence (1);[1] there are also Greek sentences which share a structure similar in structural meaning to the English structure of sentence (7). Moreover, the former class of Greek sentences is related to the latter class by a transformation of precisely the same kind as that we have described in this lesson. Greek sentences of the first kind may be represented by the formula

$$(\alpha)\quad X_n - V_{act} - Y_a$$

corresponding to formula (A) of §116. In formula (α), X and Y are nouns (or pronouns), and the subscripts $_n$ and $_a$ indicate that they are in the nominative and accusative cases, respectively. V_{act}, as before, is a verb in the active voice. The order of these elements in Greek is, of course, not fixed as it is in English. When a Greek sentence with structure (α) is transformed in the same way as we have described for English sentences,

(a) The verb is changed from active to passive.

(b) X becomes the object of a preposition; in most cases this is ὑπό, which in this function requires that X be put into the **genitive** case.

(c) Y becomes the subject and is therefore changed from accusative to nominative.

The structure of the resulting sentence is, therefore,

$$(\beta)\quad Y_n - V_{pass} - \text{ὑπό} + X_g$$

The order of these elements is, again, not fixed, *except* that the preposition ὑπό must always immediately precede the element X_g.

The transformation described in this section may be represented symbolically as follows:

ACTIVE		PASSIVE
$X_n - V_{act} - Y_a$	>	$Y_n - V_{pass} - \text{ὑπό} + X_g$

---

[1] See Lesson 7, especially §50.

119. The transformation is applied to a number of Greek sentences below, with the English equivalents given in all instances. The Greek verb forms in boldface are those of the **present** and **imperfect passive**.

	ACTIVE	PASSIVE
(1)	ἐγὼ λύω τὸν δοῦλον.	ὁ δοῦλος **λύεται** ὑπ' ἐμοῦ.
	I am loosing the slave.	The slave is being loosed by me.
(2)	σὺ λύεις ἡμᾶς.	ἡμεῖς **λυόμεθα** ὑπὸ σοῦ.
	You (sg.) are loosing us.	We are being loosed by you (sg.).
(3)	ὁ κύριος λύει με.	ὑπὸ τοῦ κυρίου **λύομαι** ἐγώ.
	The Lord is loosing me.	I am being loosed by the Lord.
(4)	τοὺς ἀνθρώπους λύετε ὑμεῖς.	οἱ ἄνθρωποι ὑφ' ὑμῶν **λύονται**.
	You (pl.) are loosing the men.	The men are being loosed by you (pl.).
(5)	ὑμᾶς λύουσιν οἱ ἀπόστολοι.	ὑμεῖς **λύεσθε** ὑπὸ τῶν ἀποστόλων.
	The apostles are loosing you (pl.).	You (pl.) are being loosed by the apostles.
(6)	ἡμεῖς λύομέν σε.	σὺ **λύῃ** ὑφ' ἡμῶν.
	We are loosing you (sg.).	You (sg.) are being loosed by us.
(7)	τὸν δοῦλον σὺ ἔλυες.	ὁ δοῦλος **ἐλύετο** ὑπὸ σοῦ.
	You (sg.) were loosing the slave.	The slave was being loosed by you.
(8)	ὁ ἄνθρωπος ἡμᾶς ἔλυεν.	ἡμεῖς **ἐλυόμεθα** ὑπὸ τοῦ ἀνθρώπου.
	The man was loosing us.	We were being loosed by the man.
(9)	οἱ μαθηταὶ ἔλυόν σε.	σὺ **ἐλύου** ὑπὸ τῶν μαθητῶν.
	The disciples were loosing you (sg.).	You (sg.) were being loosed by the disciples.
(10)	ἡμεῖς ὑμᾶς ἐλύομεν.	ὑμεῖς **ἐλύεσθε** ὑφ' ἡμῶν.
	We were loosing you (pl.).	You (pl.) were being loosed by us.
(11)	ὑμεῖς ἐλύετέ με.	ἐγὼ **ἐλυόμην** ὑφ' ὑμῶν.
	You (pl.) were loosing me.	I was being loosed by you (pl.).
(12)	ἐγὼ ἔλυον τοὺς δούλους.	οἱ δοῦλοι **ἐλύοντο** ὑπ' ἐμοῦ.
	I was loosing the slaves.	The slaves were being loosed by me.

NOTE 1: The accented forms **ἐμοῦ** and **σοῦ** are used after **ὑπό**.

NOTE 2: The final **ο** of **ὑπό** may be elided before a vowel, and if it is elided, **ὑπό** becomes **ὑπ'** before a smooth breathing but **ὑφ'** before a rough breathing: **ὑπό + ἐμοῦ = ὑπ' ἐμοῦ** but **ὑπό + ἡμῶν = ὑφ' ἡμῶν**.

120. In Greek as in English, the prepositional phrase (ὑπό + Noun or Pronoun in the genitive = *by* + Noun or Pronoun) is not an obligatory part of the structure of any of the sentences in the right-hand column of §119. Thus [ἐγώ] λύομαι, *I am being loosed*, [σύ] λύῃ, *you* (sg.) *are being loosed*, etc., are complete sentences. Thus the passive voice is often used when the writer wishes for some reason to leave "the performer of the action" unexpressed or when "the performer of the action" is unknown.

17 | THE MIDDLE VOICE

121. Greek and English are similar, as we have seen, in that each has verb forms for expressing the meanings conventionally described as those of the active voice and other verb forms for expressing the meanings conventionally described as those of the passive voice.[1] Unlike English, however, Greek verbs have a third set of forms for expressing still other meanings; these forms are described as **middle**, or are said to be in the **middle voice**, since at least some of the meanings they are used to express may be thought of as standing midway between the meanings of the active and passive voices.

122. Although English has no middle voice (there being no distinctive forms for expressing "middle meanings" in English), an examination of some English constructions which do express comparable meanings will make the Greek middle voice more readily understandable.

At first glance, the verb *bathe* in illustrative sentence (11), §45, seems to be not different from the verb *cough* in sentence (2):

(11)   The professor bathed hastily.
(2)   The judge coughed apologetically.

Bathe and *cough* in these two sentences have the same paradigmatic form ("simple past"), and their syntactic contexts are the same (each is V in S — V — [Adv]); nevertheless, the structural meanings expressed are not identical, because *bathe* and *cough* are different *kinds* of verbs (in the sense that equative verbs are not the same as transitive verbs). The difference between *bathe* and *cough* is not paradigmatic, for each has as many forms, and the same types of forms, in its paradigm as the other:

---

[1] See the previous lesson.

[98]

bathe, bathes, bathed, bathing
cough, coughs, coughed, coughing

The difference between the two verbs is *syntactic*, i.e., *cough* seldom or never occurs in some syntactic contexts in which *bathe* regularly occurs. Thus, for example, *bathe* frequently occurs in contexts like that of *misappropriate* in illustrative sentence (1) of §45:

(1)   The treasurer misappropriated the funds.
(11a)   The professor bathed the children.
                . . . the dog.
                . . . the cat.
                . . . his face.

Cough, on the other hand, occurs in such contexts only rarely:

(2a)   The judge coughed a great hacking cough.
        The judge coughed his instructions at the jury.

Bathe regularly, *cough* rarely, occurs in the passive:

(7)   The funds were misappropriated by the treasurer.
(11b)   The children were bathed by the professor.
(2b)   A great hacking cough was coughed by the judge.

Bathe also occurs in some contexts in which comparatively few other verbs ordinarily occur:

(11c)   The professor bathed himself.
(1c)   The treasurer misappropriated himself.
(2c)   The judge coughed himself.

Sentences like (1c) and (2c) would seldom or never be encountered outside a book like this one, but sentences like (11c), with verbs such as *bathe*, *wash*, *dress*, *undress*, are not at all unusual. It may be observed, moreover, that the meaning expressed by (11c) is the same as that expressed by

        The professor bathed.

123. Verbs like English *bathe* are also found in Greek, but in Greek the distinction between these and other verbs is paradigmatically marked; i.e., they have special "middle" forms to indicate the "middle" meanings which, as we have seen, must be indicated in English by the syntactic context. Even in Greek the middle voice is not complete, so to speak,

[99]

since distinctively middle forms occur only in the aorist and future tenses. In other tenses the middle voice is formally identical with the passive voice, so that we are again thrown back on syntactic considerations. In the illustrative sentences below we introduce the aorist passive as well as the aorist middle, to facilitate comparison and contrast (note that the verb in each of these sentences is λούω, not λύω):

(a)	ἡ ἀδελφὴ **ἔλουσεν** τὸ τέκνον.	The sister **bathed** the child.
(b)	ἡ ἀδελφὴ **ἐλούσατο**.	The sister **bathed**.
(c)	τὸ τέκνον **ἐλούθη** ὑπὸ τῆς ἀδελφῆς.	The child **was bathed** by the sister.

The form **ἔλουσεν** is (first) aorist active (described in Lesson 15); the form **ἐλούσατο** is (first) aorist middle, and the form **ἐλούθη** is (first) aorist passive (as one might infer from the presence of **ὑπὸ τῆς ἀδελφῆς**).

(1) The structure of (a) is

(a) $X_n - V_{act} - Y_a$

where X_n is the subject (as indicated by the nominative case); in this structure the subject indicates the *performer* of the action.[1]

(2) The structure of (c) is

(c) $Y_n - V_{pass} - ὑπό + X_g$

where Y_n is the subject (again, as indicated by the nominative case); in this structure the subject indicates the *receiver* of the action.[2]

(3) The structure of (b) is

(b) $X_n - V_{mid}$

where X_n is the subject (as indicated by the nominative case); in this structure the subject indicates *both* the performer and the receiver of the action. The distinctive mark of this structure, of course, is the middle voice of the verb. The indication of this "reflexive" meaning is only one of the functions of the middle voice; we shall discuss this and other meanings later in this lesson, but for the present we shall turn our attention to the forms themselves.

124. The forms of the (first) aorist middle are given below; to facilitate comparison and contrast, the forms of the (first) aorist active and (first)

---

[1] Cf. §§51f.   [2] Cf. §112.

aorist passive are also given (here we return to **λύω** as our model verb):

	ACTIVE	MIDDLE	PASSIVE
SG.1	ἔλυσα	ἐλυσάμην	ἐλύθην
2	ἔλυσας	ἐλύσω	ἐλύθης
3	ἔλυσεν	ἐλύσατο	ἐλύθη
PL.1	ἐλύσαμεν	ἐλυσάμεθα	ἐλύθημεν
2	ἐλύσατε	ἐλύσασθε	ἐλύθητε
3	ἔλυσαν	ἐλύσαντο	ἐλύθησαν

125. The endings of the (first) aorist middle are as follows:

SG.1	-αμην	PL.1	-αμεθα
2	-ω	2	-ασθε
3	-ατο	3	-αντο

These are added to the (first) aorist base of the verb (found by dropping -**α** of the third principal part; see §95(3,6)); for example,

DICTIONARY FORM (= FIRST PRINCIPAL PART)	THIRD PRINCIPAL PART	FIRST AORIST MIDDLE
λύω, *loose*	ἔλυσα	ἐλυσάμην
γράφω, *write*	ἔγραψα	ἐγραψάμην
διώκω, *pursue*	ἐδίωξα	ἐδιωξάμην
βαπτίζω, *baptize*	ἐβάπτισα	ἐβαπτισάμην
ἀλείφω, *anoint*	ἤλειψα	ἠλειψάμην

126. The aorist passive forms are not derived from any of the bases studied thus far. The first person singular aorist passive indicative is itself a principal part;[1] when it is a part of a regular verb, it is formed by augmenting the present base (as described in §95(1)) and by adding -**θην**. The aorist passive base is obtained by dropping -**ην** of this form; the endings are as follows:

SG.1	-ην	PL.1	-ημεν
2	-ης	2	-ητε
3	-η	3	-ησαν

---

[1] It is usually counted as the *sixth* principal part; it is, however, more convenient to take it up at this point.

The manner of forming the aorist passive of regular verbs is illustrated below:

DICTIONARY FORM	PRESENT BASE	AUGMENTED PRESENT BASE	AORIST PASSIVE
πέμπω, *send*	πεμπ-	ἐπεμπ-	ἐπέμφθην
καλύπτω, *cover*	καλυπτ-	ἐκαλυπτ-	ἐκαλύφθην
διώκω, *pursue*	διωκ-	ἐδιωκ-	ἐδιώχθην
ἄγω, *lead*	ἀγ-	ἠγ-	ἤχθην
κηρύσσω, *preach*	κηρυσσ-	ἐκηρυσσ-	ἐκηρύχθην
βαπτίζω, *baptize*	βαπτιζ-	ἐβαπτιζ-	ἐβαπτίσθην
ἀλείφω, *anoint*	ἀλειφ-	ἠλειφ-	ἠλείφθην

127. It will be observed from the forms in the right-hand column above that the addition of -θ- occasions certain phonological changes, analogous to those discussed in §§93f:

(a)   π, β, φ, or ππ + θ > φθ
(b)   κ, γ, χ, or σσ + θ > χθ
(c)   δ, θ, or ζ + θ > σθ

128. There is no way of telling, however, whether the aorist passive forms of consonant base verbs (or even of all verbs whose bases end in vowels) will be regular; it is, therefore, generally necessary to memorize these forms or to look them up in a lexicon. A few of the more common verbs with irregular first aorist passive forms are given below:

ἀκούω, *hear*	ἠκούσθην
σῴζω, *save*	ἐσώθην
εὑρίσκω, *find*	εὑρήθην
διδάσκω, *teach*	ἐδιδάχθην
λαμβάνω, *take*	ἐλήμφθην
λέγω, *say*	ἐρρέθην or ἐρρήθην

129. Verbs which have *second* aorist active forms also have second aorist middle forms, but need not have second aorist passive forms (see below, §130); similarly, verbs with first aorist active forms always have first aorist middle forms, but may or may not have first aorist passive forms. The forms of the second aorist middle are obtained by adding the following endings to the second aorist base (found by dropping **-ον** of the second aorist active):[1]

SG.1	-ομην	PL.1	-ομεθα
2	-ου	2	-εσθε
3	-ετο	3	-οντο

The second aorist middle forms of **εὑρίσκω** are given below (formed from the second aorist active **εὗρον**):

SG.1	εὑρόμην	PL.1	εὑρόμεθα
2	εὗρου	2	εὕρεσθε
3	εὕρετο	3	εὕροντο

130. The *second* aorist passive is irregular in that no rules can be given for obtaining its forms for any particular verb, nor is it possible to predict in advance that a verb will have a second aorist passive rather than a first aorist passive. The first person singular of the second aorist passive, which ends in **-ην** but not in **-θην**, must simply be learned as an irregular principal part; the second aorist passive base, like the first aorist passive base, is obtained by dropping **-ην** of this part. The endings are the same as for the first aorist passive (cf. §126). Among the most frequently occurring verbs which have second aorist passive forms are the following:

γράφω, *write*	ἐγράφην
θλίβω, *afflict*	ἐθλίβην
κόπτω, *cut*	ἐκόπην
κρύπτω, *hide*	ἐκρύβην

131. It will be noticed that all aorist forms, active, middle, and passive, first or second, have the *augment* when they are in the *indicative* mood (all forms given so far are in the indicative).

132. The Meaning of the Middle Voice. The Greek middle voice expresses several meanings, but these are not expressed by any single construction in English. In translating verb forms in the middle voice, therefore, we must be guided by the context.

---

[1] They are, of course, the same as those of the imperfect (middle and) passive. Cf. §§95(2,7) and 119 and Exercises 16-A and 16-C.

(1) The middle voice may express a *direct reflexive* meaning; i.e., the subject of a verb in the middle voice may indicate *both* the performer *and* the receiver of the action indicated by the verb. This is probably the least common meaning of the middle voice.

(2) The middle voice may express an *indirect reflexive* meaning; i.e., the subject of a verb in the middle voice may indicate *both* the performer of the action *and* "that to or for which the action is performed." When so used, a verb in the middle voice may govern a noun or pronoun in the accusative case, which functions in the same way as the direct object of a verb in the active voice.

(3) The middle voice may express a *causative meaning*; i.e., the subject of the verb in the middle voice may indicate the person who causes, or allows, an action to be performed.

EXAMPLES   ACTIVE VOICE

ἤλειψα αὐτόν.   **I anointed** him.
ἤλειψα τὴν κεφαλήν σου.   **I anointed** your head.

                                            MIDDLE VOICE

ἠλειψάμην.   **I anointed myself.** (Direct reflexive

                                            I had myself (*or* **let myself be**) **anointed.** (Causative)

ἠλειψάμην τὴν   **I anointed my** head. (Indirect reflexive)
   κεφαλήν [μου].

                                            I had my head **anointed** (*or* **let my** head **be anointed**). (Causative)

                                            PASSIVE VOICE

ἠλείφθην [ὑπὸ τοῦ   **I was anointed** [by my disciple].
   μαθητοῦ μου].

133. As we pointed out in passing (§123), the forms of the present and imperfect middle are the same as the forms of the present and imperfect passive. In the interpretation of such forms we must be guided by the context; if contextual evidence is not decisive, we are usually safe in understanding the forms as passive, since the middle voice is comparatively rare.

18

FUTURE MIDDLE AND PASSIVE
DEPONENT VERBS
THE VERB εἰμί

134. The forms of the future middle and future passive of **λύω** are given below:

	FUTURE MIDDLE	FUTURE PASSIVE
SG.1	λύσομαι	λυθήσομαι
2	λύσῃ	λυθήσῃ
3	λύσεται	λυθήσεται
PL.1	λυσόμεθα	λυθησόμεθα
2	λύσεσθε	λυθήσεσθε
3	λύσονται	λυθήσονται

135. The forms of the future middle are obtained from the second principal part (i.e., the first person singular future active); the base is found by dropping the ending **-ω** of this form, and the following endings are added:

SG.1	-ομαι		PL.1	-ομεθα
2	-η		2	-εσθε
3	-εται		3	-ονται

It will be seen that these are the same as the endings of the present passive (cf. §119 and Exercises 16-A and 16-B), which also functions as the present middle.

136. The forms of the future passive are obtained from the sixth principal part (i.e., the aorist passive); the base is found by (1) removing the augment, (2) dropping the final **-ν**, and (3) adding **-σ-**; to this base the same endings are added as for the future middle. Thus, from **ἐλύθην** we obtain (1) **λυθην** by removing the augment, then (2) **λυθη-** by dropping **-ν**, then (3) **λυθησ-** by adding **-σ-**, and finally we have **λυθήσομαι, λυθήσῃ**, etc. (If a verb has a *second* aorist passive, its future passive also has no **θ**.) The uses of the future middle are analogous to those of the aorist middle (cf. §132), and the uses of the future passive are analogous to those of other tenses in the passive (cf. Lesson 16).

137. Deponent Verbs. Some Greek verbs have no active forms, but have middle or passive forms (sometimes both) which are *syntactically* active; i.e., they are used to indicate meanings which would be expressed in English by verbs in the active voice. These verbs are called *deponent*. The most frequently occurring deponent verb is **γίνομαι**, *become, come to be, originate, arise, come about, be made, happen, take place, come to pass.* The principal parts are as follows:

PRESENT	FUTURE	AORIST (MIDDLE)	AORIST PASSIVE
γίνομαι	γενήσομαι	ἐγενόμην	ἐγενήθην

The aorist middle and aorist passive forms of this verb are synonymous (both mean *became, came to be*, etc.)

EXAMPLES: Mt 13:53 ἐγένετο ὅτε   It **came to pass** when Jesus
            ἐτέλεσεν ὁ Ἰησοῦς.   finished.

            Col. 1:25 ἐγενόμην ἐγὼ διάκονος.   I **became** a minister.

            1 Th 1:6 ὑμεῖς μιμηταὶ ἡμῶν   You **became** our imitators.
            ἐγενήθητε.

138. Some verbs are only "partly" deponent; i.e., they lack active forms in one or more tenses, but not in all tenses. The most frequently occurring verb of this type is **ἔρχομαι**, *come*, with principal parts as follows:

PRESENT	FUTURE	AORIST	AORIST PASSIVE
ἔρχομαι	ἐλεύσομαι	ἦλθον	[none]

Ἔρχομαι is deponent in the present and future (and, hence, also in the imperfect, which is formed on the present stem), but not in the aorist. This important verb is suppletive in its formation.[1]

139. The most important verbs which are deponent or partly deponent are as follows:

---

[1] Cf. §30(e).

PRESENT	FUTURE	AORIST	AORIST PASSIVE
πορεύομαι, *go, depart*	πορεύσομαι	[none in NT]	ἐπορεύθην
δέχομαι, *receive*	δέξομαι	ἐδεξάμην	[none in NT]
λαμβάνω, *take, receive*	λήμψομαι	ἔλαβον	ἐλήμφθην[1]
μανθάνω, *learn*	μαθήσομαι	ἔμαθον	[none]
ἐσθίω, *eat*	φάγομαι	ἔφαγον	[none]
ἄρχομαι, *begin*[2]	ἄρξομαι	ἠρξάμην	ἤρχθην
γινώσκω, *know*	γνώσομαι	ἔγνων[3]	ἐγνώσθην

140. The Verb εἰμί. The most frequently occurring verb in the New Testament is **εἰμί**, which, like its English equivalent *to be*, is irregular. Its forms are given below (it has no others in the indicative):

		PRESENT				IMPERFECT	
SG.1	εἰμί	I am		SG.1	ἤμην	I was	
2	εἶ	you (sg.) are, thou art		2	ἦς	you (sg.) were, thou wert	
3	ἐστίν	he, she, it is		3	ἦν	he, she, it, was	
PL.1	ἐσμέν	we are		PL.1	ἦμεν		
2	ἐστέ	you (pl.) are			or ἤμεθα	we were	
3	εἰσίν	they are		2	ἦτε	you were (pl.)	
				3	ἦσαν	they were	

		FUTURE	
SG.1	ἔσομαι	I shall be, will be	
2	ἔσῃ	you (sg.) shall be, will be, thou shalt be, wilt be	
3	ἔσται	he, she, it shall be, will be	
PL.1	ἐσόμεθα	we shall be, will be	
2	ἔσεσθε	you (pl.) shall be, will be	
3	ἔσονται	they shall be, will be	

These forms should be committed to memory. **Εἰμί** and **γίνομαι** (§137) are the most important equative verbs (cf. §§56–58, 70).

---

[1] The aorist passive and future passive forms of this verb are also passive in *meaning*.

[2] The forms of this verb are the middle and passive of ἄρχω, which in the active means *rule*.

[3] The conjugation of the aorist of γινώσκω is given in Lesson 46.

19 | FIRST AND SECOND
DECLENSIONS: REVIEW

141. In our discussion of linguistic structure (Lesson 3, §15), we referred briefly to **morphemes** as the smallest elements of language which have meaning. Although we have occasionally mentioned morphemes in succeeding lessons, we have usually been content to speak more vaguely of prefixes and suffixes, of endings, and, still more generally, of inflections. These vaguer terms serve very well for most purposes, but it is sometimes advantageous to use a more precise terminology based on a more detailed analysis. Such an analysis will entail a review of the inflections learned so far and will reduce the total number of forms which need to be learned. Further, the analysis will provide a basis for the description of the inflections which still remain to be studied.[1]

142. We shall begin with nouns. Heretofore we have regarded each form of a noun as composed of two parts, an invariable part (called the **base**) and a variable part (which we have called the **ending** or **inflection**). The base may consist of one or more morphemes (one morpheme: τιμ- in τιμή; two morphemes: παρα- and βολ- in παραβολή), but this is of no particular importance from the point of view of grammar. We shall now

---

[1] Some nouns are indeclinable, and have no inflections of any kind. For the most part these are proper names or technical terms borrowed from Hebrew or Aramaic:

τὸ πάσχα, *the Passover*	Καφαρναούμ, *Capernaum*
τὸ μάννα, *manna*	Ἰερουσαλήμ or
Βηθλεέμ, *Bethlehem*	Ἰεροσόλυμα, *Jerusalem*
Σιών, *Zion*	Σαούλ, *Saul*

Πλησίον is indeclinable, but it is not a noun at all; it is an adverb (from the adjective πλησίος, α, ον, *near*) meaning *close by, near*; used with the article, it means *neighbor*.

show that each of the *endings* in the noun paradigms studied so far may be divided into *two* morphemes, a **stem formative** and a **case-number suffix**.[1] It will be convenient to arrange the noun endings in a table, for easy reference.

BASE	SINGULAR				PLURAL			
	NOM.	GEN.	DAT.	ACC.	NOM.	GEN.	DAT.	ACC.
χαρ-	-α	-ας	-ᾳ	-αν	-αι	-ων	-αις	-ας
τιμ-	-η	-ης	-η	-ην	-αι	-ων	-αις	-ας
δοξ-	-α	-ης	-η	-αν	-αι	-ων	-αις	-ας
νεανι-	-ας	-ου	-ᾳ	-αν	-αι	-ων	-αις	-ας
μαθητ-	-ης	-ου	-η	-ην	-αι	-ων	-αις	-ας
λογ-	-ος	-ου	-ῳ	-ον	-οι	-ων	-οις	-ους
ἐργ-	-ον	-ου	-ῳ	-ον	-α	-ων	-οις	-α

143. Each of the endings in the table above may be divided into two morphemes, a stem formative and a case-number suffix, as indicated below:

(1) Either the stem formative or the ending may be lacking; if either is lacking, it is said to be **zero** (represented by #).[2] For examples, see below, (2b ii), (2e ii), (2f), and (2h).

---

[1] A detailed explanation of the method by which this division is effected is beyond the scope of this book. In general, however, morphemes are identified by contrasting words which differ minimally in form and meaning. Thus, for example, a comparison of μαθητής, μαθητήν and λόγος, λόγον leads to the isolation of morphemes -ς and -ν for the nominative and accusative cases, respectively, of the singular number, and of morphemes -η- and -ο- which serve to identify the first and second declensions, respectively. See further Nida, *Morphology*, and the relevant chapters in Gleason and Hockett (see Selected Bibliography, §6(b)). The analysis of the forms of a language into morphemes should, ideally, be preceded by a description of the language's **phonemes** (roughly speaking, the smallest elements which contrast with each other within the phonological system of the language); for the modest purposes of this book, the letters of the alphabet have been treated as if they exactly represented the phonemes.

[2] It should be observed that *zero* is introduced as a convenient device to simplify and regularize morphemic descriptions. For if we divide the endings -ης, -ην, -ος, and -ον

(2) The case-number suffixes are as follows:
  (a) Singular nominative:
    (i) # for feminine nouns of the first declension.
    (ii) -ν for neuter nouns of the second declension.
    (iii) -ς for all other nouns of the first and second declensions.

EXAMPLES   τιμή (= τιμ + η + #)   νεανίας (= νεανι + α + ς)
               ἔργον (= ἐργ + ο + ν)   λόγος (= λογ + ο + ς)
               μαθητής (= μαθητ + η + ς)

  (b) Singular genitive:
    (i) -ς for feminine nouns of the first declension.
    (ii) -ου for all other nouns of the first and second declensions.

EXAMPLES   τιμῆς (= τιμ + η + ς)   λόγου (= λογ + # + ου)
               μαθητοῦ (= μαθητ + # + ου)

  (c) Singular dative: ⁔. Iota subscript is placed under the stem formative; the long mark (–) indicates that the stem formative is lengthened if it is short: ο > ω; α and η remain unchanged.

EXAMPLES   χαρᾷ (= χαρ + α + ⁔)   λογῳ (= λογ + ο + ⁔)
               κώμῃ (= κωμ + η + ⁔)

  (d) Singular accusative: -ν for all nouns of the first and second declensions.

EXAMPLES   χαράν (= χαρ + α + ν)   μαθητήν (= μαθητ + η + ν)
               τιμήν (= τιμ + η + ν)   λόγον (= λογ + ο + ν)

  (e) Plural nominative:
    (i) -α for all neuter nouns of the second declension.
    (ii) -ι for all other nouns of the first and second declensions.

---

into two morphemes each (see §142, fn. 1), what shall we do with the endings of τιμή and λόγου? They are obviously indivisible, but for the sake of symmetry we describe the -η of τιμή as consisting of two morphemes, one, -η-, which identifies the declension, and the other, *zero*, which identifies the case and number. Obviously, it is the *absence* of any case-number suffix which serves to identify the form as nominative singular, but it is more convenient, in symbolic descriptions, to speak of the "presence" of a *zero* suffix. Similarly, we describe the ending -ου of λόγου as consisting of a *zero* stem formative and the case-number suffix -ου.

EXAMPLES ἔργα (= ἐργ + # + α) λόγοι (= λογ + ο + ι)
τιμαί (= τιμ + α + ι) νεανίαι (= νεανι + α + ι)

(f) Plural genitive: **-ων** for all nouns of the first and second declensions.

EXAMPLES χαρῶν (= χαρ + # + ων) λόγων (= λογ + # + ων)
τιμῶν (= τιμ + # + ων) ἔργων (= ἐργ + # + ων)
μαθητῶν (= μαθητ + # + ων)

(g) Plural dative: **-ις** for all nouns of the first and second declensions.

EXAMPLES χαραῖς (= χαρ + α + ις) μαθηταῖς (= μαθητ + α + ις)
τιμαῖς (= τιμ + α + ις) λόγοις (= λογ + ο + ις)

(h) Plural accusative:
  (i) **-ας** for all first declension nouns.
  (ii) **-ους** for all masculine and feminine nouns of the second declension.
  (iii) **-α** for all neuter nouns of the second declension.

EXAMPLES τιμάς (= τιμ + # + ας) λόγους (= λογ + # + ους)
μαθητάς (= μαθητ + # + ας) ἔργα (= ἐργ + # + α)

(3) The stem formatives are as follows:
  (a) **#** if the case-number suffix begins with a vowel other than ι.

EXAMPLES τιμῶν (= τιμ + # + ων) λόγους (= λογ + # + ους)

(b) **-α-** For first declension nouns, except that:
  (i) For *most* first declension nouns with bases ending in a consonant other than **-ρ-**, the stem formative is **-η-** in the *singular*.
  (ii) For *some* first declension nouns with bases ending in a consonant other than **-ρ-**, the stem formative is **-η-** in the *genitive and dative singular*. (These may be recognized from their dictionary forms.)
  (c) **-ο-** for second declension nouns.

EXAMPLES χαρά (= χαρ + α + #) τιμήν (= τιμ + η + ν)
δόξα (= δοξ + α + #) δόξης (δοξ + η + ς)
λόγος (= λογ + ο + ς)

144. Statements (2a–h) of the preceding section may be compactly arranged as follows:

				SUFFIX	DECLENSION	GENDER
(a)	(i)	SG.	NOM.	-#	1	f
	(ii)			-ν	2	n
	(iii)			-ς	$\begin{cases} 1 \\ 2 \end{cases}$	m m and f
(b)	(i)		GEN.	-ς	1	f
	(ii)			-ου	$\begin{cases} 1 \\ 2 \end{cases}$	m m, f, n
(c)			DAT.	-ͺ	1 and 2	m, f, n
(d)			ACC.	-ν	1 and 2	m, f, n
(e)	(i)	PL.	NOM.	-α	2	n
	(ii)			-ι	1 and 2	m and f
(f)			GEN.	-ων	1 and 2	m, f, n
(g)			DAT.	-ις	1 and 2	m, f, n
(h)	(i)		ACC.	-ας	1	m and f
	(ii)			-ους	2	m and f
	(iii)			-α	2	n

145. Meaning of the Morphemes. The stem formative morphemes "mean" the declension to which a noun belongs (i.e., the presence of the stem formative -α- means that the noun is of the first declension; the presence of the stem formative -o- means that the noun is of the second declension; if the stem formative is lacking, we cannot identify the declension). The case-number suffix morphemes "mean" the case and number of the noun.

NOTE 1: Some morphemes have variant forms; i.e., the case-number suffix for the accusative plural may be -ας, -ους, or -α. These variant forms of a morpheme are sometimes called **allomorphs.**

NOTE 2: The term **ending** has been and will continue to be used in this book to refer to the combination of a stem formative with a case-number suffix; in the future we shall also make use of the term **stem** to refer to the combination of a base with a stem formative.

20 | THE THIRD DECLENSION, I: MAJOR CONSONANT STEMS

146. Nouns of the third declension may be divided into subclasses as follows:

A. Nouns whose bases end in a *consonant* and which have no stem formative (or, put differently, which have *zero* as stem formative). These are collectively called **consonant stems**[1] and include:
   (1) *Major consonant stems*, which include, in turn:
      (a) *Labial stems* (nouns whose bases end in -π-, -β-, or -φ-).
      (b) *Velar stems* (nouns whose bases end in -κ-, -γ-, or -χ-).
      (c) *Dental stems* (nouns whose bases end in -τ- (but not -ντ-), -δ-, or -θ-).
   (2) *Minor consonant stems*, which include, in turn:
      (a) *Nasal stems* (nouns whose bases end in -ν- or -ντ-).
      (b) *Liquid stems* (nouns whose bases end in -λ- or -ρ-).

B. Nouns whose bases end in -υ- (preceded by a consonant) and which have no stem formative. These are called **υ-stems**.

C. Nouns whose bases end in either a consonant or a vowel and which have as stem formatives:
   (1) ι alternating with ε (ι-*stems*)
   (2) ευ alternating with ε (ευ-*stems*)
   (3) ο, η, ε (the so-called σ-*stems*[2]).

147. In the present lesson we shall consider only the first subclass, that of major consonant stems. Nouns of this subclass may be analyzed into stem

---

[1] Since nouns of this class have no stem formative, their bases and stems are identical (see §145, *Note* 2).

[2] So called because in pre-Greek times the stem ended in -σ- (we retain the name to avoid confusing these with ο-stems of the second declension).

(or base) plus case-number suffix, since the stem formative in this class is *zero*. The case-number suffixes appropriate to major consonant stems are as follows:

	MASCULINE OR FEMININE	NEUTER
SG.N.	-ς	-#
G.	-ος	-ος
D.	-ι	-ι
A.	-α	-#
PL.N.	-ες	-α
G.	-ων	-ων
D.	-σι(ν)[1]	-σι(ν)[1]
A.	-ας	-α

REMARK 1. When the case-number suffixes ς and σι(ν) are added to bases of this subclass, the usual phonological (or orthographic) modifications occur:[2]

$$\pi, \beta, \text{ or } \varphi + \varsigma = \psi \qquad \pi, \beta, \text{ or } \varphi + \sigma\iota(\nu) = \psi\iota(\nu)$$
$$\kappa, \gamma, \text{ or } \chi + \varsigma = \xi \qquad \kappa, \gamma, \text{ or } \chi + \sigma\iota(\nu) = \xi\iota(\nu)$$
$$\tau, \delta, \text{ or } \theta + \varsigma = \varsigma \qquad \tau, \delta, \text{ or } \theta + \sigma\iota(\nu) = \sigma\iota(\nu)$$

REMARK 2. The only neuter nouns in this subclass have bases ending in τ. In the nominative and accusative singular (i.e., before the case-number suffix #), this τ is changed to ς: e.g., φῶς (< φωτ + #), cf. φωτός (< φωτ + ος). EXCEPTION: In the nominative and accusative singular of neuter nouns with bases ending in ματ, the τ is simply dropped: e.g., σῶμα (< σωματ + #), cf. σώματος (< σωματ + ος).

REMARK 3. The dictionary form of a noun of the third declension is the nominative singular, as in the first two declensions. It is especially important, in the case of third declension nouns, to learn the genitive singular also, and this is cited in good dictionaries, along with the article. The stem of a third declension noun cannot always be deduced from the nominative singular, but it can be deduced from the genitive singular: e.g., σκόλοψ, σκόλοπος (stem σκολοπ-), but Ἄραψ, Ἄραβος (stem Ἀραβ-).

REMARK 4. Note that neuter nouns differ from masculine and feminine nouns only in the nominative and accusative, singular and plural.

---

[1] ν-movable (cf. §90, fn. 1).

[2] Cf. §94.

ILLUSTRATIVE PARADIGMS

148. Labial Stems. This subtype contains no neuters.

(i) π-stems:

ἡ λαῖλαψ, *storm*   stem: λαιλαπ-

SG.N. ἡ λαῖλαψ   PL.N. αἱ λαίλαπ-ες
        (= λαιλαπ + ς)   G.   τῶν λαιλάπ-ων
  G. τῆς λαίλαπ-ος   D.   ταῖς λαίλαψι(ν)
  D. τῇ λαίλαπ-ι   (= λαιλαπ + σι[ν])
  A. τὴν λαίλαπ-α   A.   τὰς λαίλαπ-ας

(ii) β-stems:

ὁ Ἄραψ, *Arab*   stem: Ἀραβ-

SG.N. ὁ Ἄραψ (= Ἀραβ + ς)   PL.N. οἱ Ἄραβ-ες
  G. τοῦ Ἄραβ-ος   G.   τῶν Ἀράβ-ων
  D. τῷ Ἄραβ-ι   D.   τοῖς Ἄραψι(ν)
  A. τὸν Ἄραβ-α   (= Ἄραβ + σι[ν])
                           A.   τοὺς Ἄραβ-ας

The only other representatives of this subtype are:

κώνωψ, κώνωπος, ὁ, *gnat*
μώλωψ, μώλωπος, ὁ, *bruise*
σκόλοψ, σκόλοπος, ὁ, *thorn*

149. Velar Stems. This subtype contains no neuters.

(i) κ-stems:

ἡ σάρξ, *flesh*   stem: σαρκ-

SG.N. ἡ σάρξ   PL.N. αἱ σάρκ-ες
        (= σαρκ + ς)   G.   τῶν σαρκ-ῶν
  G. τῆς σαρκ-ός   D.   ταῖς σαρξί(ν)
  D. τῇ σαρκ-ί   (= σαρκ + σι[ν])
  A. τὴν σάρκ-α   A.   τὰς σάρκ-ας

(ii) γ-stems:

ἡ φλόξ, *flame*   stem: φλογ-

SG.N. ἡ φλόξ   PL.N. αἱ φλόγ-ες
        (= φλογ + ς)   G.   τῶν φλογ-ῶν
  G. τῆς φλογ-ός   D.   ταῖς φλοξί(ν)
  D. τῇ φλογ-ί   (= φλογ + σι[ν])
  A. τὴν φλόγ-α   A.   τὰς φλόγ-ας

(iii)   χ -stems:

ἡ ὄρνιξ, *hen*[1]   stem: ὀρνιχ-

SG.N.	ἡ ὄρνιξ	PL.N.	αἱ ὄρνιχ-ες
	(= ὄρνιχ + ς)	G.	τῶν ὀρνίχ-ων
G.	τῆς ὄρνιχ-ος	D.	ταῖς ὄρνιξι(ν)
D.	τῇ ὄρνιχ-ι		(= ὄρνιχ + σι[ν])
A.	τὴν ὄρνιχ-α	A.	τὰς ὄρνιχ-ας

Other representatives of this type in the New Testament are as follows:

θώραξ, θώρακος, ὁ, *breastplate*   Φῆλιξ, Φήλικος, ὁ, *Felix*
κῆρυξ, κήρυκος, ὁ, *herald*   Φοῖνιξ, Φοίνικος, ὁ, *Phoenician*
λάρυγξ, λάρυγγος, ὁ, *throat*   ἀλώπηξ, ἀλώπεκος, ἡ, *fox*[2]
κόραξ, κόρακος, ὁ, *raven*   σάλπιγξ, σάλπιγγος, ἡ, *trumpet*
φύλαξ, φύλακος, ὁ, *watchman*   χοῖνιξ, χοίνικος, ἡ, *quart*
σκώληξ, σκώληκος, ὁ, *worm*   μάστιξ, μάστιγος, ἡ, *whip*

150. Three feminine nouns of this subtype are irregular; the forms of **γυνή**, *woman, wife*, occur so frequently that they, at least, should be committed to memory:

(i)   ἡ γυνή, *woman, wife*   stem: γυναικ-

SG.N.	ἡ γυνή	PL.N.	αἱ γυναῖκες
G.	τῆς γυναικός	G.	τῶν γυναικῶν
D.	τῇ γυναικί	D.	ταῖς γυναιξί(ν)
A.	τὴν γυναῖκα	A.	τὰς γυναῖκας

(ii)   ἡ νύξ, *night*   stem: νυκτ-

SG.N.	ἡ νύξ	PL.N.	αἱ νύκτες
G.	τῆς νυκτός	G.	τῶν νυκτῶν
D.	τῇ νυκτί	D.	ταῖς νυξί(ν)
A.	τὴν νύκτα	A.	τὰς νύκτας

(iii)   ἡ θρίξ, *hair*   stems: τριχ-, θριχ-

SG.N.	ἡ θρίξ	PL.N.	αἱ τρίχες
G.	τῆς τριχός	G.	τῶν τριχῶν
D.	τῇ τριχί	D.	ταῖς θριξί(ν)
A.	τὴν τρίχα	A.	τὰς τρίχας

---

[1] Only in Luke 13:34, in three MSS (ℵ D W); other MSS read ὄρνις (see §151(iii))
[2] Ἀλώπηξ has η in the nominative singular only.

151. Dental Stems:

(i)   τ-stems:

ἡ χάρις, *grace*   stem: χαριτ-

SG.N.	ἡ χάρις	PL.N.	αἱ χάριτ-ες
	(= χαριτ + ς)	G.	τῶν χαρίτ-ων
G.	τῆς χάριτ-ος	D.	ταῖς χάρισι(ν)
D.	τῇ χάριτ-ι		(= χαριτ + σι[ν])
A.	τὴν χάριτ-α	A.	τὰς χάριτ-ας

(ii)   δ-stems:

ἡ ἐλπίς, *hope*   stem: ἐλπιδ-

SG.N.	ἡ ἐλπίς	PL.N.	αἱ ἐλπίδ-ες
	(= ἐλπιδ + ς)	G.	τῶν ἐλπίδ-ων
G.	τῆς ἐλπίδ-ος	D.	ταῖς ἐλπίσι(ν)
D.	τῇ ἐλπίδ-ι		(= ἐλπιδ + σι[ν])
A.	τὴν ἐλπίδ-α	A.	τὰς ἐλπίδ-ας

(iii)   θ-stems:

ἡ ὄρνις, *hen*   stem: ὀρνιθ-

SG.N.	ἡ ὄρνις	PL.N.	αἱ ὄρνιθ-ες
	(= ὀρνιθ + ς)	G.	τῶν ὀρνίθ-ων
G.	τῆς ὄρνιθ-ος	D.	ταῖς ὄρνισι(ν)
D.	τῇ ὄρνιθ-ι		(= ὀρνιθ + σι[ν])
A.	τὴν ὄρνιθ-α	A.	τὰς ὄρνιθ-ας

(iv)   Neuter τ-stems (nouns ending in -ματ-):

τὸ σῶμα, *body*   stem: σωματ-

SG.N.	τὸ σῶμα	PL.N.	τὰ σώματ-α
	(= σωματ + #)	G.	τῶν σωμάτ-ων
G.	τοῦ σώματ-ος	D.	τοῖς σώμασι(ν)
D.	τῷ σώματ-ι		(= σωματ + σι[ν])
A.	τὸ σῶμα	A.	τὰ σώματ-α

(v)   Neuter τ-stems (other nouns):

τὸ φῶς, *light*   stem: φωτ-

SG.N.	τὸ φῶς	PL.N.	τὰ φῶτ-α
	(= φωτ + #)	G.	τῶν φώτ-ων
G.	τοῦ φωτ-ός	D.	τοῖς φωσί(ν)
D.	τῷ φωτ-ί		(= φωτ + σι[ν])
A.	τὸ φῶς	A.	τὰ φῶτ-α

The dental stems are very numerous. Those of most frequent occurrence are listed below:

MASCULINES

παῖς, παιδός, ὁ, *boy, servant*
(also παῖς, παιδός, ἡ, *girl*)
χρώς, -ωτός, ὁ, *skin*
γέλως, -ωτος, ὁ, *laughter*
ἱδρώς, -ῶτος, ὁ, *sweat*
πένης, -ητος, ὁ, *poor man*

FEMININES

ἐλπίς, -ίδος, ἡ, *hope*
ἔρις, -ιδος, ἡ, *strife*[1]
μερίς, -ίδος, ἡ, *part*
πατρίς, -ίδος, ἡ, *native land*
σφραγίς, -δος, ἡ, *seal*
χάρις, -ιτος, ἡ, *grace*[1]
ἐσθής, -ῆτος, ἡ, *clothing*
ἁγιότης, -ητος, ἡ, *holiness*
ἁπλότης, -ητος, ἡ, *singleness*
νεότης, -ητος, ἡ, *youth, newness*
τελειότης, -ητος, ἡ, *perfection*
Ἑλλάς, -αδος, ἡ, *Greece*

NEUTERS (like σῶμα)

αἷμα, -ματος, τό, *blood*
βάπτισμα, -ματος, τό, *baptism*
βῆμα, -ματος, τό, *judgment seat*
γράμμα, -ματος, τό, *letter*
θέλημα, -ματος, τό, *will*
κήρυγμα, -ματος, τό, *preaching*
κρίμα, -ματος, τό, *judgment*
ὄνομα, -ματος, τό, *name*
πλήρωμα, -ματος, τό, *fullness*
σπέρμα, -ματος, τό, *seed*
πνεῦμα, -ματος, τό, *spirit*
στόμα, -ματος, τό, *mouth*
χάρισμα, -ματος, τό, *free gift*
χρῖσμα, -ματος, τό, *anointing*

NEUTERS (like φῶς)

τέρας, -ατος, τό, *marvel, wonder*
κέρας, -ατος, τό, *horn*
πέρας, -ατος, τό, *boundary*

152. Four nouns of this subtype are irregular:

(i) ὁ πούς, *foot* stem: ποδ-

	SG.		PL.	
N.	ὁ πούς	N.	οἱ πόδες
G.	τοῦ ποδός	G.	τῶν ποδῶν
D.	τῷ ποδί	D.	τοῖς ποσί(ν)
A.	τὸν πόδα	A.	τοὺς πόδας

(ii) τὸ οὖς, *ear* stem: ὠτ-

	SG.		PL.	
N.	τὸ οὖς	N.	τὰ ὦτα
G.	τοῦ ὠτός	G.	τῶν ὤτων
D.	τῷ ὠτί	D.	τοῖς ὠσί(ν)
A.	τὸ οὖς	A.	τὰ ὦτα

---

[1] Ἔρις and χάρις may have accusative singular ἔριν, χάριν as well as ἔριδα, χάριτα.

(iii)   τὸ γόνυ, *knee*   stem: γονατ-

	SG.			PL.	
N.	τὸ	γόνυ	N.	τὰ	γόνατα
G.	τοῦ	γόνατος	G.	τῶν	γονάτων
D.	τῷ	γόνατι	D.	τοῖς	γόνασι(ν)
A.	τὸ	γόνυ	A.	τὰ	γόνατα

(iv)   τὸ ὕδωρ, *water*   stem: ὑδατ-

	SG.			PL.	
N.	τὸ	ὕδωρ	N.	τὰ	ὕδατα
G.	τοῦ	ὕδατος	G.	τῶν	ὑδάτων
D.	τῷ	ὕδατι	D.	τοῖς	ὕδασι(ν)
A.	τὸ	ὕδωρ	A.	τὰ	ὕδατα

21 | THE THIRD DECLENSION, II: MINOR CONSONANT STEMS

153. Minor consonant stems include nasal stems (i.e., nouns with stems ending in -ν- or -ντ-) and liquid stems (nouns with stems ending in -λ- or -ρ-).[1] The case-number suffixes in this subclass are the same as those given in §147, except that:

(1) In the nominative singular the case-number suffix -ς is assimilated (i.e., "dropped"), and the **vowel** preceding the final consonant of the stem is **lengthened** if it is short. Thus,

(a) Nouns with stems in -εν- or -ην- have -ην in the nominative singular, and nouns with stems in -ον- or -ων- have -ων in the nominative singular. Nouns with stems in -οντ- also lose the τ, so that they too have nominative singulars in -ων.

(b) Nouns with stems in -ερ- or -ηρ- have -ηρ in the nominative singular, and nouns with stems in -ορ- and -ωρ- have -ωρ in the nominative singular.

(2) In the dative plural of *nasal* stems (not of *liquid* stems) the suffix combines with the stem as follows:

(a) Nouns with stems in -εν- have dative plurals in -εσι(ν).

(b) Nouns with stems in -ην- have dative plurals in -ησι(ν).

(c) Nouns with stems in -ον- have dative plurals in -οσι(ν).

(d) Nouns with stems in -ων- have dative plurals in -ωσι(ν).

(e) Nouns with stems in -οντ- have dative plurals in -ουσι(ν).

---

[1] As with major consonant stems, these nouns have no stem formative, so that their stems and bases are identical.

ILLUSTRATIVE PARADIGMS

154. Nasal Stems:

(i)   ὁ ποιμήν, *shepherd*   stem: ποιμεν-

SG.N.   ὁ ποιμήν   PL.N.   οἱ ποιμέν-ες
      (= ποιμεν + ς)   G.   τῶν ποιμέν-ων
G.   τοῦ ποιμέν-ος   D.   τοῖς ποιμέσι(ν)
D.   τῷ ποιμέν-ι   (= ποιμεν + σι[ν])
A.   τὸν ποιμέν-α   A.   τοὺς ποιμέν-ας

(ii)   ὁ Ἕλλην, *Greek*   stem: Ἑλλην-

SG.N.   ὁ Ἕλλην   PL.N.   οἱ Ἕλλην-ες
      (= Ἑλλην + ς)   G.   τῶν Ἑλλήν-ων
G.   τοῦ Ἕλην-ος   D.   τοῖς Ἕλλησι(ν)
D.   τῷ Ἕλλην-ι   (= Ἕλλην + σι[ν])
A.   τὸν Ἕλλην-α   A.   τοὺς Ἕλλην-ας

(iii)   ὁ ἡγεμών, *leader*   stem: ἡγεμον-

SG.N.   ὁ ἡγεμών   PL.N.   οἱ ἡγεμόν-ες
      (= ἡγεμον + ς)   G.   τῶν ἡγεμόν-ων
G.   τοῦ ἡγεμόν-ος   D.   τοῖς ἡγεμόσιν
D.   τῷ ἡγεμόν-ι   (= ἡγεμον + σι[ν])
A.   τὸν ἡγεμόν-α   A.   τοὺς ἡγεμόν-ας

(iv)   ὁ αἰών, *age*   stem: αἰων-

SG.N.   ὁ αἰών   PL.N.   οἱ αἰῶν-ες
      (= αἰων + ς)   G.   τῶν αἰών-ων
G.   τοῦ αἰῶν-ος   D.   τοῖς αἰῶσιν
D.   τῷ αἰῶν-ι   (= αἰων + σι[ν])
A.   τὸν αἰῶν-α   A.   τούς αἰῶν-ας

(v)   ὁ ἄρχων, *ruler*   stem: ἀρχοντ-

SG.N.   ὁ ἄρχων   PL.N.   οἱ ἄρχοντ-ες
      (= ἀρχοντ + ς)   G.   τῶν ἀρχόντ-ων
G.   τοῦ ἄρχοντ-ος   D.   τοῖς ἄρχουσιν
D.   τῷ ἄρχοντ-ι   (= ἀρχοντ + σι[ν])
A.   τὸν ἄρχοντ-α   A.   τοὺς ἄρχοντ-ας

Other nouns of this type are:

ἀμπελών, -ῶνος, ὁ, *vineyard*   κανών, -όνος, ὁ, *rule*
λιμήν, -ένος, ὁ, *harbor*   λέων, -οντος, ὁ, *lion*
ἀγών, -ῶνος, ὁ, *struggle*   δράκων, -οντος, ὁ, *dragon*
δαίμων, -ονος, ὁ, *demon*

155. The following nasal stems are irregular:

(i)   ὁ κύων, *dog*   stem: κυν-

	SG.N.	ὁ κύων		PL.N.	οἱ κύνες
	G.	τοῦ κυνός		G.	τῶν κυνῶν
	D.	τῷ κυνί		D.	τοῖς κυσί(ν)
	A.	τὸν κύνα		A.	τοὺς κύνας

(ii)   ὁ ὀδούς, *tooth*   stem: ὀδοντ-

	SG.N.	ὁ ὀδούς		PL.N.	οἱ ὀδόντες
	G.	τοῦ ὀδόντος		G.	τῶν ὀδόντων
	D.	τῷ ὀδόντι		D.	τοῖς ὀδοῦσι(ν)
	A.	τὸν ὀδόντα		A.	τοὺς ὀδόντας

156. Liquid Stems.[1]

(i)   ὁ ἀήρ, *air*   stem: ἀερ-

	SG.N.	ὁ ἀήρ		PL.N.	οἱ ἀέρ-ες[2]
		(= ἀερ + ς)		G.	τῶν ἀέρ-ων
	G.	τοῦ ἀέρ-ος		D.	τοῖς ἀέρ-σι(ν)
	D.	τῷ ἀέρ-ι		A.	τοὺς ἀέρ-ας
	A.	τὸν ἀέρ-α			

(ii)   ὁ σωτήρ, *savior*   stem: σωτηρ-

	SG.N.	ὁ σωτήρ		PL.N.	οἱ σωτῆρ-ες
		(= σωτηρ + ς)		G.	τῶν σωτήρ-ων
	G.	τοῦ σωτῆρ-ος		D.	τοῖς σωτῆρ-σι(ν)
	D.	τῷ σωτῆρ-ι		A.	τοὺς σωτῆρ-ας
	A.	τὸν σωτῆρ-α			

(iii) ὁ ῥήτωρ, *orator*   stem: ῥητορ-

	SG.N.	ὁ ῥήτωρ		PL.N.	οἱ ῥήτορ-ες
		(= ῥήτορ + ς)		G.	τῶν ῥητόρ-ων
	G.	τοῦ ῥήτορ-ος		D.	τοῖς ῥήτορ-σι(ν)
	D.	τῷ ῥήτορ-ι		A.	τοὺς ῥήτορ-ας
	A.	τὸν ῥήτορ-α			

157. The following liquid stems are irregular, but are of very frequent occurrence. Their paradigms should be committed to memory.

---

[1] The only λ-stem in the New Testament is ἅλς, ἁλός, ὁ, *salt*, and this is quite rare. The usual word for *salt* is ἅλας, ἅλατος, τό, a τ-stem like τέρας; cf. §151.

[2] The plural (the usual meaning is *climates*) is not in the New Testament.

(i)   **ὁ πατήρ,** *father*   stem: πατ(ε)ρ-

     SG.N.   ὁ πατήρ   PL.N.   οἱ πατέρες
       G.   τοῦ πατρός   G.   τῶν πατέρων
       D.   τῷ πατρί   D.   τοῖς πατράσι(ν)
       A.   τὸν πατέρα   A.   τοὺς πατέρας

(ii)   **ἡ μήτηρ,** *mother*   stem: μητ(ε)ρ-

     SG.N.   ἡ μήτηρ   PL.N.   αἱ μητέρες
       G.   τῆς μητρός   G.   τῶν μητέρων
       D.   τῇ μητρί   D.   ταῖς μητράσι(ν)
       A.   τὴν μητέρα   A.   τὰς μητέρας

(iii)   **ἡ θυγάτηρ,** *daughter*   stem: θυγατ(ε)ρ-

     SG.N.   ἡ θυγάτηρ   PL.N.   αἱ θυγατέρες
       G.   τῆς θυγατρός   G.   τῶν θυγατέρων
       D.   τῇ θυγατρί   D.   ταῖς θυγατράσι(ν)
       A.   τὴν θυγατέρα   A.   τὰς θυγατέρας

(iv)   **ὁ ἀνήρ,** *man*   stem: ἀνδρ-

     SG.N.   ὁ ἀνήρ   PL.N.   οἱ ἄνδρες
       G.   τοῦ ἀνδρός   G.   τῶν ἀνδρῶν
       D.   τῷ ἀνδρί   D.   τοῖς ἀνδράσι(ν)
       A.   τὸν ἄνδρα   A.   τοὺς ἄνδρας

(v)   **ἡ χείρ,** *hand*   stem: χειρ-

     SG.N.   ἡ χείρ   PL.N.   αἱ χεῖρες
       G.   τῆς χειρός   G.   τῶν χειρῶν
       D.   τῇ χειρί   D.   ταῖς χερσί(ν)
       A.   τὴν χεῖρα   A.   τὰς χεῖρας

(vi)   **τὸ πῦρ,** *fire*   stem: πυρ-

     SG.N.   τὸ πῦρ   [no plural
       G.   τοῦ πυρός   forms in
       D.   τῷ πυρί   NT]
       A.   τὸ πῦρ

158. Third Declension Adjectives: Nasal Stems. Adjectives of this type have two sets of forms: one set serves for both masculine and feminine, and the other serves for neuter. The masculine and feminine forms are like those of nasal stem nouns described in this lesson; the neuter forms are similar, but have the case-number suffixes for neuter nouns of the third declension (see §147).

ILLUSTRATIVE PARADIGMS

(i) ἄρσην, ἄρσεν, *male*   stem: ἀρσεν-

	MASC. AND FEM.	NEUT.			MASC. AND FEM.	NEUTER
SG.N.	ἄρσην	ἄρσεν	PL.N.		ἄρσεν-ες	ἄρσεν-α
	(= ἀρσεν	(= ἀρσεν	G.		ἀρσέν-ων	ἀρσέν-ων
	+ ς)	+ #)	D.		ἄρσεσι(ν)	ἄρσεσι(ν)
G.	ἄρσεν-ος	ἄρσεν-ος			(= ἀρσεν + σι[ν])	
D.	ἄρσεν-ι	ἄρσεν-ι	A.		ἄρσεν-ας	ἄρσεν-α
A.	ἄρσεν-α	ἄρσεν (cf. nom.)				

(ii) σώφρων, σῶφρον, *sober*   stem: σωφρον-

	MASC. AND FEM.	NEUTER			MASC. AND FEM.	NEUTER
SG.N.	σώφρων	σῶφρον	PL.N.		σώφρον-ες	σώφρον-α
	(= σωφρον	(= σωφρον	G.		σωφρόν-ων	σωφρόν-ων
	+ ς)	+ #)	D.		σώφροσι(ν)	σώφροσι(ν)
G.	σώφρον-ος	σώφρον-ος			(= σωφρον + σι[ν])	
D.	σώφρον-ι	σώφρον-ι	A.		σώφρον-ας	σώφρον-α
A.	σώφρον-α	σῶφρον (cf. nom.)				

These adjectives behave syntactically like the adjectives described in Lesson 9. Other adjectives of this type are:

ἄφρων, ἄφρον, *foolish*   μείζων, μεῖζον, *greater*
ἐλάσσων, ἔλασσον, *smaller, inferior*   χείρων, χεῖρον, *worse*
κρείσσων, κρεῖσσον, *better*   ἥσσων, ἥσσον, *lesser, worse*
πλείων, πλεῖον, *more*

159. The adjectives ἐλάσσων, κρείσσων, πλείων, μείζων, ἥσσων, and χείρων are **comparatives** and are used much like their English equivalents.[1] *Than* is expressed in Greek (1) by the genitive case or (2) by the particle ἤ (note the *smooth* breathing) followed by the same case as that of the noun being compared:

Jn 5:20 μείζονα τούτων δείξει   He will show him works **greater**
αὐτῷ ἔργα.   **than these.**

---

[1] These Greek comparatives are all irregular formations; regular forms of the comparative will be discussed later. The irregular forms are of most frequent occurrence.

Mt 27:64 ἔσται ἡ ἐσχάτη πλάνη χείρων τῆς πρώτης.

The last error will be **worse than the first.**

Rev 2:19 τὰ ἔργα σου τὰ ἔσχατα πλείονα τῶν πρώτων.

Thy last works are **more than the first.**

Jn 4:1 ὁ Ἰησοῦς **πλείονας** μαθητὰς βαπτίζει ἢ Ἰωάννης.

Jesus is baptizing **more** disciples **than John.**

Jn 14:28 ὁ πατὴρ **μείζων μού** ἐστιν.

The Father is **greater than I.**

22 | THE THIRD DECLENSION, III: VOWEL STEMS AND σ-STEMS

160. For υ-stem nouns, as for the nouns studied in the preceding two lessons, bases and stems are identical, as there are no stem formatives. The case-number suffixes which are added to this stem or base are the same as those listed in §147, *except* that the accusative singular (masculine and feminine) suffix is -ν, rather than -α.

ILLUSTRATIVE PARADIGMS

(i)   ὁ ἰχθύς, *fish*   stem: ἰχθυ-

SG.N.	ὁ ἰχθύ-ς		PL.N.	οἱ ἰχθύ-ες
G.	τοῦ ἰχθύ-ος		G.	τῶν ἰχθύ-ων
D.	τῷ ἰχθύ-ι		D.	τοῖς ἰχθύ-σι(ν)
A.	τὸν ἰχθύ-ν		A.	τοὺς ἰχθύ-ας

(ii)   ἡ ἰσχύς, *strength*   stem: ἰσχυ-

SG.N.	ἡ ἰσχύ-ς		PL.N.	αἱ ἰσχύ-ες
G.	τῆς ἰσχύ-ος		G.	τῶν ἰσχύ-ων
D.	τῇ ἰσχύ-ι		D.	ταῖς ἰσχύ-σι(ν)
A.	τὴν ἰσχύ-ν		A.	τὰς ἰσχύ-ας

Other nouns of this subclass are:

> ὀσφῦς, -ύος, ἡ, *loins, waist*
> στάχυς, -υος, ὁ, *ear of corn*
> ὀφρῦς, -ύος, ἡ, *brow*
> βότρυς, -υος, ὁ, *bunch of grapes*
> ἀχλύς, -ύος, ἡ, *mist*
> ὗς, ὑός, ἡ, *sow*

161. The declension of υ-stem adjectives differs in important respects from the declension of υ-stem nouns just described. Indeed, in υ-stem adjectives the -υ- may be regarded as a stem formative rather than as part of the base. This -υ- appears only in the masculine and neuter, nominative and accusative singular; elsewhere the stem formative is -ε- (which is *not* dropped before any case-number suffix). The case-number suffixes are similar to those for υ-stem nouns, but with *further exceptions*: the genitive singular suffix (masculine and neuter) is -ως rather than -ος, and the nominative and accusative plural (masculine) suffixes are both -ις, rather than -ες and -ας. The *feminine* forms of adjectives of this class conform to the first declension.

ILLUSTRATIVE PARADIGMS

	MASCULINE	FEMININE	NEUTER
SG.N.	ὀξ-ύ-ς, *sharp*	ὀξεῖ-α-#	ὀξ-ύ-#
G.	ὀξ-έ-ως	ὀξεί-α-ς	ὀξ-έ-ως
D.	ὀξ-ε-ῖ	ὀξεί-ᾳ (α + ͅ)	ὀξ-ε-ῖ
A.	ὀξ-ύ-ν	ὀξεῖ-α-ν	ὀξ-ύ-#
PL.N.	ὀξ-έ-ῖς	ὀξεῖ-α-ι	ὀξ-έ-α
G.	ὀξ-έ-ων	ὀξει-#-ῶν	ὀξ-έ-ων
D.	ὀξ-έ-σι(ν)	ὀξεί-α-ις	ὀξ-έ-σι(ν)
A.	ὀξ-έ-ῖς	ὀξεί-#-ας	ὀξ-έ-α

Other adjectives of this class are:

βαθύς, -εῖα, -ύ, *deep*
βαρύς, -εῖα, -ύ, *heavy, burdensome*
βραδύς, -εῖα, -ύ, *slow*
βραχύς, -εῖα, -ύ, *short*
γλυκύς, -εῖα, -ύ, *sweet, fresh*
εὐθύς, -εῖα, -ύ, *straight, direct*

θῆλυς, -εῖα, -υ, *female*
πλατύς, -εῖα, -ύ *broad*
πραΰς, -εῖα, -ῢ, *meek*
ταχύς, -εῖα, -ύ, *swift*
τραχύς, -εῖα, -ύ, *rough*

162. (a) The declension of ι-stem *nouns* is similar to that of υ-stem *adjectives* (in the *masculine*), i.e., the stem formative ι appears in the nominative and accusative singular but is replaced by ε in the other forms; the case-number suffixes are as described in §161.

(b) The declension of ευ-stem nouns differs from that of ι-stems in that (1) the stem formative is ευ in the nominative singular and dative plural (elsewhere ε) and (2) the case-number suffix in the accusative singular is α rather than ν.

ILLUSTRATIVE PARADIGMS

(i)   ὁ ὄφις, *serpent*   stem: ὀφ-ι/ε-

SG.N.   ὁ ὄφ-ι-ς   PL.N.   οἱ ὄφ-ε-ις
G.   τοῦ ὄφ-ε-ως   G.   τῶν ὄφ-ε-ων
D.   τῷ ὄφ-ε-ι   D.   τοῖς ὄφ-ε-σι(ν)
A.   τὸν ὄφ-ι-ν   A.   τοὺς ὄφ-ε-ις

(ii)   ἡ πόλις, *city*   stem: πολ-ι/ε-

SG.N.   ἡ πόλ-ι-ς   PL.N.   αἱ πόλ-ε-ις
G.   τῆς πόλ-ε-ως   G.   τῶν πόλ-ε-ων
D.   τῇ πόλ-ε-ι   D.   ταῖς πόλ-ε-σι(ν)
A.   τὴν πόλ-ι-ν   A.   τὰς πόλ-ε-ις

(iii)   ὁ βασιλεύς, *king*   stem: βασιλ-ευ/ε-

SG.N.   ὁ βασιλ-εύ-ς   PL.N.   οἱ βασιλ-ε-ῖς
G.   τοῦ βασιλ-έ-ως   G.   τῶν βασιλ-έ-ων
D.   τῷ βασιλ-ε-ῖ   D.   τοῖς βασιλ-εῦ-σι(ν)
A.   τὸν βασιλ-έ-α   A.   τοὺς βασιλ-ε-ῖς

Except for ὁ ὄφις, all nouns in -ις in the New Testament are feminine; all nouns in -εύς are masculine. Some of the most important nouns in these classes are listed below:

ι-STEMS (FEMININES)

γένεσις, -εως, ἡ, *origin*
δύναμις, *power, miracle*
γνῶσις, *knowledge*
κλῆσις, *calling*
κρίσις, *judgment*
κτίσις, *creation, creature*
πρᾶξις, *deed, function, business*
πίστις, *faith, faithfulness*
τάξις, *order, position, nature*
φύσις, *nature*
ἀνάστασις, *resurrection*
αἵρεσις, *sect, faction*
ἄφεσις, *pardon, forgiveness, release*
βρῶσις, *food, eating*
θλῖψις, *affliction*
παράδοσις, *betrayal, tradition*
παράκλησις, *encouragement, comfort*
καύχησις, *boasting*

δέησις, *entreaty, prayer*
ζήτησις, *investigation, controversy*

ευ-STEMS (MASCULINES)

ἱερεύς, -έως, ὁ, *priest*
ἀρχιερεύς, *chief priest*
γραμματεύς, *scribe*
γονεύς, *parent*
γναφεύς, *fuller, bleacher*
βυρσεύς, *tanner*
ἱππεύς, *horseman*
κεραμεύς, *potter*
χαλκεύς, *coppersmith*
φαρμακεύς, *magician*
φονεύς, *murderer*
ἁλιεύς, *fisher, fisherman*

Λαοδικεύς, *Laodicean*
Ταρσεύς, *Tarsian*

Κολοσσεύς, *Colossian*	Ἀλεξανδρεύς, *Alexandrian*
Θεσσαλονικεύς, *Thessalonian*	Ἀντιοχεύς, *Antiochene*

163. The declension of the so-called σ-stems differs markedly from that of any other class of third declension nouns, so markedly, in fact, that they might reasonably be said to belong to a fourth declension. In pre-Greek times all bases in this class ended in σ (whence the name "σ-stems"); this σ was lost, however, in intervocalic position, so that it is no longer reasonable to speak of the members of this class as "consonant stems" at all.

The forms of the old σ-stems which actually occur in the historical period may be analyzed as follows:

(1) Bases may end in any consonant.

(2) Stem formatives are:

    (a) o in the nominative and accusative singular neuter of nouns.

    ε in the nominative and accusative singular neuter of adjectives.

    η in the nominative and accusative singular masculine and feminine (nouns and adjectives).

    (b) # before all case-number suffixes beginning with a vowel other than ι.

    (c) ε elsewhere.

(3) Case-number suffixes are as follows:

	MASCULINE AND FEMININE	NEUTER
SG.N.	-ς	-ς[1]
G.	-ους[2]	-ους[2]
D.	-ι	-ι
A.	-#	-ς[1]
PL.N.	-ις	-η[3]
G.	-ων	-ων
D.	-σι(ν)	-σι(ν)
A.	-ις	-η[3]

---

[1] This ς was originally not a suffix, but simply the final -σ- of the base (the neuter suffix was originally #, as in the other subtypes of the third declension).

[2] The suffix -ους arose by contraction after the loss of the σ: thus γένους < γένε-ος < γένε(σ)ος.

[3] The suffix-η arose by contraction after the loss of the σ: thus γένη < γένε-α < γένε(σ)α.

ILLUSTRATIVE PARADIGMS

(i)   Masculine nouns:

ὁ συγγενής, *kinsman*   stem: συγγεν- η/ε-

SG.N.	ὁ συγγεν-ή-ς		PL.N.	οἱ συγγεν-ε-ῖς
G.	τοῦ συγγεν-#-οῦς		G.	τῶν συγγεν-#-ῶν
D.	τῷ συγγεν-ε-ῖ		D.	τοῖς συγγεν-έ-σιν
A.	τὸν συγγεν-ῆ-#		A.	τοὺς συγγεν-ε-ῖς

(ii)   Neuter nouns:

τὸ ἔθνος, *nation*   stem: ἐθν- ο/ε-

SG.N.	τὸ ἔθν-ο-ς		PL.N.	τὰ ἔθν-#-η
G.	τοῦ ἔθν-#-ους		G.	τῶν ἐθν-#-ῶν
D.	τῷ ἔθν-ε-ι		D.	τοῖς ἔθν-ε-σιν
A.	τὸ ἔθν-ο-ς		A.	τὰ ἔθν-#-η

(iii)   Adjectives:

MASCULINE AND FEMININE	NEUTER

ἀληθής, *true*   stem: ἀληθ- η/ε-

	MASCULINE AND FEMININE	NEUTER
SG.N.	ἀληθ-ή-ς	ἀληθ-έ-ς
G.	ἀληθ-#-οῦς	ἀληθ-#-οῦς
D.	ἀληθ-ε-ῖ	ἀληθ-ε-ῖ
A.	ἀληθ-ῆ-#	ἀληθ-έ-ς
PL.N.	ἀληθ-ε-ῖς	ἀληθ-#-ῆ
G.	ἀληθ-#-ῶν	ἀληθ-#-ῶν
D.	ἀληθ-έ-σιν	ἀληθ-έ-σιν
A.	ἀληθ-ε-ῖς	ἀληθ-#-ῆ

The most important members of this class are as follows:

NOUNS (NEUTERS)	
γένος, -ους[1] *race, kind*	μέρος, -ους, *part*
βάθος, -ους, *depth*	ὄρος, -ους, *mountain*[2]
βρέφος, -ους, *babe*	πάθος, -ους, *suffering*
ἔθος, -ους, *custom*	πλῆθος, -ους, *multitude, crowd*
ἔτος, -ους, *year*	σκεῦος, -ους, *vessel*
κράτος, -ους, *strength*	τέλος, -ους, *end, goal, purpose*
μέλος, -ους, *limb, member*	σκότος, -ους, *darkness*

---

[1] T. S. Green's pocket lexicon cites the genitive of this class as -εος. It should be remembered that this is the uncontracted form, which does not occur in the New Testament.

[2] Ὄρος has genitive plural ὀρέων.

ADJECTIVES

ἀσφαλής, -ές, *sure, firm*
ἀπειθής, -ές, *disobedient*
ἀσεβής, -ές, *impious, godless*
ἀσθενής, -ές, *weak, sick*
ἐγκρατής, -ές, *disciplined*
ἐνεργής, -ές, *effective*
ἀκριβής, -ές, *exact, strict*

εὐγενής, -ές, *noble*
εὐσεβής, -ές, *pious*
εὐλαβής, -ές, *devout*
μονογενής, -ές, *only*
πλήρης, πλῆρες, *full*[1]
συγγενής, -ές, *related*
ὑγιής, -ές, *healthy*
ψευδής, -ές, *false*

---

[1] Sometimes used in the nominative singular masculine form as an indeclinable.

23 | REVIEW OF VERB INFLECTIONS
CONTRACT VERBS

164. An analysis of verb forms into morphemes, similar to the analysis of nouns described in Lesson 19, is presented in this lesson (for the verb forms studied so far). Each verb form may be regarded as consisting of a number of constituents, one or more of which may be *zero*. These constituents may be classified as **bases, prefixes, tense formants, stem formatives**, and **person-number suffixes**. (Prefixes precede bases, naturally.)

165. The **base** of a verb form may consist of one or more morphemes, The morpheme or combination of morphemes which remains invariable throughout the entire paradigm of a verb is called the **verb base**; the morpheme or combination of morphemes which remains invariable throughout the present tense (in its various voices and moods) is called the **present base**; the morpheme or combination of morphemes which remains invariable throughout the future tense (in the active and middle voices) is called the **future** (active and middle) **base**; the first and second **aorist bases** (active, middle, and passive) and others are similarly defined.

EXAMPLES[1]

> The **verb base** of λύω is λυ-;
> The **present base** of λύω is λυ-;
> The **future** (active and middle) **base** of λύω is λυσ-;

---

[1] In these examples the verb base is identical with the present base and the future base is identical with the (unaugmented) aorist (active and middle) base; neither of these identities holds for all verbs, however.

The (unaugmented) **aorist** (active and middle) **base** of λύω is λυσ-.

166. Prefixes may be either *inflectional* or *derivational*. An inflectional prefix is one which has the grammatical function of distinguishing some forms of a paradigm from other forms of the same paradigm. The only inflectional prefix we have studied so far is the *augment* (cf. §95(1)). A derivational prefix is one which occurs with every form in the paradigm of a word; it does not distinguish forms, but different words.[1] Derivational prefixes form part of the bases to which they are attached; they are sometimes, for convenience, called *prebases*. These will be discussed in Lesson 46.

167. Tense formants are added to the verb base and serve primarily to indicate the tense of the verb form, as their name implies; some of them also indicate voice. Tense formants studied so far are:

(1) -σ- (added to the verb base to form the future and aorist [active and middle] bases).

(2) -θ- (added to the verb base to form the [unaugmented first] aorist passive base).

(3) -θησ- (added to the verb base to form the future passive base). To these we may, for symmetry, add the tense formant *zero*, which we may regard as being attached to the verb base to form the present base.

168. Stem formatives are added to the verb base after the tense formants and serve principally to indicate mood; secondarily, in combination with the tense formants, stem formatives also serve to indicate tense and voice. The stem formatives which occur in the verb forms studied so far are as follows:

(1) -ο/ε/#- (i.e., -ο- before nasals [μ and ν], *zero* before a suffix beginning with a vowel other than ι, elsewhere -ε-). This stem formative occurs in the present, imperfect, second aorist, and future tenses (all voices, except for second aorist passive).

(2) -α/ε- (i.e., -α- in all persons except the third singular in the *active*

---

[1] Thus the base of παραλύω is παραλυ-, not λυ-. A morpheme which is common to several different *words* (rather than to different forms of the same word) is sometimes called a **root**.

voice, where it is **-ε-**; **-α-** combines with **-ου-** of a following suffix to give **-ω-**). This stem formative occurs in the first aorist active and middle.

(3) **-η-** (in all persons). This stem formative occurs in the aorist passive.

169. Person-number suffixes are added to verb stems (i.e., to the combination of verb base, tense formant, and stem formative[1]) and indicate, primarily, person and number; they also serve to indicate voice. The person-number suffixes may be divided into four sets:

(1)	PRIMARY A	(2) PRIMARY B	(3) SECONDARY A	(4) SECONDARY B
SG.1	-ω	-μαι	-ν, -#†	-μην
2	-ις	-η	-ς	-ου
3	-ι	-ται	-(ν)*	-το
PL.1	-μεν	-μεθα	-μεν	-μεθα
2	-τε	-σθε	-τε	-σθε
3	-ουσι(ν)*	-νται	-ν, -σαν‡	-ντο

REMARK 1: The final **ν** of certain suffixes (marked *) is enclosed in parentheses; this **ν** may be (but need not be) omitted if the following word begins with a consonant. EXAMPLES: ἔπεμψε στρατιώτας or ἔπεμψεν στρατιώτας, but always ἔπεμψεν ἄνδρας. This **ν**, called **ν-movable,** occurs only after **-ε** or **-σι**, and is **not** counted as a nasal for the purpose of determining the stem formative (cf. §168(1)).

REMARK 2: The Secondary A first singular suffix (marked †) is *zero* (#) if the preceding stem formative is **-α-**.

REMARK 3: The Secondary A third plural suffix (marked ‡) is **-σαν** if the preceding stem formative is **-η-**.

REMARK 4. (a) The **Primary** suffixes occur in the **present** and **future.**

(b) The **Primary A** suffixes occur in the **active voice.**

(c) The **Primary B** suffixes occur in the **middle** and **passive voices.**

REMARK 5 (a) The **Secondary** suffixes occur in the **imperfect** and **aorist.**

(b) The **Secondary A** suffixes occur in the **active voice** and in the **aorist passive.**

(c) The **Secondary B** suffixes occur in the **middle voice** and in the **imperfect passive.**

---

[1] See §145, *Note* 2.

170. In the illustrative paradigms in §171, the division of the forms into their component morphemes is indicated, according to the pattern set out in the table below:

	TENSES OF THE INDICATIVE	PREFIX	BASE	TENSE FORMANTS	STEM FORMATIVES	SUFFIXES
(1)	Present active	—	λυ-	(-#-)	-o/ε/#-	Primary A
(2)	Imperfect active	ἐ	λυ-	(-#-)	-o/ε/#-	Secondary A
(3)	Present middle and passive	—	λυ-	(-#-)	-o/ε/#-	Primary B
(4)	Imperfect middle and passive	ἐ-	λυ-	(-#-)	-o/ε/#-	Secondary B
(5)	Future active	—	λυ-	-σ-	-o/ε/#-	Primary A
(6)	Future middle	—	λυ-	-σ-	-o/ε/#-	Primary B
(7)	Future passive	—	λυ-	-θησ-	-o/ε/#-	Primary B
(8)	Aorist active	ἐ-	λυ-	-σ-	-α/ε-	Secondary A
(9)	Aorist middle	ἐ-	λυ-	-σ-	-α/ε-	Secondary B
(10)	Aorist passive	ἐ-	λυ-	-θ-	-η-	Secondary A

171. ILLUSTRATIVE PARADIGMS

	(1) PRESENT ACTIVE	(2) IMPERFECT ACTIVE	(3) PRESENT MIDDLE AND PASSIVE	(4) IMPERFECT MIDDLE AND PASSIVE
SG.1	λυ-#-ω[1]	ἐ-λυ-ο-ν	λυ-ο-μαι	ἐ-λυ-ο-μην
2	λυ-ε-ις	ἐ-λυ-ε-ς	λυ-#-η	ἐ-λυ-#-ου
3	λυ-ε-ι	ἐ-λυ-ε-(ν)	λυ-ε-ται	ἐ-λυ-ε-το
PL.1	λυ-ο-μεν	ἐ-λυ-ο-μεν	λυ-ο-μεθα	ἐ-λυ-ο-μεθα
2	λυ-ε-τε	ἐ-λυ-ε-τε	λυ-ε-σθε	ἐ-λυ-ε-σθε
3	λυ-#-ουσι(ν)	ἐ-λυ-ο-ν	λυ-ο-νται	ἐ-λυ-ο-ντο

	(5) FUTURE ACTIVE	(6) FUTURE MIDDLE	(7) FUTURE PASSIVE
SG.1	λυ-σ-#-ω	λυ-σ-ο-μαι	λυ-θησ-ο-μαι
2	λυ-σ-ε-ις	λυ-σ-#-η	λυ-θησ-#-η
3	λυ-σ-ε-ι	λυ-σ-ε-ται	λυ-θησ-ε-ται
PL.1	λυ-σ-ο-μεν	λυ-σ-ο-μεθα	λυ-θησ-ο-μεθα
2	λυ-σ-ε-τε	λυ-σ-ε-σθε	λυ-θησ-ε-σθε
3	λυ-σ-#-ουσι(ν)	λυ-σ-ο-νται	λυ-θησ-ο-νται

---

[1] As indicated in §§167 and 170, a *zero* tense formant may, for the sake of symmetry, be regarded as forming part of each verb form in the present and imperfect, but to conserve space this has simply been omitted in these illustrative paradigms.

(8)	AORIST ACTIVE	(9) AORIST MIDDLE	(10) AORIST PASSIVE
SG.1	ἐ-λυ-σ-α- #	ἐ-λυ-σ-α-μην	ἐ-λυ-θ-η-ν
2	ἐ-λυ-σ-α-ς	ἐ-λυ-σ-ω (<α+ου)	ἐ-λυ-θ-η-ς
3	ἐ-λυ-σ-ε-(ν)	ἐ-λυ-σ-α-το	ἐ-λυ-θ-η- #
PL.1	ἐ-λυ-σ-α-μεν	ἐ-λυ-σ-α-μεθα	ἐ-λυ-θ-η-μεν
2	ἐ-λυ-σ-α-τε	ἐ-λυ-σ-α-σθε	ἐ-λυ-θ-η-τε
3	ἐ-λυ-σ-α-ν	ἐ-λυ-σ-α-ντο	ἐ-λυ-θ-η-σαν

REMARK: The second aorist active has the stem formative and suffixes of the imperfect active, but has an irregularly formed base; the second aorist middle has the stem formative and suffixes of the imperfect middle (and passive), but has an irregularly formed base; the second aorist passive has the stem formative of the first aorist passive, but has no -θ- (cf. §§95(7), 129f).

172. Contract Verbs. We have already pointed out, in earlier lessons, the orthographic and phonological changes which take place when the tense formants **-o-**, **-θ-**, and **-θησ-** are added to bases ending in certain consonants (cf. supra, §§93, 126f); phonological changes also occur when vocalic endings (i.e., endings beginning with a vowel, however the endings are analyzed into stem formatives and suffixes) are added to verb bases ending in **-α-**, **-ε-**, or **-o-**. These phonological changes take the form of *contractions*, and the verbs in which they occur are called, collectively, **contract verbs**.

The contractions which occur may be summarized conveniently in the table below:

	ε	ει	η	ῃ	o	ου	ω
α	α	ᾳ	α	ᾳ	ω	ω	ω
ε	ει	ει	η	ῃ	ου	ου	ω
o	ου	οι	ω	οι	ου	ου	ω

When one of the vowels in the left-hand column is followed by one of the vowels or diphthongs in the top row, the resulting contraction is the vowel or diphthong at the intersection in the body of the table, e.g., **α + ε = α, α + ει = ᾳ, ε + ου = ου,** etc.

173. Further illustrations of the contractions are to be seen in the paradigms following. These are for the contract verbs **ἀγαπάω, ποιέω,** and πληρόω. The forms just cited are *uncontracted* forms; in Greek–English dictionaries these are the forms given, so that it is possible to tell at a glance what vowel has been (or should be) contracted. However, no uncontracted form occurs in the Greek New Testament. This should be carefully borne in mind: instead of ἀγαπάω we should expect to find (in the New Testament) and we should write (in the exercises) the *contracted* form ἀγαπῶ, instead of ποιέω we should have ποιῶ and instead of πληρόω we should have πληρῶ.

ILLUSTRATIVE PARADIGMS

174. ἀγαπάω, *love*:

		PRESENT ACTIVE		PRESENT MIDDLE AND PASSIVE	
		(UNCONTRACTED)	CONTRACTED	(UNCONTRACTED)	CONTRACTED
SG.	1	(ἀγαπα-ω)¹	ἀγαπῶ	(ἀγαπα-ομαι)	ἀγαπῶμαι
	2	(ἀγαπα-εις)	ἀγαπᾷς	(ἀγαπα-η)	[ἀγαπᾷ]² ἀγαπᾶσαι
	3	(ἀγαπα-ει)	ἀγαπᾷ	(ἀγαπα-εται)	ἀγαπᾶται
PL.	1	(ἀγαπα-ομεν)	ἀγαπῶμεν	(ἀγαπα-ομεθα)	ἀγαπώμεθα
	2	(ἀγαπα-ετε)	ἀγαπᾶτε	(ἀγαπα-εσθε)	ἀγαπᾶσθε
	3	(ἀγαπα-ουσι[ν])	ἀγαπῶσι(ν)	(ἀγαπα-ονται)	ἀγαπῶνται

		IMPERFECT ACTIVE		IMPERFECT MIDDLE AND PASSIVE	
SG.	1	(ἠγαπα-ον)	ἠγάπων	(ἠγαπα-ομην)	ἠγαπώμην
	2	(ἠγαπα-ες)	ἠγάπας	(ἠγαπα-ου)	ἠγαπῶ
	3	(ἠγαπα-ε[ν])	ἠγάπα³	(ἠγαπα-ετο)	ἠγαπᾶτο
PL.	1	(ἠγαπα-ομεν)	ἠγαπῶμεν	(ἠγαπα-ομεθα)	ἠγαπώμεθα
	2	(ἠγαπα-ετε)	ἠγαπᾶτε	(ἠγαπα-εσθε)	ἠγαπᾶσθε
	3	(ἠγαπα-ον)	ἠγάπων	(ἠγαπα-οντο)	ἠγαπῶντο

¹ To conserve space we have again omitted to indicate a *zero* tense formant in the present and imperfect (cf. §171(1), (2), (3), (4)) and, further, have not divided the endings into stem formatives and suffixes.

² The "regular" form ἀγαπᾷ does not occur in the New Testament; forms like ἀγαπᾶσαι replace it.

³ This form has no ν-movable, in accordance with §169, *Remark* 1.

175. ποιέω, *do, make*:

	PRESENT ACTIVE		PRESENT MIDDLE AND PASSIVE	
	(UNCONTRACTED)	CONTRACTED	(UNCONTRACTED)	CONTRACTED
SG. 1	(ποιε-ω)	**ποιῶ**	(ποιε-ομαι)	**ποιοῦμαι**
2	(ποιε-εις)	**ποιεῖς**	(ποιε-η)	**ποιῇ**
3	(ποιε-ει)	**ποιεῖ**	(ποιε-εται)	**ποιεῖται**
PL. 1	(ποιε-ομεν)	**ποιοῦμεν**	(ποιε-ομεθα)	**ποιούμεθα**
2	(ποιε-ετε)	**ποιεῖτε**	(ποιε-εσθα)	**ποιεῖσθε**
3	(ποιε-ουσι[ν])	**ποιοῦσι(ν)**	(ποιε-ονται)	**ποιοῦνται**

	IMPERFECT ACTIVE		IMPERFECT MIDDLE AND PASSIVE	
SG. 1	(ἐποιε-ον)	**ἐποίουν**	(ἐποιε-ομην)	**ἐποιούμην**
2	(ἐποιε-ες)	**ἐποίεις**	(ἐποιε-ου)	**ἐποιοῦ**
3	(ἐποιε-ε[ν])	**ἐποίει**[1]	(ἐποιε-ετο)	**ἐποιεῖτο**
PL. 1	(ἐποιε-ομεν)	**ἐποιοῦμεν**	(ἐποιε-ομεθα)	**ἐποιούμεθα**
2	(ἐποιε-ετε)	**ἐποιεῖτε**	(ἐποιε-εσθε)	**ἐποιεῖσθε**
3	(ἐποιε-ον)	**ἐποίουν**	(ἐποιε-οντο)	**ἐποιοῦντο**

176. πληρόω, *fill, fulfil*:

	PRESENT ACTIVE		PRESENT MIDDLE AND PASSIVE	
SG. 1	(πληρο-ω)	**πληρῶ**	(πληρο-ομαι)	**πληροῦμαι**
2	(πληρο-εις)	**πληροῖς**	(πληρο-η)	**πληροῖ**
3	(πληρο-ει)	**πληροῖ**	(πληρο-εται)	**πληροῦται**
PL. 1	(πληρο-ομεν)	**πληροῦμεν**	(πληρο-ομεθα)	**πληρούμεθα**
2	(πληρο-ετε)	**πληροῦτε**	(πληρο-εσθε)	**πληροῦσθε**
3	(πληρο-ουσι[ν])	**πληροῦσι(ν)**	(πληρο-ονται)	**πληροῦνται**

	IMPERFECT ACTIVE		IMPERFECT MIDDLE AND PASSIVE	
SG. 1	(ἐπληρο-ον)	**ἐπλήρουν**	(ἐπληρο-ομην)	**ἐπληρούμην**
2	(ἐπληρο-ες)	**ἐπλήρους**	(ἐπληρο-ου)	**ἐπληροῦ**
3	(ἐπληρο-ε[ν])	**ἐπλήρου**[1]	(ἐπληρο-ετο)	**ἐπληροῦτο**
PL. 1	(ἐπληρο-ομεν)	**ἐπληροῦμεν**	(ἐπληρο-ομεθα)	**ἐπληρούμεθα**
2	(ἐπληρο-ετε)	**ἐπληροῦτε**	(ἐπληρο-εσθε)	**ἐπληροῦσθε**
3	(ἐπληρο-ον)	**ἐπλήρουν**	(ἐπληρο-οντο)	**ἐπληροῦντο**

---

[1] See §174, fn. 3.

177. Apart from tenses formed on the present base (e.g., in the indicative, only the present and imperfect, active and middle passive), the forms of almost all contract verbs are perfectly regular.

(1) The final **α** of the base of **αω**-verbs is changed to **η** before a (non-zero) tense formant, unless this **α** is immediately preceded by a vowel or by **ρ**. Thus for **ἀγαπῶ** (uncontracted "dictionary form" **ἀγαπάω**) we have future **ἀγαπήσω**, aorist active **ἠγάπησα**, aorist passive **ἠγαπήθην**.

For **ἐῶ** (uncontracted "dictionary form" **ἐάω**) we have future **ἐάσω**, aorist active **εἴασα** (irregular augment).

(2) The final **ε** of the base of **εω**-verbs is changed to **η** before a (non-zero) tense formant. Thus for **ποιῶ** (uncontracted "dictionary form" **ποιέω**) we have future **ποιήσω**, aorist active **ἐποίησα** aorist passive **ἐποιήθην**.

A few **εω**-verbs retain the **ε**; these must be learned; **καλέω** has future **καλέσω**, aorist active **ἐκάλεσα** (irregular aorist passive **ἐκλήθην**).

(3) The final **ο** of the base of **οω**-verbs is changed to **ω** before a (non-zero) tense formant. Thus for **πληρῶ** (uncontracted "dictionary form" **πληρόω**) we have future **πληρώσω**, aorist active **ἐπλήρωσα**, aorist passive **ἐπληρώθην**.

24 | OTHER USES OF THE ACCUSATIVE

178. If we refer once again to §45 and compare illustrative sentences (3) and (4),

(3)   The child gave the dog a bone.
(4)   The general called the captain a fool.

we see that each contains the same parts of speech in the same arrangement, viz.,

$$N_1 - V - N_2 - N_3$$

The similarity between (3) and (4) will be seen to be merely superficial when we compare with them the sentence

(A)   The general called the captain a taxi.

Sentence (A) *looks* similar to sentence (4), but it is actually *structurally* similar to sentence (3).[1] As we saw in Lesson 11 (§84), sentence (3) has the same meaning as the structurally different sentence.

(3c)   The child gave a bone to the dog.

No such semantically equivalent structures exist for sentence (4), since

(4a)   The general called a fool to [*or* for] the captain.

does not mean the same thing as (4).[2] Such a semantically equivalent but structurally different sentence does exist for (A), however:

(Aa)   The general called a taxi for the captain.

---

[1] Assuming, of course, that the general did not in fact say to the captain, "You taxi, you!"

[2] Unless a medieval context is imagined, with "fool" = "court jester."

[140]

We infer, therefore, that (A) has the same underlying syntactic structure as (3), viz.,

$$S - V - IO - O^1$$

but that (4) has a structure we have not yet encountered.

179. The structural meanings of (4) and its constituents differ from those of (3) and its constituents. In each of them N_1 functions as the subject, with the meaning " performer of the action," but N_2 and N_3 do not have the same functions and structural meanings in (4) as they do in (3). As we saw in Lesson 11, N_3 is the direct object in sentences like (3), but in sentences like (4) N_2 is usually called the direct object. It is, moreover, a direct object of a special sort, since its structural meaning is not merely that of "receiver of the action indicated by the verb" (see §§49f), but that of "receiver of the action indicated by the verb *together with the second post-verbal noun*." This is obvious if we compare

(4)   The general called the captain a fool.

with

(4b)   The general called the captain.

The presence of *fool* alters, or completes, the meaning of the verb; it is called the **object complement**.

180. Object complements occur only with certain verbs (all of which also occur with "ordinary" direct objects, i.e., without object complements), e.g., *call, make, find, think, deem, choose, elect.* Some of these verbs also occur with indirect objects (e.g., *call, make, find*), so that it may not always be immediately apparent whether sentences containing them are structurally similar to (3) or to (4); usually, however, the meanings of the nouns N_2 and N_3 are compatible with only one interpretation (and, hence, with only one structural analysis) of a sentence, unless humor is intended:

(a)   The lady found her husband a present.
(b)   The lady found her husband a thief.
(c)   The general made the captain a major.
(d)   The general made the captain a pudding.

---

[1] See §84.

The grammatical structure of sentence (4) may be represented by the formula

$$S - V - O - OC$$

where OC stands for "object complement." Notice that the word order is an essential element in this structure; *The general made the captain a major* does not mean the same thing as *The general made the major a captain*.

181. Sentences similar to (4) in both meaning and structure also occur in Greek. The constituents of these Greek sentences may, as we might expect, occur in any order; both the direct object and the object complement are in the **accusative** case, but the direct object is always more "definite" than the object complement.[1]

In the examples below the direct object is underlined, and the object complement is doubly underlined:

Mt 4:19 ποιήσω **ὑμᾶς ἀλεεῖς**[2] ἀνθρώπων.	I will make **you fishers** of men.
Mt 23:15 ποιεῖτε **αὐτὸν υἱὸν** γεέννης.	You make **him a son** of Gehenna.
Lk 19:46 ὑμεῖς **αὐτὸν** ἐποιήσατε **σπήλαιον** λῃστῶν.	You have made **it a cave** of robbers.

182. Greek sentences with the structure

$$N_n - V - N_a^1 - N_a^2$$

must sometimes be rendered in English by sentences in which the object complement is introduced by *as, for,* or *to be*:

Acts 13:5 εἶχον **Ἰωάννην ὑπηρέτην**	They had **John as** (*or* **for**) their **minister.**
1 Jn 4:14 ὁ πατὴρ ἀπέσταλκεν **τὸν υἱὸν σωτῆρα** τοῦ κόσμου.	The Father sent **the Son to be the Savior** of the world (*or* **as the Savior** ...).

---

[1] See the discussion of predicate nominatives in §§58f.

[2] Irregular nominative and accusative plural of **ἀλιεύς**.

183. On the other hand, Greek sometimes employs ὡς, *as*, or εἰς, *for*, to introduce the object complement:

Mt 14:5 ὡς προφήτην αὐτὸν εἶχον.	They regarded (*literally*, had) **him as a prophet.**
Mt 21:46 εἰς προφήτην αὐτὸν εἶχον.	They regarded **him as a prophet.**

184. A slightly different sentence structure, in which the object complement is replaced by an adjective, also occurs in both English and Greek. In Greek sentences of this type the adjective is anarthrous and in the accusative case:

Mt 26:73 ἡ λαλιά σου **δῆλόν σε** ποιεῖ.	Your speech makes **you evident** (*i.e.*, makes it plain where you come from *or* who you are, gives you away).
Mt 28:14 ἡμεῖς ... **ὑμᾶς ἀμερίμνους** ποιήσομεν.	We shall make **you free from care.**

185. Further differences between the structures of illustrative sentences (3) and (4) come to light when they are transformed into the passive.[1] Sentence (3) has two passive transforms in English: one in which the direct object of (3) becomes the subject of the passive verb and another in which the indirect object of (3) becomes the subject of the passive verb. These two possibilities are given in §45 as illustrative sentences (8) and (10):

(3)   The child gave the dog a *bone*.

(8)   A *bone* was given the dog by the child.

(3)   The child gave the *dog* a bone.

(10)   The *dog* was given a bone by the child.

In (8) the indirect object of (3) simply remains in its old position or, as grammarians put it, is "retained"; in (10) it is the direct object of (3)

---

[1] Cf. §§117f.

which is retained. In both (8) and (10) the subject of (3) becomes the object of the preposition *by*.

Sentence (4), unlike sentence (3), has only one passive transform, which appears in §45 as illustrative sentence (9):

> (9) The captain was called a fool by the general.

Here the direct object of (4) (*captain*) becomes the subject, and the subject of (4) (*general*) becomes the object of the preposition *by*. The object complement is simply retained, and there is no passive transform of which it is the subject.

186. Greek sentences with structures similar to those of the English sentences (3) and (4) also have passive transforms. Some Greek sentences like (3) have transforms like (8), others have transforms like (10).

EXAMPLES Eph 3:3 ἐγνωρίσθη μοι τὸ   The mystery was made known to
          μυστήριον.   me (*sc.* by God).

This may be regarded as a passive transform of

          [ὁ θεὸς] ἐγνώρισέν μοι τὸ μυστήριον.   [God] made the mystery known to
                                                  me.

In Ephesians 3:3 the subject would have been the direct object of the active form of the verb.

          Rom 3:2   ἐπιστεύθησαν τὰ λόγια[1]   They have been entrusted with
          τοῦ θεοῦ.   the oracles of God (*sc.* by God).

This may be regarded as a passive transform of

          [ὁ θεὸς] ἐπίστευσεν αὐτοῖς τὰ   [God] entrusted them with his
          λόγια[1] αὐτοῦ.   oracles.

In Romans 3:2 the subject would have been the indirect object of the active form of the verb. In Ephesians 3:3 the old indirect object (**μοι**) and in Romans 3:2 the old direct object (**τὰ λόγια**) are retained in their original cases.

187. Greek sentences like (9), which may be regarded as transforms of sentences like (4), require special mention. Only the direct object of the

---

[1] **τὰ λόγια** is in the accusative case here.

active form of the verb may become the subject of the passive form, but when it does so, the object complement is not retained in the accusative, but put in the **nominative**:

Mt 21:13 ὁ οἶκός μου **οἶκος** προσευχῆς κληθήσεται.	My house will be called a **house** of prayer (*sc.* by them).

This may be regarded as a passive transform of

καλέσουσιν τὸν οἶκόν μου **οἶκον** προσευχῆς.	They will call my house a **house** of prayer.

Similarly, an adjective which has the place of the object complement is put in the nominative when the verb is made passive:

Mt 5:19 **ἐλάχιστος** κληθήσεται.	He shall be called **least** (*sc.* by them).

This may be regarded as a passive transform of

καλέσουσιν αὐτὸν **ἐλάχιστον**.	They will call him **least**.

188. In addition to verbs like **ποιέω, καλέω**, and others which govern a direct object with an object complement, there are a number of Greek verbs which govern two accusatives neither of which is an object complement. The most common of these are **διδάσκω**, *teach*, and **αἰτέω** and **ἐρωτάω**, each of which means *ask*. The use of these verbs is illustrated below:

(1) **διδάσκω**, *teach* (*someone something*):

(a) With accusative indicating the person taught:

Jn 9:34 σὺ διδάσκεις **ἡμᾶς**.	You are teaching **us**.

(b) With accusative of the thing taught:

Mt 12:14 **τὴν ὁδὸν** τοῦ θεοῦ διδάσκεις.	You are teaching **the way** of God.

(c) With two accusatives:

Acts 21:21 ἀποστασίαν διδάσκεις τοὺς 'Ιουδαίους.	You are teaching **the Jews apostasy**.

The accusative indicating the person taught becomes the subject of the passive verb:

2 Th 2:15 τὰς παραδόσεις ...   **You** were taught the traditions.
ἐδιδάχθητε.

(2) **αἰτέω**, *ask* (*someone for something*). The middle forms of this verb are synonymous with the active forms:

(a) With accusative of the person asked:

Acts 13:28 ᾐτήσαντο **Πιλᾶτον.**   They asked **Pilate.**

(b) With accusative of the thing asked for:

Mt 27:58 οὗτος ᾐτήσατο **τὸ σῶμα**   This man asked for **the body** of
τοῦ ᾽Ιησοῦ.   Jesus. [NOTE: **for** is not expressed separately.]

(c) With two accusatives:

Lk 11:11 **τὸν πατέρα** αἰτήσει   The son will ask **the father** for a
ὁ υἱὸς **ἰχθύν.**   **fish.**

Passive forms of this verb do not occur in the New Testament.

(3) **ἐρωτάω**, *ask* (*someone about something*):

(a) With accusative of the person asked:

Jn 14:16 ἐγὼ ἐρωτήσω **τὸν πατέρα.**   I shall ask **the Father.**

(b) With accusative of the thing asked about (not in the New Testament with this object alone).

(c) With two accusatives:

Mk 4:10 ἠρώτων **αὐτὸν τὰς**   They asked **him** about **the parables.** [NOTE: **about** is not expressed separately.]
παραβολάς.

Passive forms of this verb do not occur in the New Testament.

25 | PREPOSITIONS, I

189. Prepositions are function words[1] which serve to indicate the relationship of a substantive (i.e., a noun, a pronoun, or a word used as a noun) to the larger grammatical structure of which it is a part; prepositions have, therefore, functions very similar to those of case endings. There are not many prepositions in New Testament Greek and, since they are function words, they should be committed to memory.[2] However, one should not make the mistake of learning a single English meaning for each Greek preposition, at least as a general rule, for the meanings of most of the Greek prepositions are very hard to pin down. This should not be found surprising when we consider that the meanings of English prepositions also frequently seem frustratingly vague. A rather broad range of meanings is indicated by most English prepositions, as the examples below will show:

    (1)   He fought *with* the Japanese. (i.e., *against* them)
    (2)   He fought *with* the A.E.F. (i.e., *together with* it)
    (3)   He fought *with* a machine gun. (i.e., *by means of* it)
    (4)   He fought *with* courage. (i.e., *in a* courageous *manner*)

190. Greek prepositions have no inflections of their own, but they determine (or **govern**) the cases of the substantives with which they are syntactically associated. Some prepositions govern the accusative case, some govern the dative, and some govern the genitive. Other prepositions govern both the genitive *and* the accusative, and still others govern all

---

[1] Cf. §29.

[2] The lists of prepositions given in this and the following lesson include only those which occur most frequently.

three oblique cases.[1] In this lesson we shall confine ourselves to a consideration of prepositions which govern only one case.

191. Prepositions with the Accusative:

(1) ἀνά has restricted but important uses:

(a) It may mean *each, apiece,* or *by* (in a distributive sense), as in:

Mt 20:9 ἔλαβον ἀνὰ δηνάριον.	They received **a denarius each** (*or* **apiece**).
Lk 10:1 ἀπέστειλεν αὐτοὺς ἀνὰ δύο.	He sent them out **by twos**.

(b) The combination ἀνὰ μέσον means *among, between, in the midst of*; this "compound preposition" governs the genitive:

Mt 13:25 ἀνὰ μέσον τοῦ σίτου	**among the wheat**
1 Cor 6:5 ἀνὰ μέσον τοῦ ἀδελφοῦ αὐτοῦ	**between his brother** [and his opponent]

(c) The phrase ἀνὰ μέρος occurs once (in 1 Corinthians 14:27); it means *by turns, in turn.*

(2) εἰς, *into, to, for, for the purpose of*;[2] *in, on.* Note how the context affects the meaning one chooses:

Mt 9:7 ἀπῆλθεν εἰς τὸν οἶκον αὐτοῦ.	He went **into his house.**
Jn 2:2 ἐκλήθη ὁ Ἰησοῦς εἰς τὸν γάμον.	Jesus was invited **to the marriage.**
Jn 1:7 ἦλθεν εἰς μαρτυρίαν.	He came **for testimony** (*i.e.,* for the purpose of testimony).
Mt 21:46 εἰς προφήτην αὐτὸν εἶχον.	They regarded him **as a prophet** (*i.e.,* they had him **for** a prophet).
Mk 1:9 ἐβαπτίσθη εἰς τὸν Ἰορδάνην.	He was baptized **in the Jordan.**
Jn 10:42 ἐπίστευσαν εἰς αὐτόν.	They believed **in him.**
Mt 27:30 ἔτυπτον εἰς τὴν κεφαλὴν αὐτοῦ.	They struck him **on the head.**

---

[1] The genitive, dative, and accusative are collectively called the **oblique** cases.

[2] Here, as elsewhere, the semicolon separates more frequently encountered meanings from meanings less frequently met.

192. Prepositions with the Dative:

(1) **ἐν**, *in, within; by, by means of, with, on, among*:

Mt 3:1 ἐν ταῖς ἡμέραις ἐκείναις	**in those days**
Mt 22:37 ἀγαπήσεις κύριον τὸν θεόν σου **ἐν ὅλῃ τῇ καρδίᾳ σου καὶ ἐν ὅλῃ τῇ ψυχῇ σου καὶ ἐν ὅλῃ τῇ διανοίᾳ σου.**	You shall love the Lord thy God **with all your heart** and **with all your soul** and **with all your mind** (*here* **with** = **by means of**).
Mt 5:25 ἐν τῇ ὁδῷ	**on the way**
1 Cor 6:11 ἐδικαιώθητε **ἐν τῷ ὀνόματι τοῦ κυρίου ἡμῶν.**	You have been justified **by the name of our Lord.**

(2) **σύν**, *with, in company with, together with*:

Lk 20:1 οἱ ἀρχιερεῖς καὶ οἱ γραμματεῖς **σὺν τοῖς πρεσβυτέροις**	the chief priests and the scribes **with the elders**

193. Prepositions with the Genitive:

(1) **ἀντί**, *for, instead of, in place of; in behalf of*:

Mt 5:38 ὀφθαλμὸν **ἀντὶ ὀφθαλμοῦ** καὶ ὀδόντα **ἀντὶ ὀδόντος**	an eye **for an eye** and a tooth **for a tooth** (= **in place of an eye, a tooth**)
Mk 10:45 λύτρον **ἀντὶ πολλῶν**	a ransom **for many** (= **in the place of many, on behalf of many**)
Mt 2:22 Ἀρχέλαος βασιλεύει **ἀντὶ τοῦ πατρὸς αὐτοῦ Ἡρῴδου.**	Archelaus reigned **in place of his father Herod.**

(2) **ἀπό**, *from, away from, of*:

Acts 1:12 ὑπέστρεψαν **ἀπὸ ὄρους.**	They returned **from the mountain.**
Acts 1:9 νεφέλη ὑπέλαβεν αὐτὸν **ἀπὸ τῶν ὀφθαλμῶν αὐτῶν.**	A cloud took him up **from their eyes** (*i.e.*, **sight**).

(3) **ἄχρι, ἄχρις**, *until, up to*:

Acts 2:29 τὸ μνῆμα αὐτοῦ ἐστιν ἐν ἡμῖν **ἄχρι τῆς ἡμέρας ταύτης.**	His tomb is with us **to this day** (= **until this day**).
Rev 2:10 πιστὸς **ἄχρι θανάτου**	faithful **until death**

(4) **ἐκ** (**ἐξ** before vowels), *from, of, out of; by:*

 1 Jn 2:16 ἡ ἀλαζονία τοῦ βίου οὐκ The pride of life is not **of the**
 ἔστιν **ἐκ τοῦ πατρός.** **Father.**

 Rev 3:10 ἐγώ σε τηρήσω **ἐκ τῆς** I shall keep you **from the hour**
 ὥρας τοῦ πειρασμοῦ. of trial.

 Gal 2:16 οὐ δικαιοῦται ἄνθρωπος A man is not justified **by works**
 ἐξ ἔργων νόμου. of law.

(5) **ἔμπροσθεν,** *before, in the presence of:*

 Mt 10:33 ἀρνήσομαι ἐγὼ αὐτὸν I shall deny him **in the presence**
 ἔμπροσθεν τοῦ πατρός μου. **of my Father.**

(6) **ἔνεκα, ἔνεκεν, εἵνεκεν,** *for the sake of, because of:*

 Mk 8:35 ἀπολέσει τὴν ψυχὴν αὐτοῦ He shall lose his soul **for my**
 ἔνεκεν ἐμοῦ. **sake.**

 Mt 19:5 **ἔνεκα τούτου** καταλείψει **For the sake of this** a man will
 ἄνθρωπος τὸν πατέρα αὐτοῦ. leave his father.

 Acts 28:20 **εἵνεκεν τῆς ἐλπίδος** **for the sake of the hope** of
 τοῦ Ἰσραήλ Israel

(7) **ἐνώπιον,** *before, in the presence of:*

 Lk 13:20 ἐφάγομεν **ἐνώπιόν σου.** We ate **in your presence.**

 Jn 20:30 ἄλλα σημεῖα ἐποίησεν ὁ Jesus did other signs **in the**
 Ἰησοῦς **ἐνώπιον τῶν μαθητῶν.** **presence of the disciples.**

(8) **ἕως,** *until, up to, unto:*

 Mt 27:45 σκότος ἐγένετο **ἕως ὥρας** There was darkness **until the**
 ἐνάτης. **ninth hour.**

 Mk 14:34 περίλυπός ἐστιν ἡ ψυχή My soul is very sorrowful **even**
 μου **ἕως θανάτου.** **unto death.**

(9) **ὀπίσω,** *after, behind:*

 Jn 1:30 **ὀπίσω μου** ἔρχεται ἀνήρ. **After me** a man is coming.

(10) **πρό,** *before, in front of:*

 Jn 17:24 ἠγάπησάς με **πρὸ** You loved me **before the founda-**
 καταβολῆς κόσμου. **tion** of the world.

 Mk 1:2 ἀποστέλλω τὸν ἄγγελον I send my messenger **before thy**
 μου **πρὸ προσώπου σου.** **face.**

(11) **χάριν**, *because of, for the sake of* (usually follows the word it governs):

> Eph 3:14 τούτου χάριν κάμπω
> τὰ γόνατά μου.

For the sake of this I bend my knees.

(12) **χωρίς**, *apart from, without*:

> Rom 7:8 χωρὶς νόμου ἁμαρτία
> νεκρά.

Apart from law sin is dead.

> 1 Cor 4:8 χωρὶς ἡμῶν
> ἐβασιλεύσατε.

You have reigned **without us**.

194. Remarks on the Meanings of the Prepositions Listed Above:

(1) Ἔμπροσθεν and ἐνώπιον are synonymous; thus, e.g.,

> ἔμπροσθεν τοῦ θεοῦ (in Acts 10:4; 1 Thessalonians 1:3, 3:9, 13; etc.)

and

> ἐνώπιον τοῦ θεοῦ (in Luke 1:19, 12:6, etc.)

both mean *in the presence of God*. The difference is purely stylistic.

(2) Ἕως and ἄχρι(ς) are synonymous; *until the harvest* appears as ἕως τοῦ θερισμοῦ in most manuscripts of the New Testament (at Matthew 13:30) but as ἄχρι τοῦ θερισμοῦ in many others.

(3) Ἕνεκα (ἕνεκεν, εἵνεκεν) and χάριν are synonymous (=*for the sake of*). Χάριν occurs much less frequently; ἕνεκα, ἕνεκεν, and εἵνεκεν are variant spellings of the same word.

(4) Ἐκ and ἀπό are very nearly synonymous. Frequently, but not always, ἐκ means *from within*, while ἀπό means *from* in a more general way (e.g., *from the outside of, from the vicinity of*). Thus one would ordinarily expect to find ἐκ τοῦ οἴκου for *from the house* (i.e., *from inside the house*), but ἀπὸ τοῦ Χριστοῦ for *from Christ* (i.e., *away from Christ*). However, this distinction cannot be pressed, and numerous passages may be cited in which it does not hold, e.g.:

> Jn 11:1 ἀπὸ Βηθανίας, ἐκ τῆς
> κώμης Μαρίας καὶ Μάρθας

from Bethany, **from** the town of Mary and Martha

(5) Ἐν and σύν are not synonymous. When ἐν means *with*, it means *with* in the sense of *by means of*, not in the sense of *together with*. Ἐν does, when it has this "instrumental" sense, overlap the simple dative (of "means"):

Mt 3:11 ἐγὼ ὑμᾶς βαπτίζω ἐν   I baptize you **with** (*or* **in**) **water**.
ὕδατι.

Mk 1:8 ἐγὼ ἐβάπτισα ὑμᾶς **ὕδατι**.   I baptized you **with water**.

Lk 3:16 ἐγὼ **ὕδατι** βαπτίζω ὑμᾶς.   I baptize you **with water**.

Jn 1:26 ἐγὼ βαπτίζω ἐν **ὕδατι**.   I baptize **with** (*or* **in**) **water**.

195. Prepositional Phrases. The construction consisting of a preposition and the noun it governs is called a prepositional phrase. Greek prepositional phrases occur in syntactic situations similar to those in which English prepositional phrases are found, as may be seen from the examples already cited in this lesson.

(1) Greek prepositional phrases, like those of English, may be syntactically associated with verbs, as in

Mk 1:9 ἐβαπτίσθη **εἰς τὸν**   He was baptized **in the Jordan**
Ἰορδάνην.

(2) Other prepositional phrases modify nouns, as in

Mk 1:23 ἄνθρωπος **ἐν πνεύματι**   **a man with an unclean spirit**
ἀκαθάρτῳ

When a Greek prepositional phrase modifies an *articular* noun, it may simply follow the noun, as in

Eph 2:11 τὰ ἔθνη **ἐν σαρκί**   the Gentiles **in the flesh**.

However, Greek prepositional phrases, unlike English prepositional phrases, may have the ordinary attributive positions proper to adjectives, e.g., in

2 Cor 1:11 τὸ **εἰς ἡμᾶς** χάρισμα   the gift **to us**

Mt 6:23 τὸ φῶς τὸ **ἐν σοί**   the light [which is] **in you**

196. Like ordinary adjectives,[1] Greek prepositional phrases may be "substantivized" by the definite article and may then have the functions of nouns:

Lk 9:32 Πέτρος καὶ **οἱ σὺν αὐτῷ**   Peter and **the ones with him**

Rom 4:14 **οἱ ἐκ νόμου**   **those** [who live] **by the law**

Mk 13:16 **ὁ εἰς τὸν ἀγρόν**   **he** [that is] **in the field**

Acts 12:1 **οἱ ἀπὸ τῆς ἐκκλησίας**   the ones **from the church**

Cf. §71.

26 | PREPOSITIONS, II

In this lesson we shall take up prepositions governing two cases and prepositions governing three cases.

197. Prepositions Governing Two Cases. The two cases governed by prepositions in this group are always the *accusative* and the *genitive*.

(1) **διά**:

(a) With the accusative **διά** means *because of, on account of, for* (in the sense of *because of*).

Jn 4:41 ἐπίστευσαν **διὰ τὸν λόγον** αὐτοῦ.	They believed **because of his word**.
Jn 12:9 ἦλθον **διὰ τὸν 'Ιησοῦν**.	They came **on account of Jesus**.
Mk 2:27 τὸ σάββατον **διὰ τὸν ἄνθρωπον** ἐγένετο.	The Sabbath was made **for man**.

Note especially **διὰ τοῦτο**, *therefore, for this reason* (= *because of this*).

Mk 12:27 **διὰ τοῦτο** αὐτοὶ κριταὶ ἔσονται ὑμῶν.	**Therefore** they shall be your judges.
Jn 12:18 **διὰ τοῦτο** ἦλθον εἰς τὴν ὥραν ταύτην.	**For this reason** I have come to this hour.

(b) With the genitive **διά** means *through, by, by means of, during, with* (in the sense *by means of, by the agency of*).

Mk 9:30 παρεπορεύοντο **διὰ τῆς Γαλιλαίας**.	They were journeying **through Galilee**.
Acts 5:19 **διὰ νυκτὸς** ἤνοιξεν τὰς θύρας τῆς φυλακῆς.	**During the night** he opened the doors of the prison.
Rom 2:12 **διὰ νόμου** κριθήσονται.	They shall be judged **by the Law**.
Jn 1:10 ὁ κόσμος **δι' αὐτοῦ** ἐγένετο.	The world was made **by him** (*or* **through him**).

[153]

Acts 3:21 ἐλάλησεν ὁ θεὸς διὰ   God spoke **by** (= **by means of**)
στόματος τῶν ἁγίων.   **the mouth[s]** of the saints.

REMARK 1: The meaning of **διά** overlaps that of **ἐν** (cf. §§192(1), 194(5)): compare

and

Heb 9:12 **διὰ** τοῦ ἰδίου αἵματος   **by his own blood**

Heb 9:25 **ἐν** αἵματι ἀλλοτρίῳ   **by another's blood**

REMARK 2: **Διά** may indicate the agent, as in John 1:10 (cf. above), and thus overlaps **ὑπό** also (cf. §§118(b), and 197(b)). However, **διά** usually indicates the *intermediate* agent, as it does clearly in

Mt 2:15 [ἐρρήθη] **ὑπὸ** κυρίου **διὰ**   [It was spoken] **by the Lord**
τοῦ προφήτου.   **through the prophet.**

REMARK 3: The meaning of **διά** also overlaps that of **ἐκ** slightly, as in

Rom 3:30 ὁ θεὸς δικαιώσει   God shall justify the circumcision
περιτομὴν **ἐκ** πίστεως καὶ   **by faith** and the uncircum-
ἀκροβυστίαν **διὰ** τῆς πίστεως.   cision **by faith.**

NOTE: that **ἐκ** is not used to mean *by* when it governs a substantive designating a *person*.

(2) **κατά**:

(a) With the accusative **κατά** usually means *according to, in accordance with.*

Jn 8:15 ὑμεῖς **κατὰ** τὴν σάρκα   You are judging **according to**
κρίνετε.   **the flesh.**

Acts 13:22 εὗρον Δαυὶδ ἄνδρα   I have found David [to be][1] a man
κατὰ τὴν καρδίαν μου.   **after my own heart** (= ac-
    cording to my heart).

NOTE: In certain fixed phrases **κατά** with the accusative means *every*:

καθ' ἡμέραν, *every day*
κατ' ἰδίαν, *each to his own, privately*
κατ' ἔτος, *every year*
κατὰ πόλιν, *every city*

(b) With the genitive **κατά** usually means *against.*

---

[1] Cf. §182.

Mt 12:14 οἱ Φαρισαῖοι συμβούλιον ἔλαβον **κατ' αὐτοῦ.**	The Pharisees took counsel **against him.**
Mt 20:11 ἐγόγγυζον **κατὰ τοῦ οἰκοδεσπότου.**	They murmured **against the master of the house.**

Κατά sometimes has other meanings, depending on the contexts in which it is found. The lexicon should be consulted when the meanings given above are not appropriate.

(3) **μετά**:

(a) With the accusative **μετά** means *after* (almost always in a temporal sense, unlike **ὀπίσω**, which usually means *after* in the sense of *behind*).

Mk 16:12 and often **μετὰ** ταῦτα	**after** these things
Lk 1:24 **μετὰ** ταύτας τὰς ἡμέρας	**after** these days
Heb 9:3 **μετὰ** τὸ δεύτερον καταπέτασμα	**behind** the second curtain [only instance of this sense in the NT]

(b) With the genitive **μετά** means *with*.

Mk 1:13 ἦν **μετὰ τῶν θηρίων.**	He was **with the wild beasts.**

Μετά is almost entirely synonymous with **σύν**, except that it does not have the sense of *in addition to*, which **σύν** may sometimes bear. **Μετά** is commoner than **σύν** in the New Testament.

(4) **περί**:

(a) With the accusative **περί** means *around, about* (not = *concerning*).

Mt 3:4 ὁ Ἰωάννης εἶχεν ζώνην δερματίνην **περὶ τὴν ὀσφὺν αὐτοῦ.**	John had a leather girdle **around his waist.**
Mt 20:3 **περὶ τρίτην ὥραν**	**at about the third hour.**

(b) With the genitive **περί** means *about, concerning*.

Acts 2:31 ἐλάλησεν **περὶ τῆς ἀναστάσεως** τοῦ Χριστοῦ.	He spoke **about (concerning) the resurrection** of the Christ.

(5) **ὑπέρ**:

(a) With the accusative **ὑπέρ** means *above, beyond*.

Mt 10:24 οὐκ ἔστιν μαθητὴς **ὑπὲρ τὸν διδάσκαλον.**	A disciple is not **above his teacher.**
2 Cor 1:8 **ὑπὲρ δύναμιν** ἐβαρήθημεν	We were burdened **beyond our strength.**

(b) With the genitive **ὑπέρ** means *on behalf of, for the sake of, for* (in the sense *for the sake of*).

> Rom 5:8 Χριστὸς **ὑπὲρ ἡμῶν** ἀπέθανεν.
>
> Christ died **for us** (= **in behalf of us, for our sakes**).

(6) **ὑπό**:

(a) With the accusative **ὑπό** means *under*.

> Mt 8:9 ἐγώ ἄνθρωπός εἰμι **ὑπὸ ἐξουσίαν**.
>
> I am a man **under authority**.

(b) With the genitive **ὑπό** means *by* (expressing the agent, especially with verbs in the passive voice; cf. §118).

> Mt 4:1 ὁ Ἰησοῦς ἀνήχθη **ὑπὸ τοῦ πνεύματος**.
>
> Jesus was led up **by the Spirit**.

198. Prepositions Governing Three Cases. (1) **Ἐπί** with all three cases may most often be rendered by *on, upon, over*; the distinction between the various meanings of the cases with this preposition is blurred in the New Testament.

With the accusative:

> Mt 10:29 and often **ἐπὶ τὴν γῆν**   **on the earth** (*or* **on the ground**)

With the genitive:

> Mt 6:10 and often **ἐπὶ τῆς γῆς**   **on the earth** (*or* **on the ground**)

With the dative:

> Mt 16:18 **ἐπὶ ταύτῃ τῇ πέτρᾳ** οἰκοδομήσω μου τὴν ἐκκλησίαν.
>
> **On this rock** I shall build my church.

The factors that determine which case is to be used with **ἐπί** seem to be very complex. It occurs with a given case or cases of certain words with certain meanings, but not with other cases of these words in this or other meanings (thus **ἐπὶ τῇ γῇ** does not occur at all in the New Testament). These factors cannot be analyzed briefly. For our purposes it will be sufficient to learn the meanings given above and to bear in mind also the meanings of certain fixed phrases or expressions such as the following:

(a) **ἐπί** + accusative. **Ἐπὶ τὸ αὐτό** means *together*.

| Lk 17:35 ἔσονται δύο ἀλήθουσαι ἐπὶ τὸ αὐτό. | Two grinding women shall be **together.** |

'Eπί with expressions of time indicates the *extent* of the time and may usually be rendered by *for*:

Lk 4:25 ἐπὶ ἔτη τρία καὶ μῆνας ἕξ	**for** three years and six months
Lk 18:4 ἐπὶ χρόνον	**for** a while
Acts 13:31 ἐπὶ ἡμέρας πλείους	**for** many days

(b) ἐπί + genitive. 'Eπ' ἀληθείας means *in truth*; cf. Mark 12:14, 32; Luke 4:24, 20:21; etc.

'Eπί with expressions of time indicates the *point* of time and may usually be rendered by *at*, or by *when* with a paraphrase:

Mt 1:11 ἐπὶ τῆς μετοικεσίας Βαβυλῶνος	**at** the time of the Babylonian captivity
Mk 2:26 ἐπὶ 'Αβιάθαρ ἀρχιερέως	**when** Abiathar was high priest
Heb 1:2 ἐπ' ἐσχάτου τῶν ἡμερῶν	**at** the last of days

(c) ἐπί + dative. It should be noted that the phrase ἐπὶ τῷ ὀνόματι means *in the name* (Matthew 18:5 and often); however, it seems to be indistinguishable in meaning from εἰς τὸ ὄνομα and ἐν τῷ ὀνόματι.

Also note that ἐπ' ἐλπίδι means *in hope*.

(2) παρά:

(a) With the accusative παρά usually has the meaning *beside, by the side of, alongside, by.*

Mt 13:1 ὁ 'Ιησοῦς ἐκάθητο παρὰ τὴν θάλασσαν.	Jesus sat **beside the sea.**
Mt 13:4 ἔπεσεν παρὰ τὴν ὁδόν.	It fell **by the side of the path.**
Mk 10:46 Βαρτιμαῖος ἐκάθητο παρὰ τὴν ὁδόν.	Bartimaeus was sitting **by the side of the road.**

(b) With the genitive παρά means *from, from the side of* (it occurs only with substantives denoting *persons*).

| Jn 10:18 ταύτην τὴν ἐντολὴν ἔλαβον παρὰ τοῦ πατρός μου | I received this commandment **from my Father.** |
| Lk 2:1 ἐξῆλθεν δόγμα παρὰ Καίσαρος Αὐγούστου. | A decree went out **from Caesar Augustus.** |

(c) With the dative **παρά** means *with* (= *in the presence of*), *near, beside* (with a substantive denoting a *person*).

Rom 2:11 οὐκ ἔστιν προσωπολημψία **παρὰ τῷ θεῷ.**　There is no respect of persons **with God.**

1 Cor 3:19 ἡ σοφία τοῦ κόσμου τούτου μωρία **παρὰ τῷ θεῷ** ἐστιν.　The wisdom of this world is foolishness **with God.**

(3) **πρός**:
(a) With the accusative **πρός** means *to, unto* (when motion is indicated by the verb), *at, with* (when no motion is indicated), *for* (= *for the purpose of*; cf. **εἰς**).

Jn 1:42 ἤγαγεν αὐτὸν **πρὸς τὸν Ἰησοῦν.**　He led him **to Jesus.**

Jn 1:1 ὁ λόγος ἦν **πρὸς τὸν θεόν.**　The word was **with God.**

Acts 5:10 ἔπεσεν **πρὸς τοὺς πόδας αὐτοῦ.**　She fell **at his feet.**

2 Cor 10:4 τὰ ὅπλα τῆς στρατείας δυνατὰ **πρὸς καθαίρεσιν** ὀχυρωμάτων.　The weapons of our warfare are mighty **for destroying** fortresses.

(b) With the genitive (only once in the New Testament) **πρός** means *in the interest of, for*.

Acts 27:34 τοῦτο **πρὸς τῆς** ὑμετέρας σωτηρίας ὑπάρχει.　This is **for** (= **in the interest of**) **your safety.**

(c) With the dative (only six times in the New Testament) **πρός** means *at*.

Mk 5:11 ἦν ἐκεῖ **πρὸς τῷ ὄρει** ἀγέλη χοίρων μεγάλη βοσκομένη.　A great herd of swine was feeding there **at the hill.**

Lk 19:37 **πρὸς τῇ καταβάνει** τοῦ ὄρους τῶν Ἐλαιῶν　**at the descent** of the Mount of Olives

199. Remarks. (1) Many of the prepositions have alternative forms which occur before words beginning with a vowel, and some prepositions have separate forms which occur before the smooth breathing and the rough breathing. Prepositions which do *not* have such alternative forms are: **περί, πρό, εἰς, ἐν, σύν, ἔμπροσθεν, ἐνώπιον, ἕως, ὀπίσω, χάριν, χωρίς, ὑπέρ,** and **πρός**.

(2) 'Ex has the form ἐξ before vowels: ἐξ ἀνθρώπου.
"Ενεκα has the form ἕνεκεν before vowels: ἕνεκεν ἀνθρώπου. "Ενεκεν may also occur before consonants: ἕνεκεν θεοῦ.)
"Αχρι *may* have the form ἄχρις before vowels: ἄχρις οὖ, ἄχρι αὐγῆς.

The remaining contractions are usual, but not mandatory:

'Ανά has the form ἀν' before vowels: ἀν' ὀκτώ (but also ἀνὰ εἷς).
Διά has the form δι' before vowels: δι' ἐμοῦ, δι' ἡμῶν.
Παρά has the form παρ' before vowels: παρ' ἐμοί, παρ' ἡμῶν.
'Αντί has the form ἀντ' before the smooth breathing: ἀντ' ἐμοῦ
   and the form ἀνθ' before the rough breathing: ἀνθ' ὧν.
'Από has the form ἀπ' before the smooth breathing: ἀπ' ἐμοῦ
   and the form ἀφ' before the rough breathing: ἀφ' ἡμῶν.
Κατά has the form κατ' before the smooth breathing: κατ' ἐμέ
   and the form καθ' before the rough breathing: καθ' ἡμᾶς.
Μετά has the form μετ' before the smooth breathing: μετ' ἐμέ
   and the form μεθ' before the rough breathing: μεθ' ἡμῶν.
'Υπό has the form ὑπ' before the smooth breathing: ὑπ' ἐμοῦ
   and the form ὑφ' before the rough breathing: ὑφ' ὑμῶν.
'Επί has the form ἐπ' before the smooth breathing: ἐπ' ἐλπίδι
   and the form ἐφ' before the rough breathing: ἐφ' ὅσον.

(3) The *accented forms* of the personal pronouns usually occur with the prepositions (cf. §§107f); however, πρός με is commoner than πρὸς ἐμέ.

(4) The remarks in §§195f apply equally to the prepositions in this lesson:

Acts 13:13 οἱ περὶ Παῦλον	those **around** Paul
Mk 5:27 τὰ περὶ τοῦ 'Ιησοῦ	the [reports] **about** Jesus
Rom 11:21 οἱ κατὰ φύσιν κλάδοι	the **natural** branches (branches **according to nature**)

27 | μι-VERBS

200. The contract verbs introduced in Lesson 23 are among the most "regular" verbs in Greek; the verbs taken up in this lesson are undoubtedly the most irregular. However, the forms of these verbs are encountered very frequently, and so it is advisable to commit them to memory.

The μι-verbs are so called because the "dictionary form" (i.e., the first person singular, present indicative active) ends in -μι rather than in -ω. The verb εἰμί, whose forms were given in §140, is a μι-verb, but one which is irregular even among the other members of the class. The most important μι-verbs other than εἰμί are δίδωμι, *give*, τίθημι, *lay*, *put*, and ἵστημι, *stand*, *set*. The paradigms of these verbs exhibit irregularities in the present, imperfect, and aorist; these forms are set out below:

(1)
PRESENT ACTIVE

SG.	1	δίδωμι	τίθημι	ἵστημι
	2	δίδως	τίθης	ἵστης
	3	δίδωσι(ν)	τίθησι(ν)	ἵστησι(ν)
PL.	1	δίδομεν	τίθεμεν	ἵσταμεν
	2	δίδοτε	τίθετε	ἵστατε
	3	διδόασι(ν)	τιθέασι(ν)	ἱστᾶσι(ν)

(2)
IMPERFECT ACTIVE

SG.	1	ἐδίδουν	ἐτίθην	ἵστην
	2	ἐδίδους	ἐτίθεις	ἵστης
	3	ἐδίδου	ἐτίθει	ἵστη
PL.	1	ἐδίδομεν	ἐτίθεμεν	ἵσταμεν
	2	ἐδίδοτε	ἐτίθετε	ἵστατε
	3	ἐδίδοσαν	ἐτίθεσαν	ἵστασαν

(3)

AORIST ACTIVE

				FIRST[1] AORIST	SECOND AORIST
SG.	1	ἔδωκα	ἔθηκα	ἔστησα	ἔστην
	2	ἔδωκας	ἔθηκας	ἔστησας	ἔστης
	3	ἔδωκε(ν)	ἔθηκε(ν)	ἔστησε(ν)	ἔστη
PL.	1	ἐδώκαμεν	ἐθήκαμεν	ἐστήσαμεν	ἔστημεν
	2	ἐδώκατε	ἐθήκατε	ἐστήσατε	ἔστητε
	3	ἔδωκαν	ἔθηκαν	ἔστησαν	ἔστησαν

(4)

PRESENT MIDDLE AND PASSIVE

SG.	1	δίδομαι	τίθεμαι	ἵσταμαι
	2	δίδοσαι	τίθεσαι	ἵστασαι
	3	δίδοται	τίθεται	ἵσταται
PL.	1	διδόμεθα	τιθέμεθα	ἱστάμεθα
	2	δίδοσθε	τίθεσθε	ἵστασθε
	3	δίδονται	τίθενται	ἵστανται

(5)

IMPERFECT MIDDLE AND PASSIVE

SG.	1	ἐδιδόμην	ἐτιθέμην	ἱστάμην
	2	ἐδίδοσο	ἐτίθεσο	ἵστασο
	3	ἐδίδοτο	ἐτίθετο	ἵστατο
PL.	1	ἐδιδόμεθα	ἐτιθέμεθα	ἱστάμεθα
	2	ἐδίδοσθε	ἐτίθεσθε	ἵστασθε
	3	ἐδίδοντο	ἐτίθεντο	ἵσταντο

(6)

AORIST MIDDLE

SG.	1	ἐδόμην	ἐθέμην	
	2	ἔδου	ἔθου	
	3	ἔδοτο	ἔθετο	[none]
PL.	1	ἐδόμεθα	ἐθέμεθα	
	2	ἔδοσθε	ἔθεσθε	
	3	ἔδοντο	ἔθεντο	

201. The future forms (active, middle, and passive) and the aorist passive forms of these three verbs are regularly formed. The stems are derived from the second and sixth principal parts, as for other verbs (cf. §§92, 126, fn. 1). Thus we have:

---

[1] The distinction between the first and second aorists of ἵστημι is explained in §204.

FUTURE ACTIVE	1	δώσω	θήσω	στήσω
	2	δώσεις	θήσεις	στήσεις
		etc.	etc.	etc.
FUTURE MIDDLE	1	δώσομαι	θήσομαι	στήσομαι
	2	δώσῃ	θήσῃ	στήσῃ
		etc.	etc.	etc.
FUTURE PASSIVE	1	δοθήσομαι	τεθήσομαι	σταθήσομαι
	2	δοθήσῃ	τεθήσῃ	σταθήσῃ
		etc.	etc.	etc.
AORIST PASSIVE	1	ἐδόθην	ἐτέθην	ἐστάθην
	2	ἐδόθης	ἐτέθης	ἐστάθης
		etc.	etc.	etc.

202. Δίδωμι, *give*, behaves syntactically very much like its English equivalent; it governs a direct object (accusative) and an indirect object (dative); the direct object becomes the subject when the verb is transformed to the passive, the indirect object being retained in the dative (cf. §§84f, 185f). A few illustrative passages are given below:

Jn 13:34 ἐντολὴν καινὴν **δίδωμι** ὑμῖν.

I am giving you a new commandment.

Mt 10:1 **ἔδωκεν** αὐτοῖς ἐξουσίαν πνευμάτων ἀκαθάρτων.

He gave them power [over] unclean spirits.

Mk 6:7 **ἐδίδου** αὐτοῖς ἐξουσίαν τῶν πνευμάτων τῶν ἀκαθάρτων.

He was giving them power [over] the unclean spirits.

Mt 14:11 ἠνέχθη ἡ κεφαλὴ ἐπὶ πίνακι καὶ **ἐδόθη** τῷ κορασίῳ.

The head was brought on a platter and **was given** to the girl.

Acts 8:18 διὰ τῆς ἐπιθέσεως τῶν χειρῶν τῶν ἀποστόλων **δίδοται** τὸ πνεῦμα.

The Spirit **is given** by the laying on of the hands of the apostles.

203. Τίθημι has the basic meaning *put, lay,* and a number of other meanings in special contexts. The more common meanings are illustrated first:

1 Pe 2:6 **τίθημι** ἐν Σιὼν λίθον ἐκλεκτόν.

I am laying a chosen stone in Zion.

Mt 27:60 **ἔθηκεν** αὐτὸ ἐν τῷ καινῷ αὐτοῦ μνημείῳ.

He laid it in his new tomb.

Mt 12:18 **θήσω** τὸ πνεῦμά μου ἐπ' αὐτόν.

I shall put my Spirit upon him.

(1) The expression **τίθημι τὴν ψυχήν μου** means *I lay down my life*; various forms of it occur frequently in the Gospel and First Epistle of John:

Jn 10:11 ὁ ποιμὴν ὁ καλὸς **τὴν ψυχὴν αὐτοῦ τίθησιν** ὑπὲρ τῶν προβάτων.
The good shepherd **lays down his life** for the sheep.

Jn 13:37 **τὴν ψυχήν μου** ὑπὲρ σοῦ **θήσω**.
I shall lay down my life for you.

1 Jn 3:16 ἐκεῖνος ὑπὲρ ἡμῶν **τὴν ψυχὴν αὐτοῦ ἔθηκεν.**
He **laid down his life** on our behalf.

(2) It sometimes occurs with two accusatives (one being an object complement) and is then equivalent to **ποιέω**, *make* (cf. §§181ff):

θήσω τοὺς ἐχθρούς σου ὑποπόδιον τῶν ποδῶν σου. (cf. Acts 2:35).
I shall make your enemies the footstool of your feet.

When this construction is transformed into the passive, the two accusatives are changed to *nominatives* (cf. §187):

1 Tim 2:7 **ἐτέθην** ἐγὼ κῆρυξ καὶ ἀπόστολος (*as if transformed from* [ὁ θεὸς] ἔθηκέν με κήρυκα καὶ ἀπόστολον).
I was made a herald and an apostle (*as if transformed from* [God] made me a herald and an apostle).

(3) The middle voice has very much the same meanings as the active:

1 Cor 12:18 ὁ θεὸς **ἔθετο** τὰ μέλη.
God **laid** the parts (*i.e.,* **arranged** the members [of the body]).

Acts 20:28 ὑμᾶς τὸ πνεῦμα τὸ ἅγιον **ἔθετο** ἐπισκόπους.
The Holy Spirit **made** you overseers.

204. **Ἵστημι** is remarkable in having both first aorist and second aorist forms in the active voice. The first aorist active forms, as well as the forms of the present, imperfect, and future active, are used *transitively*; the second aorist active forms, together with the forms of the future middle and passive and the aorist passive, are used *intransitively*.

(1) The transitive forms of **ἵστημι** express the meanings *put, set, stand* (= *cause to stand*), *establish, place, propose*:

Mt 4:5 **ἔστησεν** αὐτὸν ἐπὶ τὸ πτερύγιον τοῦ ἱεροῦ.
He **set** him upon the pinnacle of the temple.

Acts 5:27 αὐτοὺς **ἔστησαν** ἐν τῷ   They **made** them **stand** in the
συνεδρίῳ.   council.

(2) The intransitive forms of **ἵστημι** express the meanings *stand, stand still, stand firm, stop*:

Mt 27:11 ὁ Ἰησοῦς **ἐστάθη**   Jesus **stood** before the governor.
ἔμπροσθεν τοῦ ἡγεμόνος.

Jn 20:19 ὁ Ἰησοῦς **ἔστη** εἰς τὸ   Jesus **stood** in the midst.
μέσον.

Rev 11:11 **ἔστησαν** ἐπὶ τοὺς   They **stood** upon their feet.
πόδας αὐτῶν.

Notice that **ἔστησαν** is third plural second aorist as well as third plural first aorist; cf. §200(3).

28 | PRESENT PARTICIPLES, I

205. Participles are frequently called "verbal adjectives"; as we shall notice in detail later on, they have some characteristics in common with verbs and others in common with adjectives. English verbs have *two* participles: the *present* participle always ends in *-ing*; the *past* participle may end in *-ed*, *-d*, *-t*, or *-en*, or it may be quite irregularly formed, as the illustrative examples show:

DICTIONARY FORM	PRESENT PARTICIPLE	PAST PARTICIPLE
look	looking	looked
pulverize	pulverizing	pulverized
sleep	sleeping	slept
speak	speaking	spoken
sing	singing	sung

206. A Greek verb may have as many as *ten* participles: present, future, aorist, and perfect active, present and perfect middle or passive, future and aorist middle, and future and aorist passive. We shall begin with the present participles; those of the model verb λύω are set out below:

(1)   ACTIVE VOICE

	MASCULINE	FEMININE	NEUTER
SG.N.	λύων	λύουσα	λῦον
G.	λύοντος	λυούσης	λύοντος
D.	λύοντι	λυούσῃ	λύοντι
A.	λύοντα	λύουσαν	λῦον
PL.N.	λύοντες	λύουσαι	λύοντα
G.	λυόντων	λυουσῶν	λυόντων
D.	λύουσι(ν)	λυούσαις	λύουσι(ν)
A.	λύοντας	λυούσας	λύοντα

(2)   MIDDLE OR PASSIVE VOICE

	MASCULINE	FEMININE	NEUTER
SG.N.	λυόμενος	λυομένη	λυόμενον
G.	λυομένου	λυομένης	λυομένου
D.	λυομένῳ	λυομένῃ	λυομένῳ
A.	λυόμενον	λυομένην	λυόμενον
PL.N.	λυόμενοι	λυόμεναι	λυόμενα
G.	λυομένων	λυομένων	λυομένων
D.	λυομένοις	λυομέναις	λυομένοις
A.	λυομένους	λυομένας	λυόμενα

207. The *masculine* and *neuter* forms of the present *active* participle may be analyzed into:

(1) The base λυ-.
(2) The stem formative -ο-.
(3) The morpheme -ντ-.
(4) The case-number suffixes of the third declension.[1]

Thus the masculine forms of the present active participle are exactly like those of third declension ντ-stems,[2] and the neuter forms are like ντ-stem nouns with *neuter* case-number suffixes, so that both the nominative and accusative singular neuter forms are **λῦον** (< λυ + ο + ντ + ‡) with loss of τ (as in ὄνομα < ὀνοματ + ‡), but without lengthening of ο to ω, since no ς is lost. The nominative and accusative plural neuter are both **λύοντα** (< λυ + ο + ντ + α).

208. The *feminine* forms of the present *active* participle may be analyzed into:

(1) The base λυ-.
(2) The stem formative -ο-.
(3) The morpheme -εσ-.[3]
(4) The stem vowel and case-number suffixes of the first declension as these are found in the declension of nouns like **δόξα** (cf. §§82, 143(3b ii)).

Note that constituents (2) and (3) above contract to -ουσ-, according to the rules set out in §172. Thus,

---

[1] Cf. §§147, 153.

[2] Cf. §153. Indeed, ἄρχων, ἄρχοντος is the present participle of ἄρχω, *rule*, used as a noun (= *the ruling one*).   [3] An allomorph of -ντ- (cf. §145, *Note*).

λυ + ο + εσ + α > λύουσα
λυ + ο + εσ + ης > λυούσης

209. The forms of the present middle and passive participle may be analyzed into:
(1) The base **λυ-**.
(2) The stem formative **-ο-**.
(3) The morpheme **-μεν-**.
(4) The stem vowels and case-number suffixes of the first and second declensions.

Thus, present middle and passive participles are declined exactly like adjectives of the first and second declensions, e.g., **καλός, ἡ, όν** (cf. §§64, 73, 81).

210. These analyses permit us to proceed at once to describe the present participle of contract verbs and **μι-** verbs. The forms of the contract verbs are presented first; the student should review the rules of contraction of §172.

(1) The forms of the present active participle of **ἀγαπῶ** (uncontracted **ἀγαπάω**) are given below (the uncontracted forms are given in parentheses):

MASCULINE

SG.N.	(ἀγαπα-ων[1])	ἀγαπῶν	PL.N.	(ἀγαπα-οντες)	ἀγαπῶντες
G.	(ἀγαπα-οντος)	ἀγαπῶντος	G.	(ἀγαπα-οντων)	ἀγαπῶντων
D.	(ἀγαπα-οντι)	ἀγαπῶντι	D.	(ἀγαπα-ουσι[ν][2])	ἀγαπῶσι(ν)
A.	(ἀγαπα-οντα)	ἀγαπῶντα	A.	(ἀγαπα-οντας)	ἀγαπῶντας

FEMININE

SG.N.	(ἀγαπα-ουσα[3])	ἀγαπῶσα	PL.N.	(ἀγαπα-ουσαι)	ἀγαπῶσαι
G.	(ἀγαπα-ουσης)	ἀγαπώσης	G.	(ἀγαπα-ουσων)	ἀγαπωσῶν
D.	(ἀγαπα-ουση)	ἀγαπώσῃ	D.	(ἀγαπα-ουσαις)	ἀγαπώσαις
A.	(ἀγαπα-ουσαν)	ἀγαπῶσαν	A.	(ἀγαπα-ουσας)	ἀγαπώσας

---

[1] The element **-ων** is complex; it is analyzable into **ο + ντ + ς**. As in the case of **ντ**-stem nouns of the third declension, the final **ς** is assimilated ("dropped"), with resulting lengthening of **ο** to **ω**; final **τ** is also lost.

[2] See §153(2); the final **ν** is **ν**-movable (cf. §169, *Remark* 1).

[3] See §208; **ουσα** < **ο + εσ + α**.

NEUTER

SG.N.	(ἀγαπα-ον[1])	ἀγαπῶν	PL.N.	(ἀγαπα-οντα)	ἀγαπῶντα
G.	(ἀγαπα-οντος)	ἀγαπῶντος	G.	(ἀγαπα-οντων)	ἀγαπώντων
D.	(ἀγαπα-οντι)	ἀγαπῶντι	D.	(ἀγαπα-ουσι[ν][2])	ἀγαπῶσι(ν)
A.	(ἀγαπα-ον)	ἀγαπῶν	A.	(ἀγαπα-οντα)	ἀγαπῶντα

(2) The forms of the present active participle of **ποιῶ** (uncontracted **ποιέω**) are given below (the uncontracted forms are given in parentheses):

MASCULINE

SG.N.	(ποιε-ων[3])	ποιῶν	PL.N.	(ποιε-οντες)	ποιοῦντες
G.	(ποιε-οντος)	ποιοῦντος	G.	(ποιε-οντων)	ποιούντων
D.	(ποιε-οντι)	ποιοῦντι	D.	(ποιε-ουσι[ν][2])	ποιοῦσι(ν)
A.	(ποιε-οντα)	ποιοῦντα	A.	(ποιε-οντας)	ποιοῦντας

FEMININE

SG.N.	(ποιε-ουσα[4])	ποιοῦσα	PL.N.	(ποιε-ουσαι)	ποιοῦσαι
G.	(ποιε-ουσης)	ποιούσης	G.	(ποιε-ουσων)	ποιουσῶν
D.	(ποιε-ουση)	ποιούση	D.	(ποιε-ουσαις)	ποιούσαις
A.	(ποιε-ουσαν)	ποιοῦσαν	A.	(ποιε-ουσας)	ποιούσας

NEUTER

SG.N.	(ποιε-ον[1])	ποιοῦν	PL.N.	(ποιε-οντα)	ποιοῦντα
G.	(ποιε-οντος)	ποιοῦντος	G.	(ποιε-οντων)	ποιούντων
D.	(ποιε-οντι)	ποιοῦντι	D.	(ποιε-ουσι[ν][2])	ποιοῦσι(ν)
A.	(ποιε-ον)	ποιοῦν	A.	(ποιε-οντα)	ποιοῦντα

(3) The forms of the present active participle of **πληρῶ** (uncontracted **πληρόω**) are given below (the uncontracted forms are given in parentheses):

MASCULINE

SG.N.	(πληρο-ων[3])	πληρῶν	PL.N.	(πληρο-οντες)	πληροῦντες
G.	(πληρο-οντος)	πληροῦντος	G.	(πληρο-οντων)	πληρούντων
D.	(πληρο-οντι)	πληροῦντι	D.	(πληρο-ουσι[ν][2])	πληροῦσι(ν)
A.	(πληρο-οντα)	πληροῦντα	A.	(πληρο-σντας)	πληροῦντας

---

[1] The element **-ον** is analyzable into **ο + ντ**; in this case the final **τ** is lost, but there is no lengthening of **ο** to **ω**, since there never was any final **-ς**.

[2] See fn. 2, p. 167.

[3] See fn. 1, p. 167.

[4] See fn. 3, p. 167.

FEMININE

SG.N.	(πληρο-ουσα[1])	**πληροῦσα**	PL.N.	(πληρο-ουσαι)	**πληροῦσαι**	
G.	(πληρο-ουσης)	**πληρούσης**	G.	(πληρο-ουσων)	**πληρουσῶν**	
D.	(πληρο-ουση)	**πληρούση**	D.	(πληρο-ουσαις)	**πληρούσαις**	
A.	(πληρο-ουσαν)	**πληροῦσαν**	A.	(πληρο-ουσας)	**πληρούσας**	

NEUTER

SG.N.	(πληρο-ον[2])	**πληροῦν**	PL.N.	(πληρο-οντα)	**πληροῦντα**	
G.	(πληρο-οντος)	**πληροῦντος**	G.	(πληρο-οντων)	**πληρούντων**	
D.	(πληρο-οντι)	**πληροῦντι**	D.	(πληρο-ουσι[ν][3])	**πληροῦσι(ν)**	
A.	(πληρο-ον)	**πληροῦν**	A.	(πληρο-οντα)	**πληροῦντα**	

211. There is no need to set out the paradigms of the present middle and passive participles of the contract verbs in detail. They are as follows:

For **ἀγαπῶ** (< ἀγαπάω), **ἀγαπώμενος, η, ον** (< ἀγαπα-ομενος, η, ον)
For **ποιῶ** (< ποιέω), **ποιούμενος, η, ον** (< ποιε-ομενος, η, ον)
For **πληρῶ** (< πληρόω), **πληρούμενος, η, ον** (< πληρο-ομενος, η, ον)

Each of these forms is declined like an ordinary adjective of the first and second declensions (e.g., like **καλός, ή, όν**).

212. The present participles of the **μι**-verbs studied in Lesson 27 are similarly formed, except that they have *no stem formatives*. The masculine and neuter forms of the present active participles of these verbs are thus analyzable as follows (cf. §207):

διδο + **ντ** + third declension case-number suffixes
τιθε + **ντ** + third declension case-number suffixes
ἱστα + **ντ** + third declension case-number suffixes

The element **-ντ-** is assimilated in the nominative singular masculine and in the dative plural (masculine and neuter), with modification of the final vowel of the base; the **-τ-** of **-ντ-** is lost in the nominative and accusative singular neuter.

213. The forms of the present active participle of **δίδωμι**, masculine

---

[1] See fn. 3, p. 167.
[2] See fn. 1, p. 168.
[3] See fn. 2, p. 167.

and neuter, are given below; they should be compared with the corresponding forms of the participles previously described:

MASCULINE

SG.N.	διδούς (< διδο-ντ-ς)	PL.N.	διδόντες
G.	διδόντος (< διδο-ντ-ος)	G.	διδόντων
D.	διδόντι (< διδο-ντ-ι)	D.	διδοῦσι(ν) (διδο-ντ-σι[ν])
A.	διδόντα etc.	A.	διδόντας

NEUTER

SG.N.	διδόν (< διδο-ντ- ‡)	PL.N.	διδόντα
G.	διδόντος etc.	G.	διδόντων
D.	διδόντι	D.	διδοῦσι(ν)
A.	διδόν	A.	διδόντα

214. The feminine forms of the present active participles of the μι-verbs of Lesson 27 are analyzable as:

> διδο + εσ + first declension stem vowel and suffixes (i.e., as found in δόξα)
> τιθε + εσ + first declension endings as above
> ἱστα + εσ + first declension endings as above

The initial ε of the morpheme -εσ- is contracted (in accordance with the rules of §172) with the final vowel of the base. The feminine forms of the present active participle of **δίδωμι** are given below:

FEMININE

SG.N.	διδοῦσα (< διδο-εσ-α)	PL.N.	διδοῦσαι (< διδο-εσ-αι)
G.	διδούσης (< διδο-εσ-ης)	G.	διδουσῶν (< διδο-εσ-ων)
D.	διδούσῃ etc.	D.	διδούσαις etc.
A.	διδοῦσαν	A.	διδούσας

215. The paradigms of the present active participles of **τίθημι** and **ἵστημι** are given next; compare the forms with the corresponding forms of participles previously described.

(1)   MASCULINE

SG.N.	τιθείς (< τιθε-ντ-ς)	PL.N.	τιθέντες
G.	τιθέντος (< τιθε-ντ-ος)	G.	τιθέντων
D.	τιθέντι etc.	D.	τιθεῖσι(ν) (< τιθε-ντ-σι[ν])
A.	τιθέντα	A.	τιθέντας

FEMININE

SG.N.	τιθεῖσα (< τιθε-εσ-α)		PL.N.	τιθεῖσαι (< τιθε-εσ-αι)
G.	τιθείσης (< τιθε-εσ-ης)		G.	τιθεισῶν (< τιθε-εσ-ων)
D.	τιθείσῃ etc.		D.	τιθείσαις etc.
A.	τιθεῖσαν		A.	τιθείσας

NEUTER

SG.N.	τιθέν (< τιθε-ντ-#)		PL.N.	τιθέντα
G.	τιθέντος etc.		G.	τιθέντων
D.	τιθέντι		D.	τιθεῖσι(ν)
A.	τιθέν		A.	τιθέντα

(2)

MASCULINE

SG.N.	ἱστάς (< ἱστα-ντ-ς)		PL.N.	ἱστάντες
G.	ἱστάντος (< ἱστα-ντ-ος)		G.	ἱστάντων
D.	ἱστάντι etc.		D.	ἱστᾶσι(ν) (< ἱστα-ντ-σι[ν])
A.	ἱστάντα		A.	ἱστάντας

FEMININE

SG.N.	ἱστᾶσα (< ἱστα-εσ-α)		PL.N.	ἱστᾶσαι (< ἱστα-εσ-αι)
G.	ἱστάσης etc.		G.	ἱστασῶν etc.
D.	ἱστάσῃ		D.	ἱστάσαις
A.	ἱστᾶσαν		A.	ἱστάσας

NEUTER

SG.N.	ἱστάν (< ἱστα-ντ-#)		PL.N.	ἱστάντα
G.	ἱστάντος etc.		G.	ἱστάντων
D.	ἱστάντι		D.	ἱστᾶσι(ν)
A.	ἱστάν		A.	ἱστάντα

216. The present middle and passive participles of these μι-verbs do not require special comment; they are **διδόμενος, η, ον** (< διδο-μενος, η, ον), **τιθέμενος, η, ον** (< τιθε-μενος, η, ον), and **ἱστάμενος, η, ον** (< ἱστα-μενος, η, ον). Note that none of them are formed with a vocalic stem formative.

217. The present participle of the irregular verb **εἰμί**, *I am*, is **ὤν, οὖσα, ὄν**, *being*. Its paradigm is as follows:

	MASCULINE	FEMININE	NEUTER
SG.N.	ὤν	οὖσα	ὄν
G.	ὄντος	οὔσης	ὄντος
D.	ὄντι	οὔσῃ	ὄντι
A.	ὄντα	οὖσαν	ὄν
PL.N.	ὄντες	οὖσαι	ὄντα
G.	ὄντων	οὐσῶν	ὄντων
D.	οὖσι(ν)	οὔσαις	οὖσι(ν)
A.	ὄντας	οὔσας	ὄντα

218. Verbs which are deponent in the present tense lack the active forms of the present participle; thus ἔρχομαι, *I come*, has the present participle ἐρχόμενος, η, ον, *coming*.

219. The Uses of the Present Participle. The syntactic functions of present participles in Greek are similar in many ways to those of present participles in English. In both Greek and English, for example, present participles may be used as adjectives:

(1) With anarthrous nouns:

Heb 7:8 ἀποθνήσκοντες ἄνθρωποι   **dying** men (=**mortal** men)

1 Cor 13:1 χαλκὸς ἠχῶν . . .   a **sounding** gong . . . a **clanging**
κύμβαλον ἀλαλάζον   cymbal

(2) With articular nouns:

(a) In first attributive position:

Eph 1:19 τὸ **ὑπερβάλλον** μέγεθος   the **surpassing** greatness

(b) In second attributive position:

Tit 1:9 ἐν τῇ διδασκαλίᾳ τῇ   by the **sound** teaching
ὑγιαινούσῃ   (ὑγιαίνω = **be sound, be
                                    healthy**)

1 Th 1:10 ἐκ τῆς ὀργῆς τῆς   from the **coming** wrath
ἐρχομένης

220. Present participles may also, like adjectives, be used predicatively; when they are so used, however, some form of the verb εἰμί or of some other equative verb is always expressed. The resulting periphrastic construction is exactly parallel to the English "present progressive," "past progressive," and "future progressive" tenses:

2 Cor 9:12 ἡ διακονία . . . ἐστὶν περισσεύουσα . . .	The ministry . . . **is** . . . **abounding.**
Mk 2:18 ἦσαν οἱ μαθηταὶ 'Ιωάννου καὶ οἱ Φαρισαῖοι **νηστεύοντες.**	John's disciples and the Pharisees **were fasting.**
Mt 10:22 **ἔσεσθε μισούμενοι.**	**You will be hated** (*literally,* **You will be being hated**).

This use of the present participle is much rarer in Greek than it is in English. The periphrastic construction usually emphasizes the *duration* of the action, although frequently it does not seem to differ significantly from the simple verb:

Jn 3:22f ὁ 'Ιησοῦς . . . ἐκεῖ . . . ἐβάπτιζεν, ἦν δὲ καὶ 'Ιωάννης βαπτίζων.	Jesus **was baptizing** (=**baptized**) there, and John **was** also **baptizing.**

221. Like adjectives, again, present participles may be used substantively.[1] When a participle is used substantively, it usually has the article, as in

Rom 12:7 ὁ **διδάσκων**	the **teaching one** (=the **one teaching,** the **one who is teaching,** the **one who teaches**)
2 Cor 10:17 ὁ **καυχώμενος**	the **boasting one** (=**he who boasts**)
1 Cor 14:9 τὸ **λαλούμενον**	the **thing being spoken** (=**that which is being spoken**)

In the translation of such constructions into English one must usually resort to paraphrases of the types illustrated above.

REMARK: Occasionally an anarthrous participle may be used substantively:

Rom 8:38 **μέλλοντα**	**things to come** (=**coming things**; $<$ μέλλω, **be about to, be on the point of**)
Rom 10:14 χωρὶς **κηρύσσοντος**	without **a preacher** (*literally,* without **a preaching one,** without **one who preaches**)

---

[1] Cf. §71.

222. As we noted in passing at the beginning of this lesson, participles are *verbal* adjectives; i.e., in addition to the characteristics which they share with adjectives, they also have characteristics in common with verbs. In particular, they may govern objects and have other adjuncts proper to verbs.[1]

Rom 7:20 ἡ **οἰκοῦσα** ἐν ἐμοὶ ἁμαρτία	the sin **dwelling** in me (=the sin **which dwells** in me; *literally,* the **dwelling** in me sin)
1 Cor 9:24 οἱ ἐν σταδίῳ **τρέχοντες**	the **ones running** in the stadium (=**those who run** in the stadium)
2 Cor 13:3 δοκιμὴν ζητεῖτε τοῦ ἐν ἐμοὶ **λαλοῦντος** Χριστοῦ.	You seek a proof of the Christ **who speaks** in me.
1 Cor 15:57 τῷ θεῷ χάρις **τῷ διδόντι** ἡμῖν τὸ νίκος διὰ τοῦ κυρίου ἡμῶν Ἰησοῦ Χριστοῦ.	Thanks [be] to God **who gives** us the victory through our Lord Jesus Christ.

[1] I.e., predicate nominatives, predicate adjectives, prepositional phrases, etc. Participles do not, however, have *subjects* in the usual sense.

29 | PRESENT PARTICIPLES, II

223. In addition to the adjectival and verbal functions described in the previous lesson, participles have other uses which we shall for convenience call *circumstantial*. These circumstantial uses may most readily be understood by comparing them with somewhat similar uses of English participles. Let us consider two illustrative sentences:

(a)   The apostle **baptizing the disciples** glorifies God.
(b)   The apostle, **baptizing the disciples**, glorifies God.

In the first of these sentences the construction *baptizing the disciples* is attributive, modifying *apostle*; in sentence (b), however, the participial construction modifies the *action* and describes the circumstances under which the action ("glorifying") takes place. In sentence (a) the phrase *baptizing the disciples* is semantically equivalent to a relative clause, i.e., *who is baptizing the disciples*, but in sentence (b) it is semantically equivalent to a clause such as *as he was baptizing the disciples, while he was baptizing the disciples, when he was baptizing the disciples, because he was baptizing the disciples*, or something of the sort. (The exact force of such a participial construction, in English or Greek, can only be inferred from the context.)

224. It will be observed that the difference in meaning between the English sentences (a) and (b) is indicated by the fact that the phrase *baptizing the disciples* is set off by commas in (b) but not in (a); i.e., the difference is indicated, in speech, by intonational features. The same meanings as are expressed by English present participles in these two sentences may be expressed by Greek present participles; however, the distinction between the "attributive" and "circumstantial" meanings is indicated differently in Greek. Thus

(a)   The apostle **baptizing the disciples** glorifies God.

would be rendered in Greek by

    (α) ὁ ἀπόστολος **ὁ βαπτίζων** τοὺς μαθητὰς δοξάζει τὸν θεόν.

but

    (b)   The apostle, **baptizing the disciples,** glorifies God.

would be rendered by

    (β) ὁ ἀπόστολος **βαπτίζων** τοὺς μαθητὰς δοξάζει τὸν θεόν.

The difference in meaning between (α) and (β) is not indicated by commas (in writing) or by intonational features (in speaking), but by the presence of the **article** in (α) and the absence of it in (β).

It may be laid down in general that an **articular** participle is **attributive** and that an **anarthrous** participle is **circumstantial**. Some anarthrous participles may, however, be understood as attributive; it is usually clear from the context when this is so, and such participles usually occur with anarthrous nouns. Thus, for example, 1 Corinthians 13:1 **χαλκὸς ἠχῶν** might mean *a gong as it is sounding*, but in the context it can only mean *a sounding gong*.

225. Notice that in both of the model sentences (α) and (β) in §224 the participle agrees with the subject **ἀπόστολος** in gender, case, and number. Neither attributive nor circumstantial participles are always associated with the subject, however, and when they are associated with other nouns (or pronouns), they agree with them. The following model sentences should be studied carefully:

(1) **Attributive** participial constructions occur in the following:

    (a)   **ὁ βαπτίζων** τοὺς μαθητὰς δοξάζει τὸν θεόν.
           (Same as (α), with subject unexpressed; note the translation:) **He who is baptizing** the disciples glorifies God.

    (b)   ἡ ἀδελφὴ **ἡ βαπτίζουσα** τοὺς μαθητὰς δοξάζει τὸν θεόν.
           The sister **who is baptizing** the disciples glorifies God. (Feminine subject)

    (c)   ἡ βαπτίζουσα τοὺς μαθητὰς δοξάζει τὸν θεόν.
           She who is baptizing the disciples glorifies God. (Feminine subject unexpressed, but indicated by gender of participle)

    (d)   τὸ τέκνον τὸ βαπτίζον τοὺς μαθητὰς δοξάζει τὸν θεόν.
           The child **who is baptizing** the disciples is glorifying God. (Neuter subject)

(e)   οὗτός ἐστιν ὁ οἶκος τοῦ ἀποστόλου **τοῦ βαπτίζοντος** τοὺς μαθητάς.
This is the house of the apostle **who is baptizing** the disciples.
(Masculine, genitive singular)

(f)   τὸν ἄρτον δίδωσιν τῷ ἀποστόλῳ **τῷ βαπτίζοντι** τοὺς μαθητάς.
He is giving bread to the apostle **who is baptizing** the disciples.
(Masculine, dative singular)

(g)   βλέπομεν τὸν ἀπόστολον **τὸν βαπτίζοντα** τοὺς μαθητάς.
We see the apostle **who is baptizing** the disciples. (Masculine, accusative singular)

Similar models could be constructed for plural nouns and for all genders. Note that in the above examples the words "who is" could be omitted from the translations without changing the sense; this may not always be the case.

(2) **Circumstantial** participial constructions occur in the sentences below. For the purposes of illustration, these sentences are identical to those in the preceding group except for the article. Only one of the many possible translations is given for each example, but alternative possibilities may be constructed on the analogy of others in the group:

(a)   **βαπτίζων** τοὺς μαθητὰς δοξάζει τὸν θεόν.
(Same as (β), with subject unexpressed)
While baptizing the disciples, he glorifies God.

(b)   ἡ ἀδελφὴ **βαπτίζουσα** τοὺς μαθητὰς δοξάζει τὸν θεόν.
The sister glorifies God **as she baptizes** the disciples. (Feminine subject)

(c)   **βαπτίζουσα** τοὺς μαθητὰς δοξάζει τὸν θεόν.
When she is baptizing the disciples, she glorifies God. (Feminine subject unexpressed, indicated by gender of participle)

(d)   τὸ τέκνον **βαπτίζον** τοὺς μαθητὰς δοξάζει τὸν θεόν.
The child, **baptizing** the disciples, glorifies God. (Neuter subject. Note the commas!)

(e)   οὗτός ἐστιν ὁ οἶκος τοῦ ἀποστόλου **βαπτίζοντος** τοὺς μαθητάς.
This is the house of the apostle **while he is baptizing** the disciples. (Masculine, genitive singular)

(f)   τὸν ἄρτον δίδωσιν τῷ ἀποστόλῳ **βαπτίζοντι** τοὺς μαθητάς.
He is giving the bread to the apostle **because he** [=the apostle] **is baptizing** the disciples. (Masculine, dative singular)

[177]

(g)   βλέπομεν τὸν ἀπόστολον **βαπτίζοντα** τοὺς μαθητάς.
We see the apostle **as he baptizes** the disciples.
OR: We see the apostle **baptizing** the disciples (see §226) (Masculine, accustive singular)

Again, similar models could be constructed with plural nouns and with nouns in the other genders; moreover, models could be constructed with passive (or middle) participles.

226. It should be noted that an attributive participial expression is usually best rendered in English by a *relative* clause (i.e., a clause introduced by *who, which, that*) and that a circumstantial participial expression is usually best translated by a clause introduced by *as, while, when, because*, etc., depending on the context. With certain verbs, however, it is possible to render the Greek participle directly by an English participle and to understand it as "supplementing" the main verb. In the latter case the participle agrees with the subject or the object, depending on which it has reference to:

Lk 5:4 ἐπαύσατο **λαλῶν**.   He stopped **speaking**.
Mt 24:30 ὄψονται τὸν υἱὸν . . .   They will see the Son . . .
    ἐρχόμενον.   **coming**.

This last usage is not unusual, but it is not met with very frequently in the New Testament. The verbs with which it occurs are those in the examples cited and a few others, principally **ὑπάρχω, τελέω, διαλείπω, καλῶς ποιέω, ἀκούω, βλέπω, γινώσκω, θεωρέω, εὑρίσκω.**

227. It is very important to understand that the **present participle** does not necessarily refer to **present time**. Indeed, it has no "tense" of its own at all, properly speaking, but only **aspect**: it usually refers to action *in progress* at the *same time* as the action of the main verb. A few illustrative examples will help to make this clear.

(1) **Attributive participles** (used substantively in the first two examples cited):
(a) Associated with a main verb in the *present* tense:

Rom 14:2 **ὁ ἀσθενῶν** λάχανα ἐσθίει.   **He who is weak eats** vegetables.

(b) Associated with a main verb in a *past* tense:

Jn 2:14 εὗρεν ἐν τῷ ἱερῷ τοὺς πωλοῦντας βόας.	He **found** in the temple **those who were selling** oxen.

(c) Associated with a main verb in the *future* tense:

1 Th 4:17 ἡμεῖς οἱ **ζῶντες** . . . **ἁρπαγησόμεθα** ἐν νεφέλαις.	We **who are alive** (*i.e.*, **who shall be living** [at the time]) **shall be snatched up** in the clouds.

(2) **Circumstantial participles:**

(a) Associated with a main verb in the *present* tense:

2 Cor 3:18 ἡμεῖς . . . τὴν δόξαν κυρίου **κατοπτριζόμενοι** τὴν αὐτὴν εἰκόνα **μεταμορφούμεθα**.	We, **as we reflect** the glory of the Lord, **are being transformed into** his image.

(b) Associated with a main verb in a *past* tense:

Mt 4:18 **περιπατῶν** παρὰ τὴν θάλασσαν . . . **εἶδε** δύο ἀδελφούς.	**While he was walking** by the sea, **he saw** two brothers.

(c) Associated with a main verb in the *future* tense:

Rom 12:20 **τοῦτο ποιῶν** ἄνθρακας πυρὸς **σωρεύσεις** ἐπὶ τὴν κεφαλὴν αὐτοῦ.	**By doing this you will** (*i.e.*, at a future time) **heap** coals of fire on his head.

228. The Genitive Absolute. A circumstantial participle and a noun or pronoun in the genitive case (with which the participle agrees) form the construction called the **genitive absolute**, provided that the noun or pronoun in the construction does *not* refer to a person or thing mentioned elsewhere in the sentence. The participle may have its object (in its usual case) and other adjuncts. The construction may sometimes be rendered by an English participial expression, but more frequently it is best translated by a clause introduced by *while, when, because, since*, etc., as the context indicates. The noun or pronoun in the genitive functions as the "subject" of the participle.

Rom 7:3 **ζῶντος τοῦ ἀνδρὸς** μοιχαλὶς χρηματίσει.	**While (since, because) the husband is living**, she will be called an adulteress (*literally*, **The husband being alive**, she will be called an adulteress).

Rom 5:6 Χριστὸς **ὄντων ἡμῶν**
ἀσθενῶν . . . ὑπὲρ ἀσεβῶν
ἀπέθανεν.

While we were weak (=**We being weak**), Christ died on behalf of the ungodly.

Acts 10:44 **λαλοῦντος τοῦ Πέτρου**
τὰ ῥήματα ταῦτα ἐπέπεσε τὸ
πνεῦμα τὸ ἅγιον ἐπὶ . . . τοὺς
ἀκούοντας τὸν λόγον.

While Peter was speaking these words, the Holy Spirit fell upon those who were hearing the word.

REMARK: The proviso that the noun or pronoun in the genitive not refer to a person or thing mentioned elsewhere in the sentence is sometimes ignored:

Jn 8:30 ταῦτα **αὐτοῦ λαλοῦντος**
πολλοὶ ἐπίστευσαν εἰς **αὐτόν**

While he was speaking these things, many believed in **him**.

30 | FUTURE PARTICIPLES

229. The future participles of a Greek verb are formed from its future stems in the same way as the present participles are formed from its present stem. Thus the forms of the future active participle may be analyzed into:

(1) The base (e.g., **λυ-, ἀγαπη-,**[1] **ποιη-,**[2] **πληρω-,**[3] **δω-, θη-, στη-**).

(2) The future tense formant **-σ-**.

(3) The stem formative **-ο-**.

(4) The morpheme **-ντ-** (in the masculine and neuter) or **-εσ-** (in the feminine).

(5) The case-number suffixes of the third declension (in the masculine and neuter) or of the first declension (of the type found in the paradigm of **δόξα**, in the feminine).

Thus we have:

$$\text{SG.N.} \quad \textbf{λύσων} < λυ + σ + ο + ντ + ς \ (\text{see } §207)$$
$$\text{G.} \quad \textbf{λύσοντος} < λυ + σ + ο + ντ + ος$$
$$\text{etc.}$$
$$\text{SG.N.} \quad \textbf{λύσουσα} < λυ + σ + ο + εσ + α \ (\text{see } §208)$$
$$\text{G.} \quad \textbf{λυσούσης} < λυ + σ + ο + εσ + ης$$
$$\text{etc.}$$
$$\text{SG.N.} \quad \textbf{λῦσον} < λυ + σ + ο + ντ + \#$$
$$\text{G.} \quad \textbf{λύσοντος} < λυ + σ + ο + ντ + ος$$
$$\text{etc.}$$

and

$$\textbf{ἀγαπήσων} < ἀγαπη^{1} + σ + ο + ντ + ς$$
$$\textbf{ποιήσων} < ποιη^{2} + σ + ο + ντ + ς$$
$$\textbf{πληρώσων} < πληρω^{3} + σ + ο + ντ + ς$$

---

[1] Cf. §177(1).

[2] Cf. §177(2).

[3] Cf. §177(3).

230. The bases from which the future stems of the μι-verbs are formed are **δω, θη**, and **στη**, so that their future participles in the active voice are:

$$\delta\acute{\omega}\sigma\omega\nu < \delta\omega + \sigma + o + \nu\tau + \varsigma$$
$$\delta\acute{\omega}\sigma o\nu\tau o\varsigma < \delta\omega + \sigma + o + \nu\tau + o\varsigma$$
etc.
$$\theta\acute{\eta}\sigma\omega\nu < \theta\eta + \sigma + o + \nu\tau + \varsigma$$
etc.
$$\sigma\tau\acute{\eta}\sigma\omega\nu < \sigma\tau\eta + \sigma + o + \nu\tau + \varsigma$$
etc.

231. Future middle participles are similarly formed:

$$\lambda\upsilon\sigma\acute{o}\mu\epsilon\nu o\varsigma, \eta, o\nu < \lambda\upsilon + \sigma + o + \mu\epsilon\nu + o\varsigma, \eta, o\nu \text{ (see §209)}$$
etc.
$$\dot{\alpha}\gamma\alpha\pi\eta\sigma\acute{o}\mu\epsilon\nu o\varsigma, \eta, o\nu < \dot{\alpha}\gamma\alpha\pi\eta + \sigma + o + \mu\epsilon\nu + o\varsigma, \eta, o\nu$$
etc.

232. The future participle of the verb **εἰμί** is middle in form: **ἐσόμενος, η, ον.**

233. The future passive participle occurs only once in the New Testament; it is formed on the future passive stem (cf. §§167(3), 169, 170(7)):

$$\lambda\upsilon\theta\eta\sigma\acute{o}\mu\epsilon\nu o\varsigma, \eta, o\nu < \lambda\upsilon + \theta\eta\sigma + o + \mu\epsilon\nu + o\varsigma, \eta, o\nu$$
etc.

234. The Uses of the Future Participle. The future participle occurs rather infrequently in the New Testament. Like the present participle, it may be articular or anarthrous, and it may function adjectivally, substantively, or circumstantially. The future participle represents an action as future from the point of view of the main verb; the future participle may, moreover, if the context permits, express the purpose of the action indicated by the main verb. A few illustrative examples will make these uses clear:

Mt 27:49 ἔρχεται Ἡλίας **σώσων** αὐτόν — Elijah in coming **to save** him (=**in order to save** him)

Lk 22:49 εἶδον οἱ περὶ αὐτὸν τὸ **ἐσόμενον.** — Those around him [saw] **what was going to happen** (= **what was about to be**).

1 Cor 15:37 τὸ σῶμα **τὸ γενησόμενον** the body **that will come into being** (=**that is intended to be**)

Heb 3:5 μαρτύριον **τῶν λαληθησομένων**   a testimony **of those things which are going to be spoken**

31 | AORIST PARTICIPLES

235. Verbs which have first aorists (active and middle) have first aorist active and middle participles, and verbs which have second aorists (active and middle) have second aorist active and middle participles. Similarly, verbs which have first aorists passive have first aorist passive participles, and verbs which have second aorists passive have second aorist passive participles.

236. The first aorist active participle is formed by adding (1) the participial morpheme (**-ντ-** in the masculine and neuter, **-εσ-** in the feminine) and (2) the appropriate case-number suffixes (those of the third declension for the masculine and neuter, and those of the first declension [of the type found in the paradigm of **δόξα**] for the feminine) to the **unaugmented** first aorist stem of the verb. The stem formative in this case is **-α-** rather than **-ο-**, so that the phonological modifications of the nominative singular masculine and of the dative plural masculine and neuter are like those found in the present active participle of **ἵστημι** (see §215(2)). The illustrative paradigms below will make this clear:

MASCULINE

SG.N.	λύσας (< λυ-σ-α-ντ-ς)		PL.N.	λύσαντες
G.	λύσαντος (< λυ-σ-α-ντ-ος)		G.	λυσάντων
D.	λύσαντι	etc.	D.	λύσασι(ν)
				(< λυ-σ-α-ντ-σι[ν])
A.	λύσαντα		A.	λύσαντας

FEMININE

SG.N.	λύσασα (< λυ-σ-α-εσ-α)		PL.N.	λύσασαι (< λυ-σ-α-εσ-αι)
G.	λυσάσης (< λυ-σ-α-εσ-ης)		G.	λυσασῶν (< λυ-σ-α-εσ-ων)
D.	λυσάσῃ		D.	λυσάσαις
A.	λύσασαν		A.	λυσάσας

[184]

NEUTER

SG.N.	λῦσαν (< λυ-σ-α-ντ-#)	PL.N.	λύσαντα
G.	λύσαντος	G.	λυσάντων
D.	λύσαντι	D.	λύσασι(ν)
A.	λῦσαν	A.	λύσαντα

237. The second aorist active participle is formed by adding the participial morphemes and case-number suffixes (as described above) to the **unaugmented** second aorist stem. Since the stem formative in this case is **-o-** rather than **-α-**, the second aorist active participle differs from the present active participle only in its *base*; there is, however, a further difference in the position of the *accent*. The following illustrative paradigm is of the second aorist participle of the verb **λείπω**, second aorist indicative **ἔλιπον**, unaugmented second aorist stem **λιπο-** (= base **λιπ-** + stem vowel **-o-**):

MASCULINE

SG.N.	λιπών (< λιπ-o-ντ-ς)	PL.N.	λιπόντες
G.	λιπόντος (< λιπ-o-ντ-ος)	G.	λιπόντων
D.	λιπόντι etc.	D.	λιποῦσι(ν)
			(< λιπ-o-ντ-σι[ν])
A.	λιπόντα	A.	λιπόντας

FEMININE

SG.N.	λιποῦσα (< λιπ-o-εσ-α)	PL.N.	λιποῦσαι (< λιπ-o-εσ-αι)
G.	λιπούσης	G.	λιπουσῶν
D.	λιπούσῃ	D.	λιπούσαις
A.	λιποῦσαν	A.	λιπούσας

NEUTER

SG.N.	λιπόν (< λιπ-o-ντ-#)	PL.N.	λιπόντα
G.	λιπόντος	G.	λιπόντων
D.	λιπόντι	D.	λιποῦσι(ν)
A.	λιπόν	A.	λιπόντα

238. The aorist active participles of contract verbs are formed perfectly regularly, since they do not involve contraction. Hence we have, for example,

(1) ἀγαπήσας, ἀγαπήσασα, ἀγαπῆσαν from ἀγαπάω (ἀγαπῶ), ἠγάπησα
(2) ποιήσας, ποιήσασα, ποιῆσαν from ποιέω (ποιῶ), ἐποίησα
(3) πληρώσας, πληρώσασα, πληρῶσαν from πληρόω (πληρῶ), ἐπλήρωσα

239. The aorist active participles of the μι-verbs are formed on their aorist stems; they may be obtained quite simply, however, by omitting the first syllable of each form of their present participles. Thus we have:

	PRESENT PARTICIPLE	AORIST PARTICIPLE	(AORIST STEM)
(1)	διδούς, διδοῦσα, διδόν	δούς, δοῦσα, δόν from δίδωμι	(δο-)
(2)	τιθείς, τιθεῖσα, τιθέν	θείς, θεῖσα, θέν from τίθημι	(θε-)
(3)	ἱστάς, ἱστᾶσα, ἱστάν	στάς, στᾶσα, στάν from ἵστημι	(στα-)

NOTE: ἵστημι also has a *first* aorist participle στήσας, στήσασα, στῆσαν. This is regularly formed.

240. The aorist middle participles are formed by adding the participial morpheme -μεν- to the (first or second) aorist stem and appending the case-number suffixes of the first and second declensions. The paradigms of these participles call for no special comment:

λυσάμενος, η, ον from λύω, ἔλυσα (aorist stem λυ-σ-α-)
λιπόμενος, η, ον from λείπω, ἔλιπον (aorist stem λιπ-ο-)
ἀγαπησάμενος, η, ον from ἀγαπάω, ἠγάπησα (aorist stem
  ἀγαπη-σ-α-)
ποιησάμενος, η, ον from ποιέω, ἐποίησα (aorist stem ποιη-σ-α-)
πληρωσάμενος, η, ον from πληρόω, ἐπλήρωσα (aorist stem
  πληρω-σ-α-)
δόμενος, η, ον from δίδωμι, ἔδωκα (middle ἐδόμην) (aorist
  stem δο-)
θέμενος, η, ον from τίθημι, ἔθηκα (middle ἐθέμην) (aorist
  stem θε-)
(ἵστημι has no aorist middle participle.)

241. The aorist passive participle is formed on the **unaugmented** aorist passive base (which is obtained by dropping the augment and the final -ην of the sixth principal part). To this base are added (1) the stem vowel -ε-, (2) the participial morpheme (-ντ- for the masculine and neuter, -εσ- for the feminine), and (3) the case-number suffixes (those of the third declension for the masculine and neuter, and those of the first declension [such as occur in the paradigm of δόξα] for the feminine). The phonological modifications which occur result in a paradigm quite similar to that of the present active participle of τίθημι (see §215(1)). An illustrative paradigm follows:

MASCULINE

SG.N.	λυθείς (<λυ-θ-ε-ντ-ς)	PL.N.	λυθέντες
G.	λυθέντος (<λυ-θ-ε-ντ-ος)	G.	λυθέντων
D.	λυθέντι etc.	D.	λυθεῖσι (ν)
			(<λυ-θ-ε-ντ-σι[ν])
A.	λυθέντα	A.	λυθέντας

FEMININE

SG.N.	λυθεῖσα (<λυ-θ-ε-εσ-α)	PL.N.	λυθεῖσαι (<λυ-θ-ε-εσ-αι)
G.	λυθείσης (<λυ-θ-ε-εσ-ης)	G.	λυθεισῶν
D.	λυθείσῃ etc.	D.	λυθείσαις
A.	λυθεῖσαν	A.	λυθείσας

NEUTER

SG.N.	λυθέν (<λυ-θ-ε-ντ-#)	PL.N.	λυθέντα
G.	λυθέντος	G.	λυθέντων
D.	λυθέντι	D.	λυθεῖσι(ν)
A.	λυθέν	A.	λυθέντα

REMARK: The aorist passive participles of all verbs are formed according to this rule, including those of verbs with second aorists passive (since the θ is not involved in the rule). Thus we have:

AORIST PASSIVE PARTICIPLE	VERB	SIXTH PR. PT.	AOR. PASS. STEM
γραφείς, γραφεῖσα, γραφέν	γράφω	ἐγράφην	γραφ-
ἀγαπηθείς, -θεῖσα, -θέν	ἀγαπάω	ἠγαπήθην	ἀγαπηθ-
ποιηθείς, -θεῖσα, -θέν	ποιέω	ἐποιήθην	ποιηθ-
πληρωθείς, -θεῖσα, -θέν	πληρόω	ἐπληρώθην	πληρωθ-
δοθείς, δοθεῖσα, δοθέν	δίδωμι	ἐδόθην	δοθ-
τεθείς, τεθεῖσα, τεθέν	τίθημι	ἐτέθην	τεθ-
σταθείς, σταθεῖσα, σταθέν	ἵστημι	ἐστάθην	σταθ-

242. If a verb is deponent in the future or aorist, its future and aorist participles will be middle or passive in form (sometimes both middle and passive forms are found).

Γίνομαι has aorist participles **γενόμενος** and **γενηθείς**; however, **δέχομαι** has only **δεξάμενος**; **πορεύομαι** has only **πορευθείς**. Some verbs are deponent in the present (and other paradigms) but not in the aorist; such verbs will have aorist participles with active forms; e.g. **ἔρχομαι**, with second aorist **ἦλθον**, has the second aorist participle **ἐλθών**.

243. The verb **εἰμί** has no aorist participle.

244. Since it is not always clear what the unaugmented form of certain aorist stems may be, the forms of the aorist participles of some important irregular verbs are given in full in the list below:

VERB	AORIST ACTIVE	AORIST PASSIVE	AORIST ACTIVE PARTICIPLE	AORIST PASSIVE PARTICIPLE
ἄγω, lead	ἤγαγον	ἤχθην	ἀγαγών	ἀχθείς
αἴρω, take up	ἦρα	ἤρθην	ἄρας	ἀρθείς
λέγω, say	εἶπον	ἐρρήθην	εἰπών	ῥηθείς
ἔρχομαι, come	ἦλθον	—	ἐλθών	—
ὁράω, see	εἶδον	ὤφθην	ἰδών	ὀφθείς

245. The Uses of the Aorist Participle. Aorist participles are syntactically very similar to (Greek) present participles; they may be used adjectivally, substantively, predicatively (somewhat rarely), and circumstantially. Before we consider these various functions in detail, however, something must be said about the *meaning* of the aorist participle, which does not correspond to the meaning of any simple English verb form.

246. Like the present participle, the aorist participle does not, properly speaking, have "tense"; i.e., it does not necessarily refer to past time or to any other sort of time. Like the present participle, the aorist participle indicates an *aspect* of action; more precisely, it indicates an action conceived as *indefinite*, or as a *simple event* (without reference to its being in progress, or being completed). The aorist participle may, therefore, refer to any action, whether it be past, present, or future with respect to the action of the main verb. This point may be illustrated by three passages from the New Testament (in all these the participles are "circumstantial"):

(1) Aorist participle referring to an action antecedent to that of the main verb:

Rom 5:1 **δικαιωθέντες** ἐκ πίστεως εἰρήνην ἔχομεν πρὸς τὸν θεόν. **Having been justified** by faith, we have peace with God.

(2) Aorist participle referring to an action simultaneous with that of the main verb:

Mt 19:27 **ἀποκριθεὶς** ὁ Πέτρος εἶπεν αὐτῷ . . . Peter said **in answer** to him . . .

(3) Aorist participle referring to an action subsequent to that of the main verb:

Acts 25:13 κατήντησαν εἰς Καισαρίαν ἀσπασάμενοι τὸν Φῆστον. They arrived in Caesarea [and] **greeted** Festus.

The last usage mentioned above is quite rare, and the second is found most frequently in occurrences of the phrase quoted (ἀποκριθείς . . . εἶπεν). It turns out, therefore, that *in most instances* the aorist active participle may be rendered in English—at least in a rough-and-ready way—by a phrase consisting of *having* plus an English past participle; an aorist passive participle may, *in most instances*, be rendered by a phrase consisting of *having been* plus a past participle, and an aorist middle participle, when one occurs, may be rendered similarly; for example,

λύσας = *having loosed*
λυσάμενος = *having loosed for oneself, having had* (something) *loosed*
λυθείς = *having been loosed*

In practice, of course, such rough equivalents should be paraphrased appropriately, in the light of the context; the examples given below will make this clear.

247. The various uses of aorist participles may now be illustrated:
(1) Adjectival functions:
(a) With anarthrous nouns:

Mt 12:25 βασιλεία **μερισθεῖσα**   a kingdom **divided**

(b) With articular nouns:
(i) In first attributive position:

Rom 10:5 τὴν δικαιοσύνην ἐκ νόμου **ὁ ποιήσας ἄνθρωπος** ζήσεται ἐν αὐτῇ.   **The man who has done** the righteousness which is of the law shall live by it.

(ii) In second attributive position:

Rom 16:22 ἀσπάζομαι ὑμᾶς ἐγὼ Τέρτιος **ὁ γράψας** τὴν ἐπιστολὴν ἐν κυρίῳ.   I, Tertius, **who have written** the letter in the Lord, greet you.

(c) In predicate position (this usage is rare [cf. §220]):

Lk 23:19 ἦν . . . **βληθεὶς** ἐν φυλακῇ.   He was **cast** into prison.

(2) Substantival functions:

1 Cor 7:33f **ὁ γαμήσας** μεριμνᾷ τὰ τοῦ κόσμου . . . **ἡ γαμήσασα** μεριμνᾷ τὰ τοῦ κόσμου.	**He who is married** cares for the things of the world . . . **she who is married** cares for the things of the world (*or* **the married man . . . the married woman . . .**).
2 Cor 7:12 ἕνεκεν **τοῦ ἀδικήσαντος** . . . ἕνεκεν **τοῦ ἀδικηθέντος**	for the sake of **him who did the wrong** . . . for the sake of **him who was wronged**
Rom 8:37 διὰ **τοῦ ἀγαπήσαντος** ἡμᾶς	through **him who loved** us

(3) Circumstantial functions. Like the present participle, the aorist participle may be used to express time (usually prior to that of the main verb), cause, condition, concession, etc., depending on the context:

Jn 16:8 **ἐλθὼν** ἐκεῖνος ἐλέγξει τὸν κόσμον.	**Having come**, he will convict the world (=**When he has come**, . . .).
Col. 1:3f εὐχαριστοῦμεν τῷ θεῷ . . . **ἀκούσαντες** τὴν πίστιν ὑμῶν.	We give thanks to God . . . **having heard of** your faith (=**since we have heard of** your faith).
Rom 5:9 **δικαιωθέντες** . . . ἐν τῷ αἵματι αὐτοῦ σωθησόμεθα δι' αὐτοῦ ἀπὸ τῆς ὀργῆς.	**Having been justified** by his blood, we shall be saved by him from the wrath (=**Because we have been justified**, . . .).

(4) Genitive absolute:

Mt 2:1 **τοῦ Ἰησοῦ γεννηθέντος** ἐν Βηθλεέμ . . . μάγοι ἀπὸ ἀνατολῶν παρεγένοντο . . .	**Jesus having been born** in Bethlehem . . . astrologers from the east came . . . (=**When Jesus had been born**, . . ., **After Jesus had been born**, . . .).
Rom 7:9 **ἐλθούσης τῆς ἐντολῆς** ἡ ἁμαρτία ἀνέζησεν.	**The commandment having come**, sin revived (=**When the commandment came**, . . .).

INFINITIVES, I
SOME USES OF
ANARTHROUS INFINITIVES

248. Infinitives are sometimes called **verbal nouns**; their syntactic functions are in some ways like those of verbs and in other ways like those of nouns. The infinitive of an English verb is identical to the form of the verb used in the first person singular, present tense; the infinitive *be* (first person singular, present tense, *I am*) is the only exception to this rule. The word *to*, which precedes the English infinitive in many of its uses, is sometimes called the "sign of the infinitive," but it is not properly speaking a part of it; this *to* should not be regarded as a preposition. An English verb has, as a rule, only *one* infinitive, though some so-called auxiliary verbs (*can, may, shall*) have none; it is, however, sometimes convenient to refer to the simple English infinitive (e.g., *(to) see, (to) come, (to) be*) as a "present active infinitive"; to describe various periphrastic constructions as "present passive infinitives" (e.g., *(to) be seen, (to) be called*), "perfect active infinitives" (e.g., *(to) have seen, (to) have come, (to) have been*), etc.; and to say that other such constructions "serve as infinitives" for the auxiliary verbs (e.g., *(to) be able* for *can*, *(to) be allowed to* for *may*, *(to) have to* for *must*, etc.).

249. Greek verbs, as we might expect, are more plentifully supplied with infinitives. Those of the model verb λύω, in the aspects and voices considered so far, are as follows:

	ACTIVE	MIDDLE OR PASSIVE	
PRESENT	λύειν	λύεσθαι	
		MIDDLE	PASSIVE
FUTURE	λύσειν	λύσεσθαι	λυθήσεσθαι[1]
(FIRST) AORIST	λῦσαι	λύσασθαι	λυθῆναι

[1] No future passive infinitive form occurs in the New Testament.

250. These forms may be analyzed into constituents as follows:[1]

(1) The **base** λυ-.

(2) The **tense formants**:

   (a) -σ- (in the future and first aorist, active and middle).

   (b) -θ- (in the first aorist passive).

   (c) -θησ- (in the [first] future passive).

(3) The **stem formatives**:

   (a) -#- (i.e., *zero*, in the active voice).

   (b) -ε- (in the present and future, middle and passive).

   (c) -α- (in the aorist middle).

   (d) -η- (in the aorist passive).

(4) The **infinitive suffixes**:

   (a) -ειν (in the present and future active).

   (b) -αι (in the aorist active).

   (c) -ναι (in the aorist passive).

   (d) -σθαι (elsewhere).

Note that the aorist infinitives, like the aorist participles, have **no augment**.

251. This analysis is applicable to the infinitives of contract verbs *except* in the present active infinitive, where the suffix is -εν rather than -ειν (see §250(4a)). When this allomorph -εν is added to the bases of the contract verbs, the usual rules of contraction apply (see §172). Thus, for the model verbs ἀγαπάω (ἀγαπῶ), ποιέω (ποιῶ), and πληρόω (πληρῶ), the infinitives are as follows:

	ACTIVE	MIDDLE OR PASSIVE	
PRESENT	ἀγαπᾶν (< ἀγαπα + εν)	ἀγαπᾶσθαι (< ἀγαπα + ε + σθαι)	
	ποιεῖν (< ποιε + εν)	ποιεῖσθαι (< ποιε + ε + σθσι)	
	πληροῦν (< πληρο + εν)	πληροῦσθαι (< πληρο + ε + σθαι)	

		MIDDLE	PASSIVE
FUTURE	ἀγαπήσειν	ἀγαπήσεσθαι	ἀγαπηθήσεσθαι
(Regular)	(< ἀγαπη + σ + ειν)	(< ἀγαπη + σ + ε + σθαι)	(< ἀγαπη + θησ + ε + σθαι)
	ποιήσειν	ποιήσεσθαι	ποιηθήσεσθαι
	πληρώσειν	πληρώσεσθαι	πληρωθήσεσθαι

---

[1] This analysis should be compared with those of §§165–169, 207–209, 229, 236f, and 240f.

	ACTIVE	MIDDLE	PASSIVE
(FIRST)	ἀγαπῆσαι	ἀγαπήσασθαι	ἀγαπηθῆναι
AORIST	(< ἀγαπη + σ +	(< ἀγαπη + σ +	(< ἀγαπη + θ +
(Regu-	αι)	α + σθαι)	η + ναι)
lar)	ποιῆσαι	ποιήσασθαι	ποιηθῆναι
	πληρῶσαι	πληρώσασθαι	πληρωθῆναι

252. Verbs which have second aorists have second aorist infinitives. The second aorist active infinitive is formed by adding the suffix **-ειν** to the **unaugmented** second aorist base (the position of the accent should be noted):

VERB	SECOND AORIST	SECOND AORIST BASE	SECOND AORIST ACTIVE INFINITIVE
λέγω, *say*	εἶπον	εἰπ-	εἰπεῖν
ὁράω (ὁρῶ), *see*	εἶδον	ἰδ-	ἰδεῖν
ἔρχομαι, *come*	ἦλθον	ἐλθ-	ἐλθεῖν
ἐσθίω, *eat*	ἔφαγον	φαγ-	φαγεῖν

253. The second aorist middle infinitive is formed by adding (1) the stem formative **-ε-** and (2) the suffix **-σθαι** to the *unaugmented* second aorist base (the position of the accent should be noted):

VERB	SECOND AORIST	SECOND AORIST BASE	SECOND AORIST ACTIVE INFINITIVE	SECOND AORIST MIDDLE INFINITIVE
βάλλω, *cast*	ἔβαλον	βαλ-	βαλεῖν	βαλέσθαι
λαμβάνω, *take*	ἔλαβον	λαβ-	λαβεῖν	λαβέσθαι

The second aorist passive infinitive is formed by adding (1) the stem formative **-η-** and (2) the suffix **-ναι** to the **unaugmented** second aorist passive base:

VERB	SECOND AORIST PASSIVE	SECOND AORIST PASSIVE BASE	SECOND AORIST PASSIVE INFINITIVE
γράφω, *write*	ἐγράφην	γραφ-	γραφῆναι
στρέφω, *turn*	ἐστράφην	στραφ-	στραφῆναι

254. Verbs which are deponent in the aorist have aorist infinitives which are either middle or passive in form; some verbs have both middle and passive forms:

VERB	AORIST (MIDDLE)	AORIST (PASSIVE)	AORIST INFINITIVE (MIDDLE FORM)	AORIST INFINITIVE (PASSIVE FORM)
γίνομαι, *becomes*	ἐγενόμην	ἐγενήθην	γενέσθαι	γενηθῆναι
ἀρνέομαι (ἀρνοῦμαι), *deny*	ἠρνησάμην	—	ἀρνήσασθαι	—
πορεύομαι, *go*	—	ἐπορεύθην	—	πορευθῆναι

255. The μι-verbs δίδωμι, τίθημι, and ἵστημι have irregularly formed infinitives in the present active (they have the suffix -ναι rather than -ειν), present middle or passive (they attach the suffix -σθαι directly to the base, without the stem formative -ε-), the aorist active (they have the suffix -ναι and an irregularly formed base), and the aorist middle (they attach the suffix -σθαι directly, without a stem formative). For convenience all the forms, regular and irregular, are given below:

	ACTIVE	MIDDLE OR PASSIVE	
PRESENT	διδόναι	δίδοσθαι	
	τιθέναι	τίθεσθαι	
	ἱστάναι	ἵστασθαι	
		MIDDLE	PASSIVE
FUTURE	δώσειν	δώσεσθαι	δοθήσεσθαι
	θήσειν	θήσεσθαι	τεθήσεσθαι
	στήσειν	στήσεσθαι	σταθήσεσθαι
AORIST	δοῦναι	δόσθαι	δοθῆναι
	θεῖναι	θέσθαι	τεθῆναι
	στῆναι	[none]	σταθῆναι

NOTE: ἵστημι also has the (transitive) first aorist active infinitive στῆσαι.

256. The verb εἰμί has only two infinitives, the present εἶναι and the future ἔσεσθαι.

257. The Tenses of the Infinitive. Properly speaking, only the future infinitive has tense (in that it always refers to future **time** relative to the time of the principal verb); the present and aorist infinitives express different **aspects**, rather than different tenses. The present infinitive represents an action as continuing, as repeated, or as customary; if a time is involved at all, it must be inferred from the context. The aorist infinitive represents an action as **indefinite**, i.e., as a simple event, without reference to its duration or to the existence of any result. Again, the time of the action must be inferred from the context. The future infinitive, on the other hand, does refer to time, as we have already said. Future infinitive forms occur only rarely in the New Testament.

258. The Uses of the Infinitive. Greek infinitives have many syntactic functions which are similar to those of English infinitives, so that it quite frequently turns out that a Greek infinitive can be translated by an English one;[1] it should be borne in mind, however, that there is in Greek no "sign of the infinitive" corresponding to the English *to* (in *to see, to be*, etc.) and, further, that the Greek infinitive, unlike the English infinitive, may be preceded by the article.[2] The uses of the **anarthrous** infinitive will be considered first.

259. Uses of the Anarthrous Infinitive. (1) Like the English infinitive, the Greek anarthrous infinitive may serve to complete the meaning of certain verbs which seldom or never occur without such an infinitive complement; such infinitives are, accordingly, called **complementary** infinitives. The most important verbs which govern complementary infinitives are δύναμαι, *can, be able*; θέλω, *wish, want, be willing*; βούλομαι, *wish, want, be willing* (less common than θέλω); μέλλω, *be about to, be going to*; and ὀφείλω, *ought*.

(a) Infinitive with δύναμαι:[3]

---

[1] Or, at least, by a periphrastic infinitive construction such as those mentioned in §248.
[2] Always the *neuter* article, in the *singular*; this article may be inflected for case, however.
[3] Δύναμαι is a deponent μι-verb. Its paradigm is similar in most respects to the passive of ἵστημι (cf. §200 (4, 5)), but there are a number of irregular forms:

	PRESENT	IMPERFECT		AORIST	
SG.1	δύναμαι	ἠδυνάμην or	ἐδυνάμην	ἠδυνήθην or	ἠδυνάσθην
2	δύνασαι	ἠδύνω	ἐδύνω	ἠδυνήθης	ἠδυνάσθης
3	δύναται	ἠδύνατο	etc.	etc.	etc.
				FUTURE	
PL.1	δυνάμεθα	ἠδυνάμεθα		δυνήσομαι	
2	δύνασθε	ἠδύνασθε		δυνήσῃ	
3	δύνανται	ἠδύναντο		etc.	

INFINITIVE: δύνασθαι   PARTICIPLE: δυνάμενος, η, ον

Mt 9:28 δύναμαι τοῦτο **ποιῆσαι**.

I can do this (*or* **I am able to do** this).

Mk 4:33 ἠδύναντο **ἀκούειν**.

They **could hear** (*or* they **were able to hear**).

Mk 9:39 δυνήσεται . . . κακολογεῖν με.

He **will be able to revile** me.

(b) Infinitive with **θέλω**:[1]

Mt 12:38 **θέλομεν** ἀπὸ σοῦ σημεῖον ἰδεῖν.

We **wish to see** a sign from you.

1 Th 2:18 **ἠθελήσαμεν ἐλθεῖν** πρὸς ὑμᾶς.

We **wanted to come** to you.

(c) Infinitive with **βούλομαι**:[2]

2 Cor 1:15 **ἐβουλόμην** . . . πρὸς ὑμᾶς **ἐλθεῖν**.

I wanted . . . **to come** to you.

(d) Infinitive with **μέλλω**:[3]

Mt 2:13 **μέλλει** Ἡρῴδης **ζητεῖν** τὸ παιδίον.

Herod **is going to seek** the child (*or* **is about to seek** the child).

Rev 10:4 **ἤμελλον γράφειν**.

I was about to write.

Mt 11:14 αὐτός ἐστιν Ἠλίας ὁ **μέλλων ἔρχεσθαι**.

He is Elijah **who is to come.**

(e) Infinitive with **ὀφείλω**:[4]

---

[1] **Θέλω** is regular in the present (**θέλω, θέλεις**, etc.) and future (**θελήσω, θελήσεις**, etc.) but has the augment **ἠ-** instead of **ἐ-** in the imperfect and aorist: **ἤθελον, ἤθελες**, etc. and **ἠθέλησα, ἠθέλησας**, etc. The infinitive **θέλειν** and participle **θέλων** occur.

[2] **Βούλομαι** has imperfect **ἐβουλόμην**, aorist **ἐβουλήθην** (rarely **ἠ-**); the present participle **βουλόμενος, η, ον**, and the aorist participle **βουληθείς, εῖσα, έν**, occur. The second person singular present tense is **βούλει** rather than **βούλῃ**.

[3] **Μέλλω** is regular in the present and future (**μελλήσω**), but has either **ἠ-** or **ἐ-** as augment in the imperfect (no aorist forms occur). The infinitive **μέλλειν** and the participle **μέλλων** are found. The participle **μέλλων**, when used as an adjective, means *future*: Matthew 3:7 ἀπὸ τῆς **μελλούσης** ὀργῆς, *from the future wrath, from the wrath to come.*

[4] **Ὀφείλω** (imperfect **ὤφειλον**) means *owe* (with accusative of the thing owed and dative of the person to whom it is owed) when it does not govern an infinitive.

1 Jn 3:16 ἡμεῖς ὀφείλομεν ὑπὲρ τῶν ἀδελφῶν τὰς ψυχὰς θεῖναι.	We **ought to lay down** our lives for the sake of the brethren.
Heb 2:17 ὤφειλεν . . . τοῖς ἀδελφοῖς ὁμοιωθῆναι.	He **was obliged to be like** his brethren.

REMARK: In the illustrative passages cited above, the subject[1] of the main verb is also the subject of the infinitive; when this is not the case, and whenever the subject of the infinitive is separately expressed, it is placed in the *accusative* case.[2]

Phil 1:12 γινώσκειν ὑμᾶς βούλομαι.	I **want you to know.**
1 Cor 14:5 θέλω . . . ὑμᾶς λαλεῖν γλώσσαις.	I want . . . **you to speak** with tongues.

(2) Anarthrous infinitives also occur as objects of verbs which ordinarily govern substantive objects:

Mk 12:12 ἐζήτουν αὐτὸν **κρατῆσαι.**	They **were seeking to seize** him.
Acts 8:38 ἐκέλευσεν στῆναι τὸ ἅρμα.	He **ordered** the chariot **to stop.**

(3) When the infinitive (together with its subject and object or other adjuncts, if these are present) is the object of a verb of *saying* or *thinking*, it is said to be in **indirect discourse.** This is only one of the Greek constructions which correspond to English indirect quotation. In translating such constructions, the English "sequence of tenses" should be followed:

Acts 28:6 ἔλεγον αὐτὸν εἶναι θεόν.	They **said** [that] he **was** a god.
Rom 3:28 λογιζόμεθα δικαιοῦσθαι πίστει ἄνθρωπον.	We **hold** [that] a man **is justified** by faith.

(4) An infinitive may express the purpose or result of the action indicated by the main verb; when used in this way, it is sometimes introduced by ὥστε, *so that*:

---

[1] See §§45–48.

[2] The object of the infinitive or predicate nominative (or adjective) of the infinitive are also in the accusative. There are very few exceptions to this rule.

Lk 3:12 ἦλθον τελῶναι βαπτισθῆναι.

Tax collectors came **to be baptized** (=**in order to be baptized**).

Lk 11:31 ἦλθεν . . . ἀκοῦσαι τὴν σοφίαν Σολομῶνος.

She came . . . **to hear** the wisdom of Solomon (=**in order to hear** . . .).

Mt 15:31 ἐθεράπευσεν αὐτοὺς **ὥστε** τὸν ὄχλον **θαυμάσαι.**

He healed them, **so that** the crowd **marveled** (=**with the result that** the crowd **marveled**).

In determining whether such an infinitive construction indicates purpose, result, or some other meaning, the context must always be taken into account.

33

INFINITIVES, II
FURTHER USES OF
ANARTHROUS INFINITIVES
ARTICULAR INFINITIVES

260. The following uses of the anarthrous infinitive are of less frequent occurrence than those described in the previous lesson:

(1) An anarthrous infinitive may serve as the subject of a sentence; in particular, anarthrous infinitives occur as "subjects" of impersonal verbs such as **δεῖ**, *it is necessary*, **ἔξεστιν**, *it is lawful*, etc.

Mt 17:4 καλόν ἐστιν ἡμᾶς ὧδε εἶναι.	It is good for us **to be** here (=For us **to be** here is good).
Eph 6:20 δεῖ με λαλῆσαι.	I must **speak** (=It is necessary for me **to speak**, For me **to speak** is necessary).
Acts 1:16 ἔδει πληρωθῆναι τὴν γραφήν.	The scripture had **to be fulfilled** (=It was necessary for the scripture **to be fulfilled**).

(2) Anarthrous infinitives may occur as adjuncts of certain nouns and adjectives:

Mt 3:14 ἐγώ χρείαν ἔχω ὑπὸ σοῦ βαπτισθῆναι.	I have **need to be baptized** by you.
Jn 1:12 ἔδωκεν αὐτοῖς ἐξουσίαν τέκνα θεοῦ γενέσθαι.	He gave them **power to become** children of God.
2 Tim 2:2 . . . ἱκανοὶ ἔσονται . . . ἑτέρους διδάξαι.	They shall be **able to teach** others.
Rev 5:9 ἄξιος εἶ λαβεῖν τὸ βιβλίον.	You are **worthy to take** the book.

[199]

(3) In a use similar to that just mentioned, anarthrous infinitives may be in apposition to a noun:

1 Th 4:3 τοῦτό ἐστιν τὸ **θέλημα** τοῦ θεοῦ, ὁ ἁγιασμὸς ὑμῶν, **ἀπέχεσθαι** ὑμᾶς ἀπὸ τῆς πορνείας.

This is the **will** of God, your sanctification, for you **to keep** yourself from immorality.

(4) The anarthrous infinitive may be used after the word **πρίν** or the phrase **πρὶν ἤ** both of which, in such a construction, mean *before*:

Jn 8:58 πρὶν Ἀβραὰμ **γενέσθαι**, ἐγὼ εἰμί.

Before Abraham **came to be**, I am.

Mt 1:18 πρὶν ἤ **σῆνελθεῖν** αὐτούς

before they **came together**

(5) Rarely in the New Testament, the infinitive may be used independently, as an imperative (i.e., expressing a command or request):

Rom 12:15 **χαίρειν** μετὰ χαιρόντων **κλαίειν** μετὰ κλαιόντων.

Rejoice with those who rejoice, **weep** with those who weep.

(6) Once in the New Testament the infinitive is used in a parenthetical formula:

Heb 7:9 ὡς ἔπος **εἰπεῖν**

so **to speak**

261. Uses of the Articular Infinitive. (1) Like the anarthrous infinitive, the articular infinitive may serve as the subject of a sentence:

2 Cor 9:1 περισσόν μοί ἐστιν **τὸ γράφειν** ὑμῖν.

It is superfluous for me **to write** to you (=**To write** to you is superfluous for me).

(2) Like the anarthrous infinitive, but less commonly, the articular infinitive may serve as the direct object of a verb:

Phil 4:10 ἀνεθάλετε **τὸ** ὑπὲρ ἐμοῦ **φρονεῖν**.

You have revived **caring** about me.

(3) The genitive of the articular infinitive is used:
  (a) With nouns (like the genitive of a noun or pronoun; see §§78f):

Acts 14:9 ἔχει πίστιν **τοῦ σωθῆναι**.

He has faith **to be saved**.

(b) With adjectives:

Acts 23:15 ἕτοιμοί ἐσμεν **τοῦ ἀνελεῖν** αὐτόν. — We are ready **to kill** him.

(c) To express *purpose* or *result*:

Lk 9:51 αὐτὸς τὸ πρόσωπον ἐστήρισεν **τοῦ πορεύεσθαι** εἰς Ἰερουσαλήμ. — He set his face **to go** to Jerusalem.

Acts 5:31 τοῦτον ὁ θεὸς ἀρχηγὸν καὶ σωτῆρα ὕψωσεν τῇ δεξιᾷ αὐτοῦ **τοῦ δοῦναι** μετάνοιαν τῷ Ἰσραήλ. — By his right hand God has exalted this man [to be] prince and savior **in order to give** repentance to Israel.

(d) With certain verbs:

Rom 15:22 ἐνεκοπτόμην . . . **τοῦ ἐλθεῖν** πρὸς ὑμᾶς. — I was hindered **from coming** to you.

(4) The dative of the articular infinitive (without a governing preposition) occurs only once in the New Testament; it expresses cause:

2 Cor 2:13 **τῷ μὴ εὑρεῖν** με Τίτον — **because I did** not **find** Titus

(5) Unlike the anarthrous infinitive, the articular infinitive may function as the object of a preposition.

(a) In such constructions most prepositions have their usual meanings (see §§189–199):

Gal 3:23 **πρὸ τοῦ ἐλθεῖν** τὴν πίστιν — **before** faith **came**

Acts 4:2 **διὰ τὸ διδάσκειν** αὐτοὺς τὸν λαόν — **because** they **were teaching** the people

Acts 8:40 **ἕως τοῦ ἐλθεῖν** αὐτὸν εἰς Καισάρειαν — **until** he **came** to Caesarea

2 Cor 7:12 **ἕνεκεν τοῦ φανερωθῆναι** τὴν σπουδὴν ὑμῶν — **for the sake of** your zeal **being made manifest**

Jas 4:15 **ἀντὶ τοῦ λέγειν** ὑμᾶς — **instead of** your **saying**

Acts 1:3 **μετὰ τὸ παθεῖν** αὐτόν — **after** he **suffered**

(b) In some constructions the meanings of the prepositions have been specialized:

2 Cor 8:11 ἐκ τοῦ ἔχειν

according to your **means**
(= **out of** what you **have**)

Rom 3:26 εἰς τὸ εἶναι αὐτὸν
δίκαιον

in order that he **might be**
righteous

Eph 6:11 πρὸς τὸ δύνασθαι
ὑμᾶς στῆναι

in order that you **may be able**
to stand

Lk 24:51 ἐν τῷ εὐλογεῖν αὐτὸν
αὐτούς

while he **blessed** them

34 | ADVERBS

262. In neither English nor Greek can adverbs be defined paradigmatically, since they are not inflected in either language.[1] They must, therefore, be defined syntactically. An **adverb** in English may be defined as a word which may occur as an optional[2] constituent in one of the positions indicated by·the blank spaces in the following frames:

> The green grass is moist _____.
> The elephants remembered the hunter _____.
> Horses went _____.

or, more generally, in

$$[The] + [Adj] + Noun + V_{eq} + Adj \ [+\text{_____}]$$
$$[The] + [Adj] + Noun + V_{tr} + [the] + [Adj] + Noun \ [+\text{_____}]$$
$$[The] + [Adj] + Noun + V_{int} \ [+\text{_____}]$$

in which Adj = adjective, V = verb, eq = equative, tr = transitive, and int = intransitive, and in which square brackets enclose optional constituents. By this definition[3] such words as *there, here, now, underneath, well,*

---

[1] Except for degree of comparison; cf. Lesson 35.

[2] Cf. fn. ·1, p. 42. The stipulation that an adverb is an *optional* constituent obviates the possibility of confusing adverbs with nouns, verbs, or adjectives which might occupy the positions indicated by the blanks in the frames; thus, in

> The green grass is moist *hay.*
> The elephants remembered the hunter *died.*
> Horses went *wild.*

the words *hay, died,* and *wild* are not adverbs because their presence in the sentences alters the basic sentence structures completely and they are, in sentences with these altered sentence structures, *obligatory* constituents.

[3] Cf. Charles C. Fries, *The Structure of English,* pp. 83f. (see Selected Bibliography, §6(b)).

soon, upstairs, back, and *out* qualify as adverbs in English, but such words as *very, not, even,* and several others which have traditionally been classified as adverbs do not qualify.[1]

263. An **adverb** in Greek may be defined in a similar way as an un-inflected word which may be added (in any position) as optional consti-tuents to such structures as

$$N_n - V_{tr} - N_a \qquad \text{(cf. §§51f)}$$
$$N_n - V_{int} \qquad \text{(cf. §53)}$$
$$N_n - V_{eq} - N_n \qquad \text{(cf. §57)}$$
$$Adj - t - N_n \; or \; t - N_n - Adj \qquad \text{(cf. §69)}$$
$$N_n - V_{eq} - Adj \qquad \text{(cf. §70)}$$
$$N_n - V_{tr} - N_a^1 - N_a^2 \qquad \text{(cf. §182)}$$
$$N_n - V_{tr} - N_d - N_a \qquad \text{(cf. §186)}$$

or to a dependent structure such as εἰς τό plus infinitive, *provided* that such an addition does not affect the inflectional form of any word present in the structure. From the point of view of a professional grammarian this in-cludes too much, but this is not a serious defect; the coordinating con-junctions can be sorted out in various ways, and there is no real objection to regarding them as a special class of adverbs. The real difficulty with this definition, of course, is that it cannot be immediately applied by the student; it requires a considerably greater knowledge of Greek than one is likely to have when one is taking an introductory course. Some other means, accordingly, must be found which will enable us to recognize adverbs, or at least to recognize words which are *likely* to be adverbs. Fortunately, such means do exist, since some adverbs do have character-istic forms.

264. The Formal Characteristics of Adverbs. A formal characteristic of many English adverbs is the morpheme *-ly*. This is not to say, of course, either that *all* adverbs end in *-ly* or that *all* words that end in *-ly* are ad-verbs. (In *manly, beastly, -ly* is an adjectival morpheme; in *sly fly*, it is not a morpheme at all). However, it is *usually* possible in English to form an adverb from an adjective by adding the suffix *-ly* to the adjective; some examples follow:

---

[1] Fries, *op. cit.*, pp. 92f, classes these among his "function words."

ADJECTIVE	ADVERB
quick	quickly
tedious	tediously
awkward	awkwardly
sluggish	sluggishly

The suffix -*ly* is rarely added to an adjective which itself ends in -*ly*, however (thus we have *holy*, but not *holily*, and *lovely*, but not *lovelily*); further, the addition of -*ly* to an adjective does not always produce an adverb; e.g.: *good — goodly, dead — deadly*. Many English adverbs (i.e., words which satisfy the conditions of the definition of §262) have no distinctive formal characteristics: *then, now, often, seldom, downward, never, always, thus, today*, etc.

265. A great many Greek adverbs are related to Greek adjectives in the same way that English adverbs in -*ly* are related to English adjectives. These Greek adverbs may be obtained by changing the final **-ων** of the masculine genitive plural to **-ως**. Unlike English -*ly*, this adverbial morpheme **-ως** is a constituent of some adverbs besides those derived from adjectives. A few examples are given below:

ADJECTIVES	MASCULINE GENITIVE PLURAL	ADVERBS
ἀγνός, *pure, chaste*	ἀγνῶν	ἀγνῶς, *purely, chastely*
ἀληθής, *true,*	ἀληθῶν	ἀληθῶς, *truly, indeed*
βαρύς, *heavy*	βαρέων	βαρέως, *heavily*
σώφρων, *sober*	σωφρόνων	σωφρόνως, *soberly*
πᾶς, *all*	πάντων	πάντως, *by all means*

Adverbs are formed in the same way from some participles:

ὤν, *being*	ὄντων	ὄντως, *really*
ὑπερβάλλων, *exceeding*	ὑπερβαλλόντων	ὑπερβαλλόντως, *exceedingly*
ὁμολογούμενος, *confessing*	ὁμολογουμένων	ὁμολογουμένως, *undeniably*
φειδόμενος, *sparing*	φειδομένων	φειδομένως, *sparingly*

Note, however, that the adverb corresponding to **οὗτος**, *this*, is **οὕτως**, *thus*, not **τούτως**. Adverbs in **-ως** which are not derived from adjectives are **πῶς**, *how*, and **δηλαυγῶς**, *clearly*.

266. Adverbs ending in -ως comprise by far the largest single form class of this part of speech; there are about a hundred of them in the New Testament. In addition to -ως, a few other morphemes may reasonably be said to be characteristic of adverbs. The most important of these are given below:

(1) Adverbs ending in -οτε:

πότε, *when?*   δήποτε, *at any time*
ποτέ, *at some time*   οὐδέποτε, *never*
τότε, *then*   μηδέποτε, *never*
ὅτε, *when*   πώποτε, *ever, at any time*
πάντοτε, *always*   ὁπότε, *when*

(2) Adverbs ending in -θεν:

ἀλλαχόθεν, *from another quarter*   ὅθεν, *whence*
ἄνωθεν, *from above; again*   ὄπισθεν, *from behind*
ἐκεῖθεν, *thence, from there*   οὐρανόθεν, *from heaven*
ἔμπροσθεν, *in front, ahead*   παιδιόθεν, *from childhood*
ἔνθεν, *hence, from here*   πανταχόθεν, *from all sides*
ἐντεῦθεν, *hence, therefore*   παντόθεν, *from all sides*
ἔξωθεν, *from outside*   πόθεν, *whence?*
ἔσωθεν, *from within*   πόρρωθεν, *from afar*
μακρόθεν, *from afar*

(3) Adverbs ending ing in -ω:

ἄνω, *above, up*   μήπω, *not yet*
κάτω, *below, down*   ὀπίσω, *behind*
ἔξω, *outside*   οὔπω, *not yet*
ἐπάνω, *above*   πόρρω, *far off*
ἔσω, *within*   ὑποκάτω, *below, underneath*
κατωτέρω, *lower*   μηδέπω, *not yet*

(4) Adverbs ending in -ου:

ἀλλαχοῦ, *elsewhere*   δήπου, *surely, of course*
καθόλου, *everywhere*   μήπου, *(lest) somewhere*
ποῦ, *where?*   ὁμοῦ, *together*
πού, *somewhere*   οὗ, *where*
ὅπου, *where*   οὐ, *no, not*

(5) Adverbs ending in -ις:

δίς, *twice*

τρίς, *thrice, three times*

πεντάκις, *five times*

ἑπτάκις, *seven times*

πολλάκις, *many times, often*

ἑβδομηκοντάκις, *seventy times*

ὁσάκις, *as many times*

ποσάκις, *how many times?*

μόλις, *hardly*

267. In addition to these, there are many adverbs which have no special formal characteristics. Among the more important of these are the following:

ἅμα, *together, at the same time*

ἀμήν, *amen, indeed, truly*

ἅπαξ, *once*

ἄρτι, *now, just now*

αὔριον, *tomorow*

δεῦρο, *come!*

δεῦτε, *come!* (pl. of δεῦρο)

δωρεάν, *freely, without charge*

ἐγγύς, *near*

εἶτα, *then, next, after that*

ἐκεῖ, *there*

ἐπαύριον, *tomorrow*

ἔπειτα, *thereupon, afterwards*

ἔτι, *still, yet*

εὐθύς, *immediately*

ἐχθές, *yesterday*

ἤδη, *already*

λίαν, *very*

μᾶλλον, *rather*

μάλιστα, *especially*

μή, *not*

μηκέτι, *no longer*

νῦν, *now*

νυνί, *now* (variant of νῦν)

οὐκέτι, *no longer*

οὐχί, *no*

ὀψέ, *late* (in the day)

πάλιν, *again*

πέραν, *on the other side*

πέρυσι, *last year*

πλήν, *only, nevertheless*

πρῶτον, *first*

πρωΐ, *in the morning*

σήμερον, *today*

σφόδρα, *exceedingly*

σχεδόν, *almost, nearly*

ταχύ, *quickly, swiftly*

ὕστερον, *afterwards*

ὧδε, *here*

ναί, *yes*

268. The Meanings and Uses of Adverbs. Adverbs express a variety of meanings, many of which may be classified in the traditional way as adverbs of manner (those which "answer the question" *How?*), place (*Where?*), time (*When?*), and degree (*How much?*). This classification is not exhaustive, and should on no account be mistaken for a definition. In Greek, most adverbs ending in -ως are adverbs of manner (as are most English adverbs in -*ly*), adverbs ending in -οτε are adverbs of time, and most of those in **-ου** are adverbs of place. There is no special characteristic ending for adverbs of degree (e.g., **λίαν**, *very*, **σφόδρα**, *exceedingly*), but adverbs ending in **-άκις** might be called adverbs of frequency ("answering the question" *How many times?*).

269. In their usual function adverbs are said to modify verbs, adjectives, and other adverbs. No special rules can be given for the position of adverbs, though in general they follow the verb, adjective, or adverb which they modify.

(1) Adverbs modifying verbs:

Mt 2:16 ἐθυμώθη **λίαν**. — He was **very** angry.

Mk 7:6 **καλῶς** ἐπροφήτευσεν Ἡσαΐας περὶ ὑμῶν τῶν ὑποκριτῶν. — **Well** did Isaiah prophesy concerning you hypocrites.

(2) Adverbs modifying adjectives:

Mt 4:8 εἰς ὄρος ὑψηλὸν **λίαν** — into a **very** high mountain

Lk 18:23 ἦν πλούσιος **σφόδρα**. — He was **exceedingly** rich.

(3) Adverbs modifying adverbs:

Mk 16:2 **λίαν** πρωΐ — **very** early

Adverbs may be used predicatively, as in English:

Mk 11:19 **ὀψὲ** ἐγένετο. — It was getting **late**.

Mt 1:18 τοῦ Ἰησοῦ Χριστοῦ ἡ γένεσις **οὕτως** ἦν. — The birth of Jesus Christ was **thus**.

270. (1) Adverbs may have the attributive positions and functions proper to adjectives (cf. §195(2)):

Phil 3:14 διώκω εἰς τὸ βραβεῖον τῆς **ἄνω** κλήσεως. — I press on for the prize of the **upward** call.

2 Cor 8:13 ἐν τῷ **νῦν** καιρῷ — at the **present** time

(2) Adverbs may also function as substantives (cf. §196):

Acts 18:6 ἀπὸ τοῦ **νῦν** εἰς τὰ ἔθνη πορεύσομαι. — From **now** on I shall go to the Gentiles.

Acts 5:38 τὰ **νῦν** λέγω ὑμῖν. — I tell you the **present** matters.

(3) Some adverbs are used as prepositions:
   (a) With the dative:

Mt 13:29 ἅμα αὐτοῖς	**together with** them

   (b) With the genitive:

Jn 1:28 **πέραν** τοῦ Ἰορδάνου	**beyond** the Jordan
Jn 6:23 **ἐγγὺς** τοῦ τόπου	**near** the place
Acts 8:1 **πλὴν** τῶν ἀποστόλων	**except** the apostles

35 | COMPARISON OF ADJECTIVES AND ADVERBS

271. In English, some adjectives and a few adverbs have separate forms for indicating "**degrees of comparison**"; for example,

	POSITIVE	COMPARATIVE	SUPERLATIVE
ADJECTIVE	kind	kinder	kindest
	good	better	best
ADVERB	well	better	best
	soon	sooner	soonest

The comparative and superlative degrees of most English adjectives and adverbs are indicated by means of *more* and *most* (e.g., *awkward, more awkward, most awkward; angrily, more angrily, most angrily*).

272. Comparative and superlative forms of adjectives and adverbs occur somewhat infrequently in the Greek New Testament. Such forms as do occur are of two types, which we may call *regular* and *irregular*. The regular forms of the comparative and superlative of adjectives are obtained by adding **-τερος** and **-τατος**, respectively, to the stem of the positive form (the stem vowel **o** is sometimes lengthened to **ω.**). Adjectives with irregular comparison have their comparative forms in **-(ι)ων**[1] and their superlative forms in **-ιστος**. Examples of both types of comparison are given below (the forms in square brackets do not occur in the New Testament):

POSITIVE	COMPARATIVE	SUPERLATIVE
ἅγιος, *holy*	[ἁγιώτερος, *holier*]	ἁγιώτατος, *holiest, most holy, very holy*
τίμιος, *precious*	[τιμιώτερος, *more precious*]	τιμιώτατος, *most precious, very precious*

---

[1] For the declension of these forms see §158.

POSITIVE	COMPARATIVE	SUPERLATIVE
ἀκριβής, *strict, exact*	ἀκριβέστερος, *stricter, more exact*	ἀκριβέστατος, *strictest, most exact*
ἀγαθός, *good*	κρείσσων *or* κρείττων, *better*	κράτιστος, *best, most excellent*
μέγας, *great*	μείζων, *greater*	μέγιστος, *greatest*
πολύς, *much, many*	πλείων *or* πλέων, *more*	πλεῖστος, *most*
κακός, *bad*	χείρων, *worse*	—
μικρός, *small*	μικρότερος, *smaller or* ἐλάσσων, *lesser*	[μικρότατος, *smallest*] *or* ἐλάχιστος, *least*

273. Adverbs may be formed from some comparative forms in the manner described in §265:

	POSITIVE	COMPARATIVE
ADJECTIVE	περισσός, *abundant*	περισσότερος, *more abundant*
ADVERB	περισσῶς, *exceedingly*	περισσοτέρως, *more especially*

More generally, however, the neuter **singular** (nominative or accusative) of the comparative and the neuter **plural** (nominative or accusative) of the superlative are used adverbially (the neuter singular, nominative or accusative, of the positive degree is also frequently used in this way):

	POSITIVE	COMPARATIVE	SUPERLATIVE
ADJECTIVE	ταχύς, *swift*	[ταχίων, *swifter*]	[τάχιστος,, *swiftest*]
ADVERB	ταχέως *quickly* ταχύ, *quickly*	τάχιον, *faster*	τάχιστα, *very soon*
ADJECTIVE	[ἡδύς, *pleasant*]	[ἡδίων, *more pleasant*]	[ἥδιστος, *most pleasant*]
ADVERB	ἡδέως, *gladly*	[ἥδιον, *more gladly*]	ἥδιστα, *very gladly, most gladly*
ADJECTIVE	πολύς, *much many*	πλείων, *more*	πλεῖστος, *most*
ADVERB	πολύ, *very much*	πλεῖον, *more*	[πλεῖστα, *very much*]

274. Other adverbs have irregular forms as follows:

εὖ, *well*	βέλτιον, *better*	—
ἐγγύς, *near*	ἐγγύτερον *or* ἆσσον, *nearer*	ἔγγιστα, *nearest*
[μάλα, *very*]	μᾶλλον, *more, rather*	μάλιστα, *most, especially*

275. The comparative and superlative degrees of adjectives and adverbs may also be indicated by **μᾶλλον**, *more*, and **μάλιστα**, *most*:

Acts 20:35 **μακάριόν** ἐστιν **μᾶλλον**   It is **more blessed** to give.
διδόναι.

Acts 20:38 ὀδυνώμενοι **μάλιστα**   **most sorrowful**

276. (1) *Than* with the comparative is expressed in Greek by **ἤ** followed by the same case as that of the noun or pronoun being compared, or by the genitive (cf. §159):

Jn 4:1 Ἰησοῦς **πλείονας** μαθητὰς ποιεῖ καὶ βαπτίζει **ἤ** Ἰωάννης.	Jesus is making and baptizing **more** disciples **than John.**
Jn 3:19 ἠγάπησαν οἱ ἄνθρωποι **μᾶλλον** τὸ σκότος **ἤ** τὸ φῶς.	Men loved the darkness **more** (*or* **rather**) **than the light.**
Mt 10:15 **ἀνεκτότερον** ἔσται γῆ Σοδόμων . . . **ἤ** τῇ πόλει ἐκείνῃ.	It will be **more tolerable** for the land of Sodom . . . **than for that city.**
Mt 27:64 ἔσται ἡ ἐσχάτη πλάνη **χείρων** τῆς πρώτης.	The last fraud will be **worse than the first.**
Jn 20:4 ὁ ἄλλος μαθητὴς προέδραμεν **τάχιον τοῦ** Πέτρου.	The other disciple ran ahead **faster than Peter.**

(2) *Than* is sometimes expressed by **παρά** or **ὑπέρ** with the accusative:

Heb 9:23 [καθαρίζεται] τὰ ἐπουράνια **κρείττοσιν** θυσίαις **παρὰ ταύτας.**	The heavenly things [are cleansed] by **better** sacrifices **than these.**
Lk 16:8 οἱ υἱοὶ τοῦ αἰῶνος τούτου **φρονιμώτεροι ὑπὲρ τοὺς** υἱοὺς τοῦ φωτός.	The sons of this age are **wiser than the sons** of light.

277. The superlative occurs only once in its true sense (i.e., the highest degree, as compared with others):

Acts 26:5 κατὰ τὴν **ἀκριβεστάτην**   according to the **strictest** sect
αἵρεσιν

278. The superlative forms usually have "elative" meaning; i.e., they indicate a very high degree, without any comparison with other terms being implied:

Rev 21:11 ὁ φωστὴρ αὐτῆς ὅμοιος   Its radiance was like a **very**
λίθῳ **τιμιωτάτῳ**.   **precious** stone.

Mt 21:8 ὁ **πλεῖστος** ὄχλος   the **very great** crowd

279. The comparative forms are frequently used where a superlative would be used in English:

1 Cor 13:13 **μείζων** τούτων ἡ   **The greatest** of these is love.
ἀγάπη.

Mt 8:12 τὸ σκότος τὸ **ἐξώτερον**   the **outer** (=the_ **outermost**)
                                          darkness

280. Comparative forms are also frequently used in an " elative " sense:

Phil 2:28 **σπουδαιοτέρως** ἔπεμψα   I have sent him **very eagerly**.
αὐτόν.

36 | IRREGULAR ADJECTIVES

281. Some adjectives have slight paradigmatic irregularities, while others, more important, have syntactic peculiarities which call for special remark. The former are treated first.

282. Μέγας, *great,* has irregular forms in the nominative and accusative, masculine and neuter singular. The remaining forms have the stem found in the feminine nominative singular (in the paradigm below, and in other paradigms in this lesson, forms calling for special note are underlined):

	MASCULINE	FEMININE	NEUTER
SG.N.	μέγας	μεγάλη	μέγα
G.	μεγάλου	μεγάλης	μεγάλου
D.	μεγάλῳ	μεγάλῃ	μεγάλῳ
A.	μέγαν	μεγάλην	μέγα
PL.N.	μεγάλοι	μεγάλαι	μεγάλα
G.	μεγάλων	μεγάλων	μεγάλων
D.	μεγάλοις	μεγάλαις	μεγάλοις
A.	μεγάλους	μεγάλας	μεγάλα

283. Πολύς *much* (in the singular), *many* (in the plural); *great, large* (in amount or in number):

	MASCULINE	FEMININE	NEUTER
SG.N.	πολύς	πολλή	πολύ
G.	πολλοῦ	πολλῆς	πολλοῦ
D.	πολλῷ	πολλῇ	πολλῷ
A.	πολύν	πολλήν	πολύ
PL.N.	πολλοί	πολλαί	πολλά
G.	πολλῶν	πολλῶν	πολλῶν
D.	πολλοῖς	πολλαῖς	πολλοῖς
A.	πολλούς	πολλάς	πολλά

284. A few adjectives in New Testament Greek have *contracted* forms; i.e., like the contract verbs, they have forms which, in an earlier stage of the language, had **ε** or **ο** preceding the stem vowel and case-number suffix. Since there are only a few of these contract adjectives, their forms will not be analyzed in detail, but the paradigms of two are given below as models:

	MASCULINE	FEMININE	NEUTER
SG.N.	διπλοῦς, *double*	διπλῆ	διπλοῦν
G.	διπλοῦ	διπλῆς	διπλοῦ
D.	διπλῷ	διπλῇ	διπλῷ
A.	διπλοῦν	διπλῆν	διπλοῦν
PL.N.	διπλοῖ	διπλαῖ	διπλᾶ
G.	διπλῶν	διπλῶν	διπλῶν
D.	διπλοῖς	διπλαῖς	διπλοῖς
A.	διπλοῦς	διπλᾶς	διπλᾶ
SG.N.	πορφυροῦς, *purple*	πορφυρᾶ	πορφυροῦν
G.	πορφυροῦ	πορφυρᾶς	πορφυροῦ
D.	πορφυρῷ	πορφυρᾷ	πορφυρῷ
A.	πορφυροῦν	πορφυρᾶν	πορφυροῦν
PL.N.	πορφυροῖ	πορφυραῖ	πορφυρᾶ
G.	πορφυρῶν	πορφυρῶν	πορφυρῶν
D.	πορφυροῖς	πορφυραῖς	πορφυροῖς
A.	πορφυροῦς	πορφυρᾶς	πορφυρᾶ

Declined like **διπλοῦς** are the following:

χαλκοῦς, ῆ, οῦν, *brazen, brass, bronze* χρυσοῦς, ῆ, οῦν, *gold, golden*
ἁπλοῦς, ῆ, οῦν, *simple, single* τετραπλοῦς, ῆ, οῦν, *fourfold*

Declined like **πορφυροῦς** are:

ἀργυροῦς, ᾶ, οῦν, *silver* σιδηροῦς, ᾶ, οῦν, *iron*

285. Μέλας, *black,* is declined as follows:

	MASCULINE	FEMININE	NEUTER
SG.N.	μέλας	μέλαινα	μέλαν
G.	μέλανος	μελαίνης	μέλανος
D.	μέλανι	μελαίνῃ	μέλανι
A.	μέλανα	μέλαιναν	μέλαν

	MASCULINE	FEMININE	NEUTER
PL.N.	μέλανες	μέλαιναι	μέλανα
G.	μελάνων	μελαινῶν	μελάνων
D.	μέλασι(ν)	μελαίναις	μέλασι(ν)
A.	μέλανας	μελαίνας	μέλανα

The neuter, as a substantive (**τὸ μέλαν, ος**), means *ink*.

286. Ἑκών, ἑκοῦσα, ἑκόν, *willing*, and ἄκων, ἄκουσα, ἄκον, *unwilling*, are declined like present participles (see §206(1)).

287. Πᾶς, ἄπας, and ὅλος may be treated together. Πᾶς and ἄπας are declined like first aorist participles, i.e., nominative πᾶς, πᾶσα, πᾶν, genitive παντός, πάσης, παντός, etc. (cf. §236). Ὅλος is declined like καλός. The three words are roughly synonymous; their use in the New Testament is indicated below:

(1) Ἄπας occurs comparatively infrequently.

(a) It has either of the predicate positions with articular nouns and means *all* (of), (the) *whole* (of):

Mk 16:15 εἰς τὸν κόσμον ἄπαντα	into **all** the world
Lk 8:37 ἠρώτησεν αὐτὸν ἄπαν τὸ πλῆθος.	**All** the multitude asked him.

(b) With a pronoun it means *all*:

Acts 2:7 ἄπαντες οὗτοι	**all** these

(c) With a participle it means *all* (that), *everything* (that), *all* (who), *everyone* (who):

Mt 28:11 ἄπαντα τὰ γενόμενα	**everything** that happened

(d) Without a substantive it means *all, everyone, everything*:

Acts 2:44 εἶχον ἄπαντα κοινά.	They had **everything** in common (=They held **everything** as common).
Lk 5:26 ἔκστασις ἔλαβεν ἄπαντας.	Amazement seized them **all**.

(2) Πᾶς occurs very frequently: it is found (a) with anarthrous nouns, (b) with articular nouns, (c) with participles, (d) with pronouns, and (e) alone, functioning substantively, with or without an article.

(a) With an anarthrous noun it usually precedes, but may follow (see Acts 4:29, below).

(i) In the singular it means *every* (in the sense *any*), *every kind of*, and (if the context allows it) *all*:

Mt 3:10 πᾶν δένδρον	**every** tree (*or* **every kind of** tree)
Lk 3:6 πᾶσα σάρξ	**all** flesh
Acts 4:29 μετὰ παρρησίας **πάσης**	with **all** boldness (*or* with **every kind of** boldness)

With the names of places it means *all, the whole of*:

Mt 2:3 πᾶσα Ἱεροσόλυμα	**all** Jerusalem

(ii) In the plural it means *all* (this construction is somewhat unusual, except with **ἄνθρωποι**):

1 Tim 4:10 ἔστιν σωτὴρ **πάντων** ἀνθρώπων.	He is the savior of **all** men.

(b) With an articular noun **πᾶς** may occur in either predicate position or in the first attributive position.

(i) The first predicate position is most common; the meanings *all*, (the) *whole* (of) are most usually associated with this position:

Rom 8:22 πᾶσα ἡ κτίσις	the **whole** creation (*or* **all** creation)
Mt 1:17 πᾶσαι αἱ γενεαί	**all** the generations

When **πᾶς** has this position, a demonstrative may occur in the second predicate position:

Mt 25:7 πᾶσαι αἱ παρθένοι ἐκεῖναι	**all** those virgins
Lk 1:65 πάντα τὰ ῥήματα ταῦτα	**all** these words

(ii) When **πᾶς** has the second predicate position, the noun it follows receives special emphasis; this position is not very common in the New Testament:

Mt 26:56 οἱ μαθηταὶ **πάντες**	**all** the disciples [i.e., as contrasted with others]
Jn 16:13 εἰς τὴν ἀλήθειαν **πᾶσαν**	into **all** truth [i.e., not into error]

(iii) **Πᾶς** in first attributive position contrasts the whole with the part:

Gal 5:14 ὁ **πᾶς** νόμος	the **whole body of** the law
Acts 19:7 οἱ **πάντες** ἄνδρες	the **sum total of** the men

(c) With participles (which usually have the article) **πᾶς** occurs in first predicate position; the construction is equivalent to English *everyone who . . ., everything that . . .* (in the singular), and *all those who . . ., all that . . .* (in the plural):

Mt 7:26 **πᾶς** ὁ ἀκούων μου τοὺς λόγους	**everyone who** hears my words
1 Cor 10:25 **πᾶν** τὸ ἐν μακέλλῳ πωλούμενον	**everything that** is sold in the market
Mt 11:28 **πάντες** οἱ κοπιῶντες	**all those** who labor
Mt 18:31 **πάντα** τὰ γενόμενα	**all that** happened

(d) With pronouns **πᾶς** means *all*; it may precede or follow:

Acts 2:32 **πάντες** ἡμεῖς	we **all**
Jn 1:16 ἡμεῖς **πάντες**	we **all**
Mt 23:8 **πάντες** ὑμεῖς	you **all**
Acts 20:25 ὑμεῖς **πάντες**	you **all**
Acts 4:33 **πάντες** αὐτοί	they **all**
Mt 12:15 αὐτοὶ **πάντες**	they **all**
Acts 2:7 **πάντες** οὗτοι	**all** these
Acts 1:14 οὗτοι **πάντες**	**all** these
Mt 6:32 **πάντα** ταῦτα	**all** these things
Mt 4:9 ταῦτα **πάντα**	**all** these things

(e) Without a noun it means *everybody, everything*; it may or may not have the article:

Mk 14:50 ἔφυγον **πάντες**.	**Everyone** fled (=They **all** fled).
1 Cor 9:23 **πάντα** ποιῶ.	I do **everything**.
1 Cor 10:17 οἱ **πάντες**	**everyone**
Acts 17:25 τὰ **πάντα**	**everything** (=**all things**)

(3) **῞Ολος** may occur with an anarthrous noun or in either predicate position with an articular noun. In the Greek New Testament **ὅλος** never

has the attributive position with an articular noun, nor does it occur in the plural.

(a) With an anarthrous noun it means *whole*:

Jn 7:23 **ὅλον** ἄνθρωπον ὑγιῆ ἐποίησα.	I made a **whole** man well.

(b) With an articular noun, in either first or second pedicate position, it means (the) *whole* (of), *all* (of); *all* (the):

Mk 1:33 **ὅλη** ἡ πόλις	the **whole** city
Acts 21:30 ἡ πόλις **ὅλη**	the **whole** city

Note the position of pronouns in the genitive:

Mt 6:22 **ὅλον** τὸ σῶμά σου	your **whole** body
Jn 4:53 ἡ οἰκία αὐτοῦ **ὅλη**	his **whole** household

(c) With pronouns, it means *all*:

Mt 1:22 τοῦτο **ὅλον**	**all** this

(d) Used substantively (without an article), it means *all, everything*:

Jn 19:23 δι' **ὅλου**	through **everything** (*or* through and through)

288. Ἕκαστος occurs infrequently as an adjective meaning *each, every* (i.e., *every individual*, not *any*), but more often as a pronoun: *each one, every one*.

(1) As an adjective it does not, in the Greek New Testament, occur with the article:

Lk 6:44 **ἕκαστον** δένδρον	**each** tree
Heb 3:13 **ἑκάστην** ἡμέραν	**every** day

(2) As a pronoun it may occur:
   (a) Alone:

1 Cor 14:26 **ἕκαστος** ψαλμὸν ἔχει.	**each one** has a psalm.

   (b) Followed by a genitive:

Rom 14:12 **ἕκαστος** ἡμῶν	**each** (**one**) of us
1 Cor 1:12 **ἕκαστος** ὑμῶν	**each** (**one**) of you

(c) Followed by ἴδιος:[1]

1 Cor 3:8 ἕκαστος τὸν ἴδιον μισθὸν λήμψεται κατὰ τὸν ἴδιον κόπον.	**Each one** shall receive *his own* reward according to *his own* labor.

(d) Sometimes with personal pronouns:[2]

Rev 2:23 δώσω ὑμῖν ἐκάστῳ κατὰ τὰ ἔργα ὑμῶν.	I will give **to each of you** in accordance with your works.
Rev 6:11 ἐδόθη αὐτοῖς ἐκάστῳ στολὴ λευκή.	A white robe was given **to each of them**.

(e) With a plural verb:

Jn 7:53 ἐπορεύθησαν ἕκαστος εἰς τὸν οἶκον αὐτοῦ.	**Each** went into his house.

(f) In the New Testament ἕκαστος does not occur in the plural, except in:

Phil 2:4 μὴ τὰ ἑαυτῶν ἕκαστοι σκοποῦντες, ἀλλὰ καὶ τὰ ἑτέρων ἕκαστοι	**each** looking not to their own interests, but **each** to the interests of others

REMARK: For the use of ἕκαστος with the numeral εἷς, see the following lesson.

---

[1] This is also true when ἕκαστος is adjectival; cf. Luke 6:44.

[2] This use could equally be described as adjectival.

37

THE NUMERALS
ἄλλος and ἕτερος

289. The **numerals** form an important group of adjectives. The **ordinal** numerals are declined like ordinary adjectives of the first and second declensions; the declension of each of the first four **cardinals** is given below:

	MASCULINE	FEMININE	NEUTER		ALL GENDERS
SG.N.	εἷς, *one*	μία	ἕν	PL.N.	δύο, *two*
G.	ἑνός	μίας	ἑνός	G.	δύο
D.	ἑνί	μίᾳ	ἑνί	D.	δυσί(ν)
A.	ἕνα	μίαν	ἕν	A.	δύο

(**Εἷς** has no plural forms, and the others have no singular forms.)

	MASCULINE AND FEMININE	NEUTER	MASCULINE AND FEMININE	NEUTER
PL.N.	τρεῖς, *three*	τρία	τέσσαρες, *four*	τέσσερα[1]
G.	τριῶν	τριῶν	τεσσάρων	τεσσάρων
D.	τρισί(ν)	τρισί(ν)	τέσσαρσι(ν)	τέσσαρσι(ν)
A.	τρεῖς	τρία	τέσσαρας	τέσσερα

290. The remaining cardinals below two hundred are not declined, except for those whose forms contain one of the first four as a constituent part (e.g., εἴκοσι [καὶ] εἷς, *twenty-one*, εἴκοσι [καὶ] δύο, *twenty-two*, εἴκοσι [καὶ] τρεῖς, *twenty-three*, δεκατέσσαρες, *fourteen*). The cardinals from two hundred on and the ordinals are ordinary adjectives. Χιλιάς, -άδος, and μυριάς, -άδος, are nouns (feminine) of the third declension.

291. As *symbols* for the numerals the Greeks used the letters of the alphabet, including three not ordinarily used otherwise: these are στίγμα (or δίγαμμα) for 6 (written ς), κόππα for 90 (written ϙ or ϙ), and σάν or

---

[1] Sometimes also τέσσαρα.

σαμπῖ for 900 (written ⌐ or Ͳ). When the letters were used as numerals they were marked by a horizontal stroke placed above them or by a short sloping line at their upper right; a similar short sloping line at the lower left of a symbol indicated that its value was to be multiplied by one thousand. The Greeks had no symbol for zero.

292. Not all of the numerals occur in the New Testament; for completeness, some of the missing forms are given in the list following:

VALUE	SYMBOL	CARDINALS	ORDINALS	ADVERBIALS
1	α′	εἷς, μία, ἕν, *one*	πρῶτος, η, ον, *first*	ἅπαξ, *once*
2	β′	δύο	δεύτερος, α, ον	δίς
3	γ′	τρεῖς, τρία	τρίτος, η, ον	τρίς
4	δ′	τέσσαρες, τέσσερα	τέταρτος, η, ον	τετράκις
5	ε′	πέντε	πέμπτος, η, ον	πεντάκις
6	ς′	ἕξ	ἕκτος, η, ον	
7	ζ′	ἑπτά	ἕβδομος, η, ον	ἑπτάκις
8	η′	ὀκτώ	ὄγδοος, η, ον	
9	θ′	ἐννέα	ἔνατος, η, ον	
10	ι′	δέκα	δέκατος, η, ον	
11	ια′	ἕνδεκα	ἑνδέκατος, η, ον	
12	ιβ′	δώδεκα	δωδέκατος, η, ον	
13	ιγ′	δεκατρεῖς	τρεισκαιδέκατος, η, ον	
14	ιδ′	δεκατέσσαρες	τεσσαρεσκαιδέκατος, η, ον	
15	ιε′	δεκαπέντε	πεντεκαιδέκατος, η, ον	
16	ις′	δεκαέξ		
18	ιη′	δέκα ὀκτώ or δέκα καὶ ὀκτώ		
20	κ′	εἴκοσι(ν)	εἰκοστός, ή, όν	εἰκοσάκις
24	κδ′	εἴκοσι τέσσαρες		
30	λ′	τριάκοντα		
40	μ′	τεσσαράκοντα or τεσσεράκοντα		
50	ν′	πεντήκοντα	πεντηκοστός, ή, όν	
60	ξ′	ἑξήκοντα		
70	ο′	ἑβδομήκοντα		ἑβδομηκοντάκις
80	π′	ὀγδοήκοντα		
90	ϟ′	ἐνενήκοντα		
100	ρ′	ἑκατόν		
200	σ′	διακόσιοι		
300	τ′	τριακόσιοι		
400	υ′	τετρακόσιοι		

VALUE	SYMBOL	CARDINALS
500	φ′	πεντακόσιοι
600	χ′	ἑξακόσιοι
700	ψ′	ἑπτακόσιοι
800	ω′	ὀκτακόσιοι
900	ϡ′	ἐνακόσιοι
1,000	͵α	χίλιοι, ἡ χιλιάς
2,000	͵β	δισχίλιοι
3,000	͵γ	τρισχίλιοι
4,000	͵δ	τετρακισχίλιοι
5,000	͵ε	πεντακισχίλιοι or χιλιάδες πέντε
7,000	͵ζ	ἑπτακισχίλιοι or χιλιάδες ἑπτά
10,000	M͞α	μύριοι or δέκα χιλιάδες
12,000	M͞α͵β	δώδεκα χιλιάδες
20,000	M͞β	εἴκοσι χιλιάδες or δισμύριοι
100,000,000		μυριάδες μυριάδων

293. The numerals were combined by writing one after the other; thus, the "number of the Beast" in Revelation 13:18 is ἑξακόσιοι ἑξήκοντα ἕξ, *six hundred sixty-six*; in some manuscripts of the Greek New Testament the symbols are used: χξϛ′. The number 1964 would be written ͵αϡξδ′.

294. A few examples will suffice to illustrate the use of the numerals:

Jn 6:70 ἐξ ὑμῶν **εἷς** διάβολός ἐστιν.   **One** of (=from) you is a devil.

Mk 10:8 ἔσονται οἱ **δύο** εἰς[1] σάρκα **μίαν**.   The **two** shall be **one** flesh.

Jn 8:17 **δύο** ἀνθρώπων ἡ μαρτυρία ἀληθής ἐστιν.   The testimony **of two** men is true.

Mk 16:12 μετὰ ταῦτα **δυσὶν** ἐξ αὐτῶν . . . ἐφανερώθη.   After these things he was made manifest to **two** of them.

Gal 1:18 μετὰ **τρία** ἔτη   after **three** years

Rev 15:7 **ἓν** ἐκ τῶν **τεσσάρων** ζῴων ἔδωκεν τοῖς **ἑπτὰ** ἀγγέλοις **ἑπτὰ** φιάλας χρυσᾶς.   **One** of (=from) the **four** living beings gave to the **seven** angels **seven** golden vials.

[1] See §183.

Rev 7:2 ἔκραξεν φωνῇ μεγάλῃ τοῖς   He cried with a loud voice to the
τέσσαρσιν ἀγγέλοις.   **four** angels.

Mt 18:28 ὤφειλεν αὐτῷ **ἑκατὸν**   He owed him a **hundred** denarii.
δηνάρια.

Rev 20:4 ἐβασίλευσαν μετὰ τοῦ   They ruled with Christ a **thousand**
Χριστοῦ **χίλια** ἔτη.   years.

295. Note that the numeral **εἷς** frequently occurs with **ἕκαστος** (much like English *one* with *each, every*):

Mt 26:22 ἤρξαντο λέγειν αὐτῷ   **Each one** began to say to him
εἷς ἕκαστος . . .   . . .

Acts 2:3 ἐκάθισεν ἐφ' **ἕνα ἕκαστον**   It sat upon **each one** of them.
αὐτῶν.

Eph 4:7 **ἑνὶ ἑκάστῳ** ἡμῶν ἐδόθη ἡ   Grace has been given to **each one**
χάρις.   of us.

2 Th 1:3 πλεονάζει ἡ ἀγάπη **ἑνὸς**   The love of **each one** of you all
ἑκάστου πάντων ὑμῶν.   abounds.

296. **Ἄλλος** and **ἕτερος** may be treated together. **Ἄλλος** is declined like **αὐτός** (i.e., it has **ἄλλο** in the nominative and accusative singular neuter; cf. §97), but **ἕτερος** is declined like an ordinary adjective (e.g., **μικρός**; cf. §66). **Ἄλλος** and **ἕτερος** are, in general, synonymous.

(1) In the singular, without the article, each may be translated as:
  (a) *Another*, in most instances:

Mt 13:33 **ἄλλην** παραβολὴν   He told them **another** parable.
ἐλάλησεν αὐτοῖς.

Mt 8:21 **ἕτερος** τῶν μαθητῶν εἶπεν   **Another** of the disciples said to
αὐτῷ . . .   him . . .

  (b) *Other*, before nouns which have a plural or collective sense (in English):

Mk 4:7 **ἄλλο** ἔπεσεν εἰς τὰς   **Other** (*sc.* seed) fell into the thorns.
ἀκάνθας.

Lk 8:7 **ἕτερον** ἔπεσεν ἐν μέσῳ τῶν   **Other** (*sc.* seed) fell in the midst
ἀκανθῶν.   of the thorns.

(2) In the plural, without the article, each may be translated simply *other* (or *others*, if used substantively):

| Mt 16:14 [εἶπον] **ἄλλοι** 'Ηλίαν, . . . **ἕτεροι** . . . ἕνα τῶν προφητῶν. | **Others** said Elijah, . . . **others** [said] . . . one of the prophets. |

(3) With the article, each may be translated *the other* (*the others*, if used substantively):

Jn 21:8 οἱ **ἄλλοι** μαθηταὶ τῷ πλοιαρίῳ ἦλθον.	The **other** disciples came in the boat.
Jn 20:3 ὁ **ἄλλος** μαθητής	the **other** disciple
Lk 19:20 ὁ **ἕτερος** ἦλθεν.	The **other** came.
Lk 4:43 ταῖς **ἑτέραις** πόλεσιν εὐαγγελίσασθαί με δεῖ.	I must preach the gospel to the **other** cities.

(4) **Ἕτερος**, rather than **ἄλλος**, is usually found contrasted with **εἷς**, *one*:

Lk 7:41 ὁ **εἷς** ὤφειλεν δηνάρια πεντακόσιν, ὁ **ἕτερος** πεντήκοντα.	The **one** owed five hundred denarii, the **other** fifty.
Lk 16:13 τὸν **ἕνα** μισήσει καὶ τὸν **ἕτερον** ἀγαπήσει.	He will hate the **one** and love the **other**.
Lk 18:10 **εἷς** Φαρισαῖος καὶ ὁ **ἕτερος** τελώνης	**one** a Pharisee and the **other** a tax collector

38 | THE NEGATIVES

297. Study the following illustrative examples carefully:

(1)	(a)	οὐ ποιεῖ τὸ θέλημα τοῦ θεοῦ.	He is not doing the will of God.
	(b)	ὁ μὴ ποιῶν τὸ θέλημα τοῦ θεοῦ ἁμαρτωλός ἐστιν.	He who does not do the will of God is a sinner.
	(c)	διὰ τὸ μὴ ποιεῖν τὸ θέλημα τοῦ θεοῦ ἁμαρτίαν ἔχει.	Because of not doing the will of God, he has sin.
(2)	(a)	οὐκ ἔχουσιν ἄρτον.	They do not have bread.
	(b)	οἱ μὴ ἔχοντες ἄρτον πεινῶσιν.	Those who have no bread are hungry.
	(c)	διὰ τὸ μὴ ἔχειν ἄρτον πεινῶσιν.	Because of having no bread they are hungry.
(3)	(a)	οὐχ εὗρον τὸ τέκνον.	They did not find the child.
	(b)	οἱ μὴ εὑρόντες τὸ τέκνον ἦσαν στρατιῶται τοῦ Ἡρῴδου.	Those who did not find the child were soldiers of Herod.
	(c)	διὰ τὸ μὴ εὑρεῖν τὸ τέκνον πάλιν ἐζήτησαν.	Because of not finding the child they searched again.
(4)	(a)	οὐκέτι εἰμὶ ἐν τῷ κόσμῳ.	I am no longer in the world.
	(b)	ὁ μηκέτι ὢν ἐν τῷ κόσμῳ ἐστὶν ἐν τῷ οὐρανῷ.	He who is no longer in the world is in heaven.
	(c)	εἰς τὸ μηκέτι εἶναι ἐν τῷ κόσμῳ πορεύσεται εἰς τὸν οὐρανόν.	In order no longer to be in the world, he will go to heaven.
(5)	(a)	ὀφείλομεν οὐδὲν οὐδενί.	We owe nothing to anyone (= to no one).
	(b)	θέλει ἡμᾶς ὀφείλειν μηδὲν μηδενί.	He wants us to owe nothing to anyone.
	(c)	οἱ ὀφείλοντες μηδὲν μηδενὶ μαθηταὶ ἀληθεῖς εἰσιν.	Those who owe nothing to anyone are true disciples.
(6)	(a)	ἡ ἀγάπη οὐδέποτε πίπτει.	Love never fails.

(b)	ἡ μηδέποτε πίπτουσα ἀγάπη μείζων πίστεώς ἐστιν.	Never-failing love is greater than faith.
(c)	ὁ Παῦλος εἶπεν τὴν ἀγάπην μηδέποτε πίπτειν.	Paul said that love never failed.
(7)(a)	οὐκ εἴδομεν αὐτὸν οὐκέτι ἡμεῖς.	We do not see him any longer.
(b)	οὐκ ἐδύνατο ἐκεῖ ποιῆσαι οὐδεμίαν δύναμιν.	He was not able to do any great work there. (δύναμις=great work)
(8)	οὐ μὴ διψήσει εἰς τὸν αἰῶνα.	He will not thirst at all, forever.

(The student should proceed now to do Exercise 38-A in the Workbook.)

298. Remarks. (1) **Οὐδείς** and **μηδείς** are declined like **εἷς**, *one* (cf. §289):

οὐδείς	οὐδεμία	οὐδέν
etc.		
μηδείς	μηδεμία	μηδέν
etc.		

Neither has plural forms.

(2) Other negatives are:

(a) **Οὔπω** and **μήπω**, *not yet*:

Mt 24:6 **οὔπω** ἐστὶν τὸ τέλος.	The end is **not yet**.
Rom 9:11 **μήπω** γεννηθέντων	[they] had **not yet** been born[1]

(b) **Οὐδέπω** and **μηδέπω**, *not yet*:

Jn 7:39 Ἰησοῦς **οὐδέπω** ἐδοξάσθη.	Jesus had **not yet** been glorified.
Heb 11:7 περὶ τῶν **μηδέπω** βλεπομένων	concerning things **not yet** seen

(c) **Οὐθείς** and **μηθείς** are alternative forms of **οὐδείς** and **μηδείς**.

(d) **Οὐχί** and **οὔ** (with the accent) are the words regularly used for *no*:

Jn 9:9 ἄλλοι ἔλεγον **οὐχί**.	Others said, **No**.
Jn 7:12 ἄλλοι ἔλεγον **οὔ**.	Others said, **No**.

Οὐχί may be used as a simple negative (=**οὐ**):

Jn 13:11 **οὐχί** πάντες καθαροί ἐστε.	You are **not** all clean.

---

[1] In the context this expression is a genitive absolute.

39 | QUESTIONS

299. Questions, in spoken English, are indicated primarily by special intonation patterns;[1] these are represented rather imperfectly (since there are more than one) in written English by the question mark (?). Modern Greek has, and presumably earlier Greek had, such special intonation patterns also, but these were not indicated in the written language until the ninth century of the Christian era, when the Greek question mark (;) was introduced. For recognizing questions in the New Testament, therefore, we are dependent on secondary indications of various kinds; since English also makes use of secondary indications which are generally, but not entirely, similar to those of Greek, a few English illustrative examples will be given first.

300. In English, questions are indicated secondarily by:
(1) Word order:

STATEMENT: You are the king of the Jews.
QUESTION: Are you the king of the Jews?[2]

(2) The use of auxiliary verbs as function words:

STATEMENT: He thinks so.
QUESTION: *Does* he think so?

(3) The use of other interrogative function words:
(a) Pronouns:

Who do you think you are?
Whom do you wish to see?

---

[1] Cf. Gleason, pp. 45–50, 175, 185 (see Selected Bibliography, §6(b)).

[2] Note, however, that only the primary indication (of intonation) is really necessary:

You are the king of the Jews?

with the written (?), or the intonation it indicates, is just as clearly a question.

> *Whose* dog are you?
> *What* is the matter?

(b) Adjectives:

> *Which* way did he go?

(c) Adverbs:

> *Where* do you think you're going?
> *When* does the next swan leave?
> *How* do you get that way?

301. Some of the secondary means for indicating questions in Greek are, as we have said, similar to those found in English; it should be noticed, however, that word order is not among these. A Greek sentence which contains none of the secondary question indicators which we shall describe may be either a question or a statement, regardless of word order; in interpreting it as one or the other, we must be guided by the context:

> Mk 15:2 σὺ εἶ ὁ βασιλεὺς τῶν Ἰουδαίων;   Are you the king of the Jews?

Since it would be strange to find Pontius Pilate saying to Jesus,

> You are the king of the Jews.

this sentence is naturally taken as a question, and editors have supplied a question mark (;) in printed texts of the New Testament. Only rarely are editors in disagreement:

> Jn 16:31 ἄρτι πιστεύετε;   Do you now believe?

Some editors have thought that the proper interpretation is:

> ἄρτι πιστεύετε.   You believe now.

302. Greek uses certain function words, other than the interrogatives listed in §303 to indicate that a sentence is a question; none of these function words is an auxiliary verb like English *do*, however:

(1) **Μή**, when used with the *indicative* mood, introduces a question to which a *negative* answer is expected:

> Jn 9:40 μὴ ἡμεῖς τυφλοί ἐσμεν;   Are we blind? (*or* We aren't blind, are we?)

1 Cor 12:30 **μὴ** πάντες γλώσσαις   Do all speak with tongues? (*or*
λαλοῦσιν;   All do not speak with tongues,
                                            do they?)

(2) **Μήτι**, used like **μή**, above, occurs less frequently:

Mt 12:23 **μήτι** οὗτός ἐστιν ὁ υἱὸς   Is this the son of David? (*or* This
Δαυίδ;   isn't the son of David, is it?)

Lk 6:39 **μήτι** δύναται τυφλὸς   Can a blind man lead a blind
τυφλὸν ὁδηγεῖν;   man? (A blind man can't lead a
                                            blind man, can he?)

Jn 18:35 **μήτι** ἐγὼ ᾿Ιουδαῖός εἰμι;   Am I a Jew? (I'm not a Jew, am I?
                                            Do you take me for a Jew?)

(3) **Οὐ** (**οὐκ, οὐχ**) and **οὐχί** sometimes introduce questions to which
an *affirmative* answer is expected:

Mt 13:55 **οὐχ** οὗτός ἐστιν ὁ τοῦ   Isn't this the son of the carpenter?
τέκτονος υἱός;   (This is the son of the carpenter,
                                            isn't it?)

Lk 17:17 **οὐχ** οἱ δέκα ἐκαθα-   Were not ten cleansed? (Ten were
ρίσθησαν;   cleansed, weren't they?)

Lk 4:22 **οὐχὶ** υἱός ἐστιν ᾿Ιωσὴφ   Isn't this the son of Joseph? (This
οὗτος;   is Joseph's son, isn't it?)

REMARK 1: **Οὐ** (**οὐκ, οὐχ**) and **οὐχί** need not introduce questions, of
course; especially when they immediately precede the verb in a sentence,
they may be simply negatives. Thus, except for the context, 1 Corinthians
9:1 **οὐκ εἰμὶ ἀπόστολος** might mean

I am not an apostle.

instead of

Am I not an apostle?

REMARK 2: **μή** and **οὐ** occur together (in this order), **μή** introduces the
question and **οὐ** has its ordinary negative force:

Rom 10:18 **μὴ οὐκ** ἤκουσαν;   Have they not heard? (They have
                                            heard, haven't they? *i.e.*, They
                                            haven't " not-heard," have
                                            they?)

(4) The particle **ἄρα** (sometimes accompanied by the particle **γε**)

[230]

introduces a question; it usually indicates impatience or anxiety on the part of the speaker:

Lk 18:8 ἆρα εὑρήσει τὴν πίστιν ἐπὶ τῆς γῆς; — Will he find faith upon the earth?

Acts 8:30 ἆρά γε γινώσκεις . . . — Do you know . . .

Gal 2:17 ἆρα Χριστὸς ἁμαρτίας διάκονος; — Is Christ a minister of sin?

303. Greek has interrogative pronouns, adjectives, and adverbs whose meanings and functions are quite similar to those of English.

(1) **Pronouns.** The interrogative pronoun is τίς, which is declined as follows (note the *accents*, which always appear as given here):

	MASCULINE AND FEMININE	NEUTER
SG.N.	τίς	τί
G.	τίνος	τίνος
D.	τίνι	τίνι
A.	τίνα	τί
PL.N.	τίνες	τίνα
G.	τίνων	τίνων
D.	τίσι(ν)	τίσι(ν)
A.	τίνας	τίνα

These forms correspond to English *who, whom, whose, which, what,* depending on the case, number, and gender of the Greek word to which they refer:

Mt 12:48 τίς ἐστιν ἡ μήτηρ μου, καὶ τίνες εἰσὶν οἱ ἀδελφοί μου; — **Who** is my mother, and **who** are my brothers?

Jn 18:4 τίνα ζητεῖτε; — **Whom** do you seek?

Mt 22:20 τίνος ἡ εἰκὼν αὕτη; — **Whose** is this image?

Mt 11:16 τίνι ὁμοιώσω τὴν γενεὰν ταύτην; — **To what** shall I compare this generation?

Rom 9:30 τί ἐροῦμεν; — **What** shall we say?

Jn 21:12 σὺ τίς εἶ; — **Who** are you?

Τίς usually begins a sentence or clause, but need not do so, as the last example shows.

[231]

(2) **Adjectives**. The pronoun τίς may be used adjectivally, and, in addition, the adjectives **ποῖος**, *which, what kind of,* **πόσος** *how many, how much,* and **πηλίκος**, *how great,* occur in the New Testament.

(a) **Τίς** used adjectivally:

Mt 5:46 **τίνα** μισθὸν ἔχετε;	**What** reward do you have?

(b) **Ποῖος**:

1 Cor 15:35 **ποίῳ** σώματι ἔρχονται;	**With what kind of** body do they come?
Mt 22:36 **ποία** ἐντολὴ μεγάλη ἐν τῷ νόμῳ;	**Which** is the great commandment in the law?

(c) **Πόσος**:

Mt 15:34 **πόσους** ἄρτους ἔχετε;	**How many** loaves have you?
Mk 9:21 **πόσος** χρόνος ἐστίν;	**How long** is it? (=**How much** time is it?)

Note especially:

Mt 7:11 **πόσῳ** μᾶλλον ἡ πατὴρ ὑμῶν . . . δώσει ἀγαθά;	**How much** (=**By how much**) more will your father . . . give good things?

(d) **Πηλίκος**, in the New Testament, occurs only in exclamations:

Gal 6:11 **πηλίκοις** ὑμῖν γράμμασιν ἔγραψα.	**With what large** letters I have written you!

(3) **Adverbs.** There are **ποῦ**; *where?* **πόθεν**; *whence?* **πότε**; *when?* **πῶς**; *how?* **ποσάκις**; *how many times?* and **τί**; *why?*

Jn 8:19 **ποῦ** ἐστιν ὁ πατήρ σου;	**Where** is your father?
Jn 19:9 **πόθεν** εἶ σύ;	**Whence** are you (=**Where** are you **from?**)
Lk 21:7 **πότε** ταῦτα ἔσται;	**When** will these things be?
Mt 17:17 **ἕως πότε** ἔσομαι μεθ' ὑμῶν;	**How long** (=**Until when**) shall I be with you?
Lk 11:18 **πῶς** σταθήσεται ἡ βασιλεία αὐτοῦ	**How** will his kingdom stand?
Mt 18:24 **ποσάκις** ἁμαρτήσει εἰς ἐμὲ ὁ ἀδελφός μου;	**How many times** will my brother sin against me?
Acts 9:4 **τί** με διώκεις;	**Why** are you persecuting me?

REMARK: The context enables us to tell when τί should be rendered *why?* and when it should be rendered *what?* The phrase διὰ τί, *why, on what account*, is unambiguous:

Mt 13:10 διὰ τί ἐν παραβολαῖς λαλεῖς αὐτοῖς;	**Why** do you speak to them in parables?

304. Indirect questions, in English, are introduced by the same interrogatives as are used in direct questions (*who, what, when, where,* etc.) and also by *whether* and *if.* The tense of the verb in an English indirect question depends on the tense of the main verb:

DIRECT QUESTION:	They *asked* him, "*Is* it lawful to heal on the Sabbath?"
INDIRECT QUESTION:	They *asked* him whether it *was* lawful to heal on the Sabbath.

In Greek, indirect questions may also be introduced by the same interrogatives as those used in direct questions and, in addition, by εἰ, *whether, if.* In Greek, however, the tense of the verb in the indirect question is always the same as it would be if the question were direct:

Mt 12:10 ἐπηρώτησαν αὐτὸν . . . εἰ ἔξεστιν τοῖς σάββασιν θεραπεῦσαι.	They asked him **whether it was lawful** to heal on the Sabbath.

Classical Greek made use of special **indirect** interrogative pronouns, adjectives, and adverbs, e.g., ὅστις for τίς, ὅπως for πῶς, and ὁποῖος for ποῖος. These occur (with these meanings) only very rarely in New Testament Greek. A few other types of questions do occur, and these will be considered after the remaining moods of the verb have been discussed.

40 | RELATIVE CLAUSES, I

305. The English form *who* is used in various ways; these are illustrated below:

(a)   *Who* is coming?
(b)   We shall ask them, " *Who* is coming? "
(c)   We shall ask them *who* is coming.
(d)   This is the man *who* is coming.

Sentence (a) is a question, marked as such by the introductory *who* and the special intonation patterns used for such sentences in English (indicated by the symbol [?]). In sentences (b) and (c) sentence (a) reappears; in each it has been transformed from an independent sentence into a dependent constituent (viz., an object[1]). This transformation has been managed in (b) merely by including sentence (a), together with its intonation patterns, within a larger structure; this sort of inclusion is called **direct quotation.** In (c) the inclusion of (a) has involved the alteration of the intonation patterns and might have involved the alteration of some of the forms of the words in (a).[2] This type of inclusion is called **indirect quotation.** In (a), (b) and (c), however, the words *who is coming* express a question, whether directly or indirectly, when they are accompanied by the appropriate intonation patterns. In (d), however, these same words do not express a question; rather they are descriptive of *the man.* The structural difference between the clause *who is coming* as it appears in (c)

---

[1] See §188(3).

[2] If the introductory formula of quotation were in the past tense, the question would have to be altered thus:

We asked them who *was* coming.

[234]

and as it appears in (d) may be seen from its transformational properties. Sentence (c) may be transformed easily into sentence (b), and any indirect question may in similar fashion be transformed into a direct one. Sentence (d), however, cannot be transformed in this way; the clause *who is coming* is not, therefore, an indirect question in (d). Sentence (d) can be represented as equivalent to two sentences:

(d1)   This is the man.
(d2)   The man is coming.

Sentence (d2) is grammatically attached to (d1) by replacing the common term, *the man*, by *who*; in this function *who* is said to be a **relative** pronoun, and the clause it introduces is said to be a **relative** clause.

306. In English, as we have just seen, the form *who* serves to introduce direct questions, indirect questions, and relative clauses. New Testament Greek has two forms corresponding to English *who*: τίς and ὅς. Τίς, as we saw in Lesson 39, is used to introduce direct or indirect questions; ὅς is used to introduce relative clauses.[1]

Accordingly, sentences (a), (b), (c), and (d) would appear in Greek as follows:

(a)   τίς ἔρχεται;

(b)   ἐρωτήσομεν αὐτούς, **τίς** ἔρχεται;

(c)   ἐρωτήσομεν αὐτοὺς **τίς** ἔρχεται.[2]

(d)   οὗτός ἐστιν ὁ ἀνὴρ **ὃς** ἔρχεται.

307. The forms of the relative pronoun ὅς should be carefully distinguished from those of the definite article; note that *no* forms of the relative pronoun begin with τ- and that *all* of them are accented. The relative pronoun is declined as follows:

---

[1] This distinction is almost always maintained in the New Testament. The exceptions are given by Bauer in his discussion of the two forms. The form ὅστις was used to introduce *indirect* questions in classical Greek, but this use is found only once, if at all, in the New Testament. (The interpretation of the passage [Acts 9:6] is disputed.)

[2] The Greek forms of (b) and (c) would, of course, be indistinguishable in MSS which have no punctuation; indirect questions can usually be distinguished by differences in person of the verb or by some introductory form (e.g., εἰ; see §304).

	MASCULINE	FEMININE	NEUTER
SG.N.	ὅς	ἥ	ὅ
G.	οὗ	ἧς	οὗ
D.	ᾧ	ᾗ	ᾧ
A.	ὅν	ἥν	ὅ
PL.N.	οἵ	αἵ	ἅ
G.	ὧν	ὧν	ὧν
D.	οἷς	αἷς	οἷς
A.	οὕς	ἅς	ἅ

308. The forms of ὅς correspond to English *who, whom, whose, which, that,* and *what*; the context determines which English form should be used. The gender and number of a relative pronoun are the same as the gender and number of the noun or pronoun to which the relative pronoun refers; in each of the illustrative sentences below, this noun or pronoun, called the **antecedent** of the relative, is printed in boldface type:

Jn 9:24 ἐφώνησαν τὸν **ἄνθρωπον** . . . **ὅς** ἦν τυφλός.
They called the **man who** was blind.

Lk 12:37 μακάριοι οἱ **δοῦλοι** ἐκεῖνοι, **οὕς** ὁ κύριος ἐλθὼν εὑρήσει γρηγοροῦντας.
Blessed are those **servants whom** the Lord will find watching when he comes.

Mt 17:5 οὗτός ἐστιν ὁ **υἱός** μου ὁ ἀγαπητός, ἐν **ᾧ** εὐδόκησα.
This is my beloved **son, in whom** I am well pleased.

Lk 23:29 μακάριαι . . . αἱ **κοιλίαι αἱ** οὐκ ἐγέννησαν.
Blessed are the **wombs that** have not given birth.

Eph 3:7 διὰ τοῦ **εὐαγγελίου, οὗ** ἐγενήθην διάκονος
through the **gospel, of which** I became a minister

Phil 3:18f . . . τοὺς **ἐχθροὺς** τοῦ σταυροῦ τοῦ Χριστοῦ, **ὧν** τὸ τέλος ἀπώλεια.
. . . the **enemies** of the cross of Christ, **whose** end is destruction.

Jn 4:39 εἶπέν μοι **πάντα ἅ** ἐποίησα.
He told me **everything that** I did.

309. In the passages above, the *case* of the relative pronoun is in each instance determined by the function which it has in the relative clause; usually, however, the case of the relative is assimilated or **"attracted"** to the case of the antecedent, especially if the case of the relative ought, as determined by its function in the relative clause, to be accusative, and if the case of the antecedent is genitive or dative:

Mt 24:50 ἥξει ὁ κύριος . . . ἐν ὥρᾳ ᾗ οὐ γινώσκει.	The Lord will come in an **hour which** he does not know.
Jn 7:39 εἶπεν περὶ τοῦ **πνεύματος** οὗ ἔμελλον λαμβάνειν.	He spoke about the **Spirit which** they were going to receive.
2 Cor 10:8 περὶ τῆς **ἐξουσίας** ἡμῶν ἧς ἔδωκεν ὁ κύριος	concerning our **authority which** the Lord gave

310. The long forms **ὅστις** (= **ὅς**), **ἥτις** (= **ἥ**), **ὅτι** (sometimes printed **ὅ τι** or even **ὅ, τι** [= **ὅ**]), **οἵτινες** (= **οἵ**), **αἵτινες** (= **αἵ**), and **ἅτινα** (= **ἅ**) do not differ in meaning from the short forms indicated as their equivalents;[1] it should be noted, however, that none of these long forms is ever attracted to the case of its antecedent:

Lk 2:10 εὐαγγελίζομαι ὑμῖν **χαρὰν** μεγάλην, **ἥτις** ἔσται παντὶ τῷ λαῷ.	I bring you a gospel of great **joy** (*literally*, I evangelize great joy to you), **which** shall be to all the people.
Rom 9:4 ὑπὲρ τῶν ἀδελφῶν μου . . . **οἵτινές** εἰσιν Ἰσραηλῖται	on behalf of my **brethren** . . . **who** are Israelites
Gal 5:19 τὰ **ἔργα** τῆς σαρκὸς **ἅτινά** ἐστιν πορνεία	the **works** of the flesh, **which** are fornication

311. Relative clauses occasionally precede their antecedents; this order may be altered when translating into English:

Mk 2:45 **ὃς** ἔχει δοθήσεται **αὐτῷ**.	To **him who** has it shall be given.
Mt 13:12 **ὅστις** ἔχει δοθήσεται **αὐτῷ**.	To **him who** has it shall be given.

312. The antecedent of a relative pronoun need not be expressed in Greek; in translating into English, however, it is usual to supply one:

Mk 9:40 **ὃς** οὐκ ἔστιν καθ᾽ ἡμῶν ὑπὲρ ἡμῶν ἐστιν.	**He who** is not against us is for us.
Jn 4:18 **ὃν** ἔχεις οὐκ ἔστιν σου ἀνήρ.	**The one whom** you have is not your husband.
Heb 12:6 **ὃν** ἀγαπᾷ κύριος παιδεύει.	The Lord chastens **the one whom** he loves.

---

[1] These are the only forms of **ὅστις** which occur in the New Testament except for the genitive **ὅτου**; this form occurs only in the phrase **ἕως ὅτου**, *while*.

313. The relative pronoun itself is frequently omitted in English, but it is never omitted in Greek:

> Jn 4:39 εἶπέν μοι **πάντα ἃ** ἐποίησα. He told me **everything** I did
> (=**everything that** I did).

314. When the neuter forms of the Greek relative occur without an expressed antecedent, they may often be rendered by English *what*:

> Mk 13:37 **ὃ** ὑμῖν λέγω πᾶσιν λέγω.   **What** I tell you I tell all.
>
> Jn 11:46 εἶπαν αὐτοῖς **ἃ** ἐποίησεν   They told them **what** Jesus had
> Ἰησοῦς.   done.

In this use the English *what* is sometimes called a "compound relative," as it is equivalent to *that which, those which.*

315. It is obvious that relative clauses express many of the meanings expressed by articular participles (cf. §§219, 221):

> Mt 7:24 πᾶς **ὅστις ἀκούει** μου τοὺς everyone **who hears** these words
> λόγους τούτους   of mine
>
> Mt 7:26 πᾶς **ὁ ἀκούων** μου τοὺς everyone **who hears** these words
> λόγους τούτους   of mine

Many relative clauses can readily be transformed into articular participial constructions:

> ὁ ἀνὴρ **ὃς λέγει** ταῦτα. = ὁ ἀνὴρ **ὁ λέγων** ταῦτα.

However,

> ὁ ἀνὴρ **οὗ** τοὺς λόγους **ἀκούω** . . .,
> ὁ ἀνὴρ **ᾧ ἔδωκα** τὴν ἐντολήν . . .,
> ὁ ἀνὴρ **ὃν εἶδον** . . .

cannot be transformed in this way.

316. Like participles, both anarthrous and articular, relative clauses may express various shades of meaning. Thus, in Romans 6:2 the relative clause may be held to express cause:

> Rom 6:2 **οἵτινες** ἀπεθάνομεν τῇ **Because** we have died to sin, how
> ἁμαρτίᾳ, πῶς ἔτι ζήσομεν ἐν αὐτῇ; shall we still live in it?

Relative clauses with the future indicative may express purpose:

Mt 21:41 τὸν ἀμπελῶνα ἐκδώσεται
ἄλλοις γεωργοῖς, **οἵτινες**
ἀποδώσουσιν αὐτῷ τοὺς καρπούς.

He will let out the vineyard to
other husbandmen **so that** they
will render him the fruits.

However, both these clauses may be merely descriptive; any other meanings such clauses may express must be inferred from the context.

317. Other Relatives. In addition to the relative pronouns ὅς and ὅστις, Greek has relative adjectives (sometimes used substantively, i.e., as pronouns) and relative adverbs. When these introduce relative clauses, the relative adjectives have adjectives as antecedents (unless, of course, they are being used substantively), and the relative adverbs have adverbs as antecedents; relative adverbs, however, frequently have as antecedents nouns indicating place or time. In all cases antecedents may be omitted (as with the relative pronouns), but may be inferred from the context.

   (1) **Οἷος, α, ον**, *such as, as*:

Mk 9:3 τὰ ἱμάτια αὐτοῦ ἐγένετο
στίλβοντα, **λευκὰ** λίαν, **οἷα**
γναφεὺς ἐπὶ τῆς γῆς οὐ δύναται
οὕτως λευκᾶναι.

His garments became glistening,
very **white, such as** no fuller
on earth could so bleach them.

Rev 16:18 σεισμὸς ἐγένετο **μέγας**
οἷος οὐκ ἐγένετο . . .

There was a **great** earthquake,
such as had not been . . .

Οἷος is frequently correlated with **τοιοῦτος**, *so, such*:

1 Cor 15:48 **οἷος** ὁ χοϊκὸς **τοιοῦτοι**
καὶ οἱ χοϊκοί

As was the man of dust, **so** are
those who are of dust.

2 Cor 10:11 **οἷοί** ἐσμεν τῷ λόγῳ δι'
ἐπιστολῶν ἀπόντες, **τοιοῦτοι** καὶ
παρόντες τῷ ἔργῳ.

Such as we are in word, through
letters, when absent, **so** we are
also in deed, when present.

   (2) **Ὅσος, η, ον**, *as much as, as many as, (all) who, (all) which, (all) that*:

Mt 17:12 ἐποίησαν ἐν αὐτῷ **ὅσα**
ἠθέλησαν.

They did with him **all that**
(= **as many things as**) they
wished.

Ὅσος is sometimes correlated with **τοσοῦτος**, *so much, so many*:

Heb 10:25 . . . **τοσούτῳ** μᾶλλον
ὅσῳ βλέπετε ἐγγίζουσαν τὴν
ἡμέραν.

. . . **so much** the more **as** you
see the day approaching.

(3) Ὅπου, *where*:

> Jn 12:1 ἦλθεν εἰς **Βηθανίαν ὅπου**   He came into **Bethany where**
> ἦν Λάζαρος.   Lazarus was.

Ὅπου is sometimes correlated with ἐκεῖ, *there*:

> Mt 6:21 **ὅπου** ἐστὶν ὁ θησαυρός σου,   **Where** your treasure is, **there**
> **ἐκεῖ** ἔσται ἡ καρδία σου.   your heart will be.

(4) Οὗ, **where**; synonymous with ὅπου:

> Lk 24:28 ἤγγισαν εἰς τὴν **κώμην οὗ**   They drew near to the **village**
> ἐπορεύοντο.   **where** they were going.

(5) Ὡς, *as, like*:

> Mt 17:2 ἔλαμψεν τὸ πρόσωπον   His face shone **like** the sun (*i.e.,*
> αὐτοῦ **ὡς** ὁ ἥλιος.   His face shone **brightly as** the
>   sun).

Ὡς is sometimes correlated with οὕτως, *thus, so*:

> 1 Cor 9:26 **οὕτως** τρέχω, **ὡς** οὐκ   **Thus** I run, not **as** aimlessly;
> ἀδήλως, **οὕτως** πυκτεύω **ὡς** οὐκ   **thus** I box, not **as** one beating
> ἀέρα δέρων.   the air.

(6) Ὅτε, *when*:

> Jn 16:25 ἔρχεται **ὥρα ὅτε** οὐκέτι ἐν   An **hour** is coming **when** I shall
> παροιμίαις λαλήσω ὑμῖν.   no longer speak to you in figures.

Ὅτε is sometimes correlated with τότε, *then*:

> Mt 13:26 **ὅτε** ἐβλάστησεν ὁ χόρτος   **When** the grass came up . . .
> . . . **τότε** ἐφάνη τὰ ζιζάνια   **then** the weeds appeared.

(7) Ὅθεν, *whence, from where*:

> Lk 11:24 ὑποστρέψω εἰς τὸν **οἶκον**   I shall return into the **house**
> **ὅθεν** ἐξῆλθον.   **whence** I came out.

41 | COORDINATING CONJUNCTIONS

318. A **conjunction** is an uninflected word which serves to connect other words or larger syntactic units in certain special ways which will be described in this lesson. Conjunctions are of two types, **coordinating** and **subordinating**.

(1) **Coordinating conjunctions** connect syntactic units with other syntactic units of the same grammatical type, i.e., substantive to substantive, adjective to adjective, verb to verb, phrase to phrase, clause to clause, etc. The construction formed in this way can have the same grammatical function as either of the constituents joined by the conjuntion could have alone. A few English examples will be given by way of illustration:

(a)   The boy washed the dishes.
(b)   The girl dried the silverware.

In each of these two sentences we have the familiar structure S — V — O, where S and O in each are nouns (each with the definite article) and where V in each is a transitive verb. These constituents may be joined by coordinating conjunctions in a number of ways:

(c)   The <u>boy and girl</u> washed the dishes.

Here the two nouns, *boy* and *girl*, are joined by the conjunction *and*; the resulting coordination has the article *the*, just as each of the two nouns had in (a) and (b), and the construction *the boy and girl* functions as the subject of the sentence.

(d)   <u>The boy and the girl</u> washed the dishes.

Here there is a slight difference: the constructions *the boy* and *the girl* are the grammatically similar constituents joined by *and*, and the resulting coordination of these functions as subject, just as each did in (a) and (b), respectively.

(e)   The girl washed and dried the dishes.

Here the two verbs are coordinated and together function as a single verb, having one subject (*the girl*) and one object (*the dishes*).

(f)   The boy washed the dishes and the silverware.

Here the two objects are coordinated.

(g)   The boy and the girl washed and dried the dishes and silverware.

Here there are three coordinations, but the structure of the sentence is the same as that of (a) and (b), i.e., S — V — O, only here

$$S = (t - N_1) + (t - N_2)$$
$$V = (V_1 + V_2)$$
$$O = t - (N_3 + N_4)$$

where t stands for the article *the* and where the plus stands for the co-ordinating conjunction *and.*

(h)   The boy washed the dishes and the girl dried the silverware.

Here the two original sentences, (a) and (b), are coordinated, forming a "compound" sentence.

Some coordinating conjunctions serve to join grammatical elements of any kind to other grammatical elements of the same kind, i.e., noun to noun, verb to verb, preposition to preposition, etc.; the most common English coordinating conjunctions of this type are *and* and *or.* Other coordinating conjunctions serve principally to join clauses to other clauses; some English conjunctions of this type are *but, however, yet, accordingly, nevertheless.*

(2) **Subordinating conjunctions** connect clauses to other clauses in such a way that one (the one introduced by the conjunction) functions as a subordinate constituent of the other, e.g., as its subject or object, an adjectival modifier of its subject or object, an adverbial modifier of its verb, etc.[1] Some English subordinating conjunctions are *if, because, since, although,* and *unless.*

---

[1] The relative pronouns, adjectives, and adverbs studied in Lesson 40 also have the func- tion of making one clause serve as a subordinate constituent of another. The relative pronouns, adjectives, and adverbs differ from conjunctions, however, for a relative word has a grammatical function of its own *within* its clause (i.e., it may be the subject or

EXAMPLE

(a)   The boy washed the dishes *after* the girl dried them.

The subordinating conjunction *after* makes the clause it introduces serve as an adverbial modifier.

319. Conjunctions in Greek are quite similar in their functions to those of English, but certain differences should be noticed: (1) Greek coordinating conjunctions do not necessarily stand *between* the elements they connect; (2) some Greek subordinating conjunctions are, always or under certain circumstances, followed by other moods than the indicative. (In the present lesson we shall consider only those which are followed by the indicative, for convenience.)

320. Greek Coordinating Conjunctions. (1) The most important Greek coordinating conjunctions which may join any kind of grammatical element to another element of the same kind are **καί**, **τε**, **ἤ**, **ἀλλά**, **οὔτε**, and **μήτε**.

(a) The meaning of **καί** is usually given simply as *and*, but under certain circumstances it may mean *both*, *also*, *too*, or *even*, and occasionally it may be rendered in still other ways.

(i) When **καί** is a coordinating conjunction, it stands between grammatical units of the same type, and means *and*:

(α) Connecting words:

Mt 13:55 Ἰάκωβος **καὶ** Ἰωσὴφ **καὶ** Σίμων **καὶ** Ἰούδας

James **and** Joseph **and** Simon **and** Judas

Rom 7:12 ἡ ἐντολὴ ἁγία **καὶ** δικαία **καὶ** ἀγαθή.

The commandment is holy **and** just **and** good.

Heb 1:1 πολυμερῶς **καὶ** πολυτρόπως

in many ways **and** in various ways

(β) Connecting clauses:

Jn 1:1 ἐν ἀρχῇ ἦν ὁ λόγος, **καὶ** ὁ λόγος ἦν πρὸς τὸν θεόν, **καὶ** θεὸς ἦν ὁ λόγος.

In the beginning was the Word, **and** the Word was with God, **and** the Word was God.

object of the clause, or may be an adjectival or adverbial modifier within the clause), whereas a conjunction (though counted as part of the clause it introduces) serves merely as a connector.

(ii) When **καί** occurs before two grammatical elements which are coordinated by a second **καί**, it may be translated *both* (if the context permits):

Mk 4:41 **καὶ** ὁ ἄνεμος **καὶ** ἡ θάλασσα	**both** the wind **and** the sea

(iii) When **καί** is *not* a coordinating conjunction, i.e., when it does not stand between two grammatical elements of the same type, it is an adverb with the meaning *also*, *too*, or *even* (the context will indicate which of these meanings is most satisfactory):

Mt 26:73 ἀληθῶς **καὶ** σὺ ἐξ αὐτῶν εἶ.	Certainly you **also** are one of them.

(**'Αληθῶς** and **σύ** are not of the same grammatical type, nor are **ἀληθῶς** and the construction following **καί** of the same type.)

Mt 5:46 οὐχὶ **καὶ** οἱ τελῶναι τὸ αὐτὸ ποιοῦσιν;	Do not **even** the tax collectors do the same?

(**Οὐχί** is not coordinate with all or part of the constituents following **καί**.)

Mt 6:21 ἐκεῖ ἔσται **καὶ** ἡ καρδία σου.	Your heart will be there **too**.

(b) **Τε** is peculiar, from the point of view of English, in that it does not stand *between* the two syntactic units it serves to join but *after* the second one. It is much less common than **καί**.

(i) Its usual meaning is *and*:

(α) Connecting words or phrases:

1 Cor 4:21 ἐν ἀγάπῃ πνεύματί **τε** πραΰτητος	in love **and** a spirit of gentleness

(β) Connecting clauses:

Acts 21:20 ἐδόξαζον τὸν θεόν, εἶπάν **τε** αὐτῷ . . .	They glorified God, **and** they said to him . . .

(ii) **Τε** . . . **τε** . . ., like **καί** . . . **καί** . . ., means *both . . . and* (or *not only . . . but also . . .*):

Rom 1:26f αἵ[1] **τε** θήλειαι αὐτῶν . . . : ὁμοίως **τε** οἱ ἄρσενες	**both** their females . . . **and** the males

---

[1] The article has an accent when it is followed by **τε**. See Appendix I.

(iii) **Τε . . . καί . . .** or **τε καί** has similar meanings:

Acts 5:24 ὅ τε στρατηγὸς τοῦ ἱεροῦ **καὶ** οἱ ἀρχιερεῖς	**both** the captain of the temple **and** the chief priests
Acts 1:1 ποιεῖν **τε καὶ** διδάσκειν	**both** to do **and** to teach

(c) **Ἤ** as a coordinating conjunction means *or*, but in comparisons means *than*:

    (i) As a conjunction:

        (α) Connecting words:

Mt 17:25 λαμβάνουσιν τέλη **ἤ** κῆνσον.	They receive taxes **or** tribute.

        (β) Connecting clauses:

1 Cor 1:13 μὴ Παῦλος ἐσταυρώθη ὑπὲρ ὑμῶν, **ἤ** εἰς τὸ ὄνομα Παύλου ἐβαπτίσθητε;	Was Paul crucified for you, **or** were you baptized in the name of Paul?

    (ii) **Ἤ . . . ἤ . . . (ἤ . . .)** means *either . . . or . . . (or . . .)*:

1 Cor 14:6 **ἤ** ἐν ἀποκαλύψει **ἤ** ἐν γνώσει **ἤ** ἐν προφητείᾳ **ἤ** διδαχῇ	**either** by revelation **or** by knowledge **or** by prophecy **or** by teaching

    (iii) In comparisons **ἤ** means *than* (see §§159, 276(1)):

1 Cor 7:9 κρεῖττόν ἐστιν γαμεῖν **ἤ** πυροῦσθαι.	It is better to marry **than** to burn.

(d) **Ἀλλά** indicates a contrast or difference between the two elements it connects; it usually corresponds to English *but*, but when connecting clauses or introducing sentences it may sometimes best be rendered by *however, yet, nevertheless*:

    (i) When **ἀλλά** connects words or phrases, the first is often preceded by a negative:

1 Cor 7:10 οὐκ ἐγὼ **ἀλλὰ** ὁ κύριος	not I, **but** the Lord
1 Cor 12:14 οὐκ ἔστιν ἓν μέλος **ἀλλὰ** πολλά.	It is not one member **but** many.

    (ii) Connecting clauses:

Jn 16:20 ὑμεῖς λυπηθήσεσθε, **ἀλλ'** ἡ λύπη ὑμῶν εἰς χαρὰν γενήσεται.	You will be sorrowful, **but** your sorrow will turn into joy.

(iii) **Οὐ μόνον . . . ἀλλὰ καί . . .** means *not only . . . but also* (or *but even*) . . . :

2 Cor 8:21 οὐ μόνον ἐνώπιον κυρίου **ἀλλὰ καὶ** ἐνώπιον ἀνθρώπων	**not only** in the sight of the Lord, **but even** in the sight of men

(e) **Οὔτε** (in clauses with verbs in the indicative) and **μήτε** (with other moods) means *nor*; **οὔτε . . . οὔτε . . . (μήτε . . . μήτε . . .)** means *neither . . . nor . . .* :

Rom 8:38 **οὔτε** θάνατος **οὔτε** ζωὴ **οὔτε** ἄγγελοι **οὔτε** ἀρχαί . . .	**neither** death **nor** life **nor** angels **nor** principalities . . .
Mt 11:18 ἦλθεν γάρ Ἰωάννης **μήτε** ἐσθίων **μήτε** πίνων . . .	For John came **neither** eating **nor** drinking . . .

(2) The most important Greek coordinating conjunctions which serve to join clauses or to indicate the connection of sentences with preceding sentences are **γάρ, δέ, οὖν, ἄρα, οὐδέ**, and **μηδέ**. **Γάρ, δέ**, and **οὖν** are unlike English conjunctions in that they never come first in the clauses they introduce; they usually have second place, but may come still later.

(a) **Γάρ**, *for*:
(i) Alone:

Mk 16:8 . . . ἐφοβοῦντο **γάρ**.	. . . **for** they were afraid.
2 Cor 9:7 . . . ἱλαρὸν **γὰρ** δότην ἀγαπᾷ ὁ θεός.	. . . **for** God loves a cheerful giver.

(ii) When **γάρ** occurs in combination with other conjunctions or adverbs, each usually has the meaning it would have separately. Thus,

Mt 8:9 **καὶ γὰρ** ἐγὼ ἄνθρωπός εἰμι ὑπὸ ἐξουσίαν.	**For** I **too** am a man under authority.
2 Cor 2:9 . . . εἰς τοῦτο **γὰρ καὶ** ἔγραψα.	. . . **for** to this end I **also** wrote.

However, **καὶ γάρ** may mean simply *for*:

Jn 4:23 . . . **καὶ γὰρ** ὁ πατὴρ τοιούτους ζητεῖ . . .	. . . **for** the Father seeks such . . .

(b) When **δέ** connects clauses between which some contrast is implied, it should be rendered *but* (*yet, however*); when there is no contrast, it should usually be rendered simply by *and*. Sometimes **δέ** is purely

transitional; in such cases it may be rendered *now*, *then*, or simply ignored.
  (i) **Δέ** used alone:

1 Cor 15:51 πάντες οὐ κοιμη-θησόμεθα, πάντες **δὲ** ἀλλα-γησόμεθα.	We shall not all sleep, **but** we shall all be changed.
Mt 1:2 Ἀβραὰμ ἐγέννησε τὸν Ἰσαάκ, Ἰσαὰκ **δὲ** ἐγέννησεν τὸν Ἰακώβ, . . .	Abraham begat Isaac, **and** Isaac begat Jacob, . . .
Mt 1:18 τοῦ **δὲ** Ἰησοῦ Χριστοῦ ἡ γένεσις οὕτως ἦν.	**Now** the birth of Jesus Christ was thus.

  (ii) **Δέ** in combination with other conjunctions and adverbs:
    (α) **Δὲ καί**, *but also*; *but even*, *and also*, *and even*:

Jn 3:23 ἦν **δὲ καὶ** Ἰωάννης βαπτίζων.	**And** John was **also** baptizing.

  (β) **Μέν . . . δέ . . . .** When **δέ** is used to indicate a contrast between two syntactic elements, the first element is frequently indicated by **μέν**, which, like **δέ**, never comes first in its clause. The combination **μέν . . . δέ . . .** may sometimes be rendered by *on the one hand . . . on the other . . .*, but this is usually much too emphatic; it is usually best to leave **μέν** untranslated; it simply adds emphasis to the first member of a contrast, and such emphasis is usually indicated in English only by stress (i.e., in the spoken language):

Mt 3:11 ἐγὼ **μὲν** ὑμᾶς βαπτίζω ἐν ὕδατι . . . ὁ **δὲ** ὀπίσω μου ἐρχόμενος . . .	I baptize you with water . . . **but** he who comes after me . . . [The *I* should be stressed in spoken English.]

  (γ) Certain important constructions involving **μέν . . . δέ . . .** may be considered together:

    ὁ μέν . . . ὁ δέ . . ., *the one . . . the other . . .*
    οἱ μέν . . . οἱ δέ . . ., *some . . . others . . .*

Substantives need not occur with the articles in the expressions above; i.e., the articles in these combinations may function as pronouns. Similarly, we find

    οἱ μέν . . . ἄλλοι δέ . . . ἕτεροι δέ . . ., *some . . . others . . . others . . .*
    ὃς μέν . . . ὃς δέ . . ., *the one . . . the other . . .*

Gal 4:23 ὁ μὲν ἐκ τῆς παιδίσκης . . . ὁ δὲ ἐκ τῆς ἐλευθέρας	**the one** from the slave woman . . . **the other** from the free woman
Acts 17:32 οἱ μὲν ἐχλεύαζον, οἱ δὲ εἶπον . . .	**Some** mocked, **but others** said . . . [The context demands the retention of *but*.]
Mt 16:14 οἱ μὲν Ἰωάννην τὴν βαπτιστήν, **ἄλλοι δὲ** Ἠλίαν, **ἕτεροι δὲ** Ἰερεμίαν.	**Some** [say] John the Baptist, **others** Elijah, **others** Jeremiah.
1 Cor 11:21 ὃς μὲν πεινᾷ, ὃς δὲ μεθύει.	**The one** is hungry, **the other** is drunk.
Mt 25:15 ᾧ μὲν ἔδωκεν πέντε τάλαντα ᾧ δὲ δύο ᾧ δὲ ἕν.	To **one** he gave five talents, to **another** two and to **the other** one.

(δ) **Μέν** sometimes occurs without **δέ**, introducing an implied contrast or a contrast which is actually indicated, but not by **δέ**:

1 Th 2:18 ἠθελήσαμεν ἐλθεῖν πρὸς ὑμᾶς, ἐγὼ **μὲν** Παῦλος.	We wanted to come to you— I, Paul, did (*i.e.*, more than others *or* especially).
Jn 11:6 τότε **μὲν** ἔμεινεν ἐν ᾧ ἦν τόπῳ δύο ἡμέρας. ἔπειτα . . .	Then he stayed in the place where he was for two days; afterward . . .

(Ordinarily, **δέ** would be expected to follow **ἔπειτα**.)

Μέν is also frequently followed by **οὖν**, and when so followed often occurs without **δέ**. See below.

(c) **Οὖν** occurs either alone or together with other conjunctions or adverbs.

(i) Alone it introduces a sentence expressing the consequence of or inference from what has gone before, or it may indicate a transition to a new subject; it thus corresponds to English *so, then, therefore, consequently, accordingly, now, next*.

Mt 1:17 πᾶσαι **οὖν** αἱ γενεαὶ ἀπὸ Ἀβραὰμ ἕως Δαυὶδ γενεαὶ δεκατέσσαρες.	**So** all the generations from Abraham until David are fourteen generations. [This sentence follows the "begats" of Mt 1: 2–16.]
Mt 17:10 τί **οὖν**;	Why, **then**?

(ii) With other conjunctions and adverbs:

(α) **Ἄρα οὖν** means *so then, so therefore* (see below for **ἄρα**):

Rom 8:12 **ἄρα οὖν**, ἀδελφοί, ὀφει-   **So, therefore**, brethren, we are
λέται ἐσμέν, οὐ τῇ σαρκί . . .   debtors, not to the flesh . . .

(β) **Μὲν οὖν** indicates continuity; it may be rendered *so*:

Acts 9:31 ἡ **μὲν οὖν** ἐκκλησία   **So** the church had peace.
. . . εἶχεν εἰρήνην.

Μενοῦν (written as one word) and **μενοῦνγε** may occur at the beginning
of a clause; they add emphasis:

Rom 9:20 **μενοῦνγε** σὺ τίς εἶ;   Who are **you**? [With stress on *you*]
   Who **on earth** are you?

(d) **Ἄρα** may, but need not, stand at the beginning of a clause; it
is not to be confused with the interrogative **ἆρα** (see §302(4)); in general
it is synonymous with **οὖν**, but does not occur as frequently:

(i) Alone:

Mt 12:28 **ἄρα** ἔφθασεν ἐφ' ὑμᾶς ἡ   **Then** the kingdom of God has come
βασιλεία τοῦ θεοῦ.   upon you.

Mk 4:41 τίς **ἄρα** οὗτός ἐστιν;   Who is this, **then**?

(ii) Strengthened with **γε**:

Mt 17:26 **ἄραγε** ἐλεύθεροί εἰσιν οἱ   **Therefore** the sons are free.
υἱοί.

(iii) For **ἄρα οὖν**, see above (2c iiα).

(e) **Οὐδέ** (in clauses with a verb in the indicative) and **μηδέ** (in
clauses with verbs in other moods):

(i) Alone, as conjunctions, **οὐδέ** and **μηδέ** mean *nor, and not*;
neither:

Mt 6:28 οὐ κοπιᾷ **οὐδὲ** νήθει.   They [=τὰ κρίνα, *the lilies*] toil
   not, **neither** do they spin.

2 Cor 4:2 . . . μὴ περιπατοῦντες   . . . not walking in cunning **nor**
ἐν πανουργίᾳ **μηδὲ** δολοῦντες τὸν   falsifying the word of God.
λόγον τοῦ θεοῦ.

(ii) Alone, not as conjunctions (cf. **καί** (1a iii), above), **οὐδέ** and
μηδέ mean *not even*:

Lk 7:9 **οὐδὲ** ἐν τῷ Ἰσραὴλ τοσαύτην   **Not even** in Israel have I found
πίστιν εὖρον.   such faith.

(iii) **Οὐδέ . . . οὐδέ . . . (μηδέ . . . μηδέ . . .)** corresponds to
English *neither . . . nor . . .*:

Gal 1:12 . . . **οὐδὲ** γὰρ ἐγὼ παρὰ   . . . for I **neither** received it from
ἀνθρώπου παρέλαβον αὐτὸ **οὐδὲ**   man **nor** was I taught it.
ἐδιδάχθην.

42 | SUBORDINATING CONJUNCTIONS, I

321. Subordinating conjunctions may be divided into two groups: those which are always (or almost always) followed by the indicative mood and those which are always (or almost always) followed by the subjunctive mood. A consideration of the second group is postponed to Lesson 45. The most important subordinating conjunctions of the first group are ὅτι, διότι, ὡς, καθώς, ὥσπερ, καθάπερ, ἐπεί, ἐπειδή, ἕως, ὥστε, and εἰ (εἰ will also be discussed in Lesson 45).

(1) Ὅτι is the most common subordinating conjunction;[1] depending upon its context, it means *that* (unstressed) or *because*:

(a) Ὅτι means *that* when the clause it introduces has the function of a substantive; it is especially common as a means of introducing indirect discourse:

> Phm 22 . . . ἐλπίζω γὰρ **ὅτι** διὰ τῶν προσευχῶν ὑμῶν χαρισθήσομαι ὑμῖν.
>
> . . . for I hope **that** through your prayers I shall be granted to you.

> Mt 16:18 κἀγὼ [= καὶ ἐγώ] δέ σοι λέγω **ὅτι** σὺ εἶ Πέτρος, καὶ ἐπὶ ταύτῃ τῇ πέτρᾳ οἰκοδομήσω μου τὴν ἐκκλησίαν.
>
> But I say to you also **that** you are Peter, and upon this rock I will build my church.

(b) Ὅτι means *because* when the clause it introduces cannot have a substantive function and, therefore, must be adverbial:

> Mt 20:15 ὁ ὀφθαλμός σου πονηρός ἐστιν **ὅτι** ἐγὼ ἀγαθός εἰμι;
>
> Is your eye evil **because** I am good?

(c) Ὅτι sometimes introduces *direct* discourse; when it does, it should

---

[1] It is identical in form with the neuter of the relative pronoun ὅστις; however, as a conjunction it has no antecedent.

not be translated, but merely represented by quotation marks (**ὅτι**, in this use, is roughly equivalent to English *quote* as used by some speakers to indicate the fact that they are about to begin a quotation).

Mk 1:37 καὶ λέγουσιν αὐτῷ **ὅτι** πάντες ζητοῦσίν σε.	And they said to him, [*quote,*] " Everyone is looking for you."

(2) **Διότι** usually means *because, for,* but if the context permits, it may be rendered by *therefore*:

1 Cor 15:9 ἐγὼ γάρ εἰμι ὁ ἐλάχιστος τῶν ἀποστόλων . . . **διότι** ἐδίωξα τὴν ἐκκλησίαν τοῦ θεοῦ.	For I am the least of the apostles, . . . **because** I persecuted the church of God.
Acts 20:26 **διότι** μαρτύρομαι ὑμῖν . . . ὅτι καθαρός εἰμι τοῦ αἵματος πάντων.	**Therefore** I testify to you . . . that I am innocent of the blood of everyone.

Διότι occurs much less frequently than **ὅτι**, for which it is in many respects a synonym.[1]

(3) **Ὡς**, *as,* and **καθώς**, **ὥσπερ**, and **καθάπερ**, (*just*) *as,* are used like their English equivalents; **ὡς** and **καθώς** are much more common than the others.

  (a) **Ὡς**:[2]

Lk 5:4 **ὡς** δὲ ἐπαύσατο λαλῶν, εἶπεν πρὸς Σίμωνα . . .	And **as** he stopped speaking, he said to Simon . . .

Notice that **ὡς** frequently has the meaning *while, when* (as does English *as*):

Lk 24:32 οὐχὶ ἡ καρδία ἡμῶν καιομένη ἦν ἐν ἡμῖν, **ὡς** ἐλάλει ἡμῖν ἐν τῇ ὁδῷ;	Was not our heart burning within us **as** he spoke to us on the way?
Lk 1:41 **ὡς** ἤκουσεν ἡ Ἐλισάβετ . . . ἐσκίρτησεν τὸ βρέφος . . .	**As** Elisabeth heard . . . the babe leaped . . .

---

[1] **Διότι** may also mean *that*, but this meaning is not required in the New Testament except possibly at Romans 8:21, where **ὅτι** may be the correct reading.

[2] See §317(5) for **ὡς** functioning as a relative adverb; the two functions are quite similar and are differently distinguished by different writers; it is simplest to call **ὡς** a relative adverb when it has a clearly identifiable antecedent. The distinction is, indeed, one which can be safely ignored unless one is writing a lexicon or a grammar.

(b) **Καθώς**:

Jn 5:30 **καθὼς** ἀκούω, κρίνω.
As I hear, I judge.

1 Jn 3:2 ὀψόμεθα αὐτὸν **καθώς** ἐστιν.
We shall see him **as** he is.

(c) **῞Ωσπερ**:

Rev 10:3 ἔκραξεν φωνῇ μεγάλῃ **ὥσπερ** λέων μυκᾶται.
He cried out with a loud voice, **as** a lion roars.

(d) **Καθάπερ**:

1 Cor 12:12 **καθάπερ** γὰρ τὸ σῶμα ἕν ἐστιν, καὶ μέλη πολλὰ ἔχει, πάντα δὲ τὰ μέλη τοῦ σώματος πολλὰ ὄντα ἕν ἐστιν σῶμα, οὕτως καὶ ὁ Χριστός.
For **as** the body is one and has many members, and all the members of the body, being many, are one body, so also is Christ.

Like **ὡς**, the conjunctions **καθώς**, **ὥσπερ**, and **καθάπερ** are sometimes correlated with adverbs (e.g., **καθάπερ** with **οὕτως** in 1 Corinthians 12:12, above) and may be regarded as relative adverbs themselves when they have assignable functions within the clauses they introduce (see §318(2), fn. 1).

(4) **'Επεί** and **ἐπειδή** correspond to English *since* (usually not in a temporal sense), *because*:

Lk 1:34 πῶς ἔσται τοῦτο **ἐπεὶ** ἄνδρα οὐ γινώσκω;
How shall this be, **since** I do not know a man?

1 Cor 15:21 **ἐπειδὴ** γὰρ δι' ἀνθρώπου θάνατος, καὶ δι' ἀνθρώπου ἀνάστασις νεκρῶν.
For **since** by man [came] death, by man [came] also the resurrection of the dead.

(5) **῞Εως**, *until, while*; the combination **ἕως ὅτου** has the same meanings; both **ἕως** and and **ἕως ὅτου** also occur with the subjunctive (see Lesson 45):

Mt 24:39 **ἕως** ἦλθεν ὁ κατακλυσμός
until the flood came

Jn 9:4 **ἕως** ἡμέρα ἐστίν
while it is day

Jn 9:18 οὐκ ἐπίστευσαν οὖν οἱ 'Ιουδαῖοι . . . **ἕως ὅτου** ἐφώνησαν τοὺς γονεῖς αὐτοῦ.
The Jews, therefore, did not believe . . . **until** they called his parents.

Mt 5:25 . . . **ἕως ὅτου** εἶ μετ' αὐτοῦ ἐν τῇ ὁδῷ.
. . . **while** you are with him in the way.

(6) "Ὥστε, *so that* (also used with infinitives; see §259(4)); again, if the context permits, it may mean *therefore*:

Jn 3:16 οὕτως γὰρ ἠγάπησεν ὁ θεὸς τὸν κόσμον, **ὥστε** τὸν υἱὸν τὸν μονογενῆ ἔδωκεν.

For God loved the world thus, **so that** he gave his only Son (*or, possibly*, For God thus loved the world; **therefore** he gave. . .).

Mk 2:28 **ὥστε** κύριός ἐστιν ὁ υἱὸς τοῦ ἀνθρώπου καὶ τοῦ σαββάτου.

Therefore the Son of man is lord of the Sabbath also.

43 | THE IMPERATIVE MOOD

322. Commands and requests are usually expressed in English and Greek by means of special verb forms; these verb forms are called **imperative** or are said to be "in" or "of" the **imperative mood.**[1] The imperative form of a verb, in English, is identical with its dictionary form:[2]

> *Proceed* at once.
> *Go* away.
> *Be* quiet.

Apart from forms like these, the only other English imperatives are compound or periphrastic forms:

> PASSIVE IMPERATIVE: *Be prepared.*
> PROGRESSIVE IMPERATIVE: *Keep moving.*
> *Be thinking* about it.

The force of the imperative may be softened by the addition of *please*:

> *Please* go away.
> Be quiet, *please.*

323. It may be seen from the examples cited that the English imperative has but one tense, the present; however, in certain contexts it may refer to the future:

> *Come* over tomorrow.[3]

---

[1] Commands and requests may be expressed in other ways, however; a verb form which expresses a command or a request need not be in the imperative mood, e.g.,

> *No smoking.*

[2] See §89.

[3] Some writers on English grammar refer to the construction found in

> Thou *shalt* not *covet.*

as a "future imperative," but it is simpler to regard it as a construction involving a special use of the auxiliary *shall.*

Another characteristic of the English imperative is that its forms need have no subject expressed; when a subject is expressed, it receives special stress or occupies a special position:

> *You* go away!
> Be quiet, *you*!

Whether the subject is expressed or not, it always, in English, denotes the person addressed (i.e., the second person, singular or plural).

324. This brief discussion of the English imperative mood should be borne in mind as the Greek imperative is studied, so that the two may be profitably compared and contrasted. The imperative forms of the model verb **λύω**, *free, set free, loose*, are presented in the right-hand columns in the following examples; each is given in a complete, though brief, sentence, so that at least some of the syntactic characteristics may be noted. To facilitate comparative and contrastive study even further, syntactically parallel sentences with verbs in the *indicative* mood have been given in the left-hand columns; English equivalents are indicated throughout.

(1)

		PRESENT ACTIVE INDICATIVE	PRESENT ACTIVE IMPERATIVE
SG.2		**λύεις** τοὺς δεσμίους. **You are freeing** the prisoners.	**λῦε** τοὺς δεσμίους. **Free** the prisoners! **Keep freeing** the prisoners!
	3	**λύει** τοὺς δεσμίους. **He is freeing** the prisoners.	**λυέτω** τοὺς δεσμίους. **Let him free** the prisoners! **Let him keep freeing** the prisoners!
PL.2		**λύετε** τοὺς δεσμίους. **You are freeing** the prisoners.	**λύετε** τοὺς δεσμίους. **Free** the prisoners! **Keep freeing** the prisoners!
	3	**λύουσιν** τοὺς δεσμίους. **They are freeing** the prisoners.	**λυέτωσαν** τοὺς δεσμίους. **Let them free** the prisoners! **Let them keep freeing** the prisoners.

(2)

		AORIST ACTIVE INDICATIVE	AORIST ACTIVE IMPERATIVE
SG.2		**ἔλυσας** τοὺς δεσμίους. **You freed** the prisoners.	**λῦσον** τοὺς δεσμίους. **Free** the prisoners! **Start freeing** the prisoners!

3 ἔλυσεν τοὺς δεσμίους.
He **freed** the prisoners.

λυσάτω τοὺς δεσμίους.
Let him **free** the prisoners! **Let** him **start freeing** the prisoners.

PL.2 ἐλύσατε τοὺς δεσμίους.
You **freed** the prisoners.

λύσατε τοὺς δεσμίους.
Free the prisoners! **Start freeing** the prisoners!

3 ἔλυσαν τοὺς δεσμίους.
They **freed** the prisoners.

λυσάτωσαν τοὺς δεσμίους.
Let them **free** the prisoners! **Let** them **start freeing** the prisoners!

(3) PRESENT MIDDLE INDICATIVE

PRESENT MIDDLE IMPERATIVE

SG.2 λύῃ τοὺς δεσμίους.
You **are having** the prisoners **set free.**

λύου τοὺς δεσμίους.
Have the prisoners **set free**! **Keep having** the prisoners **set free**!

3 λύεται τοὺς δεσμίους.
He **is having** the prisoners **set free.**

λυέσθω τοὺς δεσμίους.
Let him **have** the prisoners **set free**! **Let** him **keep having** the prisoners **set free**!

PL.2 λύεσθε τοὺς δεσμίους.
You **are having** the prisoners **set free.**

λύεσθε τοὺς δεσμίους.
Have the prisoners **set free**! **Keep having** the prisoners **set free**!

3 λύονται τοὺς δεσμίους.
They **are having** the prisoners **set free.**

λυέσθωσαν τοὺς δεσμίους.
Let them **have** the prisoners **set free**! **Let** them **keep having** the prisoners **set free**!

(4) AORIST MIDDLE INDICATIVE

AORIST MIDDLE IMPERATIVE

SG.2 ἐλύσω τοὺς δεσμίους.
You **had** the prisoners **set free.**

λῦσαι τοὺς δεσμίους.
Have the prisoners **set free**! **Start having** the prisoners **set free**!

3 ἐλύσατο τοὺς δεσμίους.
He **had** the prisoners **set free.**

λυσάσθω τοὺς δεσμίους.
Let him **have** the prisoners **set free**! **Let** him **start having** the prisoners **set free**!

	AORIST MIDDLE INDICATIVE	AORIST MIDDLE IMPERATIVE
PL.2	ἐλύσασθε τοὺς δεσμίους. You **had** the prisoners **set free**.	λύσασθε τοὺς δεσμίους. **Have** the prisoners **set free**! **Start having** the prisoners **set free**!
3	ἐλύσαντο τοὺς δεσμίους. They **had** the prisoners **set free**.	λυσάσθωσαν τοὺς δεσμίους. **Let** them **have** the prisoners **set free**! **Let** them **start having** the prisoners **set free**!

(5)

	PRESENT PASSIVE INDICATIVE	PRESENT PASSIVE IMPERATIVE
SG.2	λύῃ. You **are being set free**.	λύου. **Be set free**! **Keep on being set free**!
3	λύεται ὁ δέσμιος. The prisoner **is being set free**.	λυέσθω ὁ δέσμιος. **Let** the prisoner **be set free**! **Let** the prisoner **keep on being set free**!
PL.2	λύεσθε. You **are being set free**.	λύεσθε, **Be set free**! **Keep on being set free**!
3	λύονται οἱ δέσμιοι. The prisoners **are being set free**.	λυέσθωσαν οἱ δέσμιοι. **Let** the prisoners **be set free**! **Let** the prisoners **keep on being set free**.

(6)

	AORIST PASSIVE INDICATIVE	AORIST PASSIVE IMPERATIVE
SG.2	ἐλύθης. You **have been set free**.	λύθητι. **Be set free**! **Start being set free**!
3	ἐλύθη ὁ δέσμιος. The prisoner **has been set free**.	λυθήτω ὁ δέσμιος. **Let** the prisoner **be set free**! **Let** the prisoner **start being set free**!
PL.2	ἐλύθητε. You **have been set free**.	λύθητε. **Be set free**! **Start being set free**!
3	ἐλύθησαν οἱ δέσμιοι. The prisoners **have been set free**.	λυθήτωσαν οἱ δέσμιοι. **Let** the prisoners **be set free**! **Let** the prisoners **start being set free**!

325. A number of important facts about the Greek imperative mood can be discovered by the student for himself, through a careful examination of the illustrative material in the preceding section.[1] Some of the less obvious points are explained below.

326. The Forms of the Imperative. Like other verb forms, the forms of the imperative may be analyzed into constituents, as follows:[2]

(1) The **base** (e.g., λυ-).

(2) **Prefixes.** The forms of the imperative mood never have the augment. Prefixes which do occur with the imperative will be discussed in later lessons.

(3) **Tense formants:**

(a) -σ- (attached to the base in the first aorist, active and middle).

(b) -θ- (attached to the base in the first aorist passive).

(4) **Stem formatives:**

(a) -ε- (*zero* if the following suffix begins with a vowel); this stem formative occurs in all voices of the *present* imperative and in the active and middle voices of the *second aorist* imperative.

(b) -α- (*zero* if the following suffix begins with a vowel other than ι); this stem formative occurs in the *first aorist* imperative in the active and middle voices.

(c) -η- (in all forms); this stem formative occurs in the first and second aorist passive imperative.

(5) **Suffixes** may be divided into four sets:

	(a) PRIMARY A	(b) PRIMARY B	(c) SECONDARY A	(d) SECONDARY B
SG.1	[no form]	[no form]	[no form]	[no form]
2	-ε	-ου	-ον, -τι, (-θι)*	-ι
3	-τω	-σθω	-τω	-σθω
PL.1	[no form]	[no form]	[no form]	[no form]
2	-τε	-σθε	-τε	-σθε
3	-τωσαν	-σθωσαν	-τωσαν	-σθωσαν

REMARK: The Secondary A suffix of the second person singular (marked with an asterisk in the tabulation above) is -τι if the preceding vowel is η; if, however, the consonant immediately preceding this η is other than φ, θ, or χ, this suffix is -θι. Thus, for example, the second singular aorist

---

[1] See Exercise 43-A.   [2] Cf. §§164–169.

passive imperative of **λύω** is **λύθητι**, that of **γράφω** is **γράφητι**, but that of **κρύπτω** is **κρύβηθι**.

327. Verbs with second aorists in the indicative have second aorists in the imperative;[1] the forms of these have special bases (as in the indicative) with the stem formatives and suffixes of the present tense: **λείπω**, second aorist **ἔλιπον**, has the following forms:

	SECOND AORIST ACTIVE	SECOND AORIST MIDDLE
SG.2	λίπε	λίπου
3	λιπέτω	λιπέσθω
PL.2	λίπετε	λίπεσθε
3	λιπέτωσαν	λιπέσθωσαν

328. Verbs which are deponent or partly deponent in the indicative will be deponent (or partly deponent, in corresponding tenses) in the imperative:

		PRESENT IMPERATIVE	AORIST IMPERATIVE	
γίνομαι has:	SG.2	γίνου, *be*	γένου	or γενήθητι, *be*
	3	γινέσθω	γενέσθω	γενηθήτω
	PL.2	γίνεσθε	γένεσθε	γενήθητε
	3	γινέσθωσαν	γενέσθωσαν	γενηθήτωσαν
ἔρχομαι has:	SG.2	ἔρχου, *come*	ἐλθέ, *come*	
	3	ἐρχέσθω	ἐλθέτω	
	PL.2	ἔρχεσθε	ἔλθετε	
	3	ἐρχέσθωσαν	ἐλθέτωσαν	

329. The forms of the imperative of the **μι**-verbs **δίδωμι**, **τίθημι**, and **ἵστημι** involve irregularities of various types:

(1)

		PRESENT ACTIVE IMPERATIVE		
		δίδωμι	τίθημι	ἵστημι
SG.2		δίδου, *give*	τίθει, *put*	ἵστη, *establish*
3		διδότω	τιθέτω	ἱστάτω
PL.2		δίδοτε	τίθετε	ἵστατε
3		διδότωσαν	τιθέτωσαν	ἱστάτωσαν

---

[1] Some second aorist stems have first aorist endings: from **εἶπον** we have **εἶπόν** (as well as **εἰπέ**), **εἴπατε, εἰπάτω, εἰπάτωσαν**; from **ἦλθον** we have **ἐλθέ** but **ἐλθάτω** as well as **ἐλθέτω**, etc. (Note the accent of **εἰπόν, εἰπέ, ἐλθέ, λαβέ, ἰδέ**.)

(2)

AORIST ACTIVE IMPERATIVE

SG.2	δός, *give*	θές, *put*	στῆθι (-στα), *stand*
3	δότω	θέτω	στήτω
PL.2	δότε	θέτε	στῆτε
3	δότωσαν	θέτωσαν	στήτωσαν

(3)

PRESENT MIDDLE AND PASSIVE IMPERATIVE

SG.2	δίδοσο, *have given;*	τίθεσο, *have put;*	ἵστασο, *have established;*
	be given	*be put*	*be established*
3	διδόσθω	τιθέσθω	ἱστάσθω
PL.2	δίδοσθε	τίθεσθε	ἵστασθε
3	διδόσθωσαν	τιθέσθωσαν	ἱστάσθωσαν

(4)

AORIST MIDDLE IMPERATIVE

SG.2	[not found]	θοῦ, *have put*	[none]
3		θέσθω	
PL.2		θέσθε	
3		θέσθωσαν	

(5)

AORIST PASSIVE IMPERATIVE

SG.2	δόθητι, *be given*	τέθητι, *be put*	στάθητι, *be established*
3	δοθήτω	τεθήτω	σταθήτω
PL.2	δόθητε	τέθητε	στάθητε
3	δοθήτωσαν	τεθήτωσαν	σταθήτωσαν

330. The imperative forms of the verb εἰμί are as follows:

PRESENT IMPERATIVE

SG.2.	ἴσθι, *be*
3	ἔστω or ἤτω
PL.2	ἔστε
3	ἔστωσαν or ἤτωσαν

331. The formation of the present imperative of contract verbs is left as an exercise (Exercise 43-B); the aorist imperative forms of the contract verbs are regular.

332. The Meanings of the Imperative. (1) Perhaps the first thing which strikes an English-speaking reader of the illustrative sentences in §324 is the fact that Greek has imperative forms for the **third person**, singular and plural, as well as for the second person. These third person forms, which express a strong wish on the part of the speaker that something be done by or to a third person or persons, must be rendered in English by compound forms like those given in the translations: *let him loose, let them be loosed,* etc. These compound English forms are not regarded as imperatives in English, of course, and they may, when translated from English to Greek, occasionally be rendered by Greek forms other than imperatives (some of these will be taken up in Lesson 44).

(2) Next it should be noticed that the difference in meaning between the present imperative and the aorist imperative is not one of **time**, but of **aspect**. The present imperative is progressive or durative, referring to an action already in progress, while the aorist is indefinite or "ingressive," referring, usually, to an action which is to be commenced. This distinction is expressed in the English translations by paraphrases: *keep on loosing, keep on having set free, keep on being set free, start setting free,* etc.[1] This distinction may be illustrated by further examples taken from the New Testament itself:

1 Cor 14:1 **διώκετε** τὴν ἀγάπην.	**Pursue** love (*i.e.,* **Keep on pursuing** love *or* **Keep** love **as your goal**).
1 Th 5:16 πάντοτε **χαίρετε**.	Always **rejoice** (=Always **be rejoicing**).
1 Cor 7:2 ἑκάστη τὸν ἴδιον ἄνδρα **ἐχέτω**.	Let each woman **have** (=**continue to have**) her own husband.
Rev 2:11 ὃ βλέπεις **γράψον** εἰς βιβλίον.	**Write** (=**start writing**) what you see in a book.

This distinction between present and aorist turns out, however, to be one which cannot always be pressed; the imperatives in the Lord's Prayer (Matthew 6:9–13) are all aorists, but it would be strange to translate them by *start to give us our daily bread, let thy will start to be done,* etc.:

Mt 6:10a **ἁγιασθήτω** τὸ ὄνομά σου.	**Hallowed be** thy name (=**Let** thy name **be hallowed**).

[1] It must be confessed that the model verb **λύω** is not a very good choice for illustrating this distinction; it is hard to imagine a context for such a remark as *Let them keep on being set free!*

Mt 6:10b **ἐλθέτω**[1] ἡ βασιλεία σου.	Thy kingdom **come** (=**Let** thy kingdom **come**).
Mt 6:11a **γενηθήτω** τὸ θέλημά σου, ὡς ἐν οὐρανῷ, καὶ ἐπὶ γῆς.	Thy will **be done** (=**Let** thy will **be done, happen, take place**) as in heaven, also on earth.
Mt 6:11b τὸν ἄρτον ἡμῶν τὸν ἐπιούσιον **δὸς** ἡμῖν σήμερον.	**Give** us today our daily bread.

The safest rule, then, for translating the Greek imperatives is to use the simplest English forms unless the context indicates that the aspect of the verb is of special significance.

(3) The **negatives** used with the imperative mood are μή and its compounds; the translation of these negative commands or prohibitions parallels that of positive commands: the present imperative is thus used in a prohibition in which someone is commanded to *stop* doing what he is doing, whereas the aorist imperative is used in prohibitions in which someone is commanded *not to start* doing something:

Jn 5:14 μηκέτι **ἁμάρτανε**.	**Sin** no longer (=**Stop sinning** any more).
Mt 24:18 ὁ ἐν τῷ ἀγρῷ μὴ **ἐπιστρεψάτω** ὀπίσω.	**Let** him who is in the field **not turn** back (=**not start to turn**).

As before, this distinction cannot be pressed in every instance. The aorist imperative occurs only quite rarely with negatives; its place is taken, in such constructions, by the aorist subjunctive.[2]

[1] Most MSS have **ἐλθάτω**, with first aorist ending.

[2] See Lesson 44.

44 | THE SUBJUNCTIVE MOOD, I: INDEPENDENT USES

333. The **subjunctive mood** is very nearly obsolete in English. It still occurs frequently in "unreal" conditions, such as the *if*-clause in

> If I *were* you, I'd get a haircut.

It is also found in poetry and in old-fashioned stories:

> ". . . *be* he 'live or *be* he dead,
> I'll grind his bones to make my bread."
> "Though he *strike* me dead, I'll still tell the truth."

The forms of the English subjunctive are mostly identical with those of the indicative, except that the third person singular of the present subjunctive has no -*s* (cf. "*he strike*" in the last illustrative sentence); the present subjunctive of *to be* is *be*, and the past subjunctive is *were* (cf. the other illustrative sentences).

334. The subjunctive mood in New Testament Greek occurs very frequently and has many uses, most of which do not correspond to uses of the English subjunctive. The forms of the Greek subjunctive, moreover, are usually, though not always, easily distinguished from those of the Greek indicative. Happily, the forms of the subjunctive add very little to the load which the Greek verb imposes on the memory; those of the model verb **λύω** are given below. The corresponding indicative forms are given also, to facilitate comparison.

(1)	PRESENT ACTIVE		(2) PRESENT MIDDLE AND PASSIVE	
	INDICATIVE	SUBJUNCTIVE	INDICATIVE	SUBJUNCTIVE
SG.1	λύω	**λύω**	λύομαι	**λύωμαι**
2	λύεις	**λύῃς**	λύῃ	**λύῃ**
3	λύει	**λύῃ**	λύεται	**λύηται**
PL.1	λύομεν	**λύωμεν**	λυόμεθα	**λυώμεθα**
2	λύετε	**λύητε**	λύεσθε	**λύησθε**
3	λύουσι(ν)	**λύωσι(ν)**	λύονται	**λύωνται**

(3)	AORIST ACTIVE		(4)	AORIST MIDDLE	
	INDICATIVE	SUBJUNCTIVE		INDICATIVE	SUBJUNCTIVE
SG.1.	ἔλυσα	λύσω		ἐλυσάμην	λύσωμαι
2	ἔλυσας	λύσῃς		ἐλύσω	λύσῃ
3	ἔλυσε(ν)	λύσῃ		ἐλύσατο	λύσηται
PL.1	ἐλύσαμεν	λύσωμεν		ἐλυσάμεθα	λυσώμεθα
2	ἐλύσατε	λύσητε		ἐλύσασθε	λύσησθε
3	ἔλυσαν	λύσωσι(ν)		ἐλύσαντο	λύσωνται

(5)		AORIST PASSIVE	
	INDICATIVE		SUBJUNCTIVE
SG.1	ἐλύθην		λυθῶ
2	ἐλύθης		λυθῇς
3	ἐλύθη		λυθῇ
PL.1	ἐλύθημεν		λυθῶμεν
2	ἐλύθητε		λυθῆτε
3	ἐλύθησαν		λυθῶσι(ν)

(6) Greek has no future subjunctive and no imperfect subjunctive.

335. The analysis of the subjunctive forms into constituents follows that already made for indicative and imperative forms:[1]

(1) The **base** (e.g., λυ-).

(2) **Prefixes.** The forms of the subjunctive mood never have the augment. Prefixes which do occur with the subjunctive will be discussed in Lesson 46.

(3) **Tense formants:**

(a) -σ- (attached to the base in the first aorist, active and middle).

(b) -θ- (attached to the base in the first aorist passive).

(4) **Stem formative:** -ω/η/#- (i.e., -ω- before nasals [μ and ν], *zero* before a suffix beginning with a vowel other than ι, elsewhere -η-).[2]

(5) **Suffixes:**

	PRIMARY A	PRIMARY B
SG.1	-ω	-μαι
2	-ις (ι subscript)	-η
3	-ι (ι subscript)	-ται
PL.1	-μεν	-μεθα
2	-τε	-σθε
3	-ωσι(ν)	-νται

---

[1] See §§164–169, 326.   [2] Cf. §168(1).

REMARK 1: There are no secondary suffixes in the subjunctive. Note that the Primary A suffixes differ from those of §169(1) only in the third plural and that the Primary B suffixes are identical with those of §169(2).

REMARK 2: *Important:* The vowel of the ending (i.e., the vowel ω or η) always has the circumflex accent (thus: ῶ or ῇ) in the aorist passive subjunctive.

336. Verbs which have second aorists in the indicative also have second aorists in the subjunctive; the suffixes are the same as for first aorists. The second aorist active and middle subjunctive forms of **λείπω** (aorist indicative active **ἔλιπον**) and the second aorist passive subjunctive forms of **γράφω** (aorist indicative passive **ἐγράφην**) are given below for illustration:

	(1) SECOND AORIST ACTIVE SUBJUNCTIVE	(2) SECOND AORIST MIDDLE SUBJUNCTIVE	(3) SECOND AORIST PASSIVE SUBJUNCTIVE
SG.1	λίπω	λίπωμαι	γραφῶ
2	λίπῃς	λίπῃ	γραφῇς
3	λίπῃ	λίπηται	γραφῇ
PL.1	λίπωμεν	λιπώμεθα	γραφῶμεν
2	λίπητε	λίπησθε	γραφῆτε
3	λίπωσι(ν)	λίπωνται	γραφῶσι(ν)

337. Verbs which are deponent in the indicative are deponent in corresponding paradigms of the subjunctive: **γίνομαι** has present subjunctive **γίνωμαι, γίνῃ γίνηται, γινώμεθα, γίνησθε, γίνωνται**, and aorist subjunctive **γένωμαι, γένῃ, γένηται, γενώμεθα, γένησθε, γένωνται**, or **γενηθῶ, γενηθῇς, γενηθῇ, γενηθῶμεν, γενηθῆτε, γενηθῶσιν**; **ἔρχομαι** has present subjunctive **ἔρχωμαι, ἔρχῃ, ἔρχηται, ἐρχώμεθα, ἔρχησθε, ἔρχωνται**, but aorist subjunctive **ἔλθω, ἔλθῃς, ἔλθῃ, ἔλθωμεν, ἔλθητε, ἔλθωσι(ν)**.

338. In the present subjunctive of contract verbs contraction occurs in accordance with the rules given in §172 (cf. Exercise 44-B of the *Workbook*).[1]

---

[1] The αω-verbs have their present subjunctive paradigms identical to their present indicative paradigms except for the second singular middle and passive (indicative **ἀγαπᾶσαι** [cf. §174, fn. 2], subjunctive **ἀγαπᾷ**); the οω-verbs, in the New Testament,

339. The μι-verbs τίθημι and ἵστημι are regular in the subjunctive, so that their paradigms may be given in outline only:[1]

(1)		τίθημι	(2)		ἵστημι
	PRESENT	PRESENT		PRESENT	PRESENT
	ACTIVE	MID. & PASS.		ACTIVE	MID. & PASS.
SG.1	τιθῶ	τιθῶμαι		ἱστῶ	ἱστῶμαι
2	τιθῇς	τιθῇ		ἱστῇς	ἱστῇ
3	τιθῇ	τιθῆται		ἱστῇ	ἱστῆται
	etc.	etc.		etc.	etc.

	AORIST	AORIST	AORIST	AORIST	AORIST	AORIST
	ACTIVE	MIDDLE	PASSIVE	ACTIVE	MIDDLE	PASSIVE
SG.1	θῶ	θῶμαι	τεθῶ	στῶ	στῶμαι	σταθῶ
2	θῇς	θῇ	τεθῇς	στῇς	στῇ	σταθῇς
3	θῇ	θῆται	τεθῇ	στῇ	στῆται	σταθῇ
	etc.	etc.	etc.	etc.	etc.	etc.

340. The subjunctive of δίδωμι, however, contains some irregularities:

	PRESENT	PRESENT	AORIST	AORIST	AORIST
	ACTIVE	MID. & PASS.	ACTIVE	MIDDLE	PASSIVE
SG.1	διδῶ	διδῶμαι	δῶ	δῶμαι	δοθῶ
2	διδῷς, -οῖς	διδῷ	δῷς, δοῖς	δῷ	δοθῇς
3	διδῷ, -οῖ	διδῶται	δῷ, δοῖ, δώῃ	δῶται	δοθῇ
PL.1	διδῶμεν	διδώμεθα	δῶμεν	δώμεθα	δοθῶμεν
2	διδῶτε	διδῶσθε	δῶτε	δῶσθε	δοθῆτε
3	διδῶσι(ν)	διδῶνται	δῶσι(ν)	δῶνται	δοθῶσι(ν)

The irregularity in the subjunctive of δίδωμι consists in the fact that it has ω instead of η (in all forms, except those of the aorist passive).

341. The subjunctive forms of the verb εἰμί are as follows:

SG.1	ὦ	PL.1	ὦμεν
2	ᾖς	2	ἦτε
3	ᾖ	3	ὦσι(ν)

also have their present subjunctive and indicative alike (although, for the subjunctive, this goes against the rules of contraction). Outside the New Testament regular forms occur.

[1] Note that the circumflex accent occurs on all endings except -ώμεθα.

342. We now turn to the various uses of the Greek subjunctive as they occur in the New Testament. It should be borne in mind that forms of the Greek subjunctive will rarely have to be translated by forms of the English subjunctive.

343. The Hortatory Subjunctive.[1] The subjunctive is used in the first person (usually plural, but occasionally singular) in main clauses to express exhortations. This "hortatory" subjunctive is sometimes introduced by ἄφες or ἄφετε (aorist imperative forms of ἀφίημι; they may usually be rendered **let** or left untranslated), δεῦρο or δεῦτε (to be rendered **come**, if translated at all).

Jn 14:31 ἄγωμεν ἐντεῦθεν.	**Let us go** hence.
Gal 5:26 μὴ γινώμεθα κενόδοξοι.	**Let's** not **become** conceited.
Mt 7:4 ἄφες ἐκβάλω τὸ κάρφος.	**Let me cast out** the mote.

344. The Prohibitory Subjunctive. The **aorist** subjunctive is used in the second and third persons (singular and plural) in main clauses to express a prohibition or negative command (in all such cases, of course, the negative μή is used).

Heb 3:8 μὴ σκληρύνητε τὰς καρδίας ὑμῶν.	**Do not harden** your hearts.
1 Cor 16:11 μή τις οὖν αὐτὸν ἐξουθενήσῃ.	So **let no** one **despise** him.

Two points should be remembered about the prohibitory subjunctive:

(1) It occurs only rarely in the third person (as in 1 Corinthians 16:11; it also occurs in 2 Thessalonians 2:3 and 2 Corinthians 11:16).

(2) More important is its relationship to the **imperative** mood. We saw in Lesson 43 (§332(3)) that the **present imperative** is used in a prohibition in which someone is told to *stop* doing what he is already doing, and that the **aorist imperative** is used in prohibitions in which someone is commanded *not to start* doing something. The aorist imperative, it was also pointed out, occurs only infrequently with negatives: in its place the

---

[1] The names "hortatory," "prohibitory," "deliberative," and so on refer to the *meanings* of the subjunctive in various uses; they are traditional, but are at best convenient labels. As names they are quite unimportant.

prohibitory (**aorist**) **subjunctive** is used. Some examples will make this clear:

PRESENT IMPERATIVE	μὴ κηρύσσετε	**Don't preach. Stop preaching.**
AORIST SUBJUNCTIVE	μὴ κηρύξητε	**Don't preach. Don't start preaching.**

In doing the exercise in the *Workbook*, the student should not use the aorist imperative with μή, but the aorist subjunctive. On the other hand, he should not use the **present** subjunctive with μή to express a prohibition, as it was not so used in the New Testament.

345. The Deliberative Subjunctive. The subjunctive (usually the aorist) or the future indicative may be used in deliberative questions, i.e., questions of possibility, desirability, or necessity, rather than questions of fact:

Lk 3:10 τί οὖν **ποιήσωμεν**;	What then **shall we do**?
Lk 11:5 τίς ἐξ ὑμῶν **ἕξει** φίλον	Which of you **shall have** (fut.
. . . καὶ **εἴπῃ** αὐτῷ . . .	ind.) a friend and **shall say** (aor. subj.) to him . . .

The deliberative subjunctive is occasionally introduced by **θέλεις, θέλετε,** or **βούλεσθε** (all mean *do you wish*):

Lk 22:9 ποῦ **θέλεις** ἑτοιμάσωμεν;	Where, **do you wish, shall we make ready**?

346. Like the future indicative, the aorist subjunctive is sometimes used with **οὐ μή** to express an emphatic negative statement (cf. §297(8)).

Mt 23:39 οὐ μή με **ἴδητε** ἀπ' ἄρτι.	**You will not see** me at all from now on.

45 | THE SUBJUNCTIVE MOOD, II
RELATIVE CLAUSES, II
SUBORDINATING CONJUNCTIONS, II

347. The subjunctive mood occurs most frequently in **dependent** clauses; the various types of these are considered in this lesson.

348. The subjunctive is used in **indefinite** relative clauses. An indefinite relative clause is one which refers to a supposed event rather than to an actual one; generally speaking, indefinite relative clauses in English are introduced by indefinite relative pronouns, adjectives, and adverbs, e.g., *whoever, whosoever, whatever, whenever, however* (not the conjunction, of course), *whichever, wherever,* and so on. The indefinite relatives in Greek are expressed by the same relatives already given in Lesson 40, with the addition of **ἄν** or **ἐάν** (usually written as a separate word; instead of **ὅτε ἄν**, however, the form **ὅταν**, *whenever*, is used).

Mt 5:19 **ὅς ἐάν** οὖν **λύσῃ** μίαν τῶν ἐντολῶν τούτων τῶν ἐλαχίστων καὶ **διδάξῃ** οὕτως τοὺς ἀνθρώπους ἐλάχιστος κληθήσεται ἐν τῇ βασιλείᾳ τῶν οὐρανῶν.

Therefore **whoever breaks** one of the least of these commandments and **teaches** men so will be called least in the kingdom of heaven.

Mt 20:4 **ὃ ἐάν ᾖ** δίκαιον δώσω ὑμῖν.

Whatsoever is just I will give you.

Mt 20:27 **ὃς ἄν θέλῃ** ἐν ὑμῖν εἶναι πρῶτος, ἔσται ὑμῶν δοῦλος.

Whoever wishes to be first among you shall be your servant.

Mt 21:22 πάντα **ὅσα ἄν αἰτήσητε** ἐν τῇ προσευχῇ πιστεύοντες, λήμψεσθε.

Everything **whatsoever you ask for** in prayer while believing, you shall receive.

Mt 6:23 **ὅτι**[1] **ἐάν** με **αἰτήσῃς** δώσω σοι.

Whatever you ask me **for** I will give you.

---

[1] Not the conjunction, but the neuter of **ὅστις** (cf. §310).

Mt 12:50 ὅστις γὰρ ἂν ποιήσῃ τὸ θέλημα τοῦ πατρός μου τοῦ ἐν οὐρανοῖς, αὐτός μου ἀδελφὸς καὶ ἀδελφὴ καὶ μήτηρ ἐστίν.	For **whosoever does** the will of my Father in heaven, he is my brother and my sister and my mother.
Mt 25:31 **ὅταν** δὲ **ἔλθῃ** ὁ υἱὸς τοῦ ἀνθρώπου ἐν τῇ δόξῃ αὐτοῦ καὶ πάντες οἱ ἄγγελοι μετ' αὐτοῦ, τότε καθίσει ἐπὶ θρόνου δόξης αὐτοῦ.	And **whenever** the Son of man **comes** in his glory, and all the angels with him, then he will sit upon the throne of his glory.

349. The subjunctive is used in subordinate clauses introduced by ἵνα, ὅπως, and μή, and sometimes in clauses introduced by ἕως, ἄχρι(ς), and μέχρι(ς).

(1) **Ἵνα** means *that, in order that, so that*. Clauses introduced by ἵνα usually indicate the *purpose* of the action expressed in the main clause, but may indicate its *result* or *content*. The meanings which may be expressed by ἵνα-clauses, in fact, are the same as those which may be expressed by the infinitive (see Lessons 32 and 33).

Rom 3:8 ποιήσωμεν τὰ κακὰ **ἵνα ἔλθῃ** τὰ ἀγαθά.	Let us do evil things **in order** that good things **may come**. (Purpose)
Rom 11:11 λέγω οὖν, μὴ ἔπταισαν **ἵνα πέσωσιν**;	I say then, have they stumbled **so that they fell**? (Result)
1 Jn 5:3 αὕτη γάρ ἐστιν ἡ ἀγάπη τοῦ θεοῦ, **ἵνα** τὰς ἐντολὰς αὐτοῦ **τηρῶμεν**.	For this is the love of God, **that we keep** his commandments. (Content)
Phil 2:27 ὁ θεὸς ἠλέησεν αὐτὸν . . . καὶ ἐμέ, **ἵνα** μὴ λύπην ἐπὶ λύπην **σχῶ**.[1]	God had mercy upon him . . . and me, **in order that** I **might** not **have** sorrow upon sorrow.

(2) **Ὅπως** is synonymous with ἵνα, but occurs less frequently. It almost always introduces purpose clauses. Ὅπως is sometimes followed by ἄν, which does not change the translation.

Mt 5:16 οὕτως λαμψάτω τὸ φῶς ὑμῶν ἔμπροσθεν τῶν ἀνθρώπων, **ὅπως ἴδωσιν** ὑμῶν τὰ καλὰ ἔργα καὶ **δοξάσωσιν** τὸν πατέρα ὑμῶν τὸν ἐν τοῖς οὐρανοῖς.	Let your light thus shine before men, **so that** they **may see** your good works and **glorify** your Father in heaven.

---

[1] **Σχῶ** is the aorist subjunctive of ἔχω; its base is formed by dropping the augment of the aorist indicative, **ἔσχον**, and substituting subjunctive endings for indicative ones.

Rom 3:4 γινέσθω δὲ ὁ θεὸς ἀληθής, πᾶς δὲ ἄνθρωπος ψεύστης . . . **ὅπως ἂν δικαιωθῇς** ἐν τοῖς λόγοις σου.

Let God be true and every man a liar . . . **so that** you may **be justified** by your words.

Mt 6:17f σὺ δὲ νηστεύων ἄλειψαί σου τὴν κεφαλὴν καὶ τὸ πρόσωπόν σου νίψαι, **ὅπως** μὴ **φανῇς** τοῖς ἀνθρώποις νηστεύων.

But you, when fasting, anoint your head and wash your face, **so that** you **may** not **appear** to men as fasting.

(3) **Μή** is used as the negative of the subjunctive in ἵνα- and ὅπως-clauses as it is elsewhere (cf. the last examples in (1) and (2) above); it may also, however, serve as a conjunction itself, with the meaning *lest, in order that . . . not*. It frequently follows verbs meaning *fear, be afraid, have a care*. In this use it is sometimes strengthened by the addition of **πως** or **ποτε**; these combinations are sometimes written **μήπως, μήποτε**, sometimes **μή πως, μή ποτε**.

Mk 13:35f γρηγορεῖτε οὖν . . . **μὴ** ἐλθὼν ἐξαίφνης **εὕρῃ** ὑμᾶς καθεύδοντας.

Watch therefore, . . . **lest** coming suddenly he **finds** you sleeping.

2 Cor 12:20 φοβοῦμαι γὰρ **μή πως** ἐλθὼν οὐχ οἵους θέλω **εὕρω** ὑμᾶς.

For I fear **lest** when I come I **may find** you not as I wish.

Mt 27:64 κέλευσον οὖν ἀσφαλισθῆναι τὸν τάφον ἕως τῆς τρίτης ἡμέρας, **μήποτε** ἐλθόντες οἱ μαθηταὶ **κλέψωσιν** αὐτόν.

Therefore command that the tomb be made secure until the third day, **in order that** the disciples may **not steal** him when they come (=**lest** the disciples . . .).

REMARK: Except with verbs of fearing, the constructions with ἵνα μή, ὅπως μή are to be preferred to those with μή, μήπως, μήποτε.

(4) **Ἕως**, *until*, is used with the aorist subjunctive (with or without the particle **ἄν**) to indicate that the beginning of an event is dependent on circumstances (cf. §321(5)).

Mt 2:13 ἴσθι ἐκεῖ **ἕως ἂν εἴπω** σοι.

Be there **until** I **tell** you.

Mt 10:23 οὐ μὴ τελέσητε τὰς πόλεις τοῦ Ἰσραὴλ **ἕως ἔλθῃ** ὁ υἱὸς τοῦ ἀνθρώπου.

You will not finish (*sc.* going through) the cities of Israel **until** the Son of man **comes**.

Clauses with similar meanings are introduced by **ἕως οὗ, ἕως ὅτου, ἄχρι(ς), ἄχρις οὗ, μέχρι(ς), μέχρις οὗ.**

350. The subjunctive is used in certain types of **conditional clauses.** A conditional clause, obviously, is one which expresses a condition; conditional clauses are grammatically dependent and are adjoined to other clauses which express the result or conclusion following from the condition. The clause which expresses the conclusion is independent in form; i.e., it could stand alone, grammatically, as a sentence. A sentence consisting of a conditional clause and a clause expressing the conclusion following from this condition is called a conditional sentence. Conditional sentences in English are very similar in structure to conditional sentences in Greek. In English, the conditional clause is usually introduced by *if*, and its verb may be in any tense; the form of the conclusion may be quite varied:

> If he does this, he does well.
> If he does this, he will do well.
> If he does this, let him do well!
> If he does this, will he do well?
> If he did this, he did well.
> If he did this, he would have done well.

Many other examples could be constructed, of course.

351. Conditional sentences in Greek may be most conveniently classified according to the form of each of their constituent clauses.

	CONDITION	CONCLUSION
TYPE A:	Εἰ with a verb in the indicative (*any* tense); if there is a negative, it is usually οὐ.	A clause with verb in the indicative, imperative, or subjunctive in one of its independent uses (*i.e.*, the four discussed in §§343–346).
TYPE B:	’Εάν with a verb in the subjunctive; if there is a negative, it is usually μή.	Same as for Type A.
TYPE C:	Εἰ with a verb in a *past tense* of the indicative; negative usually μή.	A clause with a verb in a *past tense* (not necessarily the same tense as in the εἰ-clause) of the indicative, and with the particle ἄν.

[273]

REMARK: Other types of conditional sentences involve the optative mood; these, which are not frequently found in the New Testament, will be taken up in Lesson 50.

352. Conditional clauses of **Type A** express conditions which are believed (by the speaker) to be actual or possible:

Gal 5:18 εἰ δὲ πνεύματι **ἄγεσθε**, οὐκ ἐστὲ ὑπὸ νόμον.

But **if** you **are led** by the Spirit, you are not under law.

Jn 15:20 εἰ ἐμὲ **ἐδίωξαν**, καὶ ὑμᾶς διώξουσιν.

If they **persecuted** me, they will also persecute you.

Mt 26:33 εἰ πάντες **σκανδαλισθήσονται** ἐν σοί, ἐγὼ οὐδέποτε σκανδαλισθήσομαι.

If all **shall be offended** in you, I shall never be offended.

Jn 1:25 τί οὖν βαπτίζεις **εἰ σὺ οὐκ εἶ** ὁ Χριστὸς οὐδὲ Ἠλίας οὐδὲ ὁ προφήτης;

Why are you baptizing, then, **if** you **are not** the Christ nor Elijah nor the prophet?

353. Conditional clauses of **Type B** express conditions which are believed by the speaker to be generally true in the present or probably realizable in the future (future conditions are more often expressed by clauses of **Type B** than by clauses of **Type A**).

Mt 8:2 **ἐὰν θέλῃς** δύνασαί με καθαρίσαι.

If you **wish** (*i.e.*, if you **ever** wish), you can cleanse me.

1 Cor 4:19 ἐλεύσομαι δὲ ταχέως πρὸς ὑμᾶς, **ἐὰν** ὁ κύριος **θελήσῃ**.

But I shall come to you swiftly, **if** the Lord **wills** (*i.e.*, if he **shall** wish it).

Jn 13:8 **ἐὰν μὴ νίψω** σε, οὐκ ἔχεις μέρος μετ' ἐμοῦ.

If I do **not wash** you (*i.e.*, **ever** *or* in the future), you have no part with me.

354. Conditional clauses of **Type C** express hypothetical conditions, i.e., conditions which the speaker himself believes to be contrary to fact:

Mk 13:20 **εἰ μὴ ἐκολόβωσεν** κύριος τὰς ἡμέρας, οὐκ **ἂν ἐσώθη** πᾶσα σάρξ.

If the Lord **had not shortened** the days [but he did], all flesh **would** not **have been saved** (=no one would have been saved).

Jn 8:42 εἰ ὁ θεὸς πατὴρ ὑμῶν ἦν, ἠγαπᾶτε ἂν ἐμέ.

If God **were** your Father [*i.e.*, but he isn't], you **would have loved** me.

REMARK. Occasionally ἄν is omitted from the conclusion; in such cases the context, or the presence of μή in the conditional clause, indicates the hypothetical nature of the condition:

Jn 9:33 εἰ μὴ ἦν οὗτος παρὰ θεοῦ, οὐκ ἠδύνατο ποιεῖν οὐδέν.

If this man **were not** from God [but he is], he **would** not **have been able** to do anything.

355. The phrase εἰ μή may be used without a verb with the meaning *except, but*; it acts as a "compound conjunction," and the element which it joins to the sentence has the grammatical form (case, etc.) which it would have if joined to the sentence by an ordinary coordinating conjunction:

Mt 11:27 οὐδεὶς ἐπιγινώσκει τὸν υἱὸν εἰ μὴ ὁ πατήρ.

No one knows the Son **except** the Father. [ὁ πατήρ coordinate with οὐδείς]

Mt 17:8 οὐδένα εἶδον εἰ μὴ τὸν Ἰησοῦν μόνον.

They saw no one **but** Jesus only.

356. Conditional clauses are sometimes described as **concessive** clauses when they contain the adverb καί; it usually follows εἰ but precedes ἐάν. Both καὶ ἐάν and εἰ καί may be rendered *although, even if, even though, though*.

357. Indefinite relative clauses (see §348) are described by some writers as "conditional relative clauses," because they imply a condition. This may be seen from a comparison of Mark 10:43 and 9:35:

Mk 10:43 ὃς ἂν θέλῃ μέγας γενέσθαι ἐν ὑμῖν, ἔσται ὑμῶν διάκονος.

Whosoever will be great among you shall be your minister.

Mk 9:35 εἴ τις θέλει πρῶτος εἶναι ἔσται πάντων ἔσχατος καὶ πάντων διάκονος.

If anyone wishes to be first, he shall be last of all and servant of all.

The terminology, "indefinite relative clause," is used in this book as it is less confusing.

46 | COMPOUND VERBS
SOME "IRREGULAR" VERBS

358. Compound Verbs. In our analysis of verb forms into morphemes[1] we have so far encountered only one prefix, namely, the **augment** (ἐ- or, for some verbs, ἠ-[2]). This prefix is peculiar in that it appears only as a constituent of verb forms and, moreover, only in past tenses of the indicative mood. No prefix of this type occurs in English, but many prefixes do occur as constituents of nouns, verbs, adjectives, and adverbs. Among these are *be-* in *besmear, befriend, befall; under-* in *undertake, understand, underwear; un-* in *unclad, ungodly, undo*, and *uneasily*.[3] When a prefix of this second type[4] occurs with an inflected word (e.g., a verb), it occurs with *all* forms of it and thus forms with it a "new word" rather than just a grammatical form (e.g., a tense form) of the old word.[5]

359. Prefixes of this second, more familiar, type are also found in Greek. The most common ones are identical in form to some of the prepositions studied in Lessons 25 and 26: ἀνα-, ἀντι-, ἀπο-, δια-, εἰσ-, ἐκ-, ἐν-, ἐπι-, κατα-, μετα-, παρα-, περι-, προ-, προσ-, συν-, ὑπο-, and ὑπερ-.

---

[1] Cf. Lessons 23, 28, 30, 31, 32, 43, and 44.

[2] E.g., θέλω always, μέλλω and δύναμαι frequently, and βούλομαι rarely. When the augment takes the form of a modification of the initial vowel of a verb base, it is not, of course, a prefix.

[3] Whether or not these particular prefixes are also morphemes is not now in question.

[4] Called *prebases* by some writers (e.g., A. A. Hill, *Introduction to Linguistic Structures*, pp. 119f, 123f, 127, 129, 166, 446f), who reserve the term *prefix* for the Greek augment and similar preposed elements. (See Selected Bibliography, §6(b).)

[5] Thus *understand* is not part of the paradigm of *stand*, but a different word. The prefix *under-* occurs throughout its paradigm: *understand, understands, understanding, understood.*

[276]

For convenience we shall speak of verbs which have one or more of these prefixes as constituents as *compound verbs*. The exact form which a given prefix has in a particular compound depends on various phonological factors:

(1) When these prefixes are joined to verb forms beginning with a consonant (but see (4), below), they have the forms given above:

ἀνα + βαίνω = ἀναβαίνω
ἀντι + λέγω = ἀντιλέγω
ἀπο + δίδωμι = ἀποδίδωμι
δια + λύω = διαλύω

(2) When a prefix ending with a vowel is joined to a verb form beginning with a vowel, the final vowel of the prefix is dropped.

(a) If the initial vowel of the verb form has a *smooth* breathing, no further change is made in the prefix:

ἀνα + ἔρχομαι = ἀνέρχομαι   δια + ἔρχομαι = διέρχομαι
ἀντι + ἔχομαι = ἀντέχομαι   ἐπι + ἐρωτάω = ἐπερωτάω
ἀπο + ἔχω = ἀπέχω   κατα + εὐλογέω = κατευλογέω

(b) If the initial vowel of the verb form has a *rough* breathing, the prefixes ἀντι-, ἀπο-, ἐπι-, κατα-, μετα-, and ὑπο- have the forms ἀνθ-, ἀφ-, ἐφ-, καθ-, μεθ-, and ὑφ-, respectively:

ἀντι + ἵστημι = ἀνθίστημι   ἀπο + ἵστημι = ἀφίστημι
ἐπι + ἵστημι = ἐφίστημι   κατα + ἵστημι = καθίστημι
μετα + ἱστάνω = μεθιστάνω   ὑπο + ἵστημι = ὑφίστημι

EXCEPTION to (2): The final vowels of περι- and προ- are never dropped:

περι + ἔχω = περιέχω   προ + ἡγέομαι = προηγέομαι
περι + ἵστημι = περιΐστημι   προ + εἶπον = προεῖπον

(3) When the prefix ἐκ- is joined to a verb form beginning with a vowel it has the form ἐξ-:

ἐκ + ἀγοράζω = ἐξαγοράζω   ἐκ + ἡγέομαι = ἐξηγέομαι

(4) If the prefixes ἐν- and συν- are joined to verb forms beginning with certain consonants, they assume special forms as noted below:

(a) Before μ, π, β, φ, or ψ, they have the forms ἐμ- and συμ-, respectively:

ἐν + μένω = ἐμμένω   συν + πέμπω = συμπέμπω
ἐν + βάλλω = ἐμβάλλω   συν + φέρω = συμφέρω

(b) Before γ, κ, χ, or ξ, they have the forms ἐγ- and συγ-, respectively:

ἐν + γράφω = ἐγγράφω   συν + χαίρω = συγχαίρω
συν + καλέω = συγκαλέω

(c) Before λ they have the forms ἐλ- and συλ-, respectively:

ἐν + λείπω = ἐλλείπω   συν + λέγω = συλλέγω

(d) Before ζ and σ, ἐν- does not change, but συν- has the form συ-:

συν + ζητέω = συζητέω   συν + στρέφω = συστρέφω

360. The foregoing rules may be conveniently summarized in tabular form:

BEFORE CONSONANTS (but see the four columns at the right)	BEFORE VOWELS WITH SMOOTH BREATHING	BEFORE VOWELS WITH ROUGH BREATHING	BEFORE μ, π, β, φ, ψ	BEFORE γ, κ, χ, ξ,	BEFORE λ	BEFORE σ, ζ
ἀνα-	ἀν-	ἀν-				
ἀντι-	ἀντ-	ἀνθ-				
ἀπο-	ἀπ-	ἀφ-				
δια-	δι-	δι-				
εἰσ-						
ἐκ-	ἐξ-	ἐξ-				
ἐν-	..	..	ἐμ-	ἐγ-	ἐλ-	
ἐπι-	ἐπ-	ἐφ-				
κατα-	κατ-	καθ-				
μετα-	μετ-	μεθ-				
παρα-	παρ-	παρ-				
περι-						
προ-						
προσ-						
συν-	..	..	συμ-	συγ-	συλ-	συ-
ὑπο-	ὑπ-	ὑφ-				
ὑπερ-						

REMARK 1: Verbs are frequently found with *two* prefixes:

ἀντι + ἀνα + πληρόω = ἀνταναπληρόω
ἐν + κατα + λείπω = ἐγκαταλείπω
ἐπι + συν + ἄγω = ἐπισυνάγω

REMARK 2: Some compound verbs in the New Testament are formed from simple (i.e., uncompounded) verbs which do not occur in the New Testament:

ἀνα + βαίνω = ἀναβαίνω; βαίνω does not occur in the New Testament
ἀπο + κτείνω = ἀποκτείνω; κτείνω does not occur in the New Testament

361. Occasionally it is possible to infer the meaning of a compound verb from the meanings of its constituents:[1]

ἀνα-, *up* + βαίνω, *go* = ἀναβαίνω, *go up, ascend*
δια-, *through* + ἔρχομαι, *go* = διέρχομαι, *go through*
εἰσ-, *into* + ἔρχομαι, *go* = εἰσέρχομαι, *go into, enter*
μετα-, *with* + ἔχω, *have* = μετέχω, *partake, share*

Unfortunately, however, the meaning of compounds is not usually so transparent. The model verb λύω, *loose, set free, untie, destroy*, for example, has a number of compounds, but no clear meanings for the prefixes involved can be derived by "subtracting" the "root" meaning of λύω from the meanings of the compounds:

ἀναλύω (transitive) *loose, untie*; (intransitive) *depart, return*
ἀπολύω, *set free, release, pardon, let go, send away, dismiss*
διαλύω, *break up, dissolve, decay, destroy*
ἐκλύομαι (ἐκλύω occurs only in the passive in the New Testament), *be weary, give out, be ungirded*
ἐπιλύω, *explain, interpret*
καταλύω, *throw down, destroy, demolish, abolish*; (intransitive) *halt, rest*
παραλύω, *undo, weaken, disable, paralyze*

Λύω and its compounds are typical so far as this situation is concerned, so that students are advised to check the meanings of compounds in the lexicon.

---

[1] B. M. Metzger has a discussion of compounds and gives the most frequently encountered meanings of some of the prefixes in his *Lexical Aids for Students of New Testament Greek*, appendix II, pp. 102–109 (see Selected Bibliography, §5).

362. Compound verbs are conjugated exactly like uncompounded verbs except in the past tenses of the indicative mood. In these tenses the augment comes *between* the prefix and the actual verb base.[1] The compound verb ἀναλύω, for example, is conjugated as follows:

	PRESENT INDICATIVE ACTIVE	FUTURE INDICATIVE ACTIVE	IMPERFECT INDICATIVE ACTIVE	AORIST INDICATIVE ACTIVE
SG.1	ἀναλύω	ἀναλύσω	ἀνέλυον	ἀνέλυσα
2	ἀναλύεις	ἀναλύσεις	ἀνέλυες	ἀνέλυσας
	etc.	etc.	etc.	etc.

	IMPERFECT INDICATIVE MIDDLE & PASSIVE	AORIST INDICATIVE MIDDLE	AORIST INDICATIVE PASSIVE
SG.1	ἀνελυόμην	ἀνελυσάμην	ἀνελύθην
2	ἀνελύου	ἀνελύσω	ἀνελύθης
	etc.	etc.	etc.

The other tenses of the indicative have no augment, and so they cause no difficulty; similarly, no augment appears in the tenses of the imperative or subjunctive, or in the various infinitives and participles.

REMARK: It should be noticed that, in the paradigms given above, ἀνα- becomes ἀν- before the augmented forms; this change is in accordance with the rules given in §§359f. Similar changes occur in other prefixes:

PRESENT INDICATIVE ACTIVE	AORIST INDICATIVE ACTIVE
ἀπολύω	ἀπέλυσα
διαλύω	διέλυσα
ἐκζητέω	ἐξεζήτησα
ἀφίστημι	ἀπέστην
etc.	etc.

Note also present indicative ἀπέχω, future indicative (middle) ἀφέξομαι, where no augment is involved (the simple verb ἔχω has a smooth breathing in the present, but a rough breathing in the future: ἕξω).

---

[1] If a verb has two prefixes, the augment follows both of them:

PRESENT: ἀνταναπληρόω   AORIST: ἀντανεπλήρωσα

363. Some "Irregular" Verbs. Though the student has probably long since concluded, like Dean Inge, that with few exceptions all Greek verbs are irregular to the verge of impropriety, it is nevertheless true that some verbs are "more irregular" than others. We shall consider three groups of these in the following sections.

364. Verbs with Liquid or Nasal Futures (and Aorists). Verbs whose bases end in a liquid (λ or ρ) or a nasal (μ or ν) usually do not have the tense formant -σ- in the future or aorist.[1]

(1) The future of most such verbs is formed by affixing a tense formant -ε- to the base (which may or may not be modified from the form it has in the present); the resulting forms are, therefore, exactly similar to present tense forms of contract verbs in -έω (since, in εω-verbs, the base itself ends in an "extra" -ε-). Thus we have:

	PRESENT	FUTURE
SG.1	κρίνω, *judge*	κρινῶ (< κριν + ε + # + ω)
2	κρίνεις	κρινεῖς (< κριν + ε + ε + ις)
3	κρίνει	κρινεῖ (< κριν + ε + ε + ι)
	etc.	etc.

(2) The aorist indicative of these verbs is formed by adding the stem formative -α/ε- (see §168(2)) and the appropriate suffixes directly to the augmented base (which, aside from the augment, may or may not differ from the base of the present stem):

PRESENT INDICATIVE	AORIST INDICATIVE
κρίνω	ἔκρινα (< ἐ + κριν + α + #)
κρίνεις	ἔκρινας (< ἐ + κριν + α + ς)
κρίνει	ἔκρινε(ν) (< ἐ + κριν + ε + [ν])
etc.	etc.

The aorist subjunctive, infinitives, and participles are similarly formed (without the augment, of course):

---

[1] See §167(1a). This statement is, of course, to be understood descriptively, not historically; what the liquid and nasal futures may have been like in pre-Mycenaean times is not now under consideration.

AORIST SUBJUNCTIVE: κρίνω, κρίνῃς, κρίνῃ, etc. [like the
                           present subjunctive, for this verb]
AORIST INFINITIVE (ACTIVE): κρῖναι
                (MIDDLE):   κρίνασθαι
                (PASSIVE):   κριθῆναι [does not involve nasal base]
AORIST PARTICIPLE (ACTIVE): κρίνας, κρίνασα, κρίναν
                (MIDDLE):   κρινάμενος, η, ον
                (PASSIVE):   κριθείς [does not involve nasal base]

365. The most important verbs which have futures or aorists of this type
(or both) are as follows:

(1) λ-stems:

PRESENT	FUTURE	AORIST
ἀγγέλλω, *announce*	ἀγγελῶ	ἤγγειλα
-στέλλω[1]	-στελῶ	-ἔστειλα
-τέλλω[2]	-τελοῦμαι[3]	-ἔτειλα
βάλλω, *put, place, cast*	βαλῶ	ἔβαλον
ψάλλω, *sing*	ψαλῶ	—

(2) ρ-stems:

αἴρω, *take up, away*	ἀρῶ	ἦρα
ἐγείρω, *raise*	ἐγερῶ	ἤγειρα
καθαίρω, *cleanse*	καθαρῶ	ἐκάθαρα
φθείρω, *corrupt*	φθερῶ	ἔφθειρα

(3) ν-stems:

κερδαίνω, *gain*	κερδανῶ or κερδήσω	ἐκέρδανα or ἐκέρδησα
κλίνω, *lean*	κλινῶ	ἔκλινα
κρίνω, *judge*	κρινῶ	ἔκρινα
-κτείνω[4]	-κτενῶ	-ἔκτεινα
μένω, *remain*	μενῶ	ἔμεινα
ποιμαίνω, *shepherd*	ποιμανῶ	ἐποίμανα
-τείνω[5]	-τενῶ	-ἔτεινα
φαίνω, *shine*	φανοῦμαι[3]	ἔφανα

---

[1] Only in compounds, e.g., ἀποστέλλω, *send.*

[2] Only in compounds, e.g., ἀνατέλλω, *rise.*

[3] Deponent future.

[4] Only in compounds, e.g., ἀποκτείνω, *kill.*

[5] Only in compounds, e.g., ἐκτείνω, *stretch out.*

(4) Mixed (Suppletives):

PRESENT	FUTURE	AORIST
αἱρέω, *take*	-ἑλῶ[1] or αἱρήσομαι	-εἷλον or -εἷλα[1]
λέγω, *say*	ἐρῶ	εἷπον
-θνήσκω[2]	-θανοῦμαι[2]	-ἔθανον[2]

(5) In addition to these, some verbs in -ίζω have their futures in -ιῶ (instead of -ίσω); for example:

ἐλπίζω, *hope*	ἐλπιῶ	ἤλπισα

366. Verbs with Root Aorists. "Root" aorists are so called because they are formed by adding the personal suffixes directly to the verb base (or "root") without any intervening stem formatives. The most important verbs in the New Testament which have root aorists are γινώσκω, χαίρω, and the compounds of βαίνω. The so-called second aorist forms of ἵστημι are in fact root aorist forms (cf. §200(3)), as are the shorter aorist forms of the other μι-verbs (e.g., δός, θές, etc.). Further, the aorist active forms of βαίνω and χαίρω are very similar to the aorist passive forms of ordinary verbs, and the aorist active forms of γινώσκω are somewhat similar to the aorist active forms of δίδωμι. The paradigms of ἀναβαίνω and γινώσκω in the aorist active are given below:[3]

AORIST INDICATIVE

SG.1	ἀνέβην	PL.1	ἀνέβημεν	SG.1	ἔγνων	PL.1	ἔγνωμεν
2	ἀνέβης	2	ἀνέβητε	2	ἔγνως	2	ἔγνωτε
3	ἀνέβη	3	ἀνέβησαν	3	ἔγνω	3	ἔγνωσαν

AORIST IMPERATIVE

SG.2	ἀνάβηθι or ἀνάβα	PL.2	ἀνάβητε	SG.2	γνῶθι	PL.2	γνῶτε
3	ἀναβήτω	3	ἀναβήτωσαν	3	γνώτω	3	γνώτωσαν

---

[1] The simple verb has only the future middle; the irregular forms occur only in compounds, e.g., ἀναιρέω, ἀνελῶ, ἀνεῖλον or ἀνεῖλα, *destroy, kill*; ἀφαιρέω, ἀφελῶ ἀφεῖλον, *take away, cut off*.

[2] Only in compounds, e.g., ἀποθνήσκω, *die*.

[3] No middle forms occur; the aorist passive of γινώσκω (ἐγνώσθην) is regular.

AORIST SUBJUNCTIVE

SG.1	ἀναβῶ	PL.1	ἀναβῶμεν	SG.1	γνῶ	PL.1	γνῶμεν
2	ἀναβῇς	2	ἀναβῆτε	2	γνῷς	2	γνῶτε
3	ἀναβῇ	3	ἀναβῶσι(ν)	3	γνῷ or	3	γνῶσι(ν)
					γνοῖ		

AORIST INFINITIVE

ἀναβῆναι   γνῶναι

AORIST PARTICIPLE

ἀναβάς, -ᾶσα, -άν   γνούς, γνοῦσα, γνόν

REMARK: Ἐχάρην, root aorist of χαίρω, is conjugated like ἀνέβην

367. Other Mι-verbs:

(1) Conjugated like ἵστημι are:

πίμπλημι, *fill, fulfill*; in the New Testament only in aorist and aorist passive forms (regularly derived from the principal parts ἔπλησα and ἐπλήσθην).

πίμπραμαι, *burn with fever*; *swell up*; the single form πίμπρασθαι occurs in the New Testament.

δύναμαι, *be able* (see fn. 3, p. 195).

ἐπίσταμαι, *understand*. Found only in present tense (indicative and participle) in the New Testament; the imperfect is ἠπιστάμην.

κάθημαι, *sit*; the forms are like those of ἵσταμαι, but with καθη- replacing ἱστα-. The imperfect is ἐκαθήμην, future καθήσομαι.

NOTE: The second singular present imperative is κάθου.

κεῖμαι, *lie*; the forms are like those of ἵσταμαι, but with κει- replacing ἱστα-.

(2) Conjugated like τίθημι are the compounds of ἵημι. These are:

ἀνίημι, *loosen, abandon, give up*; ἀφίημι, *let go, forgive, abandon*; καθίημι, *let down*; παρίημι, *neglect, weaken*; συνίημι, *understand*. The most important of these is ἀφίημι, which may serve as a model for the others. The forms of ἀφίημι are like those of τίθημι, but with ἀφι- replacing τιθ-: ἀφίημι, ἀφίης, ἀφίησι(ν), ἀφίεμεν, ἀφίετε, *but* ἀφιᾶσι(ν); similarly, where τίθημι has simply θ- or ἐθ-, ἀφίημι has ἀφ-: ἀφῆκα, etc.; ἀφῶ, etc.; ἀφήσω, etc.; ἄφες; the aorist passive is ἀφέθην.

(3) Δείκνυμι, *show*, and its compounds are conjugated more or less like δίδωμι. Where δίδωμι has a variety of stems, e.g., διδω-, διδο-,

διδου-, δείκνυμι has only one: δεικνυ-. Thus we have, in the present indicative active, δείκνυμι, δείκνυς, δείκνυσι(ν), δείκνυμεν, δείκνυτε, δεικνύασι(ν). A number of forms occur, however, which indicate that the verb was passing over into the λύω type: thus we find δεικνύεις for δείκνυς, δεικνύειν for δεικνύναι, etc., and in particular the present subjunctive forms δεικνύω, δεικνυῇς, etc., and δεικνυῶμαι, etc. The future, aorist, and aorist passive paradigms are formed from the principal parts δείξω, ἔδειξα, ἐδείχθην.

REMARK: A few other verbs are found in the New Testament with forms like those of δείκνυμι; most of them, however, also have forms like those of λύω, and the latter predominate. The most important verb in this group is ἀπόλλυμι, which in the active voice means *ruin, destroy, kill, lose*, and in the middle voice means *be destroyed, be lost, perish, die*. The forms which occur in the New Testament (in the tenses so far studied) are given below:

			ACTIVE		MIDDLE
INDICATIVE:					
	PRESENT	SG.3	ἀπολλύει	SG.3	ἀπόλλυται
				PL.1	ἀπολλύμεθα
				3	ἀπόλλυνται
	IMPERFECT			PL.3	ἀπώλλυντο
	FUTURE	SG.1	ἀπολῶ	SG.1	—
		3	ἀπολέσει	3	ἀπολεῖται
				PL.2	ἀπολεῖσθε
				3	ἀπολοῦνται
	AORIST	SG.1	ἀπώλεσα	SG.1	—
		3	ἀπώλεσεν	3	ἀπώλετο
				PL.3	ἀπώλοντο
SUBJUNCTIVE:					
	AORIST	SG.3	ἀπολέσῃ	SG.3	ἀπόληται
		PL.3	ἀπολέσωσιν	PL.3	ἀπόλωνται
IMPERATIVE:					
	PRESENT	SG.2	ἀπόλλυε		
PARTICIPLES:					
	PRESENT				ἀπολλύμενος
	AORIST		ἀπολέσας		ἀπολόμενος
INFINITIVES:					
	AORIST		ἀπολέσαι		ἀπολέσθαι

(4) **Φημί**, *say, affirm,* has only first singular present indicative **φημί**; third **φησί(ν)**; third plural **φασί(ν)**; and third singular imperfect and aorist **ἔφη**.

368. Irregular Contract Verbs:

(1) **Ζάω**, *live* (originally an **ηω**-verb). The following forms are found in the New Testament: Present indicative (and subjunctive) **ζῶ, ζῇς, ζῇ, ζῶμεν, ζῆτε, ζῶσι(ν)**; imperfect first singular **ἔζων**; second plural **ἐζῆτε**; future **ζήσω** or **ζήσομαι**, etc., aorist **ἔζησα**, etc.; present infinitive **ζῆν**, present participle **ζῶν, ζῶσα, ζῶν**.

(2) **Χράομαι**, *use* (originally an **ηω**-verb). The forms are generally like those of the middle and passive of **τιμάω**, except that in the present subjunctive **χράομαι** has third singular **χρῆται**.

(3) A few verbs in **-έω** have uncontracted forms (as well as, usually, some contracted forms). The most important of these is **δέομαι**, *ask, beg, pray, beseech* (**δέη, δεῖται, δεόμεθα, δεῖσθε, δέονται; ἐδεόμην; ἐδεήθην**).

47 | THE PERFECT AND PLUPERFECT

369. In our study of the Greek verb we have thus far considered four of its principal parts:[1] the first person singular indicative of (a) the present active,[2] (b) the future active, (3) the aorist active, and (d) the aorist passive. In this lesson we shall take up the remaining principal parts, the **perfect active** and the **perfect middle and passive**[3] (first person singular indicative, in both cases). From these principal parts are obtained the perfect and pluperfect forms of the verb.[4] Some of the more common regular verbs are listed below, with these two principal parts given:

PRESENT ACTIVE	PERFECT ACTIVE	PERFECT MIDDLE AND PASSIVE
λύω, *loose*	λέλυκα	λέλυμαι
ποιέω, *do, make*	πεποίηκα	πεποίημαι
γεννάω, *beget*	γεγέννηκα	γεγέννημαι
βαπτίζω, *baptize*	βεβάπτικα	βεβάπτισμαι
τηρέω, *keep*	τετήρηκα	τετήρημαι

The chief distinguishing features of the forms in the two right-hand columns are the prefixed syllables λε-, πε-, γε-, βε-, τε-; these are called **reduplicating syllables**; the presence of reduplication in a verb form is a certain[5] indication that the form is perfect or pluperfect.

---

[1] See §§89, 92, 95(4), and 126.

[2] Or, for deponent verbs, the present middle (and passive), future middle, and aorist middle. If a verb is deponent in some tenses but not in all, the principal parts will show this.

[3] Usually regarded as the fourth and fifth principal parts. Cf. §126, fn. 1.

[4] As with the present and imperfect, the perfect and pluperfect use two sets of forms to express the three Greek voices.

[5] Certain, that is, provided it takes the form described in this lesson. Some verbs have reduplicated *present* stems, but these always have ι instead of ε as the vowel of the re-

370. In general, the reduplicating syllable consists of the initial consonant of the verb base plus the vowel **ε**; the exceptions to this general rule are as follows:

(1) If the verb base begins with **φ**, **θ**, or **χ**, the reduplicating syllable is **πε-**, **τε-**, or **κε-**, respectively:

PRESENT ACTIVE	PERFECT ACTIVE	PERFECT MIDDLE AND PASSIVE
φανερόω, *reveal*	πεφανέρωκα	πεφανέρωμαι
θεραπεύω, *heal*	τεθεράπευκα	τεθεράπευμαι
χωρίζω, *divide*	κεχώρικα	κεχώρισμαι

(2) If the verb base begins with **ψ**, **ζ**, or **ξ**, or with two consonants other than a consonant plus **λ** or **ρ**, the reduplicating syllable is simply **ἐ-**:

	ψωμίζω, *feed*	ἐψώμικα	ἐψώμισμαι
	ζητέω, *seek*	ἐζήτηκα	ἐζήτημαι
	ξενίζω, *entertain*	ἐξένικα	ἐξένισμαι
	-στέλλω	-ἔσταλκα	-ἔσταλμαι
	γινώσκω, *know*	ἔγνωκα	ἔγνωσμαι
	κτίζω, *create*	—	ἔκτισμαι
BUT	πληρόω, *fill*	πεπλήρωκα	πεπλήρωμαι

(3) If the verb base begins with **ρ**, the reduplicating syllable is sometimes regularly formed (i.e., **ῥε-**), but is usually **ἐρ-**:

ῥαντίζω, *sprinkle*	—	ῥεράντισμαι
ῥίπτω, *throw*	—	ἔρριμμαι

(4) If the verb base begins with a vowel, reduplication takes the same form as the augment (see §95(1)):

ἀγαπάω, *love*	ἠγάπηκα	ἠγάπημαι
ἑτοιμάζω, *prepare*	ἡτοίμακα	ἡτοίμασμαι
ἡγέομαι, *regard*	—	ἥγημαι
αἰτέω, *ask*	ᾔτηκα	—
εὑρίσκω, *find*	εὕρηκα	—
ὁρίζω, *appoint*	—	ὥρισμαι

(5) The reduplication of a number of important verbs is irregular:

---

duplicating syllable: e.g., **δίδωμι**, **τίθημι**, **ἵστημι** (< **σίστημι**), **γινώσκω** (< **γιγνώσκω**), etc.

PRESENT ACTIVE	PERFECT ACTIVE	PERFECT MIDDLE AND PASSIVE
αἴρω, *take up*	ἦρκα	ἦρμαι
ἀκούω, *hear*	ἀκήκοα	—
ἀνοίγω, *open*	ἀνέῳγα	ἀνέῳγμαι (ἠνέῳγμαι, ἤνοιγμαι)
ἐγείρω, *raise*	—	ἐγήγερμαι
ἔχω, *have*	ἔσχηκα	—
ἵστημι, *establish*	ἕστηκα	—
δίδωμι, *give*	δέδωκα	δέδομαι
τίθημι, *put*	τέθεικα	τέθειμαι
-ἵημι	-εἷκα	-εἷμαι
-ὄλλυμι	-ὄλωλα	—
λαμβάνω, *take*	εἴληφα	εἴλημμαι
ὁράω, *see*	ἑώρακα and ἑόρακα	—

371. The perfect and pluperfect forms of regular verbs may be analyzed into constituent morphemes as follows:

(1) The **base** (e.g., λυ-).

(2) **Prefixes.** (a) The reduplicating syllable, as described above, is prefixed to the base in all perfect and pluperfect forms.

(b) The augment (as described in §95(1)) is prefixed to the reduplicating syllable in pluperfect indicative forms; however, this augment is frequently omitted.

(3) **Tense formant: -κ-** (added to the reduplicated verb base to form the perfect active base). NOTE: Some verbs do not have this -κ- in their perfect (or pluperfect) forms (e.g., γέγραφα < γράφω) and other verbs have shortened or lengthened forms of the verb base before it (e.g., βεβάπτικα < βαπτίζω and μεμάθηκα < μανθάνω [base μαθ-, seen in the second aorist ἔμαθον]).

(4) **Stem formatives:**

(a) -α/ε- (added to the perfect active base to form the perfect active stem; the allomorph -ε- occurs only in the third person singular).

(b) -ει- (added to the perfect active base to form the pluperfect active stem).

REMARK: Neither tense formants nor stem formatives occur in the perfect and pluperfect middle and passive. The perfect middle and passive base is thus identical with the perfect middle and passive stem, and consists merely of the reduplicated verb base.

(5) **Suffixes:**
(a) Indicative:

	PRIMARY A	PRIMARY B	SECONDARY A	SECONDARY B
SG.1	-#	-μαι	-ν	-μην
2	-ς	-σαι	-ς	-σο
3	-(ν)	-ται	-#	-το
PL.1	-μεν	-μεθα	-μεν	-μεθα
2	-τε	-σθε	-τε	-σθε
3	-σι(ν)	-νται	-σαν	-ντο

The Primary A suffixes are added to the perfect active stem to form the perfect active indicative; the Primary B suffixes are added to the perfect middle and passive stem to form the perfect middle and passive indicative; the Secondary A suffixes are added to the (sometimes augmented) pluperfect active stem to form the pluperfect active indicative, and the Secondary B suffixes are added to the (sometimes augmented) perfect (=pluperfect) middle and passive stem to form the pluperfect middle and passive indicative.

(b) Imperative: No perfect active imperative forms occur in the New Testament. The following perfect middle and passive forms occur:

> πεφίμωσο (Mk 4:39), *be muzzled* (second singular)
> ἔρρωσο (Acts 23:30), *be strong, farewell* (second singular)
> ἔρρωσθε (Acts 15:29), *be strong, farewell* (second plural)

The first of these forms is from **φιμόω**, the last two from **ῥώννυμαι.**

(c) Subjunctive: No perfect subjunctive form occurs in the New Testament; where necessary, its place is taken by a perfect participle plus a subjunctive form of **εἰμί.**

(d) Infinitives:
    (i) **-έναι**, added to the perfect active base to form the perfect active infinitive: e.g., **λελυκέναι, γεγραφέναι, πεποιηκέναι.**
    (ii) **-σθαι**, added to the perfect middle and passive base to form the perfect middle and passive infinitive: e.g., **λελύσθαι, πεποιῆσθαι.**

(e) Participles:
    (i) **-ώς,** (masculine), **-υῖα,** (feminine), **-ός** (neuter), added to the perfect active base to form the perfect active participle: e.g., **λελυκώς, λελυκυῖα, λελυκός**; genitive singular, **λελυκότος, λελυκυίας, λελυκότος**; dative plural **λελυκόσι(ν), λελυκυίαις, λελυκόσι(ν).**
    (ii) **-μένος, -μένη, -μένον,** added to the perfect middle and pas-

sive base to form the perfect middle and passive participle: e.g., λελυμένος, πεποιημένος.

REMARK: If the perfect middle and passive stem (or base) of a verb ends in a consonant,[1] this consonant and the initial consonant of the following suffix combine as indicated in the table below:[2]

	μ	σ	τ	σθ
π, β, φ	μμ	ψ	πτ	φθ
κ, γ, χ	γμ	ξ	κτ	χθ
τ, δ, θ	σμ	σ	στ	σθ
λ	λμ	λσ	λτ	λθ
ρ	ρμ	ρσ	ρτ	ρθ
ν	μμ	νσ	ντ	νθ

Note that this table does not provide for combinations of consonants with **ντ** (e.g., in -νται, -ντο), because the forms in which such combinations would occur have been replaced, in Hellenistic Greek, by periphrastic expressions. See the examples (in the third person plural) in the following section.

372. ILLUSTRATIVE PARADIGMS:

	(1) λύω	(2) γράφω	(3) τάσσω
		PERFECT ACTIVE	
SG.1	λέλυκα	γέγραφα	τέταχα
2	λέλυκας	γέγραφας	τέταχας
3	λέλυκε(ν)	γέγραφε(ν)	τέταχε(ν)
PL.1	λελύκαμεν	γεγράφαμεν	τετάχαμεν
2	λελύκατε	γεγράφατε	τετάχατε
3	λελύκασι(ν)	γεγράφασι(ν)	τετάχασι(ν)

---

[1] In general, the final consonant of the verb base (see §90) as this appears when final -ω of the first principal part is dropped. The verb base cannot, however, always be found in this way: thus the base of βαπτίζω is βαπτιδ-, and the base of κηρύσσω is κηρυκ-.

[2] The final consonant of the stem is given in the left-hand column, and the initial consonant of the suffix is given in the top row; the combination of the two appears in the intersection of a column and a row, thus:

π, β, or φ + μ > μμ : γεγραφ + μαι > γέγραμμαι
κ, γ, or χ + σ > ξ : τεταγ + σαι > τέταξαι
τ, δ, or θ + τ > στ : πεπειθ + ται > πέπεισται
λ + σθ > λθ : εσταλ + σθε > ἔσταλθε

PLUPERFECT ACTIVE

SG.1	(ἐ)λελύκειν	(ἐ)γεγράφειν	(ἐ)τετάχειν
2	(ἐ)λελύκεις	(ἐ)γεγράφεις	(ἐ)τετάχεις
3	(ἐ)λελύκει	(ἐ)γεγράφει	(ἐ)τετάχει
PL.1	(ἐ)λελύκειμεν	(ἐ)γεγράφειμεν	(ἐ)τετάχειμεν
2	(ἐ)λελύκειτε	(ἐ)γεγράφειτε	(ἐ)τετάχειτε
3	(ἐ)λελύκεισαν	(ἐ)γεγράφεισαν	(ἐ)τετάχεισαν

PERFECT MIDDLE AND PASSIVE

SG.1	λέλυμαι	γέγραμμαι	τέταγμαι
2	λέλυσαι	γέγραψαι	τέταξαι
3	λέλυται	γέγραπται	τέτακται
PL.1	λελύμεθα	γεγράμμεθα	τετάγμεθα
2	λέλυσθε	γέγραφθε	τέταχθε
3	λέλυνται	γεγραμμένοι εἰσίν	τεταγμένοι εἰσίν

PLUPERFECT MIDDLE AND PASSIVE

SG.1	(ἐ)λελύμην	(ἐ)γεγράμμην	(ἐ)τετάγμην
2	(ἐ)λέλυσο	(ἐ)γέγραψο	(ἐ)τέταξο
3	(ἐ)λέλυτο	(ἐ)γέγραπτο	(ἐ)τέτακτο
PL.1	(ἐ)λελύμεθα	(ἐ)γεγράμμεθα	(ἐ)τετάγμεθα
2	(ἐ)λέλυσθε	(ἐ)γέγραφθε	(ἐ)τέταχθε
3	(ἐ)λέλυντο	γεγραμμένοι ἦσαν	τεταγμένοι ἦσαν

PERFECT ACTIVE INFINITIVE

λελυκέναι   γεγραφέναι   τεταχέναι

PERFECT ACTIVE PARTICIPLE

λελυκώς, -υῖα, -ός   γεγραφώς,   τεταχώς, -υῖα, -ός
                             -υῖα, -ός

PERFECT MIDDLE AND PASSIVE INFINITIVE

λελύσθαι   γεγράφθαι   τετάχθαι

PERFECT MIDDLE AND PASSIVE PARTICIPLE

λελυμένος, -η, -ον   γεγραμμένος, -η,   τεταγμένος, -η,
                             -ον   -ον

REMARK 1: In the perfect and pluperfect forms of compound verbs, the augment (if present) and the reduplicating syllable follow all other prefixes:

PRESENT	PERFECT ACTIVE	PLUPERFECT ACTIVE
ἀπολύω, *dismiss*	ἀπολέλυκα	ἀπελελύκειν

REMARK 2: The verb οἶδα deserves special attention. It has only perfect and pluperfect *forms*, but these are used to express simple present and past meanings. Since this is a very important verb, its forms should be committed to memory:

	PRESENT (PERFECT FORM)	PAST (PLUPERFECT FORM)	FUTURE	SUBJUNCTIVE
SG.1	οἶδα, *I know*	ᾔδειν, *I knew*	εἰδήσω [only form in NT]	εἰδῶ
2	οἶδας	ᾔδεις		εἰδῇς
3	οἶδε(ν)	ᾔδει		εἰδῇ
PL.1	οἴδαμεν	ᾔδειμεν		εἰδῶμεν
2	οἴδατε	ᾔδειτε		εἰδῆτε
3	οἴδασι(ν)	ᾔδεισαν		εἰδῶσι(ν)

	IMPERATIVE	INFINITIVE	PARTICIPLE
PL.2	ἴστε [only form in NT]	εἰδέναι	εἰδώς, -υῖα, -ός

REMARK 3: Ἕστηκα, the perfect active of ἵστημι, is intransitive and is always translated as if present: *I stand, I am standing.* The perfect active participle of ἵστημι is irregular: ἑστώς, ἑστῶσα, ἑστός (genitive singular ἑστῶτος, ἑστώσης, ἑστῶτος), *standing* (intransitive). (The regular form, ἑστηκώς, -υῖα, -ός, also occurs.) The perfect active infinitive of ἵστημι is ἑστάναι.

373. The Meaning of the Perfect and Pluperfect. The Greek perfect may usually be adequately rendered by the English perfect (*have* plus past participle; e.g. *I have seen, I have come*, etc.). The Greek perfect differs from the Greek aorist in that it emphasizes the **continuing result** of the action which was completed in past time. Thus *he is risen* usually represents ἐγήγερται (perfect passive of ἐγείρω: literally, *he has been raised*: Mark 6:14, 1 Corinthians 15:12, 13, 14, 16, 17; 2 Timothy 2:8), which points to the *result* of the resurrection. Paul says (1 Corinthians 9:1), Ἰησοῦν . . . ἑώρακα = *I have seen . . . Jesus* (ἑώρακα is perfect active of ὁράω); hence he *is* an apostle, as a continuing result. The English perfect does not emphasize a result, but simply indicates that the speaker or writer does not intend to interpose a distinct interval between the events of which he uses the perfect tense and the time of speaking or writing. The English

[293]

perfect, accordingly, sometimes represents a Greek aorist, sometimes a Greek perfect.

The Greek pluperfect represents an action as complete at a point in past time, and as having then an existing result. The Greek pluperfect will always be represented by an English pluperfect (e.g., *I had seen, I had come*, etc.), but the English pluperfect will sometimes correspond to other Greek tenses, e.g., the aorist, in

Jn 19:30 ὅτε οὖν **ἔλαβεν** τὸ ὄξος ὁ 'Ιησοῦς εἶπεν, Τετέλεσται.	When therefore Jesus **had received** the vinegar, he said, " It is finished."

374. Summary of Principal Parts. Since we have now completed the study of the principal parts of Greek verbs, it is convenient to conclude this lesson with a short table indicating the manner of forming the principal parts of regular verbs, i.e., verbs which end as indicated in the left-hand column below, in the first person singular, present active indicative:

PRESENT	FUTURE	AORIST	PERFECT	PERFECT MID. & PASS.	AORIST PASSIVE
-άω	-ήσω	-ησα	-ηκα	-ημαι	-ήθην
-άω[1]	-άσω	-ασα	-ακα	-αμαι	-άθην
-έω	-ήσω	-ησα	-ηκα	-ημαι	-ήθην
-όω	-ώσω	-ωσα	-ωκα	-ωμαι	-ώθην
-ίζω	-ίσω[2]	-ισα	-ικα	-ισμαι	-ίσθην
-άζω	-άσω	-ασα	-ακα	-ασμαι	-άσθην
-ύω	-ύσω	-υσα	-υκα	-υμαι	-ύθην

---

[1] Contract verbs in -αω have -α- throughout, if the -αω is immediately preceded by a vowel or ρ.

[2] Some verbs in -ίζω have futures in -ιῶ ("contract futures"; see §365(5)).

48

REFLEXIVE AND RECIPROCAL PRONOUNS INDEFINITE PRONOUNS, ADJECTIVES, AND ADVERBS

375. The Reflexive Pronouns. The ordinary personal pronouns (see above, Lesson 15) may be used, in Greek as in English, with reflexive meaning:

> Mt 11:29 ἄρατε τὸ ζυγόν μου ἐφ' ὑμᾶς.
>
> Take my yoke upon **you** (= upon **yourselves**).

As a general rule, however, Greek uses special forms to express the reflexive meaning. Note that, in the paradigms below, no nominative forms occur:

	FIRST PERSON SINGULAR		SECOND PERSON SINGULAR	
N.	—		—	
G.	ἐμαυτοῦ	(of) myself	σεαυτοῦ	(of) yourself
D.	ἐμαυτῷ	(to, for) myself	σεαυτῷ	(to, for) yourself
A.	ἐμαυτόν	myself	σεαυτόν	yourself

	THIRD PERSON SINGULAR					
N.	—		—		—	
G.	ἑαυτοῦ	(of) himself	ἑαυτῆς	(of) herself	ἑαυτοῦ	(of) itself
D.	ἑαυτῷ	(to, for) himself	ἑαυτῇ	(to, for) herself	ἑαυτῷ	(to, for) itself
A.	ἑαυτόν	himself	ἑαυτήν	herself	ἑαυτό	itself

	PLURAL, ALL PERSONS			
	MASCULINE	FEMININE	NEUTER	
N.	—			
G.	ἑαυτῶν	ἑαυτῶν	ἑαυτῶν	(of) ourselves, yourselves, themselves
D.	ἑαυτοῖς	ἑαυταῖς	ἑαυτοῖς	(to, for) ourselves, etc.
A.	ἑαυτούς	ἑαυτάς	ἑαυτά	ourselves, yourselves, etc.

NOTE 1: The feminine forms of ἐμαυτοῦ and σεαυτοῦ (i.e., ἐμαυτῆς, σεαυτῆς, etc.) do not occur in the New Testament. They would be required if the speaker or person addressed were female.

NOTE 2: It will be noticed from the paradigms above that a single set of forms was used for the reflexive pronoun of all three persons in the *plural*. In translating these forms, therefore, one must refer to the subjects of the clauses in which they stand.

NOTE 3: The reflexive pronouns of English are formally identical with pronouns used for emphasis. They are easily distinguished, however, since the emphatic forms (corresponding to forms of αὐτός in Greek) are always appositive.

Jn 17:19 ἐγὼ ἁγιάζω ἐμαυτόν[1]	I consecrate **myself.**
Lk 23:39 σῶσον **σεαυτὸν** καὶ ἡμᾶς.	Save **yourself** and us.
Mk 4:17 οὐκ ἔχομεν ῥίζαν ἐν ἑαυτοῖς.	They have no root in **themselves.**
Lk 15:20 ἦλθεν πρὸς τὸν πατέρα ἑαυτοῦ.	He came to **his** (= **his own**) father.
Jude 18 κατὰ τὰς ἑαυτῶν ἐπιθυμίας	according to **their own** desires
1 Jn 1:18 ἑαυτοὺς πλανῶμεν.	We deceive **ourselves.**

376. The adjective ἴδιος, α, ον, *private, one's own, peculiar to oneself*, is sometimes used as a possessive adjective corresponding in meaning to the genitive forms of αὐτός, but is usually reflexive:

Mt 25:14 ἄνθρωπος . . . ἐκάλεσεν τοὺς **ἰδίους** δούλους.	A man . . . called **his** servants (*i.e.*, **his own**).

῎Ιδιος is sometimes used for the first and second persons as well as for the third:

1 Th 2:14 τὰ αὐτὰ ἐπάθετε . . . ὑπὸ τῶν **ἰδίων** συμφυλετῶν.	You suffered the same things from **your own** countrymen.

῎Ιδιος is sometimes used in addition to the genitive forms of the personal pronouns, for emphasis:

---

[1] Both the Greek and the English pronouns are reflexive. They would be emphatic in such a sentence as

ἐγὼ **αὐτὸς** ἁγιάζω αὐτούς.	I consecrate them **myself** (= I **myself** consecrate them).

Acts 2:8 . . . ἡμεῖς ἀκούομεν ἕκαστος   . . . we hear, each in **our own**
τῇ **ἰδίᾳ** διαλέκτῳ ἡμῶν.   tongue.

Ἴδιος is also used substantively:

Jn 13:1 ἀγάπησας τοὺς **ἰδίους** . . .   having loved **his own** . . .

The adverbial use of the dative **ἰδίᾳ**, *separately, privately, individually*, and of the phrase **κατ᾽ ἰδίαν**, *in private, by oneself, privately*, should also be noted:

1 Cor 12:11 . . . διαιροῦν **ἰδίᾳ**   distributing to each one **indi-**
ἑκάστῳ . . .   **vidually**

Mt 14:23 ἀνέβη . . . **κατ᾽ ἰδίαν**   He went up **by himself**.

377. The Reciprocal Pronoun. The meaning of the English phrase *each other* is usually expressed in Greek by the reciprocal pronoun **ἀλλήλων**:

	MASCULINE	FEMININE	NEUTER
N.	—	—	—
G.	ἀλλήλων	ἀλλήλων	ἀλλήλων
D.	ἀλλήλοις	ἀλλήλαις	ἀλλήλοις
A.	ἀλλήλους	ἀλλήλας	ἄλληλα

1 Jn 1:7 κοινωνίαν ἔχομεν μετ᾽   We have fellowship with **each**
ἀλλήλων.   **other**.

Jas 5:16 προσεύχεσθε ὑπὲρ   Pray on behalf of **each other**.
ἀλλήλων.

Rev 11:10 δῶρα πέμψουσιν   They will send gifts to **each**
ἀλλήλοις   **other**.

1 Cor 16:20 ἀσπάσασθε **ἀλλήλους**   Greet **one another** (= **each**
ἐν φιλήματι ἁγίῳ.   **other**) with a holy kiss.

The meaning of the English *each other* is also sometimes expressed in Greek by the third person plural of the reflexive pronoun, and sometimes by the phrase **εἰς τὸν ἕνα**:

1 Cor 6:7 κρίματα ἔχετε μεθ᾽   You have lawsuits with **each**
ἑαυτῶν.   **other**.

1 Th 5:11 οἰκοδομεῖτε **εἰς τὸν ἕνα**.   Build up **one another**.

378. Indefinite Pronouns, Adjectives, and Adverbs. The indefinite pronoun and adjective in New Testament Greek is **τις**, whose case forms are identical to those of the interrogative pronoun and adjective τίς except for accent (see above, §303(1)):[1]

		MASCULINE AND FEMININE	NEUTER
SG.	N.	τις	τι
	G.	τινός (or τινος)	τινός (or τινος)
	D.	τινί (or τινι)	τινί (or τινι)
	A.	τινά (or τινα)	τι
PL.	N.	τινές (or τινες)	τινά (or τινα)
	G.	τινῶν (or τινων)	τινῶν (or τινων)
	D.	τισί(ν) (or τισι[ν])	τισί(ν) (or τισι[ν])
	A.	τινάς (or τινας)	τινά (or τινα)

(1) When used as a pronoun the indefinite τις, τι corresponds to English *any, anyone, anybody, anything, some, someone, somebody, something, one, a certain one, a certain person, a certain man, a certain thing, certain, certain ones, certain people*; in selecting one of these possible translations one must be guided by the context:

Mt 12:29 πῶς δύναταί **τις** εἰσελθεῖν εἰς τὴν οἰκίαν τοῦ ἰσχυροῦ;	How can **anyone** enter into the strong man's house?
Jn 3:3 ἐὰν μή **τις** γεννηθῇ ἄνωθεν . . .	Unless **one** is born again . . .
Mt 9:3 ἰδού **τινες** τῶν γραμματέων εἶπαν ἐν ἑαυτοῖς . . .	**Some** (*or* **certain**) of the scribes said among themselves . . .
Lk 9:49 εἴδαμέν **τινα** ἐν τῷ ὀνόματί σου ἐκβάλλοντα δαιμόνια.	We saw **someone** casting out demons in your name.
Lk 1:40 ἔχω σοί **τι** εἰπεῖν.	I have **something** to say to you.
Heb 3:4 πᾶς γὰρ οἶκος κατασκευάζεται ὑπό **τινος**.	For every house is built by **someone**.
1 Th 5:15 ὁρᾶτε μή **τις** κακὸν ἀντὶ κακοῦ **τινι** ἀποδῷ.	See that **no one** (= **not anyone**) returns evil for evil **to anyone**.

---

[1] The forms of the interrogative pronoun always have an *acute* accent (which falls on the first syllable, in the case of dissyllabic forms); the forms of the indefinite pronoun have either *no* accent or an accent on the second syllable (of dissyllabic forms). For complete rules, see Appendix I. In doing the exercises, the student should write accents for the interrogative forms, but omit them from the indefinite forms, unless otherwise directed by his instructor.

(2) The indefinite **τις, τι** may also function as an adjective (with anarthrous nouns); it then means *any, some, a certain, certain*:

Lk 15:11 ἄνθρωπός **τις** εἶχεν δύο υἱούς.	**A certain** man had two sons.
Lk 18:2 κριτής **τις** ἦν ἔν **τινι** πόλει.	**A certain** judge was in **a certain** city.
Acts 15:36 μετὰ δέ **τινας** ἡμέρας εἶπεν πρὸς Βαρνάβαν Παῦλος . . .	And after **some** days Paul said to Barnabas, . . .
1 Tim 5:24 **τινῶν** ἀνθρώπων αἱ ἁμαρτίαι πρόδηλοί εἰσιν.	The sins of **some** men are conspicuous.

379. Indefinite Adverbs. The indefinite adverbs which occur in the New Testament are **ποτέ** (or **ποτε**), *at some time or other, once, formerly, at times* (cf. the interrogative **πότε**; *when?*), **πού** (or **που**), *somewhere, about* (with numbers) (cf. the interrogative **ποῦ**; *where?*), and **πώς** (or **πως**), *somehow* (cf. the interrogative **πῶς**; *how?*) [1] The use of these adverbs requires some explanation:

(a) **ποτέ** (or **ποτε**):

(i) When the context points to future time, **ποτέ** means *ever, at any time, at some time, once*:

Lk 22:32 σύ **ποτε** ἐπιστρέψας στήρισον τοὺς ἀδελφούς σου.	**Once** you are converted, strengthen your brethren.

(ii) When the context points to past time, **ποτέ** means *once, formerly*:

Rom 7:9 ἐγὼ δὲ ἔζων χωρὶς νόμου **ποτέ**.	But I was **formerly** alive apart from the Law.
Jn 9:13 ἄγουσιν αὐτὸν πρὸς τοὺς Φαρισαίους, τόν **ποτε** τυφλόν.	They led him who was **once** blind to the Pharisees.

(iii) In combination with other words:

(α) **ἤδη ποτέ**, *now at last*:

Rom 1:10 . . . δεόμενος εἴ πως **ἤδη ποτὲ** εὐοδωθήσομαι ἐν τῷ θελήματι τοῦ θεοῦ ἐλθεῖν πρὸς ὑμᾶς.	. . . asking whether perhaps **now at last** I shall succeed by God's will to come to you.

---

[1] Note that the indefinite adverbs are either unaccented or accented differently from the interrogative adverbs.

(β) **οὐ . . . ποτέ**, *never, not ever*:

    2 Pet 1:21 . . . οὐ γὰρ θελήματι   . . . for a prophecy **never** was
    ἀνθρώπου ἠνέχθη προφητεία **ποτέ**   brought by man's will

(γ) **τίς . . . ποτέ**; *who in the world?* (introducing a rhetorical
question anticipating a negative answer):

    1 Cor 9:7 **τίς** στρατεύεται ἰδίοις   **Who in the world** serves as a
    ὀψωνίοις **ποτέ**;   soldier at his own expense?

(δ) **μή ποτε** (or **μήποτε**). With the indicative, *never*:

    Heb 9:17 . . . ἐπεὶ **μήποτε** ἰσχύει.   . . . since it is **never** in force.

With the subjunctive, *lest, that . . . not* (cf. the use of **μή** as a conjunctive
§349(3)):

    Mt 15:32 ἀπολῦσαι αὐτοὺς νήστεις   I do not wish to send them away
    οὐ θέλω, **μήποτε** ἐκλυθῶσιν ἐν τῇ   hungry, **lest** they faint on the
    ὁδῷ.   way.

As an interrogative adverb (cf. **μή**, §302(1)), with the indicative:

    Jn 7:26 **μήποτε** ἀληθῶς ἔγνωσαν οἱ   Have the authorities really come
    ἄρχοντες;   to know?

  (b) **ποῦ** (or **που**):
    (i) Rarely alone, with the meaning *somewhere*:

    Heb 4:4 εἴρηκεν γάρ **που** περὶ τῆς   For he has **somewhere** spoken
    ἑβδόμης οὕτως.   thus concerning the seventh
                              day.

    (ii) With numbers and numeral expressions, meaning *about*:

    Rom 4:19 . . . ἑκατονταετής **που**   . . . being **about** a hundred years
    ὑπάρχων.   old.

    (iii) In combination with other words:
      (α) **δή που** (or **δήπου**), *surely, of course*:

    Heb 2:16 οὐ γὰρ **δήπου** ἀγγέλων   For **surely** he is not concerned
    ἐπιλαμβάνεται.   with angels.

    (β) **μή που** (or **μήπου**), *lest . . . somewhere*:

| Acts 27:29 . . . φοβούμενοί τε μή
που κατὰ τραχεῖς τόπους
ἐκπέσωμεν . . . | . . . and fearing **lest** we might
somewhere run on rough
places . . . |

(c) **πώς** (or **πως**), *somehow, in some way;* in the New Testament only in the combinations **μή πως** (**μήπως**) and **εἴ πως**:

(i) **μή πως** (**μήπως**), *so that . . .* (*perhaps*) *not, lest . . .* (*perhaps*).

| 1 Cor 9:27 ὑπωπιάζω μου τὸ σῶμα
καὶ δουλαγωγῶ, **μή πως** ἄλλοις
κηρύξας αὐτὸς ἀδόκιμος γένωμαι. | I pommel my body and subdue it
lest (**perhaps**) after preaching
to others I myself should be dis-
qualified. |

(ii) **εἴ πως**, *if perhaps, if somehow; whether perhaps, whether somehow:*

| Rom 1:10 . . . δεόμενος **εἴ πως** ἤδη
ποτὲ εὐοδωθήσομαι ἐν τῷ θελήματι
τοῦ θεοῦ ἐλθεῖν πρὸς ὑμᾶς. | . . . asking **whether somehow** I
may now at last succeed, by
God's will, in coming to you. |

49 | THE VOCATIVE
OTHER USES OF THE CASES

380. The Vocative Case. The fifth and last of the Greek cases is called the **vocative**. The vocative does not exist as a separate case form for all nouns and does not exist as a separate case form at all except in the singular number.

The vocative exists as a separate case form for:

(1) Some **masculine** nouns of the **first** declension; the case-number suffix is -α,[1] except for ᾅδης, *Hell, Hades*, which has vocative ᾅδη:

EXAMPLES   δεσπότης, *lord*, has vocative δέσποτα
ἐπιστάτης, *master*, has vocative ἐπιστάτα
ὑποκριτής, *hypocrite*, has vocative ὑποκριτά
Ἀγρίππας, *Agrippa*, has vocative Ἀγρίππα

(2) About thirty **masculine** nouns of the **second** declension; the case-number suffix is -ε:[1]

EXAMPLES   κύριος, *lord*, has vocative κύριε
θάνατος, *death*, has vocative θάνατε

(3) The following nouns of the **third** declension have vocatives which occur in the New Testament; there is no case-number suffix, but the base of each noun is altered as indicated:

EXAMPLES   γυνή, *woman*, has vocative γύναι
πατήρ, *father*, has vocative πάτερ
θυγάτηρ, *daughter*, has vocative θύγατερ
ἀνήρ, *man*, has vocative ἄνερ
βασιλεύς, *king*, has vocative βασιλεῦ

(4) The **masculine** form of adjectives of the first and second declensions may have a vocative in -ε:

---

[1] With stem vowel *zero*. See §143(3a).

EXAMPLE   Lk 1:3 κράτιστε Θεόφιλε   **most excellent** Theophilus

REMARK: The definite article has no vocative form. Nouns in the vocative are sometimes preceded by ὦ, *oh, O*, but this is an interjection, not a form of the article.

381. The Meaning of the Vocative. The vocative case indicates the person (or personified thing) addressed by the speaker:

Lk 2:29 νῦν ἀπολύεις τὸν δοῦλόν σου, **δέσποτα.**	**Lord**, now lettest thou thy servant depart.
Lk 8:24 **ἐπιστάτα, ἐπιστάτα,** ἀπολλύμεθα.	**Master, master,** we are perishing.
Mt 7:5 **ὑποκριτά,** ἔκβαλε πρῶτον ἐκ τοῦ ὀφθαλμοῦ σου τὴν δοκόν.	**You hypocrite**, first take the log out of your eye.
Mt 15:28 ὦ **γύναι,** μεγάλη σου ἡ πίστις.	O **woman**, great is your faith.
Mt 20:30 ἐλέησον ἡμᾶς **υἱὲ** Δαυίδ.	Have mercy on us, **son** of David!
Mt 27:46 **θεέ** μου, **θεέ** μου, ἱνατί με ἐγκατέλιπες;	My **God**, my **God**, why hast thou forsaken me?
Acts 26:27 πιστεύεις, **βασιλεῦ** 'Αγρίππα . . .;	Do you believe, **King Agrippa,** . . .?

382. Other Uses of the Cases. (1) **The nominative.** The principal function of the nominative case is to indicate the subject of a sentence or clause (see §48); the only other function we have noticed up to now is that of indicating the predicate nominative (see §57). In addition to these functions, the nominative also serves:

(a) In place of the vocative (whether the noun involved actually has a vocative or not); when the nominative is so used, it may have an article:

Jn 20:28 **ὁ κύριός** μου καὶ **ὁ θεός** μου.	My **Lord** and my **God**!
Mk 5:41 **τὸ κοράσιον,** σοὶ λέγω, ἔγειρε.	**Little girl**, I say to you, arise.

(b) In introducing or citing names or titles:

Jn 13:13 ὑμεῖς φωνεῖτέ με **ὁ διδάσκαλος** καὶ **ὁ κύριος.**	You call me **teacher** and **lord**.
Rev 9:11 ὄνομα ἔχει **'Απολλύων.**	He has the name **Apollyon**.

(2) **The accusative.** The principal function of the accusative case is to indicate the direct object of a verb (see §49). Other uses of the accusative which have been discussed in previous lessons are those of object complement (with certain verbs; see §§181f), second object with certain verbs (§188), "retained" object with some of the same verbs when they are in the passive voice (§185), object of various prepositions (§§191, 197, 198), and subject of an infinitive (§259, *Remark*). In addition to these uses the accusative case appears in various adverbial uses:

(a) With expressions usually rendered in English by phrases such as "with respect to . . .", etc.; sometimes called "accusative of respect":

Mt 27:57 τοὔνομα (= τὸ ὄνομα) Ἰωσήφ	Joseph **by name**
Jn 6:10 ἀνέπεσαν οὖν οἱ ἄνδρες τὸν ἀριθμὸν ὡς πεντακισχίλιοι.	The men therefore sat down, **in number** about five thousand (about five thousand **in respect to the number**).
Mt 23:37 ποσάκις ἠθέλησα ἐπισυναγαγεῖν τὰ τέκνα σου, **ὃν τρόπον** ὄρνις ἐπισυνάγει τὰ νοσσία ὑπὸ τὰς πτέρυγας, καὶ οὐκ ἠθελήσατε.	How often would I have gathered your children together **as** (= **in which manner**) a hen gathers her brood under her wings, and you would not.

(b) With expressions indicating "extent of time":

Jn 2:12 ἔμειναν οὐ **πολλὰς ἡμέρας**.	They stayed not **many days**.
Lk 21:37 ἦν δὲ **τὰς ἡμέρας** ἐν τῷ ἱερῷ διδάσκων, **τὰς δὲ νύκτας** ἐξερχόμενος . . .	And **every day** he was teaching in the temple, but **at night** he went out . . .

In translating adverbial accusative expressions, one must be guided by the context; most such expressions (especially the last three cited above) are quite stereotyped in form.

(3) **The genitive.** The principal function of the genitive case is to indicate that one noun or pronoun stands in a relationship of "modification" or dependence to another (see §80); the genitive is also used as the object of certain prepositions (§§193, 197f), in comparisons (§§159, 276(1)), and in the construction called the "genitive absolute," with participles (§228). Three other important uses of the genitive remain to be noticed here:

(a) The genitive is used to indicate the direct object (i.e., the single object) of certain verbs, the most important of which are listed below:[1]

> ἀκούω, *hear* (also with the accusative)
> ἀνέχομαι, *endure, bear, put up with* (rarely with the accusative)
> ἅπτομαι, *touch, take hold of*
> ἄρχω, *rule* (in the middle voice, *begin*)
> γεύομαι, *taste, experience* (sometimes with the accusative)
> ἐπιθυμέω, *desire, long for* (sometimes with the accusative)
> ἐπιλαμβάνομαι, *take hold of, catch*
> κρατέω, *take hold of, grasp* (also with the accusative)
> μιμνήσκομαι, *remember*
> μνημονεύω, *remember* (also with the accusative)
> περισσεύω, *abound in, have an abundance of*
> ὑστερέω, *be in need of, lack, be inferior to*

(b) The genitive is used as a second object of a few verbs which have a direct object in the accusative:

> κατηγορέω, *accuse* (τινος τι, *someone* [genitive] *of something* [accusative])
> πίμπλημι, *fill* (τι τινος. *something with something*)[2]
> πληρόω, *fill* (τι τινος. *something with something*)

	Lk 14:24 οὐδεὶς τῶν ἀνδρῶν ἐκείνων . . . γεύσεται μου **τοῦ δείπνου**.	None of those men . . . shall taste **my dinner**.
	Jn 20:17 μή **μου** ἅπτου.	Do not touch **me**.
	Jn 10:16 καὶ **τῆς φωνῆς** μου ἀκούσουσιν.	And they will hear my **voice**.
BUT:	Acts 9:4 ἤκουσεν **φωνὴν** λέγουσαν αὐτῷ . . .	He heard a **voice** saying to him . . .
	Mt 26:75 ἐμνήσθη ὁ Πέτρος **τοῦ ῥήματος** Ἰησοῦ.	Peter remembered **the saying** of Jesus.
	Col 4:18 μνημονεύετε μου **τῶν δεσμῶν**.	Remember my **bonds**.

---

[1] For the details of the syntax of these and similar verbs, the student should consult a lexicon or reference grammar. In the present textbook, the student should assume that a transitive verb requires an object in the accusative unless it is explicitly said to do otherwise.

[2] For the conjugation of this verb, see §367(1).

BUT: 2 Tim 2:8 μνημονεύετε Ἰησοῦν Χριστόν.

Remember **Jesus Christ**.

Mk 15:3 κατηγόρουν **αὐτοῦ** οἱ ἀρχιερεῖς πολλά.

The chief priests were accusing **him** of many things.

REMARK: Most of the verbs listed under (a) above are not used in the passive; when those listed under (b) are used in the passive, the accusative becomes the subject and the genitive object is simply retained:

Mt 27:48 . . . λαβὼν σπόλλον πλήσας τε **ὄξους** . . .

. . . taking a sponge and filling it **with vinegar** . . . [It, if expressed, would be in the accusative.]

Acts 2:4 ἐπλήσθησαν πάντες **πνεύματος ἁγίου**.

They were all filled **with the Holy Spirit**.

(c) The genitive is used with certain adjectives, the most important of which are as follows:

κοινωνός, ή, όν, *sharing*
μεστός, ή, όν, *full*
πλήρης, ες, *full*

ἄξιος, α, ον, *worthy*
ἔνοχος, ον, *guilty, liable*
ξένος, η, ον, *strange*

Jn 19:29 σκεῦος ἔκειτο **ὄξους** μεστόν.

A vessel **full of vinegar** was sitting.

Lk 4:1 Ἰησοῦς δὲ **πλήρης πνεύματος ἁγίου** ὑπέστρεψεν ἀπὸ τοῦ Ἰορδάνου.

And Jesus, **full of the Holy Spirit**, returned from the Jordan.

Mt 3:8 ποιήσατε οὖν καρπὸν **ἄξιον τῆς μετανοίας**.

Therefore bear fruit **worthy of repentance**.

Mt 26:66 **ἔνοχος θανάτου** ἐστίν.

He is **guilty of death** (*i.e.*, He is deserving of death, by reason of guilt).

(d) The genitive is used in several adverbial expressions; for example:

χειμῶνος, *in winter*
ἡμέρας, *by day*
ἡμέρας καὶ νυκτός, *day and night*
νυκτός, *at night*
σαββάτου, *on the Sabbath*
ἡμέρας μέσης, *at midday*

μέσης νυκτός, *at midnight, in the middle of the night*
τοῦ λοιποῦ, *further*

(4) **The dative.** We have seen that the dative case is used to indicate (i) the indirect object of verbs (see §83), (ii) the object of certain prepositions (§§192, 197f), and (iii) various other meanings, e.g., those of means or instrument, manner, and "respect" or "interest" (§85). The dative has a number of other functions, the most important of which are indicated below:

(a) The dative is used as the direct object (i.e., as the single object, corresponding to a single direct object in the accusative with other verbs) with certain verbs, among which are the following:

ἀκολουθέω, *follow*
ἀπειθέω, *disobey*
ἀπιστέω, *disbelieve*
διακονέω, *serve (at table), wait on, care for, help, serve as a deacon* (an accusative, indicating the thing served, may occur)
δουλεύω, *serve, obey, be subject to, be a slave*
ἐγγίζω, *approach, draw near to*
εὐχαριστέω, *thank, give thanks*[1]
λατρεύω, *serve* (in carrying out religious duties)
πιστεύω, *believe*[2]
προσκυνέω, *worship* (sometimes with the accusative)
ὑπακούω, *obey*
χράομαι, *make use of, employ, use* (sometimes with the accusative)

Mt 9:9 ἀκολούθει μοι	**Follow me.**
Rom 11:30 ὑμεῖς ποτὲ **ἠπειθήσατε** τῷ θεῷ.	You formerly **disobeyed God.**
Lk 24:11 καὶ **ἠπίστουν αὐταῖς.**	And **they refused to believe them.**
Mt 6:24 οὐδεὶς δύναται **δυσὶ κυρίοις δουλεύειν.**	No one can **serve two masters.**

[1] The thing for which thanks is given is indicated by περί τινος, ὑπέρ τινος, or ἐπί τινι; outside the New Testament an accusative also occurs in this meaning.

[2] Πιστεύω also admits other constructions, as follows: πιστεύω + accusative, *believe (a thing)*; πιστεύω εἰς τινά or ἐπί τινι, *believe in someone or something*; πιστεύω τι τινι, *entrust something to someone.*

Lk 7:12 ἤγγισεν τῇ πύλῃ τῆς πόλεως.	He **approached the gate** of the city.
1 Cor 1:4 εὐχαριστῶ τῷ θεῷ πάντοτε περὶ ὑμῶν.	I **thank God** always concerning you.
Mt 4:10 αὐτῷ μόνῳ λατρεύσεις.	**Him only shall you serve.**
Mt 21:32 οἱ δὲ τελῶναι καὶ αἱ πόρναι ἐπίστευσαν αὐτῷ.	But the tax collectors and the harlots **believed him**.
Jn 4:23 οἱ ἀληθινοὶ προσκυνηταὶ **προσκυνήσουσιν τῷ πατρὶ** ἐν πνεύματι καὶ ἀληθείᾳ.	The true worshippers **shall worship the Father** in Spirit and truth.
Mt 8:27 καὶ οἱ ἄνεμοι καὶ ἡ θάλασσα αὐτῷ ὑπακούουσιν.	Both the winds and the sea **obey him**.
1 Cor 9:12 οὐκ ἐχρησάμεθα τῇ ἐξουσίᾳ ταύτῃ.	**We have** not **used this authority**.

(b) The dative is used with certain adjectives, of which the most important are given below:

ἀπειθής, ές, *disobedient*
ἐναντίος, ον, *hostile, contrary*
ὅμοιος, α, ον, *like, similar*
πιστός, ή, όν, *faithful* (previously noted in §85)
σωτήριος, ον, *saving, preserving, bringing salvation*
φανερός, ά, όν, *manifest, evident, known, plain, visible*
ὠφέλιμος, ον, *useful, beneficial, advantageous*

Acts 26:19 οὐκ ἐγενόμην **ἀπειθὴς τῇ οὐρανίῳ ὀπτασίᾳ**.	I did not become **disobedient to the heavenly vision**.
Mk 6:48 . . . ἦν γὰρ ὁ ἄνεμος **ἐναντίος αὐτοῖς**	. . . for the wind was **contrary to them**
Mt 13:44 **ὁμοία** ἐστὶν ἡ βασιλεία τῶν οὐρανῶν **θησαυρῷ**.	The kingdom of heaven is **like a treasure**.
Acts 16:15 κεκρίκατέ με **πιστὴν τῷ κυρίῳ** εἶναι.	You have judged me to be **faithful to the Lord**. [A woman is speaking.]
Tit 2:11 ἐπεφάνη γὰρ ἡ χάρις τοῦ θεοῦ **σωτήριος πᾶσιν ἀνθρώποις**.	For the grace of God has appeared, **bringing salvation to all men**.
Acts 7:13 **φανερὸν** ἐγένετο **τῷ Φαραὼ** τὸ γένος Ἰωσήφ.	The kindred of Joseph was made **known to Pharaoh**.

Tit 3:8 ταῦτά ἐστιν καλὰ καὶ ὠφέλιμα τοῖς ἀνθρώποις.

These things are good and **profitable for men**.

(c) To the special uses of the dative noted in (iii), above (cf. §85), the following expressions of time may be added:

Mk 14:12	τῇ πρώτῃ ἡμέρᾳ	*on the first day*
Lk 12:20	νυκτί	*at night*
Mt 14:25	τετάρτῃ φυλακῇ	*in the fourth watch*
Lk 12:39	ποίᾳ ὥρᾳ	*at what hour*
Mk 6:21	τοῖς γενεσίοις αὐτοῦ	*on his birthday*
Mt 24:20	τῷ σαββάτῳ	*on the Sabbath*

50 | THE OPTATIVE MOOD

383. The **optative mood** is used very infrequently in the New Testament; the forms are indicated below:

	(1) PRESENT ACTIVE	(2) PRESENT MIDDLE AND PASSIVE
SG.1	λύοιμι	λυοίμην
2	λύοις	λύοιο
3	λύοι	λύοιτο
PL.1	λύοιμεν	λυοίμεθα
2	λύοιτε	λύοισθε
3	λύοιεν	λύοιντο

	(3) (FIRST) AORIST ACTIVE	(4) (FIRST) AORIST MIDDLE	(5) AORIST PASSIVE
SG.1	λύσαιμι	λυσαίμην	λυθείην
2	λύσαις	λύσαιο	λυθείης
3	λύσαι	λύσαιτο	λυθείη
PL.1	λύσαιμεν	λυσαίμεθα	λυθείημεν
2	λύσαιτε	λύσαισθε	λυθείητε
3	λύσαιεν	λύσαιντο	λυθείησαν

384. Forms for other than "regular" verbs are indicated below:

	(1) SECOND AORIST ACTIVE	(2) SECOND AORIST MIDDLE	(3) PRESENT OPTATIVE OF εἰμί
SG.1	λίποιμι	λιποίμην	εἴην
2	λίποις	λίποιο	εἴης
3	λίποι	λίποιτο	εἴη
PL.1	λίποιμεν	λιποίμεθα	εἴημεν
2	λίποιτε	λίποισθε	εἴητε
3	λίποιεν	λίποιντο	εἴησαν

385. Contracted forms of the optative (i.e., present optative forms of contract verbs) do not occur in the New Testament. For the μι-verbs only the following forms can be cited:

PRESENT MIDDLE AND PASSIVE (of δύναμαι; deponent)	SG.1	δυναίμην
	PL.3	δύναιτο
AORIST ACTIVE (of δίδωμι)	SG.3	δῴη
AORIST MIDDLE (of ὀνίνημι, *help, profit, benefit*)	SG.1	ὀναίμην

386. The forms of the optative may be analyzed into morphemes (along the lines laid down in §§164–169) as follows:

(1) **Base** (e.g., λυ-).

(2) **Tense formants:**

(a) -σ- (in the first aorist active and middle).

(b) -θ- (in the first aorist passive).

(3) **Stem formatives:**

(a) -οι- (in all voices of the present tense and in the second aorist active and middle).

(b) -αι- (in the first aorist active and middle).

(c) -ειη- (in the aorist passive).

(4) **Suffixes:**

	(a) PRIMARY A	(b) PRIMARY B	(c) SECONDARY A	(d) SECONDARY B
SG.1	-μι		-ν	-μην
2	-ς		-ς	-ο
3	-#	[none]	-#	-το
PL.1	-μεν		-μεν	-μεθα
2	-τε		-τε	-σθε
3	-εν		-σαν	-ντο

REMARK: The Primary A suffixes given above are found in the present and (first and second) aorist optative active; the Secondary A suffixes are found in the aorist optative passive; the Secondary B suffixes are found in the present optative middle and passive and in the (first and second) aorist optative middle.

387. Uses of the Optative. (1) The optative is used in independent clauses to express a wish or prayer:

Lk 20:16 μὴ γένοιτο.   **May it** not **happen**! [= **God forbid**, in most English versions]

Phm 20 ἐγώ σου **ὀναίμην**.   **May I benefit** from you!

1 Th 5:23 ὁ θεὸς τῆς εἰρήνης   **May** the God of peace **sanctify**
ἁγιάσαι ὑμᾶς ὁλοτελεῖς, καὶ   you wholly; and **may** your
ὁλόκληρον ὑμῶν τὸ πνεῦμα καὶ ἡ   spirit and soul and body **be**
ψυχὴ καὶ τὸ σῶμα ἀμέμπτως ἐν τῇ   **kept** sound and blameless at
παρουσίᾳ τοῦ κυρίου ἡμῶν Ἰησοῦ   the coming of our Lord Jesus
Χριστοῦ **τηρηθείη**.   Christ.

(2) The optative is used in independent clauses to express what *would*
happen if some supposed condition were fulfilled. The particle **ἄν** always
accompanies the optative when it is used with this meaning. (When the
optative is used in this meaning it is said, in traditional terminology, to be
"potential.")

Acts 17:18 τί **ἄν θέλοι** ὁ σπερμο-   What **would** this babbler **wish**
λόγος οὗτος λέγειν;   to say? [*i.e.,* if he could only
                                    manage it]

Acts 8:31 πῶς γὰρ **ἄν δυναίμην** ἐὰν   For how **would I be able** unless
μή τις ὁδηγήσει με;   someone will guide me? [Here
                                    the condition is actually ex-
                                    pressed.]

(3) The optative (again traditionally called the "potential optative")
may be used in the *if*-clause of a conditional sentence if it expresses a
hypothetical assumption. ("*If*" in such clauses is rendered by **εἰ**.)

Acts 20:16 . . . ἔσπευδεν γάρ, **εἰ**   . . . for he was hastening to be in
δυνατὸν **εἴη** αὐτῷ, τὴν ἡμέραν τῆς   Jerusalem on the day of Pente-
πεντηκοστῆς γενέσθαι εἰς   cost, **if it were** possible for him.
Ἱεροσόλυμα.

1 Pet 3:14 ἀλλ' **εἰ** καὶ **πάσχοιτε** διὰ   But even **if** you **should suffer**
δικαιοσύνην, μακάριοί ἐστε.   (=**were to suffer**) for right-
                                    eousness' sake, you are blessed.

(4) The optative may be used in subordinate clauses (after introductory
verbs of *saying*, etc., in past tenses) in indirect discourse, representing an
original indicative or subjunctive in direct discourse. This use of the
optative (the "oblique optative"), like that described in (2), above, occurs
in the New Testament only in Luke's writings; elsewhere, in indirect discourse, the original mood and tense of the direct discourse are simply
retained.

[312]

Lk 8:9 ἐπηρώτων δὲ αὐτὸν οἱ μαθηταὶ   And his disciples asked him what
αὐτοῦ τίς αὕτη **εἴη** ἡ παραβολή   this parable **was** (=**might be**).

In direct discourse the Greek and English would be:

τίς αὕτη **ἐστὶν** ἡ παραβολή;   What **is** this parable?

An example of indirect discourse without the optative is:

Mt 20:10 ἐλθόντες οἱ πρῶτοι ἐνό-   When the first ones came, they
μισαν ὅτι πλεῖον **λήμψονται**.   supposed that they **would re-
                                        ceive** more.

In direct discourse the Greek and English would be:

πλεῖον **λημψόμεθα**.   We **shall receive** more.

REMARK: As explained earlier (§259(3)), the infinitive with its subject in the accusative may also represent indirect discourse:

Acts 28:6 ἔλεγον αὐτὸν **εἶναι** θεόν.   They said that he **was** a god
                                        (*literally*, They said him **to be**
                                        a god).

388. In the New Testament the negative used with the optative mood is always **μή** (or one of its compounds).

APPENDICES

THE GREEK ACCENTS

389. Modern Greek, like Modern English, is pronounced with a **stress accent**; i.e., the difference between accented and unaccented syllables is primarily one of dynamic force. In this book it is recommended that New Testament Greek be pronounced with a stress accent as, indeed, it is entirely possible that it was pronounced.[1] In earlier Greek, however, the difference between accented and unaccented syllables was one of **musical pitch**, and it was to represent this system of pitch accent that the familiar accent signs were devised.[2] Originally, then, the Greek acute accent (´) indicated high pitch and the grave accent (`) indicated low pitch (i.e., the pitch characteristic of unaccented syllables); the circumflex accent (˜, ^, or ⁀) indicated a high pitch falling to a low pitch in the same syllable (or on the same vowel or diphthong).

Since the accents bear little "functional load," in that they do not serve to distinguish many grammatically significant forms, they may be safely ignored by beginners. More advanced students will find the rules given here quite sufficient for almost all purposes.[3]

390. Definitions:

(1) **Vowel length.** For the purposes of accentuation, vowels and diphthongs are classified as *long* or *short*:

---

[1] See E. M. Sturtevant, *The Pronunciation of Greek and Latin* (Baltimore: The Waverly Press, 1940), pp. 94–105.

[2] The invention of the accent signs is usually ascribed to Aristophanes of Byzantium (ca. 275–180 B.C.). These signs did not, however, come into general use even in literary texts until the third Christian century, and the earlier MSS of the New Testament are quite innocent of them.

[3] For further details see A. J. Koster, *A Practical Guide for the Writing of the Greek Accents* (Leiden: E. J. Brill, 1962), and the bibliography given there.

(a) ε and o are always *short*.

(b) η and ω are always *long*.

(c) α, ι, and υ are sometimes long, sometimes short.

(d) Diphthongs are *long* (including the "improper" diphthongs ᾳ, ῃ, and ῳ) except for final[1] οι and αι, which are treated as short in all words other than forms of the optative mood.

(2) **The syllable.** A Greek word has as many syllables as it has vowels and diphthongs:[2] ἀλήθεια = ἀ-λή-θει-α (four syllables)

A syllable is said to be long if it contains a long vowel or diphthong, but short if it contains a short vowel or diphthong:

νόμος (two short syllables)   νόμοι (two short syllables)
ἤδη (two long syllables)   δοῦλοι (one long, one short)

(3) **Designations of the syllables.** The last syllable of a word is called the **ultima**; the syllable immediately preceding the ultima is called

---

[1] I.e., coming at the very end of a word:

οι is final (and is short) in λόγοι.
οι is not final (and is long) in λόγοις.
αι is final (and is short) in φωναί.
αι is not final (and is long) in φωναῖς.

[2] The method used to divide words into syllables is itself unimportant. In general, it is similar to that used for English:

(a) A single consonant goes with the following vowel: λυ-σό-με-θα

(b) Any group of consonants that can begin a word (in Greek) goes with the following vowel:

πι-στεύ-ο-μεν   ἄ-θλη-σις   μι-κρός   τί-κτω   κρύ-πτω

(c) A consonant plus μ or ν goes with the following vowel:

πρᾶ-γμα   μι-μνή-σκο-μαι

(d) Other consonant groups are divided:

ἐλ-πίς   ἔρ-χο-μαι

(e) Compounds are divided at the point of junction:

εἰσ-ῆλ-θον   προσ-έρ-χε-ται

the **penult**; and the syllable immediately preceding the penult is called the **antepenult.**

391. General Rules of Accent:

(1) (a) A word may be accented only on one of its last three syllables.

(b) No word may have more than one accent, unless it is followed by an enclitic (see §400 (3,4)).

(2) (a) The acute accent may stand only on one of the last three syllables of a word.

(b) The circumflex accent may stand only on one of the last two syllables of a word.

(c) The grave accent may stand only on the last syllable of a word.

(3) (a) The acute accent may stand on either a long or a short syllable.

(b) The circumflex accent may stand only on a long syllable.

(c) The grave accent may stand on either a long or a short syllable.

(4) If the ultima is *short*:

(a) The antepenult, if accented, may have only the acute accent:

ἄνθρωπος   ἀπόστολος   λυόμεθα   λυώμεθα   πνεύματος

(b) The penult, if accented, *must* have the circumflex if it is itself long, but the acute if it is itself short:

ζῆλος   μῶμος   πρᾶγμα   πνεῦμα   δοῦλος   νόμος   θέμα

(c) The short ultima may itself have an acute accent, provided that a mark of punctuation or an enclitic (see §400) immediately follows; if a word other than an enclitic follows immediately, the acute is changed to a grave (note, however, that the interrogative τίς, τί always retains the acute):

υἱός;   υἱὸς θεοῦ;   υἱοί;   υἱοὶ θεοῦ;   τίς δύναται αὐτοῦ ἀκούειν;

(5) If the ultima is *long*:

(a) The antepenult cannot have an accent.

(b) The penult, if accented, may have only the acute:

δούλους   νόμου   προφήτης

(c) The long ultima may itself have either the circumflex or the acute; if it has the acute, this is changed to a grave as described in (4c), above.

υἱούς   υἱοὺς θεοῦ

392. Special Rules of Accent. It should be noticed that the general rules just given do not say how a word must be accented, but only how it may be accented, or, at most, how it must be accented in rather particular circumstances. To determine where the accent of a particular word actually belongs, further information is necessary.

393. Rules of Accent for Nouns. In noun forms the accent remains on the syllable which bears it in the nominative singular, unless it is prevented from doing so by the operation of one or more of the General Rules of Accent (§391). In order to accent a noun form correctly, therefore, it is necessary to know where the accent is in the nominative singular; since no general rule exists for determining this, it must be learned for each noun separately.

A few examples will make clear how the rule of accent for nouns operates:

EXAMPLE 1: The nominative singular of **ἄνθρωπος** has an acute accent on the antepenult; in the genitive and dative singular forms of this word, however, the ultima is long, so that (by General Rule (5a) of §391) the antepenult cannot receive an accent. Accordingly, the accent is moved to the penult in these forms (**ἀνθρώπου, ἀνθρώπῳ**) and is returned to the antepenult in the accusative singular (**ἄνθρωπον**), in which the ultima is again short. The fluctuation of the accent in the plural forms (**ἄνθρωποι, ἀνθρώπων, ἀνθρώποις, ἀνθρώπους**) is explained in the same way.

EXAMPLE 2: The nominative singular of **δοῦλος** has a circumflex accent on the penult, but in the genitive and dative singular this must be changed to an acute (**δούλου, δούλῳ**), since a circumflex can stand on the penult only when the ultima is short.

EXAMPLE 3: The nominative singular of **προφήτης** has an acute accent on the penult; in the nominative plural, however, this must be changed to a circumflex (**προφῆται**) since, by the rule of accent for nouns, it must remain in the position it has in the nominative singular, but also since, by General Rule (4b), §391, an accented long penult must have a circumflex if the ultima is short.

394. More detailed rules are necessary for accenting certain classes of nouns:

(1) In the first and second declensions, an acute on the ultima in the nominative singular is changed to a circumflex in the genitive and dative (singular and plural):

SG.N.	τιμή	μαθητής	ὁδός	ἱερόν
G.	τιμῆς	μαθητοῦ	ὁδοῦ	ἱεροῦ
D.	τιμῇ	μαθητῇ	ὁδῷ	ἱερῷ
A.	τιμήν	μαθητήν	ὁδόν	ἱερόν
PL.N.	τιμαί	μαθηταί	ὁδοί	ἱερά
G.	τιμῶν	μαθητῶν	ὁδῶν	ἱερῶν
D.	τιμαῖς	μαθηταῖς	ὁδοῖς	ἱεροῖς
A.	τιμάς	μαθητάς	ὁδούς	ἱερά

(2) In the **first declension**:

(a) If α is short in the ending of the nominative singular, it is also short in the accusative singular. Thus ἀλήθεια, being accented on the antepenult, must have final -α short; accordingly, its accusative singular is ἀλήθειαν. Similar, if α is long in the ending of the nominative singular, it is also long in the accusative singular. Thus βασιλεία, with an acute accent on its (long) penult, must have final -α long; accordingly, its accusative singular is βασιλείαν.

(b) Regardless of the position of the accent in the nominative singular, nouns of the first declension have a circumflex on the ultima in the genitive plural. (This constitutes an important exception to the basic rule for noun accent given at the beginning of §393.)

SG.N.	τιμή	μαθητής	κώμη	προφήτης	θάλασσα
PL.G.	τιμῶν	μαθητῶν	κωμῶν	προφητῶν	θαλασσῶν

(c) The α in the ending -ας (however analyzed; i.e., whether accusative plural or genitive singular) is always long:

SG.N.	ἀλήθεια	προφήτης	θάλασσα
G.	ἀληθείας	(προφήτου)	(θαλάσσης)
PL.A.	ἀληθείας	προφήτας	θαλάσσας

(3) In the **second declension**, the vowel α is short in the suffix of the nominative and accusative plural, neuter. Thus δῶρον has plural δῶρα.

(4) (a) All the rules of accent given for nouns of the first and second declensions also apply to **adjectives of the first and second declensions**, except for (2b), above (i.e., the feminine genitive plural of adjectives is accented exactly like the masculine and neuter genitive plural). For the accentuation of participles, see §396 (4-6).

(b) Contracted adjectives (see §284) have the circumflex accent on the ultima in all case forms.

(5) In the **third declension**:

(a) The vowel α is short in the suffixes of the accusative singular and plural (masculine and feminine) and in the nominative and accusative plural, neuter:

SG.N.	ἐσθής	φῶς
A.	ἐσθῆτα	φῶς
PL.N.	(ἐσθῆτες)	φῶτα
A.	ἐσθῆτας	φῶτα

(b) ι-stems (see §162) have an acute accent on the antepenult in the genitive singular and plural. (This constitutes an important exception to General Rule (5a), §391.)

SG.N.	πόλις	δύναμις
G.	πόλεως	δυνάμεως
PL.G.	πόλεων	δυνάμεων

(c) Monosyllables of the third declension accent the ultima (circumflex in the genitive plural, otherwise acute) in the genitive and dative, but retain the position of the accent of the nominative singular in the other forms:

SG.N.	πούς	χείρ	θρίξ
G.	ποδός	χειρός	τριχός
D.	ποδί	χειρί	τριχί
A.	πόδα	χεῖρα	τρίχα
PL.N.	πόδες	χεῖρες	τρίχες
G.	ποδῶν	χειρῶν	τριχῶν
D.	ποσί(ν)	χερσί(ν)	θριξί(ν)
A.	πόδας	χεῖρας	τρίχας

(Note that the accent of **χείρ** becomes circumflex in the accusative singular and nominative and accusative plural, in accordance with General Rule (4b), §391).

(d) Some monosyllables do not follow the preceding rule in the genitive plural:

SG.N.	οὖς	παῖς	φῶς
PL.G.	ὤτων	παίδων	φώτων

(e) **Πᾶς** follows the "rule of monosyllables" only in the singular, masculine and neuter:

	MASCULINE	FEMININE	NEUTER
SG.N.	πᾶς	πᾶσα	πᾶν
G.	παντός	πάσης	παντός
D.	παντί	πάσῃ	παντί
A.	πάντα	πᾶσαν	πᾶν
PL.N.	πάντες	πᾶσαι	πάντα
G.	πάντων	πασῶν	πάντων
D.	πᾶσι(ν)	πάσαις	πᾶσι(ν)
A.	πάντας	πάσας	πάντα

(f) **Γυνή**, though not a monosyllable, follows the rule (see §150(i) for the forms).

(g) Feminine (first declension) forms of adjectives which, in the masculine and neuter, are of the third declension, have the circumflex on the ultima in the genitive plural (cf. **πᾶς**, above).

395. Rules of Accent for Verbs. The accent of verb forms is said to be *recessive*; i.e., subject to the restrictions of the General Rules of Accent, §391, it falls as far forward as possible.

λύομεν   ἐπίστευον   ἐλύσαμεν   λυόμεθα   ἔλυσα   ἐλύθητε

In each of the forms above the ultima is short, so that the accent falls as far forward as possible, i.e., on the antepenult (cf. General Rules (1a), (2a), and (4a)).

πιστεύω   πιστεύει   ἐλύθη   πιστεύοι (third singular optative)

In each of these forms the ultima is long, so that the antepenult cannot be accented; the accent cannot fall farther forward than the penult, which is, accordingly, accented (cf. General Rules (5a, b), §391, and, for the optative form, Definition (1d), §390).

λῦε   κλαῖε

In each of these forms the ultima is short, so that the accent would stand on the antepenult if there were one; since there is no antepenult, the accent stands on the penult and since, in each case, the penult is long, it bears a circumflex.[1]

---

[1] The υ of **λύω** is not, unfortunately, long in all forms in its paradigm, so that the nature of the accent must be learned from observation (cf. **λελύσθαι** among the examples given in the next group, in which the υ is short).

396. A number of exceptions must now be noticed:

(1) All aorist infinitives (except first aorist middle infinitives and second aorist active infinitives) and all perfect infinitives are accented on the *penult* (with the acute or circumflex, according as the penult is short or long):

πιστεῦσαι	(first aorist active)
λυθῆναι	(first aorist passive)
καλέσαι	(first aorist active)
λελυκέναι	(perfect active)
λελύσθαι	(perfect middle and passive)
γενέσθαι	(second aorist middle [in form; the verb is, of course, deponent])
γραφῆναι	(second aorist passive)

(2) First aorist middle infinitives are regular (for second aorist middle infinitives, see (1), above):

λύσασθαι

(3) Second aorist active infinitives have a circumflex on the ultima:

εἰπεῖν   ἰδεῖν   ἐλθεῖν   λαβεῖν   βαλεῖν

(4) Most participles (see (5) and (6), below) have regular verb accent in the nominative singular masculine.

(a) Active participles are declined like adjectives of the first and third declensions (see §394(5g)).

(b) Middle and passive participles are declined like adjectives of the first and second declensions (see §394(4a)).

(5) (a) Second aorist active participles and (b) all aorist passive participles have the acute accent on the ultima in the nominative singular masculine. This determines the position of the accent in the rest of the paradigm:

ἐλθών	ἐλθοῦσα	ἐλθόν	λυθείς	λυθεῖσα	λυθέν
ἐλθόντος	ἐλθούσης	ἐλθόντος	λυθέντος	λυθείσης	λυθέντος
etc.	etc.	etc.	etc.	etc.	etc.

(6) Perfect middle and passive participles have the acute on the penult in all cases:

λελυμένος   λελυμένη   λελυμένον

(7) In verb forms which are augmented, the accent cannot fall farther forward than the augment:

> ἀπῆλθον (the penult contains the augment, so that the accent cannot precede it; since it is long and the ultima is short, it bears the circumflex)

> ἄπελθε (since this imperative form has no augment, the accent moves to the antepenult in accordance with the normal rule)

(8) In the aorist passive subjunctive there is always a circumflex accent on the ending (see §§334(5), 335, *Remark* 2).

(9) A few imperative forms are irregularly accented:

> εἰπέ   εἰπόν   ἐλθέ[1]   ἰδέ[2]   λαβέ

(10) For the accents of other irregular forms (e.g., participles of εἰμί, δίδωμι, τίθημι, and ἵστημι), see the paradigms given in the text.

397. Rules of Accent for Contracted Forms. All the rules of accent already given apply to the *uncontracted* forms of verbs; the proper accentuation for the *contracted* forms may be found as follows:

(1) If there is no accent on either of the vowels (or vowel plus diphthong) being contracted, the resulting contraction has no accent, and the accent remains where it stood on the uncontracted form:

> (Uncontracted) ἐπλήρο-ον > (Contracted) ἐπλήρουν

(2) If there is an accent on the first of the two vowels (or vowel plus diphthong) being contracted, the resulting contraction has a *circumflex* accent:

> (Uncontracted) ποιέ-ει > (Contracted) ποιεῖ

(3) If there is an accent on the second of the two vowels (or vowel plus diphthong) being contracted, the resulting contraction has the *same* accent (in verbs, always an acute):

> (Uncontracted) ἀγαπα-όμεθα > (Contracted) ἀγαπώμεθα

---

[1] The compounds are regular; see ἄπελθε in (7) above.

[2] The forms ἴδε and ἴδου (so accented) are not treated as verbs; both mean *behold!*, *lo!*, and do not govern an object in the accusative.

398. The accentuation of pronouns should be learned from the paradigms given in the text. (Note especially that the interrogative τίς, τί *always* retains the acute.)

399. The accentuation of prepositions, conjunctions, and adverbs is invariable except that an acute on the ultima is changed to a grave in accordance with General Rule (4c), §391. The accentuation of these forms should be learned, since in a few instances it is exceptional (e.g., ὥστε, which by General Rule (4b), §391, would be expected to have the circumflex).

400. Proclitics and Enclitics:[1]

  (1) The proclitics are:

    (a) The forms ὁ, ἡ, οἱ, and αἱ of the article.

    (b) The negative οὐ (οὐκ, οὐχ; however, οὔ, *no*, is not enclitic).

    (c) The prepositions εἰς, ἐν, and ἐκ (ἐξ).

    (d) The conjunctions εἰ and ὡς.

  (2) Proclitics normally have no accent, but may receive an accent when followed directly by an enclitic (see below, (4e)); however, when two or more proclitics occur together, none of them has an accent.

  (3) The enclitics are:

    (a) The present indicative forms of εἰμί and φημί, except for the second singular forms εἶ and φῇς (φῇς does not occur in the New Testament).

    (b) The forms of the indefinite pronoun τις, τι (§378).

    (c) The unaccented forms of the personal pronouns:

      μου   μοι   με   σου   σοι   σε

    (d) The indefinite adverbs πού, ποτέ, and πώς.

    (e) The conjunction τε.

    (f) The emphatic particle γε.

  (4) Rules for accenting enclitics and words followed by enclitics:

    (a) When a word accented on the ultima is followed by an enclitic, it retains its accent, and the enclitic receives no accent:

---

[1] Proclitics "lean on" the following word and form an accentual unit with it; enclitics "lean on" the preceding word and form an accentual unit with it.

ὁ υἱός μου
ὁ υἱὸς τοῦ ἀδελφοῦ μου
θεοί ἐστε

(b) When a word having an *acute* accent on its penult is followed by an enclitic, it retains its accent and:
(i) The enclitic, if monosyllabic, receives no accent.
(ii) The enclitic, if disyllabic, receives an accent on its ultima (acute if the ultima is short, circumflex if it is long):

ὁ λόγος μου
ὁ θεὸς ἀγάπη ἐστίν.
αὕτη ἐστὶν ἡ ἀγγελία.

(Here the acute of **ἐστίν** is changed to a grave, in accordance with General Rule (4c), §391).

μετὰ πρεσβυτέρων τινῶν

(c) If a word with an *acute* on its *antepenult* or with a *circumflex* on its *penult* is followed by an enclitic, it receives a second accent (an acute) on its ultima; the enclitic receives no accent:

ἄνθρωπός τις   ἄνθρωποί τινες
ὁ δοῦλός σου   δοῦλοί τινες

(d) When several enclitics occur together, all but the last have an acute accent (the last receives no accent):

ἀνήρ τίς ἐστιν . . .
ὑμεῖς φίλοι μού ἐστε.

(e) When an enclitic follows a proclitic, the proclitic receives an acute:

εἴ τις

(f) Exceptions to the rules for enclitics:
(i) Enclitics may receive an accent when they begin a sentence or clause (or, more generally, when they follow a mark of punctuation); in this position **ἐστίν** is accented **ἔστιν**:

Mt 19:12a εἰσὶν γὰρ εὐνοῦχοι . . .
Acts 17:18 τινὲς δὲ καὶ τῶν Ἐπικουρίων καὶ Στωικῶν . . .

[327]

(ii) After ἀλλά, εἰ, καί, οὐ, τοῦτο, and ὡς, the forms of εἰμί retain their accent, but ἐστίν is accented ἔστιν:

1 Cor 15:44 εἰ ἔστιν σῶμα ψυχικόν . . .

Mt 19:12b καὶ εἰσὶν εὐνοῦχοι . . .

1 Jn 4:6 οὐκ ἔστιν ἐκ τοῦ θεοῦ.

Jn 3:28 οὐκ εἰμὶ ἐγὼ ὁ Χριστός.

Mt 27:46 τοῦτ' ἔστιν (= τοῦτο ἔστιν)

PRINCIPAL PARTS OF VERBS

401. Verbs whose first principal parts end as indicated in the first column below **regularly** form their remaining principal parts as indicated in the other columns:

PRESENT ACTIVE	FUTURE ACTIVE	AORIST ACTIVE	PERFECT ACTIVE	PERFECT MID. & PASS.	AORIST PASSIVE
-υω	-υσω	-υσα	-υκα	-υμαι	-ύθην
(-αυω, ευω, -ουω similarly)					
-βω, -πω, -φω, -πτω	-ψω	-ψα	-φα	-μμαι	-φθην
-γω, -κω, -χω, -σσω, -ττω	-ξω	-ξα	-χα	-γμαι	-χθην
-δω, -θω, -ζω	-σω	-σα	-κα	-σμαι	-σθην
-αίνω	-ανῶ	-ανα	-αγκα	-αμμαι	-άνθην
-ύνω	-υνῶ	-υνα	—	-υμμαι	-ύνθην

Contract verbs:

-άω	-ασω	-ασα	-ακα	-αμαι	-άθην
(α preceded by ρ or a vowel)					
-άω	-ησω	-ησα	-ηκα	-ημαι	-ήθην
(α not preceded by ρ or a vowel)					
-έω	-ησω	-ησα	-ηκα	-ημαι	-ήθην
-όω	-ωσω	-ωσα	-ωκα	-ωμαι	-ώθην

402. The most important verbs which do not form their principal parts as indicated above are listed in the table following. Compound verbs are not included in this table; in the case of compounds formed from simple verbs which do not occur in the New Testament, the simple verb is given, preceded by a hyphen (e.g., **-βαίνω, -θνῄσκω**). Deponent forms are given in the columns marked "active" if no more appropriate heading exists (thus, for γίνομαι, ἐγενόμην is given as aorist active, while ἐγενήθην is given as aorist passive).

PRESENT ACTIVE	FUTURE ACTIVE	AORIST ACTIVE	PERFECT ACTIVE	PERFECT MID. & PASS.	AORIST PASSIVE
ἄγω, *lead*	ἄξω	ἤγαγον	(ἦχα)[1]	ἦγμαι	ἤχθην
αἱρέω, *take*	αἱρήσομαι	-εῖλον		-ἥρημαι	-ἡρέθην
		-ἑλῶ (in compounds)			
αἴρω, *raise, take up*	ἀρῶ	ἦρα	ἦρκα	ἦρμαι	ἤρθην
ἀκούω, *hear*	ἀκούσω	ἤκουσα	ἀκήκοα	(ἤκουσμαι)	ἠκούσθην
ἁμαρτάνω, *sin*	ἁμαρτήσω	ἡμάρτησα ἥμαρτον	ἡμάρτηκα	ἡμάρτημαι	ἡμαρτήθην
ἀνοίγω, *open*	ἀνοίξω	ἤνοιξα ἠνέῳξα ἀνέῳξα	ἀνέῳγα	ἀνέῳγμαι ἠνέῳγμαι ἤνοιγμαι	ἠνοίχθην ἠνεῴχθην ἀνεῴχθην
-βαίνω	-βήσομαι	-ἔβην	-βέβηκα		
(ἀναβαίνω, *go up, ascend*; many other compounds)					
βάλλω, *throw, put*	βαλῶ	ἔβαλον	βέβληκα	βέβλημαι	ἐβλήθην
γίνομαι, *become happen*	γενήσομαι	ἐγενόμην	γέγονα	γεγένημαι	ἐγενήθην
γινώσκω, *know*	γνώσομαι	ἔγνων	ἔγνωκα	ἔγνωσμαι	ἐγνώσθην
γράφω, *write*	γράψω	ἔγραψα	γέγραφα	γέγραμμαι	ἐγράφην
δείκνυμι, *show*	δείξω	ἔδειξα		δέδειγμαι	ἐδείχθην
δέομαι, *ask, beseech*					ἐδεήθην
διδάσκω, *teach*	διδάξω	ἐδίδαξα			ἐδιδάχθην
δίδωμι, *give*	δώσω	ἔδωκα	δέδωκα	δέδομαι	ἐδόθην
δύναμαι, *be able*	δυνήσομαι	ἐδυνάμην ἠδυνάμην			ἠδυνήθην ἠδυνάσθην
ἐγείρω, *raise*	ἐγερῶ	ἤγειρα		ἐγήγερμαι	ἠγέρθην
εἰμί, *be*	ἔσομαι	ἤμην			
ἐλπίζω, *hope*	ἐλπιῶ	ἤλπισα	ἤλπικα		
ἐργάζομαι, *work*		ἠργασάμην		εἴργασμαι	-εἰργάσθην
ἔρχομαι, *come*	ἐλεύσομαι	ἦλθον	ἐλήλυθα		
ἐσθίω, ἔσθω, *eat*	φάγομαι	ἔφαγον			
εὑρίσκω, *find*	εὑρήσω	εὗρον	εὕρηκα		εὑρέθην
ἔχω, *have*	ἕξω	ἔσχον	ἔσχηκα		
(Imperfect εἶχον)					

---

[1] Forms given in parentheses do not occur in the New Testament.

PRESENT ACTIVE	FUTURE ACTIVE	AORIST ACTIVE	PERFECT ACTIVE	PERFECT MID. & PASS.	AORIST PASSIVE
ζάω (ζήω), *live*	ζήσω ζήσομαι	ἔζησα			
θέλω, *wish, want*	θελήσω	ἠθέλησα			
-θνῃσκω	-θανοῦμαι	-ἔθανον	τέθνηκα		

(ἀποθνῃσκω, *die*; the perfect does not have the prefix.)

| -ἵημι | -ἥσω | -ἧκα | -εἷκα | -ἕωμαι -εἷμαι | -ἕθην |

(ἀφίημι, *leave, forgive*, is the most important compound.)

| ἵστημι, *stand* | στήσω | ἔστην ἔστησα | ἔστηκα | | ἐστάθην |

(Perfect participle: ἑστώς as well as ἑστηκώς)

| καθαρίζω, *cleanse* | καθαριῶ | ἐκαθέρισα | | κεκαθέρισμαι | ἐκαθερίσθην |

(Forms also occur with α for ε after the θ.)

καλέω, *call*	καλέσω	ἐκάλεσα	κέκληκα	κέκλημαι	ἐκλήθην
κόπτω, *cut*	κόψω	ἔκοψα		κέκομμαι	ἐκόπην
κρίνω, *judge*	κρινῶ	ἔκρινα	κέκρικα	κέκριμαι	ἐκρίθην
(κρύπτω), -κρύβω, *hide*	(κρύψω)	ἔκρυψα		κέκρυμμαι	ἐκρύβην
-κτείνω	-κτενῶ	-ἔκτεινα			-ἐκτάνθην

(ἀποκτείνω, *kill*, is the only compound.)

λαμβάνω, *take*	λήμψομαι	ἔλαβον	εἴληφα	εἴλημμαι	ἐλήμφθην
λέγω, *say*	ἐρῶ	εἶπον	εἴρηκα	εἴρημαι	ἐρρέθην ἐρρήθην
λείπω, *leave*	λείψω	ἔλιπον	(λέλοιπα)	λέλειμμαι	ἐλείφθην
μανθάνω, *learn*	(μαθήσο- μαι)	ἔμαθον	μεμάθηκα		
μέλλω, *intend*	μελλήσω				

(Imperfect ἤμελλον or ἔμελλον)

| μένω, *remain* | μενῶ | ἔμεινα | μεμένηκα | | |
| μιμνῄσκω, *remind* | -μνήσω | -ἔμνησα | | μέμνημαι | ἐμνήσθην |

[οἶδα, *know*; perfect forms with present meaning; see §372, *Remark* 2.]

| -ὄλλυμι | -ὀλέσω -ὀλῶ | -ὤλεσα | -ὄλωλα | | |

(ἀπόλλυμι, *destroy*, is the usual compound.)

| ὁράω, *see* | ὄψομαι | εἶδον | ἑόρακα ἑώρακα | | ὤφθην |

(Imperfect ἑώρων)

| πάσχω, *suffer* | (πείσομαι) | ἔπαθον | πέπονθα | | |
| πείθω, *persuade* | πείσω | ἔπεισα | πέποιθα | πέπεισμαι | ἐπείσθην |

PRESENT ACTIVE	FUTURE ACTIVE	AORIST ACTIVE	PERFECT ACTIVE	PERFECT MID. & PASS.	AORIST PASSIVE
πεινάω, *hunger*	πεινάσω	ἐπείνασα			
πίνω, *drink*	πίομαι	ἔπιον	πέπωκα		ἐπόθην
πίπτω, *fall*	πεσοῦμαι	ἔπεσον	πέπτωκα		
σπείρω, *sow*	σπερῶ	ἔσπειρα		ἔσπαρμαι	ἐσπάρην
-στέλλω	-στελῶ	-ἔστειλα	-ἔσταλκα	-ἔσταλμαι	-ἐστάλην
(ἀποστέλλω, *send*, is the most important compound.)					
στηρίζω, *strengthen*	στηρίξω	ἐστήριξα		ἐστήριγμαι	ἐστηρίχθην
στρέφω, *turn*	στρέψω	ἔστρεψα		ἔστραμμαι	ἐστράφην
σῴζω, *save*	σώσω	ἔσωσα	σέσωκα	σέσῳ(σ)μαι	ἐσώθην
τελέω, *finish*	τελέσω	ἐτέλεσα	τετέλεκα	τετέλεσμαι	ἐτελέσθην
-τέλλω	-τελοῦμαι	-ἔτειλα	-τέταλκα	-τέταλμαι	
(ἀνατέλλω, *rise*, and a few other compounds)					
-τέμνω		-ἔτεμον		-τέτμημαι	-ἐτμήθην
(περιτέμνω, *circumcise*, is the most important compound.)					
τίθημι, *put, place*	θήσω	ἔθηκα	τέθεικα	τέθειμαι	ἐτέθην
τίκτω, *bear, give birth to*	τέξομαι	ἔτεκον			ἐτέχθην
-τρέπω	-τραπή-σομαι	-ἔτρεψα			-ἐτράπην
(ἀνατρέπω, *overturn, upset*, and a few other compounds)					
τρέφω, *nourish, nurture*	(θρέψω)	ἔθρεψα	(τέτροφα)	τέθραμμαι	-ἐτράφην
τρέχω, *run*	(θρέξομαι)	ἔδραμον			
-τρίβω	-τρίψω	-ἔτριψα		-τέτριμμαι	-ἐτρίβην
(συντρίβω, *shatter, crush*)					
τυγχάνω, *happen*		ἔτυχον	τέτυχα		
φαίνω, *shine*	φανοῦμαι φανήσομαι	ἔφανα			ἐφάνην
φέρω, *bear, bring, carry*	οἴσω	ἤνεγκον ἤνεγκα	-ἐνήνοχα		ἠνέχθην
φεύγω, *flee*	φεύξομαι	ἔφυγον	πέφευγα		
χαίρω, *rejoice*	ἐχάρην[1]	χαρήσομαι			

[1] It matters little whether this form is counted as a "root" aorist (see §366; so E. Schwyzer, *Griechische Grammatik*, I, 755) or as a deponent aorist passive (so Bauer); the inflection is the same, in any case.

SELECTED BIBLIOGRAPHY

SELECTED BIBLIOGRAPHY

1. Text. Numerous editions of the Greek text of the New Testament are available; the two following are especially recommended:

E. Nestle (ed.). *Novum Testamentum Graece.* Stuttgart: Priviligierte Württembergische Bibelanstalt, 1963.

> This is the twenty-fifth edition; earlier editions are satisfactory for many purposes. Nestle's edition is available in several formats, including one in large type, one with wide page margins, one with an interleaved Latin (Vulgate) text, and one with an interleaved German text.

G. D. Kilpatrick (ed.). Ἡ Καινὴ Διαθήκη. London: British and Foreign Bible Society, 1958.

> This edition differs from Nestle's most obviously in the style of type, which is somewhat easier on the eyes. The apparatus is not quite as detailed as that of Nestle, but for many purposes this does not affect its usefulness.

For the study of the first three gospels (and, to a less extent, of the fourth also) a synopsis is indispensable; the first of the two recommended below is more detailed, but the second is somewhat more convenient to use:

Kurt Aland (ed.). *Synopsis Quattuor Evangeliorum; Locis Parallelis Evangeliorum Apocryphorum et Patrum Adhibitis.* Stuttgart: Priviligierte Württembergische Bibelanstalt, 1964.

A. Huck, H. Lietzmann, and F. L. Cross (eds.). *Synopsis of the First Three Gospels.* Oxford: Basil Blackwell, 1959.

[335]

Selected Bibliography

2. Lexicons:

Walter Bauer. *A Greek–English Lexicon of the New Testament and Other Early Christian Literature.* Chicago: The University of Chicago Press, 1957.

> This is a translation and adaptation, by W. F. Arndt and F. W. Gingrich, of the fourth German edition; for students who can use German with some facility, a fifth edition is available. An exhaustive and detailed work, it gives numerous illustrative Biblical citations and thus serves, to a great extent, the purpose of a concordance; it also contains references to relevant articles and books.

T. S. Green. *A Greek–English Lexicon to the New Testament.* New York: Harper and Row, [n.d.].

A. Souter. *A Pocket Lexicon to the Greek New Testament.* New York: Oxford University Press, 1916.

> Neither Green's lexicon nor Souter's is in any sense a substitute for Bauer's, but beginning students may find it convenient to have one of them. Green's lexicon contains more grammatically useful information (gender of nouns, principal parts of verbs, etc.) than Souter's.

3. Grammars:

F. Blass and A. Debrunner. *A Greek Grammar of the New Testament and Other Early Christian Literature.* Chicago: The University of Chicago Press, 1961.

> This is a detailed reference grammar, recently translated (1961) by R. W. Funk from the German edition (the "9th–10th") of 1954–1959. Professor Funk has also included additional bibliographical material of value. This book is indispensable for advanced studies in the language of the New Testament.

C. F. D. Moule. *An Idiom Book of New Testament Greek* (2nd ed.). London: Cambridge University Press, 1959.

> This is not a grammar in the usual sense, but treats selected topics from New Testament grammar in a way which is sometimes illuminating.

James Hope Moulton. *A Grammar of New Testament Greek.* Edinburgh: T. & T. Clark.

> This is a very detailed and valuable work in three volumes. The first volume (*Prolegomena*) was issued in 1906 (3rd edition, 1908) and the second (*Accidence and Word-Formation*; edited by W. F. Howard) in 1929. The third volume (*Syntax*) is the work of Dr. Nigel Turner, and appeared in 1963.

Both Blass–Debrunner and Turner's *Syntax* contain elaborate bibliographies.

4. Concordances:

W. F. Moulton and A. S. Geden. *A Concordance to the Greek Testament.* Edinburgh: T. & T. Clark, 1953.

Alfred Schmoller. *Handkonkordanz zum griechischen Neuen Testament.* Stuttgart: Priviligierte Württembergische Bibelanstalt, 1949.

J. B. Smith. *Greek–English Concordance to the New Testament.* Scottdale, Pennsylvania: Herald Press, 1955.

> The concordance of Moulton and Geden is generally to be preferred, as Schmoller's is not exhaustive. Smith's concordance does not cite words in context but only lists passages by chapter and verse numbers; Smith's work does, however, give much valuable statistical information.

5. Works on the Vocabulary of the New Testament:

B. M. Metzger. *Lexical Aids for Students of New Testament Greek.* London: Allenson & Co., Ltd., 1955.

> This is primarily a list of words which occur in the New Testament ten times or more, arranged in decreasing order of frequency. Sections on word formation, irregular verbs, and prepositions are included.

The Analytical Greek Lexicon. New York: Harper and Row, [n.d.].

> Every *form* which occurs in the New Testament is listed and explained very briefly.

[337]

G. Kittel *et al. Bible Key Words.* Tr. and ed. J. R. Coates *et al.* New York: Harper & Row, 1952–.

> Five volumes have appeared so far in this series, which contains important articles from the *Theologisches Wörterbuch zum Neuen Testament* (see below).

G. Kittel *et al. Theologisches Wörterbuch zum Neuen Testament.* Stuttgart: W. Kohlhammer, 1933–.

> This work will be completed in eight volumes. It is now being translated in its entirety by G. W. Bromiley, as the *Theological Dictionary of the New Testament.* (The first volume of the translation was published in Grand Rapids, Michigan, by the Wm. B. Eerdmans Publishing Company in 1964.)

R. Morgenthaler. *Statistik des neutestamentlichen Wortschatzes.* Zürich and Frankfurt a. M.: Gotthelf-Verlag, 1958.

> This book is indispensable for word-frequency studies.

6. Works on Linguistics:

(a) General:

Edward Sapir. *Language.* New York: Harcourt, Brace & World, 1921.

(b) Somewhat more specialized:

Charles C. Fries. *The Structure of English.* New York: Harcourt, Brace & World, 1952.

Henry A. Gleason. *An Introduction to Descriptive Linguistics* (2nd ed.). New York: Rinehart and Winston, 1961.

A. A. Hill. *Introduction to Linguistic Structures.* New York: Harcourt, Brace & World, 1958.

Charles F. Hockett. *A Course in Modern Linguistics.* New York: The Macmillan Company, 1958.

E. A. Nida. *Morphology* (2nd ed.). Ann Arbor, Michigan: The University of Michigan Press, 1949.

(c) Popular:

E. A. Nida. *Learning a Foreign Language.* New York: American Bible Society, 1950.

E. A. Nida. *Linguistic Interludes.* Glendale, California: Summer Institute of Linguistics, 1947.

INDICES

SUBJECT INDEX

The numerals refer to the sections of the grammar, not to the pages.

Subject Index

Constructions, definition, 17

Contract verbs, 172; irregular, 368; -αω, 174; -εω, 175; -οω, 176

Contraction, of vowels and diphthongs, 172

Dative case, 81, 382(4); forms, 82; syntax, 83f; meanings, 84f; with verbs, 382(4a); with adjectives, 382(4b)

Declension, definition, 34, 36; first, 34; second, 34; third, 146

Definite article: *see* Article

Deliberative subjunctive, 345

Demonstratives, 102; syntax, 103

Devices, grammatical: *see* Grammatical devices

Dictionary, 22, 25; *see also* sections 2 and 3 in the Selected Bibliography

Dictionary form, for nouns, 35, 81, fn. 2, 147, *Remark* 3; for adjectives, 65; for verbs, 89; contract verbs, 173; μι-verbs, 200ff

Diphthongs, 6f

Direct object: *see* Object

Distributional characteristics, 33(2)

Enclitics, 108, 391(1b), 400(3,4)

Endings, first aorist middle, 125; primary active, 90; imperfect, 95(2); *see also* Suffixes

Equative verbs, 56f, 69f

Form, relationship between meaning and, 19

Formal characteristics, 33, 264f

Formants, *see* tense formants

"Frames," syntactic, 33(2)

Function words, 29, 56, 189, 301f

Future active, 91

Gender, 36f

Genitive absolute, 228, 247(4)

Genitive case, 73, 382(3); forms, first and second declensions, 74; syntax, 74; with

article, 76f; position, 76–78; meaning, 79f; with verbs, 382(3a,b); with adjectives, 382(3c)

Government, 30, 190

Grammar, 15, 20, 25, 32

Grammatical analysis, 20; "traditional," 21; "scientific," 22, 26, 32

Grammatical devices, 20, 23, 25, 29–32

Hortatory subjunctive, 343

Imperative, 322; aspect, 332(2); forms, 326; meaning, 332; morphemes, 326; tenses, 323–331

"Improper diphthongs," 7

Indeclinable nouns, 141, fn. 1

Indefinite adverbs, 379

Indefinite pronouns, 378

Indefinite relative clauses, 357

Indirect discourse, 259(3)

Indirect object: *see* Object

Infinitive, 89, 248–261; anarthrous, 259; uses, 259f; with ὥστε, 259(4); tenses, 257; aspect, 257; uses, 258–261; forms 249–256; morphemes, 250; complementary, 259(1); as object of verbs, 259(2); with subject accusative, 259(1), *Remark*; in indirect discourse, 259(3); expressing purpose or result, 259(4): articular, 261; genitive, 261(3); dative, 261(4); with prepositions, 261(5)

Infix, 30

Inflections, 30f, 33(1)

Interrogative adjectives, 303(2)

Interrogative adverbs, 303(3)

Interrogative particles, 302

Interrogative pronouns, 303(1)

Intonation pattern, 18, 23, 299

Iota-subscript, 7

Irregular verbs, 363

Language, definition of, 13

Liquid stems, nouns, 153, 156; irregular, 157; verbs, 364f

[344]

GREEK INDEX

The numerals refer to the sections of the grammar, not to the pages.

ἀγαπάω, 173f, 177(2), 238, 251, 210(1), 211
αἰώνιος, 67
ἀλλά, 320(1d)
ἀλλήλων, 377
ἄλλος, 296
ἄν, 348, 349(2), 351, Type C; 354, *Remark*
ἀνά, 191(1)
ἀναβαίνω, 366
ἀνέβην, 366
ἀνήρ, 157(iv)
ἀντί, 193(1), 199(2)
ἅπας, 287(1)
ἀπό, 193(2), 194(4), 199(2)
ἄρα, 302(4)
ἄρα, 320(2d)
Ἀραψ, 148(ii)
αὐτός, 97–101, 103(3), 104–106
αω-verbs: *see* ἀγαπάω

β-stems, 146A(1a), 148(ii)
βούλομαι, 259(1c), fn. 2 (page 196)

γ-stems, 146A(1b), 149(ii)
γάρ, 320(2)
γίνομαι, 56–58, 70, 137
γινώσκω, 366
γόνυ, 152(iii)
γυνή, 150(i)

δ-stems, 146A(1c), 151(ii); irregular, 152(i)
δέ, 320(2b)

δεῖ, 260(1)
διά, 197(1)
δίδωμι, 200, 202, 212–214, 216, 239
διότι, 321(2)
δύναμαι, 259(1a), fn. 3 (page 195)

ἐάν, 348
ἑαυτοῦ, 375
ἔγνων, 366
ἐγώ, 107(1)
εἰ, 351
εἰμί, 56–58, 70, 140, 217, 232, 256, 330, 341
εἰς, 191(2), 199(1)
εἷς, 288, *Remark*, 289, 295
ἐκ, 193(4), 194(4), 197(1), *Remark* 3, 199(2)
ἕκαστος, 288
ἐκεῖνος, 102(2), 103
ἐλπίς, 151(ii)
ἐμαυτοῦ, 375
ἐμέ, 107(1), 199(3)
ἐμοί, 107(1), 199(3)
ἐμός, 110
ἐμοῦ, 107(1), 199(3)
ἔμπροσθεν, 193(5), 194(1), 199(1)
ἐν, 192(1), 199(1)
ἕνεκα, 193(6), 194(3), 199(2)
ἐνώπιον, 193(7), 194(2), 199(1)
ἐξ: *see* ἐκ
ἔξεστιν, 260(1)
ἐπεί, 321(4)
ἐπειδή, 321(4)
ἐπί, 198(1)
ἕτερος, 296

[347]

Greek Index

οὗτος, 102(1), 103
ὀφείλω, 259(1e), fn. 4 (page 196)
οω-verbs: *see* πληρόω

π-stems, 146A(1a), 148(i)
παρά, 276(2), 198(2a,b,c)
πᾶς, 287(2)
πατήρ, 157(i)
περί, 197(4a,b), 199(1)
πληρόω, 173, 176, 177(3), 210(3), 211,
   238, 251
ποιέω, 173, 175, 177(1), 210(2), 211, 238,
   251
πολύς, 283
πούς, 152(i)
πρίν (ἤ), 260(4)
πρό, 193(10), 199(1)
πρός, 199(3)
πῦρ, 157(vi)

ρ-stems, nouns, 146A(2b), 153(1), 156;
   irregular, 157; verbs, 365(2)

σ-stems, 146C(3), 163; origin, 163, fns.
   1–3 (page 129)
σάρξ, 149(i)
σέ, 107(2), 199(3)
σε, 107(2), 108
σεαυτοῦ, 375
σοί, 107(2), 199(3)
σοι, 107(2), 108
σός, 110
σοῦ, 107(2), 199(3)
σου, 107(2), 108

σύ, 107(2)
σύν, 192(2), 194(5), 199(1)
σῶμα, 147, *Remark* 2, *Exception*; 151(iv)

τ-stems, 146A(1c), 147, *Remark* 2; 151(i,iv,
   v); irregular, 152(ii,iii,iv)
τε, 320(1b)
τίθημι, 200, 203, 212, 215(1), 216, 239
τίς, 303(1)
τις, 378

υ-stems, nouns, 146B, 160; adjectives, 161
ὕδωρ, 152(iv)
ὑμᾶς, 107(4)
ὑμεῖς, 107(4)
ὑμέτερος, 110
ὑμῖν, 107(4)
ὑμῶν, 107(4)
ὑπέρ, 197(5a,b), 199(1), 276(2)
ὑπό, 118–120, 197(1), *Remark* 2, 197(6)

φλόξ, 149(ii)
φῶς, 147, *Remark* 2, 151(iv)

χ-stems, 146A(1b), 149(iii)
χάρις, 151(i)
χάριν, 193(11), 199(1)
χωρίς, 193(12), 199(1)
χείρ, 157(v)

ὡς, 321(3)
ὥσπερ, 321(3)
ὥστε, 321(6)